Italian–Two and Three Years

Joseph A. Tursi

Chairman, Department of French and Italian
State University of New York at Stony Brook

Paul D. Cincinnato

Director of Foreign Languages
Farmingdale Public Schools, New York

Dedicated to serving

AMSCO

our nation's youth

When ordering this book, please specify:
either **R 207 P** *or* ITALIAN—TWO AND THREE YEARS

AMSCO SCHOOL PUBLICATIONS, INC.

315 Hudson Street New York, N.Y. 10013

ISBN 0-87720-594-9

The cover photograph of Venice is by Inge Morath from Magnum. Text illustrations are by Ann Toulmin-Rothe.

PRINTED IN THE UNITED STATES OF AMERICA

PREFACE

L'Italiano: Lingua e Cultura is a comprehensive text for the student who has already completed a basic course in Italian. Through well-organized and concise preliminary lessons, the text reviews and reenforces what the student has learned in the first year. More complicated structural concepts are then introduced in carefully graded fashion. The book is broadly suitable for Italian classes on the intermediate level, both in secondary schools and colleges.

To permit flexible use of the material and easy reference to topics, the authors have organized the text into five major parts: Verbs, Grammatical Structures, Idioms, Vocabulary, and Civilization. A part is divided into individual lessons, each of which presents a specific topic in simple outline form. Both teachers and students will find this outline form of the text particularly helpful because it keeps explanations brief, clear, and to the point.

Following each lesson is a varied and extensive set of exercises to promote student review and mastery of the topic of the lesson. Many types of exercises have been prepared so that they also give the teacher a rich variety of models from which additional exercises may be developed, depending on the individual preferences of the teacher.

Within each part, cumulative review exercises provide medial practice and testing. A set of mastery exercises at the end of each part offers a comprehensive review of the entire part.

In Part V–Civilization, the authors have kept in mind the needs and interests of the American student. Thus, Lesson 8 deals with the influence of the Italian language on English. Lesson 13 treats two topics of special interest to the student: the role of Italians and Americans of Italian descent in the history of the United States, and the important contributions of Italy to the cultural medium of the motion picture.

The authors have taken great care to integrate Italian culture with the presentation of the Italian language. They recommend that the teacher expand upon the cultural items in the book and relate this cultural material as much as possible to the development of language skills. For example, language and culture can be integrated in the culturally based completion paragraphs in the exercises following most civilization lessons. Once the student has completed these cultural passages and the teacher has corrected them, the teacher can use them as language comprehension passages by developing a series of related questions to which the student may be asked to respond orally or in writing. Language and culture can also be integrated in these passages through the development of guided compositions based on the themes of the passages.

With *L'Italiano: Lingua e Cultura*, the authors have attempted to provide much-needed new materials for the teaching of Italian language and culture beyond the first year. Because the book reflects the eclectic methodological trends now prevalent in the teaching of foreign languages, it should give teachers a systematic yet flexible aid in their work. Students should find the book a genuine help in their continuing study of Italian.

The authors appreciate the significant contributions to their book of Ms. Concetta R. Giuliano, Acting Chairman of Foreign Languages at Edward R. Murrow High School, New York City, and Mrs. Simona Morini, editor at Rizzoli International Publications, Inc., New York City.

Joseph A. Tursi
Paul D. Cincinnato

CONTENTS

Part IV—Vocabulary

Part V—Civilization

Part I—Verbs

1. Present Indicative of Regular *-ARE* and *-ERE* Verbs

The present indicative of regular **-are** and **-ere** verbs is formed by:

1. dropping the infinitive ending (**-are**, **-ere**)
2. adding to the stem the following endings:

   -are verbs: **-o, -i, -a, -iamo, -ate, -ano**

   -ere verbs: **-o, -i, -e, -iamo, -ete, -ono**

compr*are*, to buy	**vend*ere***, to sell
I buy, *I am buying,* *I do buy*, etc.	*I sell,* *I am selling,* *I do sell*, etc.
io compr*o* tu compr*i* Lei, lui, lei compr*a* (egli, essa) noi compr***iamo*** voi compr***ate*** Loro, loro compr***ano*** (essi, esse)	io vend*o* tu vend*i* Lei, lui, lei vend*e* (egli, essa) noi vend***iamo*** voi vend***ete*** Loro, loro vend***ono*** (essi, esse)

The pronouns **lui, lei,** and **loro** are used in informal conversation at present in Italy.

The pronouns **egli, essa, essi,** and **esse** are used in more formal situations and reserved more often for formal writing. Therefore, the **lui, lei,** and **loro** forms will be used in this book instead of the **egli, essa, essi,** and **esse** forms.

Note

1. Verbs ending in **-iare**, such as **studiare**, retain the **-i** in all forms: **io studio, Lei studia, voi studiate, loro studiano.** Note that the **tu** and **noi** forms do not double the **-i**: **tu studi, noi studiamo.**
2. Verbs ending in **-care** and **-gare**, such as **giocare** and **pagare**, must retain the hard **c** and **g** sounds. Therefore, an **h** is added to the **tu** and **noi** forms: **tu giochi, tu paghi, noi giochiamo, noi paghiamo.**
3. Verbs ending in **-giare**, **-ciare**, or **-sciare** retain the **i** but do not double it in the **tu** and **noi** forms: **tu mangi, tu cominci, tu lasci, noi mangiamo, noi cominciamo, noi lasciamo.**

COMMON -ARE VERBS

abitare, to live, to reside
accompagnare, to accompany
aiutare, to help
alzare, to raise
ammirare, to admire
arrivare, to arrive
ascoltare, to listen (to)
aspettare, to wait
attraversare, to cross
baciare, to kiss
ballare, to dance
bussare, to knock
cambiare, to change
camminare, to walk
cantare, to sing
celebrare, to celebrate
cenare, to have supper
cercare, to seek, to look for
chiamare, to call
comprare, to buy
desiderare, to wish, to desire
dimenticare, to forget
domandare, to ask (for information)
entrare, to enter
festeggiare, to celebrate
giocare, to play (a game)
guadagnare, to earn
guardare, to look at
imparare, to learn
incontrare, to meet
insegnare, to teach
invitare, to invite
lasciare, to leave (something)
lavare, to wash
lavorare, to work
mandare, to send
mangiare, to eat
pagare, to pay
parlare, to speak, to talk
pensare, to think
portare, to bring, to carry, to wear
pranzare, to dine
preparare, to prepare
raccontare, to narrate
restare, to remain
salutare, to greet
spiegare, to explain, to unfold
stirare, to iron, to press
studiare, to study
suonare, to play (a musical instrument), to sound, to ring
telefonare, to telephone
trovare, to find
viaggiare, to travel
visitare, to visit

COMMON -ERE VERBS

accendere, to light, to turn on
chiedere, to ask
chiudere, to close
commettere, to commit
comprendere, to understand
conoscere, to know
correre, to run
credere, to believe
cuocere, to cook
decidere, to decide
difendere, to defend
dividere, to divide
godere, to enjoy
leggere, to read
mettere, to place, to put
nascere, to be born
nascondere, to hide
perdere, to lose
prendere, to take
promettere, to promise
proteggere, to protect
rendere, to render, to give
ricevere, to receive
ripetere, to repeat
rispondere, to answer, to respond
rompere, to break
scendere, to descend, to go down
scrivere, to write
spendere, to spend (money)
stringere, to tighten, to press
vedere, to see
vendere, to sell
vincere, to win
vivere, to live, to reside

EXERCISES

A. Choose the correct form of the verb in parentheses:

1. Voi (canti, cantate, canto) molte canzoni.
2. Carla (scende, scendi, scendono) le scale.
3. Loro (prende, prendi, prendono) un gelato ogni giorno.
4. Tu (cerchiamo, cerca, cerchi) la matita?
5. I ragazzi (prepara, prepariamo, preparano) una bella cena.
6. Noi non (metto, mettono, mettiamo) i libri sulla tavola.
7. Signora, perchè non (risponde, rispondi, rispondete)?
8. Io (lasciamo, lasci, lascio) tutto a casa.
9. Lui (studio, studia, studiate) pochissimo.
10. Voi (vediamo, vedete, vedono) quelle riviste?
11. Giorgio, tu (spiega, spiego, spieghi) tutto molto bene.
12. Marisa (legge, leggiamo, leggete) ad alta voce.
13. Carlo ed io (laviamo, lavate, lavo) i piatti ogni sera.
14. Loro non (scrive, scrivono, scrivo) molto.
15. Il signor Gianni (chiama, chiamano, chiami) spesso gli amici.

B. Rewrite each sentence, using the subjects indicated:

1. Abito accanto alla scuola.	(voi, Loro, tu)
2. Michele risponde bene in classe.	(io, Luisa ed io, I miei compagni)
3. Invitate molti studenti alla festa?	(Lei, La signorina, Le ragazze, noi)
4. Cerchiamo dei posti buoni.	(La signora, Tu e Piero, I tuoi amici)
5. Luisa scende le scale della chiesa.	(lui, Giovanni e Luigi, voi)

C. Change the subject and the verb to the singular:

1. I giovani raccontano una novella.	_____ una novella.
2. Loro entrano alle sei.	_____ alle sei.
3. Voi spendete troppo.	_____ troppo.
4. Noi paghiamo molto per la frutta.	_____ molto per la frutta.
5. Loro godono una bella giornata al mare?	_____ una bella giornata al mare?

D. Complete each sentence by using the present indicative of the verb in parentheses:

1. (giocare)	Noi _____ al calcio.
2. (conoscere)	Questi ragazzi non _____ molte ragazze.
3. (mangiare)	Tu _____ sempre pasta asciutta.
4. (correre)	La signora Rudi _____ sempre.
5. (spendere)	Quando faccio la spesa _____ sempre molto denaro.
6. (viaggiare)	Tu e Paolo _____ ogni anno?
7. (baciare)	La mamma _____ suo figlio ogni mattina.
8. (vincere)	Laura ed Anna _____ sempre qualche cosa.
9. (portare)	Il signor Rosa _____ un bel cappello oggi.
10. (aiutare)	Susanna ed io _____ Giorgio a studiare.
11. (vedere)	Lui _____ tutti i programmi possibili alla televisione.
12. (attraversare)	Chi _____ la strada da solo?
13. (telefonare)	Voi mi _____ spesso.
14. (credere)	Io non _____ che domani farà bel tempo.
15. (guadagnare)	Mio fratello _____ molto ogni settimana.

E. Answer the following questions in complete Italian sentences:

1. Parli italiano?
2. Studiano molto i ragazzi?
3. Abitate lontano dalla scuola?
4. Chi telefona ogni sera alle otto?

5. Scrivete molte lettere?
6. Quando canta Maria?
7. Chi corregge i compiti degli studenti?
8. Che cosa porta la signorina Biondi?
9. Chi aspetti?
10. Chi non risponde mai in classe?
11. Cosa guardi alla televisione?
12. Chi paga il conto al ristorante?
13. Lavora molto il padre di Laura?
14. Cosa chiedete a vostra madre ogni giorno?
15. Che desideri fare stasera?

F. Complete the Italian sentences:

1.	We knock at the door.	_____ alla porta.
2.	Joe admires the photographs.	Peppe _____ le fotografie.
3.	You (tu) think too much!	_____ troppo!
4.	You put the sofa in the living room.	Lei _____ il divano nel salotto.
5.	Today we visit the museum.	Oggi _____ il museo.
6.	Who answers the phone?	Chi _____ al telefono?
7.	Where does he study?	Dove _____ ?
8.	She is walking with Maria.	_____ con Maria.
9.	Are you washing the dishes, Miss?	_____ i piatti, signorina?
10.	When do they sell the bicycles?	Quando _____ le biciclette?
11.	Do they dance well?	_____ bene?
12.	What is he looking at?	Cosa _____ ?
13.	Do you (tu) write to Anthony?	_____ ad Antonio?
14.	The boy is singing a song.	Il ragazzo _____ una canzone.
15.	Carlo always loses the books.	Carlo _____ sempre i libri.

2. Present Indicative of Regular *-IRE* Verbs

Note

1. Verbs ending in **-ire** fall into two categories: those conjugated like **partire** and those conjugated like **finire**. The personal endings are the same for both groups, except that those verbs conjugated like **finire** add **-isc** to the stem before the personal endings in the three singular forms and in the third person plural only. The **noi** and **voi** forms do not add **-isc**. A general rule for determining which **-ire** verbs take **-isc** is the following: When there is one consonant before **-ire (spe*d*ire, fi*n*ire, pu*l*ire)**, add **-isc** to the stem. When there are two constants before **-ire (o*ff*rire, se*nt*ire, se*rv*ire)**, do not add **-isc** to the stem.

2. The endings for **-ire** verbs are: **-o, -i, -e, -iamo, -ite, -ono.**

part*ire*, to depart	**fin*ire***, to finish
I depart, *I am departing,* *I do depart,* etc.	*I finish,* *I am finishing,* *I do finish,* etc.
io part***o*** tu part***i*** Lei, lui, lei part***e*** (egli, essa) noi part***iamo*** voi part***ite*** Loro, loro part***ono*** (essi, esse)	io fin***isco*** tu fin***isci*** Lei, lui, lei fin***isce*** (egli, essa) noi fin***iamo*** voi fin***ite*** Loro, loro fin***iscono*** (essi, esse)

COMMON VERBS LIKE *PARTIRE*

aprire, to open
coprire, to cover
dormire, to sleep
offrire, to offer
seguire, to follow
sentire, to hear, to feel
servire, to serve
soffrire, to suffer

COMMON VERBS LIKE *FINIRE*

ardire, to dare to
capire, to understand
condire, to season
disobbedire, to disobey
fornire, to furnish
guarire, to heal
obbedire, to obey
preferire, to prefer
proibire, to forbid, to prohibit
pulire, to clean
punire, to punish
spedire, to send, to mail
suggerire, to suggest

EXERCISES

A. Write the correct form of verbs *a* and *b* in the present indicative:

Example: Carlo non *finisce* niente.
a. capire *b*. sentire
a. capisce *b*. sente

1.	Tu *parti* tardi sabato mattina.	*a*. dormire	*b*. pulire
2.	Giorgio *ascolta* i suoi genitori.	*a*. seguire	*b*. disobbedire
3.	*Mangio* i ravioli.	*a*. preferire	*b*. servire
4.	Non *sentiamo* mai niente.	*a*. capire	*b*. condire
5.	*Bevono* tutto.	*a*. fornire	*b*. offrire
6.	*Scrivete* la lettera.	*a*. finire	*b*. spedire
7.	Non *manda* niente a nessuno.	*a*. proibire	*b*. servire
8.	*Vedi* il libro sul banco?	*a*. aprire	*b*. capire
9.	Non *prometto* niente a mio fratello.	*a*. suggerire	*b*. offrire
10.	*Compriamo* i piatti per la festa.	*a*. pulire	*b*. fornire

B. Complete the following sentences, using the verb in the model sentence:

1. *Capisci* la lezione.
   Lidia non _____ niente.
   Quelle ragazze _____ tutto.
2. Sandro *apre* le finestre.
   Noi _____ la porta quando fa caldo.
   Voi _____ i libri?
3. La maestra *punisce* alcuni alunni.
   Io _____ il mio cane.
   Le madri _____ i loro figli quando sono cattivi.

4. Non *suggerite* mai niente al vostro professore.
   La signorina _____qualcosa alle sue amiche.
   Cosa _____ a tua madre?
5. Cosa *preferite* fare stasera?
   Maria _____ mangiare invece di studiare.
   Tu e Gino _____ giocare o studiare?
6. *Partiamo* domani alle sei di mattina.
   (io) Non _____ per l'Italia prima di ottobre.
   I miei genitori _____ lunedì per Milano.
7. Ma perchè non *pulisci* la macchina?
   Giorgio ed io _____ la nostra macchina sportiva.
   Ragazzi, perchè _____ questa tavola?
8. *Dormite* così tranquilli!
   Anita ed Anna _____ invece di lavorare.
   (io) Non _____ mai.
9. *Spediamo* questo pacco a Paola.
   Margherita _____ la lettera ai genitori.
   (voi) Perchè non _____ una cartolina a Susanna?
10. *Senti* sempre i tuoi dischi!
    Lui _____ tanti programmi.
    Canio e Lucio _____ tutto quello che dice il professore.

C. Complete the Italian sentences:

1. He is suffering very much.	_____ molto.
2. The boys clean their room every Saturday.	I ragazzi _____ la loro camera ogni sabato.
3. The man obeys the doctor.	L'uomo _____ al dottore.
4. I open the door slowly.	_____ la porta lentamente.
5. They prefer to go out early.	_____ uscire presto.
6. That dog follows George everywhere.	Quel cane _____ Giorgio dappertutto.
7. Marisa furnishes the anchovies and the antipasto.	Marisa _____ le acciughe e l'antipasto.
8. My cousins send many post-cards from France.	I miei cugini _____ molte cartoline dalla Francia.
9. The doctor says that you (voi) heal very rapidly.	Il dottore dice che _____ rapidamente.
10. Mothers serve their children.	Le madri _____ i loro figli.

D. Answer the following questions in complete Italian sentences:

1. Chi pulisce la lavagna ogni giorno?
2. Obbediamo le leggi della città?
3. Apri la porta per le signore?
4. Tuo fratello capisce tutto ciò che legge?
5. Voi due dormite tardi la domenica?
6. Chi soffre in classe?
7. Chi punisce gli studenti cattivi?
8. Cosa preferisci studiare?
9. Chi guarisce i malati?
10. Spedite molte cartoline?

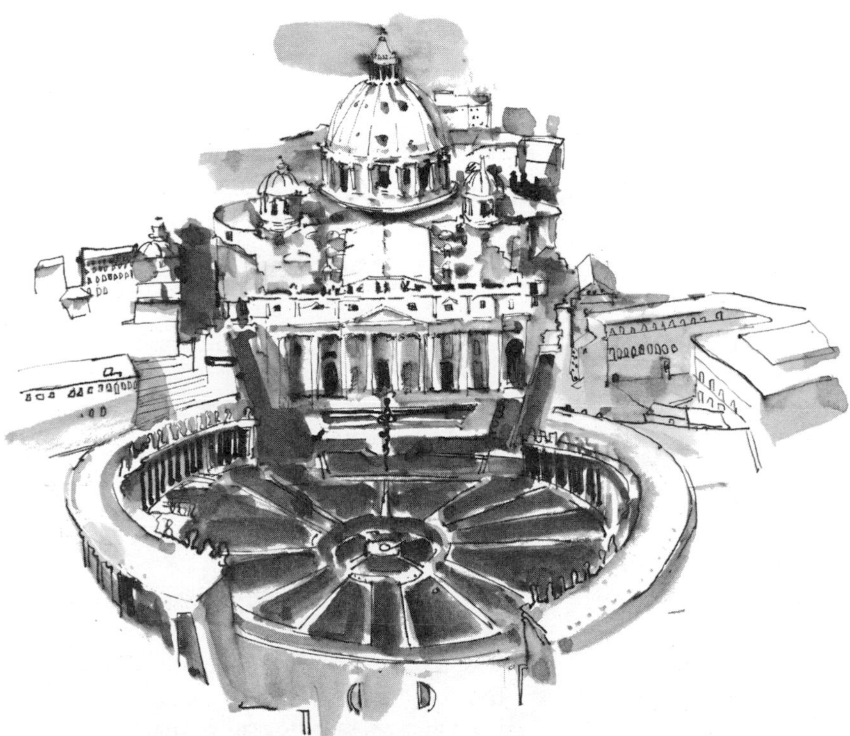

Veduta panoramica di *Piazza San Pietro* a Roma con la facciata della basilica dello stesso nome. Sia la piazza che la basilica fanno parte del Vaticano che è la sede della religione cattolica.

3. Present Indicative of Irregular Verbs

The following verbs are irregular in the present indicative:

andare, to go	vado, vai, va, andiamo, andate, vanno
apparire, to appear	apparisco (appaio), apparisci (appari), apparisce (appare), appariamo, apparite, appariscono (appaiono)
avere, to have	ho, hai, ha, abbiamo, avete, hanno
bere, to drink	bevo, bevi, beve, beviamo, bevete, bevono
cogliere, to pick, to gather	colgo, cogli, coglie, cogliamo, cogliete, colgono
condurre, to lead	conduco, conduci, conduce, conduciamo, conducete, conducono
dare, to give	do, dai, dà, diamo, date, danno
dire, to say	dico, dici, dice, diciamo, dite, dicono
dovere, to have to, must	devo (debbo), devi, deve, dobbiamo, dovete, devono (debbono)
essere, to be	sono, sei, è, siamo, siete, sono
fare, to make, to do	faccio, fai, fa, facciamo, fate, fanno
morire, to die	muoio, muori, muore, moriamo, morite, muoiono
parere, to seem, to appear	paio, pari, pare, pariamo, parete, paiono
piacere, to please	piaccio, piaci, piace, piacciamo, piacete, piacciono
porre, to put, to place	pongo, poni, pone, poniamo, ponete, pongono
possedere, to possess	possiedo (posseggo), possiedi, possiede, possediamo, possedete, possiedono (posseggono)
potere, to be able, may, can	posso, puoi, può, possiamo, potete, possono
rimanere, to remain, to stay	rimango, rimani, rimane, rimaniamo, rimanete, rimangono
riuscire, to succeed, to go out again	riesco, riesci, riesce, riusciamo, riuscite, riescono
salire, to ascend, to climb, to go up	salgo, sali, sale, saliamo, salite, salgono
sapere, to know	so, sai, sa, sappiamo, sapete, sanno

scegliere, to select, to choose	scelgo, scegli, sceglie, scegliamo, scegliete, scelgono
sedere, to sit	seggo (siedo), siedi, siede, sediamo, sedete, seggono (siedono)
stare, to be	sto, stai, sta, stiamo, state, stanno
tacere, to be silent	taccio, taci, tace, taciamo, tacete, tacciono
tenere, to hold, to have	tengo, tieni, tiene, teniamo, tenete, tengono
tradurre, to translate	traduco, traduci, traduce, traduciamo, traducete, traducono
udire, to hear	odo, odi, ode, udiamo, udite, odono
uscire, to go out	esco, esci, esce, usciamo, uscite, escono
valere, to be worth	valgo, vali, vale, valiamo, valete, valgono
venire, to come	vengo, vieni, viene, veniamo, venite, vengono
volere, to want, to wish	voglio, vuoi, vuole, vogliamo, volete, vogliono

Note

Some of the preceding irregular verbs tend to be regular in the **noi** and **voi** forms. However, there is no set rule to determine which of these verbs become regular in those forms.

EXERCISES

A. Complete each sentence below by choosing the appropriate verb from the following list:

dobbiamo	venite	vai
muoiono	ode	colgono
salgo	sei	dite
stanno		

1. Carlo non _____ tanto bene.
2. Teresa ed io _____ studiare per l'esame di domani.
3. A che ora _____ tu e Luisa domani?
4. Molte persone _____ di fame ogni giorno.
5. Per andare sopra _____ molte scale.
6. I ragazzi _____ dei fiori nel parco.
7. Sergio, _____ qui per guardare la televisione o no?
8. Tu e Viola _____ molte cose strane.
9. Scusino, signorine, come _____ oggi?
10. Tu _____ dal macellaio sabato mattina?

B. Rewrite each sentence, using the subject indicated in parentheses:

1. *Siamo* a New York da lunedì. (tu)
2. Carlo *rimane* a casa ogni sera. (io)
3. *Dice* sempre la stessa cosa! (loro)
4. D'estate *bevo* molto latte. (Giorgio)
5. *Scegliete* molti abiti nel negozio d'abbigliamenti? (Le ragazze)
6. *Puoi* mangiare questi spaghetti. (Lei, signore)
7. *Sa* sciare bene. (noi)
8. *Do* questo libro a Teodoro. (Tu e Mario)
9. *Ha* molti giornali. (io)
10. *Escono* presto la mattina. (tu)

C. Replace the verbs in italics with the correct form of each verb in parentheses:

1. Non *siete* nel salotto. (bere) (stare) (andare)
2. Perchè *dici* quelle cose? (scegliere) (fare) (spedire)
3. *Comprono* un foglio di carta. (volere) (cogliere) (avere)
4. *Studi* ogni mattina alle otto? (venire) (uscire) (apparire)
5. *Voglio* fare i compiti. (potere) (dovere) (sapere)

D. Complete the sentences in Italian:

1. *He must* viaggiare in treno. ----- viaggiare in treno.
2. *I am silent* quando parla mio padre. ----- quando parla mio padre.
3. *It's worth* molto denaro. ----- molto denaro.
4. *They appear* ogni anno a Natale. ----- ogni anno a Natale.
5. *She selects* i migliori fiori. ----- i migliori fiori.
6. *We do not succeed* a trovare i biglietti. ----- a trovare i biglietti.
7. *You* (*voi*) *are* troppo noiosi. ----- troppo noiosi.
8. *Are you* (*tu*) bene? ----- bene?
9. *The ladies have* molto da fare. ----- molto da fare.
10. *He does not do* niente tutto il giorno. ----- niente tutto il giorno.

E. *Progressive Substitution*. The drill begins with a complete Italian sentence. Complete each of the following sentences, substituting the new word or words given and using as much of the preceding sentence as possible. For example, begin with this sentence: Parlo italiano.

INCOMPLETE SENTENCES	COMPLETED SENTENCES
Noi _____.	Noi *parliamo italiano.*
_____ francese.	*Noi parliamo* francese.
_____ parlate _____.	*Voi* parlate *francese.*

Bevo un bicchiere di latte.

1. Tu _____.
2. Lui _____.
3. _____ bevono _____.
4. _____ di limonata.
5. Voi _____.
6. _____ scelgono _____.
7. _____ dei fiori.
8. Io _____.
9. _____ cogliamo _____.
10. _____ della carta.
11. Tu _____.
12. _____ del pane.
13. _____ fa _____.
14. Loro _____.
15. _____ avete _____.

F. Complete the following sentences, using the verb in italics in its correct form:

Example: *Parli* con Luisa?
Sì, *parlo* con Luisa.

1. *Sai* che l'Italia è piccola? (io) Sì, lo _____.
2. Chi *parla* tanto? I ragazzi _____ tanto.
3. Cosa *volete* ascoltare? (noi) _____ ascoltare i dischi.
4. Cosa *bevi?* (io) _____ del latte.
5. *Riesci* mai a pensare agli studi? (io) No, non _____ mai a pensare agli studi.
6. *Uscite* spesso? (noi) Sì, _____ spesso.
7. Chi *fa* tanto rumore? Mia sorella _____ tanto rumore.
8. *Posso* andare con Franco oggi? No, (tu) non _____ andare con Franco oggi.
9. Cosa *avete* in quella scatola? (noi) Non _____ niente in quella scatola.
10. Chi *va* con noi? Giorgio e Carlo _____ con noi.
11. *Vieni* da Luigi? (io) Sì, _____ da Luigi.
12. *Sali* molte scale tutti i giorni? No, (io) non _____ molte scale.
13. Come *pare* Maria? _____ malata.
14. *Dovete* telefonare a vostra madre? No, (noi) non le _____ telefonare.
15. Ti *siedi* accanto a Paolo a scuola? Sì, mi _____ accanto a Paolo.

4. The Imperative (Familiar Commands)

AFFIRMATIVE	
Singular	Plural
parlare, (tu) parl*a* to speak (speak)	(noi) parl*iamo* (let's speak) (voi) parl*ate* (speak)
vèndere, (tu) vend*i* to sell (sell)	(noi) vend*iamo* (let's sell) (voi) vend*ete* (sell)
finire, (tu) fin*isci* to finish (finish)	(noi) fin*iamo* (let's finish) (voi) fin*ite* (finish)

NEGATIVE	
Singular	Plural
parlare (tu) non parl*are* (don't speak)	(noi) non parl*iamo* (let's not speak) (voi) non parl*ate* (don't speak)
vendere (tu) non vend*ere* (don't sell)	(noi) non vend*iamo* (let's not sell) (voi) non vend*ete* (don't sell)
finire (tu) non fin*ire* (don't finish)	(noi) non fin*iamo* (let's not finish) (voi) non fin*ite* (don't finish)

Note

1. The forms of the imperative (familar commands) in the affirmative of regular verbs are the same as the corresponding forms of the present indicative, with the exception of the **tu** form of **-are** verbs, which changes from **-i** to **-a.**

PRESENT INDICATIVE	IMPERATIVE
tu cant*i*	(tu) cant*a*

2. The **tu** affirmative form is made negative by adding **non** to the infinitive.

AFFIRMATIVE	NEGATIVE
(tu) **canta**	(tu) ***non*** **cantare**

3. The **noi** and **voi** forms of the imperative are made negative by adding **non** to the affirmative.

AFFIRMATIVE	NEGATIVE
(noi) **cantiamo**	(noi) ***non*** **cantiamo**
(voi) **cantate**	(voi) ***non*** **cantate**

4. The verbs **avere** and **essere** have irregular imperatives in the **tu** and **voi** forms.

avere, to have	**essere**, to be
(tu) **abbi**, have	(tu) **sii**, be
(noi) **abbiamo**, let's have	(noi) **siamo**, let's be
(voi) **abbiate**, have	(voi) **siate**, be

5. Four irregular **-are** verbs have an irregular **tu** form.

andare, to go	**dare**, to give	**fare**, to do	**stare**, to be
(tu) **va'**	(tu) **da'**	(tu) **fa'**	(tu) **sta'**

Note

The verb **dire** follows the same pattern.

(tu) **di'**

REVIEW OF THE IMPERATIVE (For the polite forms, see Verb Lesson 17.)

ballare, to dance

FAMILIAR	POLITE
Affirmative	
(tu) Balla! (voi) Ballate! (noi) Balliamo!	(Lei) Balli! (Loro) Ballino!
Negative	
(tu) Non ballare! (voi) Non ballate! (noi) Non balliamo!	(Lei) Non balli! (Loro) Non ballino!

vendere, to sell

FAMILIAR	POLITE
(tu) Vendi! (voi) Vendete! (noi) Vendiamo!	(Lei) Venda! (Loro) Vendano!

finire (isc), to finish

FAMILIAR	POLITE
(tu) Finisci! (voi) Finite! (noi) Finiamo!	(Lei) Finisca! (Loro) Finiscano!

partire, to depart

FAMILIAR	POLITE
(tu) Parti! (voi) Partite! (noi) Partiamo!	(Lei) Parta! (Loro) Partano!

EXERCISES

A. Write the three forms of the imperative–**tu, noi, voi**–for each of the following verbs in the affirmative:

1. comprare
2. aprire
3. dovere
4. leggere
5. uscire
6. giocare
7. scendere
8. bere
9. guardare
10. obbedire

B. Translate into Italian:

1. let's eat
2. don't speak (tu)
3. go (voi)
4. close the door (tu)
5. let's enjoy
6. don't drink (tu)
7. promise (voi)
8. give (tu)
9. let's not study
10. have (voi)

C. Complete the English sentences:

1. Guarda la televisione!	----- at television!
2. Non disturbare tuo fratello!	----- your brother!
3. Scegliamo questi fiori rossi!	----- these red flowers!
4. Abbiate pazienza, ragazzi!	----- patience, children!
5. Pulisci bene, Carlo!	----- well, Charles!
6. Cantiamo ad alta voce!	----- sing loudly!
7. Non dormite tardi domani!	----- late tomorrow!
8. Sii buona, Maria!	-----, Mary!
9. Non spedire quel pacco!	----- that package!
10. Pensa bene a quel che dici!	----- well about what you are saying!

D. Rewrite each expression so as to give your brother the following familiar commands:

Example: cercare il giornale
Cerca il giornale!

1. prendere il gelato
2. non dimenticare i panini
3. ballare con Carla
4. dare un regalo a Peppe
5. non portare i compagni a casa
6. venire presto stasera
7. fare attenzione in classe
8. non porre i libri sul tavolo
9. camminare insieme a Luca
10. dire la verità

E. Rewrite each expression so as to give your friends the following familiar commands:

Example: arrivare in orario
Arrivate in orario!

1. essere pazienti
2. non avere fretta
3. chiamare Federico
4. correggere i compiti
5. non perdere la giacca
6. cogliere i fiori
7. obbedire al babbo
8. non bussare alla porta
9. rispondere bene
10. finire di parlare

5. The Present Perfect of *Avere* Verbs

This present perfect is formed by combining the present indicative of **avere** and the past participle of the verb.

The endings of past participles of regular verbs are:

-ato for **-are** verbs	compr***ato***
-uto for **-ere** verbs	vend***uto***
-ito for **-ire** verbs	dorm***ito***

	comprare, to buy	**vendere**, to sell	**dormire**, to sleep
	I bought, *I have bought,* *I did buy,* etc.	*I sold,* *I have sold,* *I did sell,* etc.	*I slept,* *I have slept,* *I did sleep,* etc.
io	***ho*** compr***ato***	***ho*** vend***uto***	***ho*** dorm***ito***
tu	***hai*** compr***ato***	***hai*** vend***uto***	***hai*** dorm***ito***
Lei, lui, lei	***ha*** compr***ato***	***ha*** vend***uto***	***ha*** dorm***ito***
noi	***abbiamo*** compr***ato***	***abbiamo*** vend***uto***	***abbiamo*** dorm***ito***
voi	***avete*** compr***ato***	***avete*** vend***uto***	***avete*** dorm***ito***
Loro, loro	***hanno*** compr***ato***	***hanno*** vend***uto***	***hanno*** dorm***ito***

Note

1. Verbs conjugated like **finire** have the same past participle as those conjugated like **dormire**: **finire** = fin***ito***

2. The following verbs have irregular past participles:

Verb	Past Participle
aggiungere, to add	***aggiunto***, added
apparire, to appear	***apparso***, appeared
appendere, to hang	***appeso***, hung
aprire, to open	***aperto***, opened
bere, to drink	***bevuto***, drunk
chiedere, to ask	***chiesto***, asked
chiudere, to close	***chiuso***, closed

cogliere, to gather — ***colto***, gathered
commettere, to commit — ***commesso***, committed
comprendere, to understand — ***compreso***, understood
concludere, to conclude — ***concluso***, concluded
condurre, to lead — ***condotto***, led
conoscere, to know — ***conosciuto***, known
convincere, to convince — ***convinto***, convinced
coprire, to cover — ***coperto***, covered
correggere, to correct — ***corretto***, corrected
correre, to run — ***corso***, run
cuocere, to cook — ***cotto***, cooked
decidere, to decide — ***deciso***, decided
difendere, to defend — ***difeso***, defended
dire, to say — ***detto***, said
dividere, to divide — ***diviso***, divided
fare, to do, to make — ***fatto***, done, made
leggere, to read — ***letto***, read
mettere, to put, to place — ***messo***, put, placed
offrire, to offer — ***offerto***, offered
perdere, to lose — ***perso***, lost
porre, to place — ***posto***, placed
prendere, to take — ***preso***, taken
promettere, to promise — ***promesso***, promised
proporre, to propose — ***proposto***, proposed
proteggere, to protect — ***protetto***, protected
raggiungere, to arrive, to reach — ***raggiunto***, arrived, reached
rendere, to render, to give back — ***reso***, rendered
ridere, to laugh — ***riso***, laughed
riflettere, to reflect — ***riflesso***, reflected
rispondere, to answer — ***risposto***, answered
rompere, to break — ***rotto***, broken
scegliere, to select — ***scelto***, selected
scommettere, to bet — ***scommesso***, bet
scrivere, to write — ***scritto***, written
soffrire, to suffer — ***sofferto***, suffered
spendere, to spend — ***speso***, spent
stringere, to bind, to clasp — ***stretto***, bound, clasped
togliere, to take from — ***tolto***, taken from
vedere, to see — ***visto (veduto)***, seen
vincere, to win — ***vinto***, won

3. In the present perfect, the present indicative of **avere** is treated as the main verb and the past participle is added to it.

Non ho parlato in classe.	I haven't spoken in class.

EXERCISES

A. Rewrite the sentences, changing each of the verbs in parentheses to the present perfect:

1. Roberto *ha spedito* una lettera. (scrivere, leggere, trovare)
2. Perchè *hai preso* quella bottiglia? (servire, rompere, portare)
3. Gli studenti *hanno ascoltato* il programma. (vedere, guardare, seguire)
4. Cosa *avete venduto?* (prendere, coprire, suggerire)
5. Non *ho dormito* bene. (fare, lavorare, udire)

B. Change the italicized verbs to the present perfect:

1. *Metto* il burro sul pane.
2. *Lavori* tutto il giorno?
3. Non *attraversano* la strada da soli.
4. Il professore *corregge* gli esami.
5. *Finite* di mangiare prima delle otto?
6. La signora *telefona* a suo marito.
7. Chi *sceglie* questi broccoli?
8. *Cerco* il mio cane nel parco.
9. *Pulisci* la camera ogni sabato?
10. Non *spendete* mai molto denaro.
11. *Devono* ascoltare un programma alla radio.
12. Chi *canta* ad alta voce?
13. *Aprite* la porta immediatamente?
14. Mio padre *racconta* molte storie.
15. Non *capisci* mai niente!

C. Change the italicized verbs to the present indicative:

Example: *Ho abbracciato* mia nonna.
Abbraccio mia nonna.

1. *Hai capito* la lezione?
2. *Ho tolto* la giacca dalla sedia.
3. *Hanno udito* delle cose strane.

4. *Hai giocato* con i bambini?
5. Signore, *ha finito* di leggere?
6. Lei *ha cenato* dai nonni.
7. *Abbiamo detto* una bugia a Luigi.
8. *Avete messo* le scarpe vicino alla porta.
9. Gianni *ha suggerito* di uscire stasera.
10. *Ho cambiato* la macchina.

D. Answer the following questions in Italian, changing the verbs from the present indicative to the present perfect:

Example: *Compri* il giornale dal giornalaio?
Sì, *ho comprato* il giornale dal giornalaio.

1. A che ora *finiscono* il lavoro?
2. Chi *chiude* la finestra?
3. *Comprendi* questo film?
4. Tu e Giorgio *preparate* la colazione?
5. I genitori *soffrono* molto?
6. Chi *mette* i guanti sul tavolo?
7. *Hai* molto da fare?
8. La signorina *sa* fare quel lavoro?
9. *Posso* salutare quel soldato?
10. *Ceniamo* alle otto o alle nove? (Voi)

E. Translate into Italian, using the present perfect:

1. They ran to the store.
2. He danced with Regina.
3. I promised to write a letter.
4. You (tu) closed the door.
5. Didn't you (voi) see the hat?
6. Sir, have you punished the dog?
7. The carabiniere shouted "Alt!"
8. Rose did not wash the dishes.
9. Did they believe the story?
10. I slept late this morning.

6. The Present Perfect of *Essere* Verbs

The endings of past participles of regular verbs conjugated with **essere** are the same as those conjugated with **avere**.

-ato for **-are** verbs	arriv***ato***
-uto for **-ere** verbs	cad***uto***
-ito for **-ire** verbs	part***ito***

The present perfect of "**essere**" verbs is formed by combining the present indicative of **essere** and the past participle of the verb.

arrivare, to arrive	
I arrived, I have arrived, I did arrive, etc.	
Masculine Subject	Feminine Subject
io ***sono*** arriv***ato***	io ***sono*** arriv***ata***
tu ***sei*** arriv***ato***	tu ***sei*** arriv***ata***
Lei ***è*** arriv***ato***	Lei ***è*** arriv***ata***
lui ***è*** arriv***ato***	lei ***è*** arriv***ata***
noi ***siamo*** arriv***ati***	noi ***siamo*** arriv***ate***
voi ***siete*** arriv***ati***	voi ***siete*** arriv***ate***
Loro ***sono*** arriv***ati***	Loro ***sono*** arriv***ate***
loro ***sono*** arriv***ati***	loro ***sono*** arriv***ate***

Note

1. Like adjectives, past participles conjugated with **essere** agree in gender and number with the subject.

Maria *è caduta* ieri.	Mary fell yesterday.
I ragazzi *sono arrivati* alle sette.	The boys arrived at seven o'clock.

2. Transitive verbs (those that take an object) are almost always conjugated with **avere**.

Ho **comprato** un **libro**. (comprato: transitive verb; libro: direct object)	I bought a book.
Luigi *ha* **venduto** la **bicicletta**. (venduto: transitive verb; bicicletta: direct object)	Louis sold the bike.

Intransitive verbs (those that do not take an object) and all reflexive verbs (**vestirsi, lavarsi, svegliarsi**, etc.) are conjugated with **essere**.

Maria *è* **andata** a scuola. (andata: intransitive verb)	Mary has gone to school.
Siamo **tornati** alle due. (tornati: intransitive verb)	We returned at two o'clock.
Mi *sono* **alzato** presto. (alzato: reflexive verb)	I got up early.

3. The following common verbs are conjugated with **essere** (instead of **avere**) in the present perfect:

Infinitive	Past Participle
andare, to go	***andato(-a, -i, -e)***, gone
venire, to come	***venuto***, came
arrivare, to arrive	***arrivato***, arrived
partire, to depart, to leave (town)	***partito***, departed, left
entrare, to enter	***entrato***, entered
uscire, to leave (the house)	***uscito***, left
salire, to go up	***salito***, gone up
scendere, to go (come) down	***sceso***, gone (come) down
tornare, to return	***tornato***, turned, returned
ritornare, to return, to come back	***ritornato***, returned, come back
cadere, to fall	***caduto***, fallen
restare, to remain, to stay	***restato***, remained, stayed
rimanere, to remain, to stay	***rimasto***, remained, stayed
nascere, to be born	***nato***, been born
morire, to die	***morto***, died
essere, to be	***stato***, been
stare, to be	***stato***, been

succedere, to happen	***successo***, happened
diventare, to become	***diventato***, become
piacere, to like, to be pleasing to	***piaciuto***, liked, been pleasing to
vivere, to live, to reside	***vissuto***, lived, resided
riuscire, to succeed	***riuscito***, succeeded
apparire, to seem, to appear	***apparso***, seemed, appeared
durare, to last	***durato***, lasted

EXERCISES

A. Rewrite the following sentences, changing the verb to the present perfect:

1. Le mie cugine *entrano* alle sei.
2. Giorgio *va* dal tabaccaio.
3. Carla ed io *usciamo* presto la mattina.
4. *Riuscite* a trovare dei posti buoni?
5. La bambina *nasce* a settembre.
6. *Torno* in Africa da solo.
7. A che ora *viene* Anna?
8. *Parti* per la Germania a febbraio?
9. Signora, Lei rimane a casa stasera?
10. Gloria e Susanna *diventano* bellissime!

B. Translate the italicized words into English:

1. Il problema *è diventato* serio.
2. *Sono caduti* nella neve.
3. *Siete entrati* poco fa?
4. Dove *sei andato*?
5. Cosa *è successo*?
6. *Sono tornato* prima di mio fratello.
7. Dante *è nato* a Firenze.
8. I soldati *sono morti* per la patria.
9. A che ora *sei scesa*?
10. *Sono apparse* qui per la prima volta.

C. Complete the sentences in Italian:

1. She went down to the second floor.	_____ al secondo piano.
2. I came to school early.	_____ a scuola presto.

3. His brother was born in Rome.	_____ a Roma.
4. The girls left for Spain last week.	_____ per la Spagna la settimana scorsa.
5. The film lasted two hours.	_____ due ore.
6. We succeeded in going to the movies.	_____ ad andare al cinema.
7. At what time did my aunt arrive?	A che ora _____ mia zia?
8. They have become famous.	_____ famosi.
9. Did you fall in the snow, sir?	_____ nella neve, signore?
10. Where have you (tu) been?	Dove _____?

D. Rewrite the following sentences, substituting for each masculine subject the equivalent feminine subject:

Example: Il ragazzo è uscito.
La ragazza è uscita.

1. Mio fratello è caduto.
2. Gli uomini sono saliti proprio ora.
3. Lo zio di Mario è diventato povero.
4. Non sono ancora arrivati.
5. I fratelli sono stati al mercato.
6. Quando è nato?
7. Con chi è rimasto?
8. Il maestro è entrato pochi minuti fa.
9. Il nonno è tornato in Italia.
10. Sono andato con Federico alla spiaggia.

E. Answer the following questions in Italian:

1. Dove sei andato(a) ieri sera?
2. Ti è piaciuto il dramma?
3. Siete ritornati un'altra volta?
4. A che ora sei arrivato(a) a casa?
5. Quando sono entrati(e) in chiesa?
6. Sei nato(a) in Italia o negli Stati Uniti?
7. La signora è scesa stamattina?
8. Siete rimasti(e) molto tempo a Milano?
9. Tu e Franco siete stati al mare?
10. I tuoi compagni sono già partiti?

7. The Imperfect Indicative

REGULAR VERBS

The imperfect indicative of regular verbs is formed by:

1. dropping the infinitive ending **(-are, -ere, -ire)**
2. adding to the stem the following endings:

-are verbs:	**-avo,**	**-avi,**	**-ava,**	**-avamo,**	**-avate,**	**-avano**
-ere verbs:	**-evo,**	**-evi,**	**-eva,**	**-evamo,**	**-evate,**	**-evano**
-ire verbs:	**-ivo,**	**-ivi,**	**-iva,**	**-ivamo,**	**-ivate,**	**-ivano**

	comprare, to buy	**vendere,** to sell	**finire**, to finish
	I was buying, *I used to buy,* *I bought,* etc.	*I was selling,* *I used to sell,* *I sold,* etc.	*I was finishing,* *I used to finish,* *I finished,* etc.
io	compr***avo***	vend***evo***	fin***ivo***
tu	compr***avi***	vend***evi***	fin***ivi***
Lei, lui, lei	compr***ava***	vend***eva***	fin***iva***
noi	compr***avamo***	vend***evamo***	fin***ivamo***
voi	compr***avate***	vend***evate***	fin***ivate***
Loro, loro	compr***avano***	vend***evano***	fin***ivano***

Note

1. Except for the fact that each conjugation retains its characteristic vowel (*-a* in **-are** verbs, *-e* in **-ere** verbs, *-i* in **-ire** verbs), the endings for the imperfect indicative are the same for all verbs.
2. Verbs like **finire** do not add **-isc** in the imperfect, as is done for the present tense.

IRREGULAR VERBS

andare, to go	andavo, andavi, andava, andavamo, andavate, andavano
bere, to drink	bevevo, bevevi, beveva, bevevamo, bevevate, bevevano
condurre, to lead	conducevo, conducevi, conduceva, conducevamo, conducevate, conducevano
dare, to give	davo, davi, dava, davamo, davate, davano
dire, to say	dicevo, dicevi, diceva, dicevamo, dicevate, dicevano
essere, to be	ero, eri, era, eravamo, eravate, erano
fare, to do	facevo, facevi, faceva, facevamo, facevate, facevano
porre, to put	ponevo, ponevi, poneva, ponevamo, ponevate, ponevano
stare, to be	stavo, stavi, stava, stavamo, stavate, stavano
tradurre, to translate	traducevo, traducevi, traduceva, traducevamo, traducevate, traducevano

USES OF THE IMPERFECT

1*a*. To express a *continuous* action in the past.

Giovanni ***scriveva*** una lettera.	John was writing a letter.

b. To express two past actions going on at the same time.

Cosa ***facevi*** mentre Tina ***mangiava***?	What were you doing while Tina was eating?

2. To express a *repeated* or *customary* action in the past.

Lo ***vedevo*** tutte le mattine.	I saw (used to see) him every morning.
Paolo ***andava*** in chiesa ogni domenica.	Paul went (used to go) to church every Sunday.

3. To *describe persons* or *things* in the past.

Aveva una faccia triste.	She had a sad face.
Era una macchina vecchia.	It was an old car.

4. When the word *would* means *used to*.

Mio padre mi ***portava*** spesso a caccia.	My father would (used to) take me hunting often.

5. With the present perfect.
   The imperfect describes what was going on in the past when a definite action occurred (present perfect).

Giorgio ***ha telefonato*** (present perfect) mentre ***studiavo.*** (imperfect)	George telephoned while I was studying.
Sara ***è entrata*** (present perfect) mentre noi ***uscivamo.*** (imperfect)	Sara entered while we were going out.

Note

The imperfect of **avere** is generally translated by *had*, and the imperfect of **essere** by *was* or *were*. The imperfect of **potere** is often translated as *could*.

avevo	I had
eravamo	we were
poteva	he could

EXERCISES

A. Rewrite each sentence, replacing the verb in italics with the imperfect of the verbs in parentheses:

1. *Lavoravano* in Egitto. (viaggiare, essere, soffrire)
2. *Mangiavi* molto pane da piccolo. (comprare, fare, prendere)
3. *Scrivevo* alcune lettere. (cercare, spedire, scegliere)
4. *Parlavate* con Luigi. (ridere, bere, uscire)
5. *Amavamo* la musica di Verdi. (ascoltare, sentire, godere)

B. Rewrite the following sentences in the imperfect:

1. *Parla* con Tommaso.
2. *Faccio* il mio lavoro attentamente.

3. Giacomo, dove *vai*?
4. *Conosciamo* molte ragazze francesi.
5. *Date* un regalo a vostra zia per Natale?
6. Il signor Remi *traduce* dall'italiano all'inglese.
7. *Metti* i fagioli nel frigorifero.
8. *Guardo* spesso i programmi di varietà alla televisione.
9. Maria *sta* bene.
10. Luigi *scrive* spesso a sua madre.
11. *Preferite* andare in Canadà o nel Messico?
12. Quei giovani *amano* la musica popolare.
13. *È* una bella giornata.
14. *Ho* un bel paio di guanti!
15. *Puoi* andare dal tabaccaio?

C. Change the infinitive to the correct form of the imperfect, the present perfect, and the present indicative:

1. lui (*essere*)
2. tu (*comprare*)
3. Loro (*capire*)
4. noi (*abbracciare*)
5. Gina (*andare*)
6. voi (*chiedere*)
7. lei (*vedere*)
8. io (*servire*)
9. Lei (*dire*)
10. loro (*mettere*)

D. Translate the italicized words into Italian:

1. *You* (*tu*) *were walking* lungo la spiaggia.
2. *Maria was reading* il giornale quando io sono arrivato.
3. *We would listen to* la radio tutto il giorno.
4. *They were singing and laughing* allo stesso tempo.
5. *I used to drink* latte.
6. *He seemed young* venti anni fa.
7. *Lidia and Arturo worked* mentre io ballavo.
8. *We did not disobey* la nonna quando eravamo piccoli.
9. *You* (*voi*) *used to run* dappertutto.
10. *She would do* il suo compito con diligenza.
11. Cosa *was he saying*?
12. *I had* un mal di testa.
13. *They couldn't defend* il soldato.
14. *We would play* a scacchi ogni martedì.
15. *He waited for me* sempre vicino alla stazione.

E. Translate the italicized words into English:

1. Non *poteva* cantare.	He _____ (to) sing.
2. *Scrivevo* una lettera.	_____ a letter.
3. *Ridevamo* spesso.	_____ often.
4. *Era* una bella giornata.	_____ a beautiful day.
5. Cosa *diceva*?	What _____ you _____ ?
6. Non *pulivate* mai la vostra camera!	You never _____ your room!
7. Mi *credeva* sempre.	He always _____ me.
8. *Volevamo* partire presto.	_____ to leave early.
9. La signorina *sceglieva* i migliori abiti.	The young lady _____ the best clothes.
10. Non *fumavi* anni fa?	_____ years ago?

F. Answer the following questions in complete sentences in Italian:

1. Faceva bel tempo quando sei arrivato(a) a Napoli?
2. Chi ascoltava i dischi ogni giorno?
3. Quando andavi al mare?
4. Chi aspettavate?
5. Mangiavi mentre studiavi?
6. Cosa dicevi mentre parlavo al telefono?
7. Facevo rumore mentre dormivo?
8. C'erano molti ragazzi nel parco?
9. Dove andavi ieri sera con Franca?
10. Perchè non eravate in classe?

I due lati [sides] di *una moneta coniata* [coined] *a Siracusa*, in Sicilia, circa il 479 a.C., quando la città faceva parte della Magna Grecia.

8. The Future Tense

The future tense of all three conjugations is formed by dropping the final **-e** of the infinitive and adding the following endings: **-ò**, **-ai**, **-à**, **-emo**, **-ete**, **-anno**.

In regular **-are** verbs, the **-a** changes to an **-e**:

Infinitive	Future
parl*a*re	io parl*e*rò

	parlare, to speak	**rispondere**, to answer	**pulire**, to clean
	I shall (*will*) *speak, I am going to speak,* etc.	*I shall* (*will*) *answer, I am going to answer,* etc.	*I shall* (*will*) *clean, I am going to clean,* etc.
io	parl***erò***	rispond***erò***	pul***irò***
tu	parl***erai***	rispond***erai***	pul***irai***
Lei, lui, lei	parl***erà***	rispond***erà***	pul***irà***
noi	parl***eremo***	rispond***eremo***	pul***iremo***
voi	parl***erete***	rispond***erete***	pul***irete***
Loro, loro	parl***eranno***	rispond***eranno***	pul***iranno***

Note

1. **-care** and **-gare** verbs add an **-h** before the **-e** of the endings:

cer*care*	cerc***herò***
pa*gare*	pag***herò***

2. In **-sciare**, **-ciare**, and **-giare** verbs, the **-ia** changes to an **-e**:

la*sciare*	lasc***erò***
cominc*iare*	cominc***erò***
mang*iare*	mang***erò***

USES OF THE FUTURE

1. The future is generally used in Italian, as in English, to refer to an anticipated event.

Pranzerai con Luigi domani?	Will you dine with Louis tomorrow?

2. The future is also used in a subordinate clause referring to future time, introduced by conjunctions such as **appena, quando**, or by **se**.

Andremo al cinema ***quando*** **saremo** a Roma.	We will go to the movies when we are in Rome.
Comprerò questa giacca ***se*** **ribasseranno** il prezzo.	I'll buy this jacket if they reduce the price.

VERBS IRREGULAR IN THE FUTURE TENSE

1. **essere**, to be   sarò, sarai, sarà, saremo, sarete, saranno

2. The following verbs drop the **-a** or **-e** before **-re** of the infinitive ending before adding the endings of the future:

andare, to go	andrò, andrai, andrà, andremo, andrete, andranno
avere, to have	avrò, avrai, avrà, avremo, avrete, avranno
cadere, to fall	cadrò, cadrai, cadrà, cadremo, cadrete, cadranno
dovere, to have to, must	dovrò, dovrai, dovrà, dovremo, dovrete, dovranno
potere, to be able, can	potrò, potrai, potrà, potremo, potrete, potranno
sapere, to know	saprò, saprai, saprà, sapremo, saprete, sapranno
vedere, to see	vedrò, vedrai, vedrà, vedremo, vedrete, vedranno

3. The following verbs drop the **-e** of the infinitive ending before adding the endings of the future:

dare, to give	darò, darai, darà, daremo, darete, daranno
fare, to do	farò, farai, farà, faremo, farete, faranno
stare, to be	starò, starai, starà, staremo, starete, staranno

4. The following verbs assume an **-rr** before the future endings. These follow no particular pattern:

bere, to drink	berrò, berrai, berrà, berremo, berrete, berranno
rimanere, to remain	rimarrò, rimarrai, rimarrà, rimarremo, rimarrete, rimarranno

tenere, to hold, to keep	terrò, terrai, terrà, terremo, terrete, terranno
venire, to come	verrò, verrai, verrà, verremo, verrete, verranno
volere, to wish, to want	vorrò, vorrai, vorrà, vorremo, vorrete, vorranno

EXERCISES

A. Write the correct form of the future of the verbs in parentheses:

1. (dare) Il babbo _____ un regalo a Stefano.
2. (abitare) Io _____ vicino ai miei genitori.
3. (sentire) Tu ed io _____ un bel concerto venerdì.
4. (volere) Gli Americani _____ visitare il Vaticano.
5. (potere) Voi _____ uscire più tardi.
6. (accompagnare) Tu _____ Lola alla cattedrale.
7. (rispondere) Il professore _____ alla tua domanda.
8. (cantare) Due tenori _____ stasera nell'opera di Puccini.
9. (rimanere) La signorina non _____ sola.
10. (partire) Il treno _____ dalla stazione di Firenze alle tre precise.
11. (perdonare) Mio padre non mi _____ mai.
12. (finire) Gli ambasciatori non _____ a tempo.
13. (dire) Io non _____ niente ai miei amici.
14. (apparire) Noi _____ alla televisione la settimana prossima.
15. (avere) Giorgio, _____ molto da fare domani?

B. Rewrite the following sentences, changing the verbs from the imperfect to the future:

1. *Venivano* dopo il programma delle sette.
2. Mirella mi *scriveva* da Venezia spesso.
3. Il presidente *parlava* ai giornalisti.
4. *Vedevi* gli attori al teatro.
5. *Offrivano* una sigaretta ad Antonio.
6. *Era* una bella giornata.
7. Viviana *faceva* colazione prima di me.
8. *Telefonavo* a casa ogni venerdì sera.
9. *Conoscevano* molti turisti a Napoli.
10. *Dovevi* studiare molto per gli esami?

C. Complete the Italian sentences:

1. *He will prepare* la cena.	_____ la cena.
2. *We shall sell* la bicicletta.	_____ la bicicletta.
3. *Will she fly* in un aviogetto?	_____ in un aviogetto?
4. *They will follow* questa macchina.	_____ questa macchina.
5. *Will she phone* fra poco?	_____ fra poco?
6. *Will you* (*tu*) *keep* questi libri per me?	_____ questi libri per me?
7. *You* (*tu*) *will eat* dei cannelloni squisiti a Bari.	_____ dei cannelloni squisiti a Bari.
8. *We shall walk* fino al Lido.	_____ fino al Lido.
9. I miei cugini *will receive* molte cartoline.	I miei cugini _____ molte cartoline.
10. Pietro *will read* due romanzi.	Pietro _____ due romanzi.

D. Translate the italicized words into English:

1. *Offriranno* molto denaro al giovane.
2. *Andrai* a teatro con Giacomo?
3. *Non arriverò* prima delle dodici.
4. *Metterete* del vino buono a tavola?
5. Il signor Bianchi non *prenderà* un gelato.
6. Lo *farò* molto volentieri.
7. Mia sorella ed io *cercheremo* delle riviste italiane.
8. I professori *correggeranno* i compiti.
9. Sandra *verrà* alla trattoria con noi.
10. Non *cadremo* più nella neve.

E. Answer each question in complete sentences in Italian. The verb in the answer *must* be in the future:

1. A chi telefoni?
2. Cosa scegliete come piatto principale?
3. Che tempo fa?
4. Possono vedere quello spettacolo?
5. Carla sposa Giovanni o Alberto?
6. Riesci a convincere tua madre?
7. Cercate qualche cosa in farmacia?
8. Cosa chiediamo al macellaio?
9. Rimango qui stasera?
10. Cosa porti alla scampagnata?

9. Review of Verb Lessons 1–8

A. Fill in horizontally the three missing forms, using the verb already given:

	Present Indicative	Present Perfect	Imperfect	Future
Example:	cammino	ho camminato	camminavo	camminerò
1.	esci	_____	_____	_____
2.	abbiamo	_____	_____	_____
3.	_____	è partita	_____	_____
4.	_____	_____	giocavate	_____
5.	_____	_____	_____	arriveranno
6.	cado	_____	_____	_____
7.	siete	_____	_____	_____
8.	_____	hai bevuto	_____	_____
9.	_____	_____	pagavamo	_____
10.	_____	ha fatto	_____	_____
11.	vengono	_____	_____	_____
12.	_____	_____	_____	potrò
13.	_____	_____	mangiavi	_____
14.	_____	_____	_____	comprerà
15.	rispondiamo	_____	_____	_____

B. Write the correct form of each verb in the tense indicated:

1. accettare (*future*)	Clara non _____ niente da Carlo.
2. studiare (*imperative*)	Giorgio, _____ la lezione bene!
3. arrivare (*imperfect*)	Le signorine _____ sempre in ritardo.
4. scegliere (*present perfect*)	Noi _____ le banane fresche.
5. fare (*present*)	Io _____ troppo in classe.
6. volere (*imperfect*)	Tu _____ andare al mercato con me?
7. lasciare (*imperative*)	Ragazzi, _____ i libri sul tavolo!
8. vendere (*present perfect*)	Mia zia _____ la macchina da cucire.
9. nascere (*present perfect*)	La bambina _____ alle otto di mattina.
10. mettere (*imperative*)	(Noi) _____ tutto su questo scaffale!
11. vedere (*future*)	Voi non _____ nessuno alla spiaggia.
12. potere (*imperfect*)	Loro _____ ballare abbastanza bene.

13.	spendere (*present perfect*)	Io _____ troppo per questo abito.
14.	credere (*imperative*)	Susanna, non _____ a quelle storie!
15.	viaggiare (*future*)	I giovani _____ lungo la costa.

C. Answer the questions by following the example shown:

Example: Oggi mangio molto. E ieri?
Ieri ho mangiato molto.

1. Oggi pulisco la camera. E domani?
2. Adesso non faccio niente. E quando ero piccolo?
3. Stasera bevete un vino buono. E la settimana prossima?
4. Promettiamo di scrivere a Maria. E ieri?
5. Ora fa freddo. E giovedì scorso?
6. Stamattina le ragazze rimangono in classe. E ieri sera?
7. Oggi sono stanca. E ieri?
8. Trovo tutto fatto bene. E l'anno scorso?
9. Quest'anno leggo molto. E l'anno prossimo?
10. Stamattina vuole andare dal macellaio. E domani?

D. Translate the italicized words into Italian:

1. Chi *is speaking* in classe?
2. Tommaso *was walking* con Pietro.
3. Roberto, *don't take* il pane di Marco!
4. Per Natale, *I will buy* un panettone.
5. Caterina *went out* con il fratello.
6. *Let's telephone* a mio zio in Francia!
7. *It was warm* ieri.
8. Peppe e Maria, *wash* i piatti!
9. *He came* alla biblioteca da solo.
10. *We are eating* polpette e spaghetti.
11. Giovanni *will pay* il conto.
12. Noi *used to sing* ogni sera.
13. *Don't buy* questa carta! (*tu*)
14. *They do spend* troppo.
15. *I gave* il regalo a Lisa.
16. Lui *has had* molti problemi.
17. *I'll buy* quel giornale per papà.
18. *She arrived* alle otto precise.
19. *Were you* (*voi*) *watching* la televisione ieri sera?
20. *Show* (*voi*) la fotografia a Michele!

10. The Conditional

The conditional is formed by dropping the final **-e** of the infinitive and adding the endings: **-ei, -esti, -ebbe, -emmo, -este, -ebbero.**

As in the future, the **-a** of **-are** verbs changes to an **-e.**

	salutare, to greet	**prendere**, to take	**coprire**, to cover
	I would (should) greet, etc.	*I would (should) take,* etc.	*I would (should) cover,* etc.
io	salut***erei***	prend***erei***	copr***irei***
tu	salut***eresti***	prend***eresti***	copr***iresti***
Lei, lui, lei	salut***erebbe***	prend***erebbe***	copr***irebbe***
noi	salut***eremmo***	prend***eremmo***	copr***iremmo***
voi	salut***ereste***	prend***ereste***	copr***ireste***
Loro, loro	salut***erebbero***	prend***erebbero***	copr***irebbero***

Note

1. Verbs that are regular in the future are also regular in the conditional. The stem is the same for both tenses.
2. The rule that applies to **-care**, **-gare**, **-sciare**, **-ciare**, and **-giare** verbs in the future applies also to the conditional.

Infinitive	Future	Conditional
cer***care***	cer***cherò***	cer***cherei***
pa***gare***	pa***gherò***	pa***gherei***
la***sciare***	la***scerò***	la***scerei***
comin***ciare***	comin***cerò***	comin***cerei***
man***giare***	man***gerò***	man***gerei***

3. Verbs irregular in the future are similarly irregular in the conditional.

Infinitive	Conditional
essere	***sarei***
dare	***darei***
fare	***farei***
stare	***starei***
andare	***andrei***
avere	***avrei***
cadere	***cadrei***
dovere	***dovrei***
potere	***potrei***
sapere	***saprei***
vedere	***vedrei***
bere	***berrei***
rimanere	***rimarrei***
tenere	***terrei***
venire	***verrei***
volere	***vorrei***

4. Although the conditional is often translated as *would* both in English and in Italian, it may be translated occasionally as *should.*

Dovrei mandarle questo regalo.	I *should* send her this gift.

5. Remember that when *would* is used in the sense of *used to*, it is translated by the imperfect tense.

Ci ***visitava*** spesso.	He *would* (used to) visit us often.

EXERCISES

A. Write the correct form of the conditional of the verbs in parentheses:

1. (ritornare) Io _____ prima di tutti.
2. (aprire) Maria _____ quella scatola volentieri.
3. (venire) Loro _____ con voi a sentire la sinfonia.
4. (aiutare) Noi _____ quei poveri malati!
5. (chiedere) Voi _____ un appuntamento per le due?
6. (dare) (tu) _____ un buon voto al tuo professore?
7. (garantire) Il commesso _____ questa lavatrice.
8. (lasciare) Lei _____ tutto per andare in Germania.

9.	(volere)	Scusi, signore, ma _____ altro da mangiare?
10.	(sapere)	(io) _____ bene cosa dire a lui.
11.	(essere)	Mia cugina _____ a casa stasera.
12.	(pagare)	(tu) _____ il conto almeno questa volta?
13.	(dormire)	Loro _____ tardi ogni mattina!
14.	(abitare)	(voi) _____ a Milano durante l'estate?
15.	(mettere)	I miei compagni ed io _____ dello zucchero su tutto!

B. Rewrite each sentence, replacing the verb in italics with the conditional of the verbs in parentheses:

1. *Giocherebbe* ogni giorno. (viaggiare, cuocere, chiacchierare)
2. *Dormiresti* all'aperto? (mangiare, bere, rimanere)
3. *Dovrebbero* ordinare dei manicotti. (volere, potere, desiderare)
4. Dove *andreste* questa estate? (volare, rimanere, abitare)
5. *Porteremmo* dei guanti d'inverno. (comprare, fare, perdere)

C. Change the following sentences from the present indicative to the conditional:

1. *Termino* il lavoro in tempo.
2. *Vuole* accompagnarmi.
3. *Abbracciamo* Sophia Loren volentieri.
4. *Rompete* tutti i bicchieri?
5. *Preferisci* pescare o remare?
6. *Rimangono* sempre attaccati alla madre!
7. *Sali* molte scale nella basilica.
8. Roberto *può* viaggiare da solo.
9. Le due sorelle *comprano* degli abiti azzurri.
10. *Sai* che ore sono, per caso?

D. Translate the italicized words into Italian:

1. *We should visit* mia zia.	_____ mia zia.
2. *You* (*tu*) *wouldn't understand* il romanzo.	_____ il romanzo.
3. *They would drink* limonata tutto il giorno.	_____ limonata tutto il giorno.
4. *Would we know* fare una torta?	_____ fare una torta?
5. *Would you* (*voi*) *see* quel film?	_____ quel film?
6. *I would buy* una cravatta.	_____ una cravatta.
7. *He would leave* in treno.	_____ in treno.

8. *She would be able to* giocare con noi. ----- giocare con noi.
9. *We would listen to* la musica italiana. ----- la musica italiana.
10. *Would* i ragazzi *laugh?* I ragazzi -----?

E. Translate into English:

1. Sapresti il nome di quel signore?
2. Dovrei telefonare a mia madre.
3. Scommetto che vorresti venire a Capri.
4. Giorgio sa che bruceremmo questi fogli di carta.
5. Le mie sorelle non laverebbero neanche un piatto!
6. Questo professore non mi piacerebbe mai.
7. Non capirei niente nella classe di biologia.
8. Morireste di paura nella foresta.
9. Giovanni mi terrebbe questi libri?
10. Non tradurrebbero mai dal francese all'italiano!
11. Carlotta non fumerebbe quelle sigarette americane!
12. Sai bene che avresti molto da fare.
13. Quel dottore guarirebbe chiunque.
14. Manderei delle rose rosse a quella ragazza!
15. Andreste al matrimonio di Guido e Maddalena?

Un tipico *caffè all'aperto* frequentato da molti Italiani nei mesi caldi. In Italia ce ne sono migliaia, ma questo disegno in particolare rappresenta un caffè della città di Trieste.

11. The Past Absolute

REGULAR VERBS

The past absolute (also called the preterit indicative or past definite) of regular verbs is formed by:

1. dropping the infinitive ending (**-are**, **-ere**, **-ire**).
2. adding to the stem the following endings:

   -are verbs: ***-ai***, ***-asti***, ***-ò***, ***-ammo***, ***-aste***, ***-arono***

   -ere verbs: ***-etti*** (***-ei***), ***-esti***, ***-ette*** (***-è***), ***-emmo***, ***-este***, ***-ettero*** (***-erono***).

   -ire verbs: ***-ii***, ***-isti***, ***-ì***, ***-immo***, ***-iste***, ***-irono***.

	pensare, to think	**godere**, to enjoy	**capire**, to understand
	I thought, etc.	*I enjoyed*, etc.	*I understood*, etc.
io	pens***ai***	god***etti*** (god***ei***)	cap***ii***
tu	pens***asti***	god***esti***	cap***isti***
Lei, lui, lei	pens***ò***	god***ette*** (god***è***)	cap***ì***
noi	pens***ammo***	god***emmo***	cap***immo***
voi	pens***aste***	god***este***	cap***iste***
Loro, loro	pens***arono***	god***ettero*** (god***erono***)	cap***irono***

Note

1. The characteristic vowel of each conjugation (**a**, **e**, **i**) is retained in the past absolute, with the exception of the third person singular of **-are** verbs (**pensò**). Other than the characteristic vowel of each conjugation, the endings are the same for **-are**, **-ere**, and **-ire** verbs.
2. Many verbs of the **-ere** conjugation have a second form for the first and third persons singular and the third person plural. However, these forms are not used as often in current Italian. For example, **godei** is not used as often as **godetti**; **godè** is not used as often as **godette**, etc.

IRREGULAR VERBS

1. The following verbs have special forms throughout the past absolute:

bere, to drink	bevetti (bevvi), bevesti, bevette (bevve), bevemmo, beveste, bevettero (bevvero)*
condurre, to lead, to drive	condussi, conducesti, condusse, conducemmo, conduceste, condussero
dare, to give	diedi (detti), desti, diede (dette), demmo, deste, diedero (dettero)
dire, to say	dissi, dicesti, disse, dicemmo, diceste, dissero
essere, to be	fui, fosti, fu, fummo, foste, furono
fare, to do	feci, facesti, fece, facemmo, faceste, fecero
stare, to be	stetti, stesti, stette, stemmo, steste, stettero

2. In the past absolute of all other irregular verbs, the second person singular and the first and second persons plural follow the regular pattern of the conjugations to which the verbs belong: **-are**, **-ere**, **-ire**.

In the following verbs, the first and third persons singular and the third person plural have special forms:

avere, to have	***ebbi***, avesti, ***ebbe***, avemmo, aveste, ***ebbero***
cadere, to fall	***caddi***, cadesti, ***cadde***, cademmo, cadeste, ***caddero***
conoscere, to know	***conobbi***, conoscesti, ***conobbe***, conoscemmo, conosceste, ***conobbero***
decidere, to decide	***decisi***, decidesti, ***decise***, decidemmo, decideste, ***decisero***
leggere, to read	***lessi***, leggesti, ***lesse***, leggemmo, leggeste, ***lessero***
mettere, to put	***misi***, mettesti, ***mise***, mettemmo, metteste, ***misero***
nascere, to be born	***nacqui***, nascesti, ***nacque***, nascemmo, nasceste, ***nacquero***
prendere, to take	***presi***, prendesti, ***prese***, prendemmo, prendeste, ***presero***

*Note that *bere* also has the following forms, which are not used as often in current Italian: io **bevei**, lui **bevè**, loro **beverono**.

rimanere, to remain	***rimasi***, rimanesti, ***rimase***, rimanemmo, rimaneste, ***rimasero***
rispondere, to respond, to answer	***risposi***, rispondesti, ***rispose***, rispondemmo, rispondeste, ***risposero***
sapere, to know	***seppi***, sapesti, ***seppe***, sapemmo, sapeste, ***seppero***
scegliere, to choose	***scelsi***, scegliesti, ***scelse***, scegliemmo, sceglieste, ***scelsero***
scendere, to descend	***scesi***, scendesti, ***scese***, scendemmo, scendeste, ***scesero***
scrivere, to write	***scrissi***, scrivesti, ***scrisse***, scrivemmo, scriveste, ***scrissero***
spendere, to spend	***spesi***, spendesti, ***spese***, spendemmo, spendeste, ***spesero***
uccidere, to kill	***uccisi***, uccidesti, ***uccise***, uccidemmo, uccideste, ***uccisero***
vedere, to see	***vidi***, vedesti, ***vide***, vedemmo, vedeste, ***videro***
***venire**, to come	***venni***, venisti, ***venne***, venimmo, veniste, ***vennero***
vivere, to live	***vissi***, vivesti, ***visse***, vivemmo, viveste, ***vissero***
volere, to wish, to want	***volli***, volesti, ***volle***, volemmo, voleste, ***vollero***

USES OF THE PAST ABSOLUTE

The past absolute is used in formal speech or writing to describe an action or event that took place solely in the past, in a definite period of time.

Giulio Cesare ***combattè*** molte battaglie.	Julius Caesar fought many battles.
Dante ***scrisse*** "La Divina Commedia."	Dante wrote "The Divine Comedy."

In conversation and informal writing, such an action or event is generally expressed by the present perfect.

***Divenire** is conjugated like **venire**.

EXERCISES

A. Write the correct form of the past absolute of the verbs in parentheses:

1.	(dovere)	Il re _____ partire dalla Francia.
2.	(uccidere)	I leoni _____ molti cristiani.
3.	(dare)	Mio padre mi _____ molti regali quando ero bambino.
4.	(telefonare)	Quando eri a Roma non _____ ad Antonio nemmeno una volta!
5.	(preferire)	(io) _____ andare al concerto e non al balletto.
6.	(prendere)	(noi) _____ la strada a sinistra per andare a Bologna.
7.	(scoprire)	Colombo _____ il Nuovo Mondo nel 1492.
8.	(leggere)	Carducci e Manzoni _____ molti libri da bambini.
9.	(vivere)	Lord Byron _____ a Roma per parecchi anni.
10.	(aspettare)	Tu e Giovanni _____ molto per la guida?

B. Change the italicized verb from the present perfect to the past absolute:

1. Giacomo Leopardi *è nato* a Recanati.
2. Giuseppe Verdi *ha scritto* "il Trovatore."
3. *Ho scelto* molti dischi.
4. *Hai trovato* tutto a posto?
5. Gli emigranti *sono venuti* in America anni fa.
6. Quando eravate in Italia *avete visitato* il Panteon?
7. La cattedrale di Firenze *è stata* costruita nel 1360.
8. Dove *ha messo* la sedia?
9. *Abbiamo pagato* il conto al ristorante.
10. I compagni *hanno deciso* di vendere la macchina.
11. *È uscita* per andare al Ponte Vecchio.
12. A Roma *ho bevuto* un chinotto freddo.
13. La festa di San Gennaro *ha avuto* luogo a Napoli.
14. Giulietta non *ha risposto* alle lettere di Romeo.
15. I cristiani *hanno costruito* molte catacombe.

C. Write sentences, using the following items in the order given. The main verb or verbs must be conjugated in the past absolute:

Example: (io) / andare / Italia / solo
Andai in Italia da solo.

1. (noi) / potere / uscire
2. Maria / ricevere / pacco / Carlo
3. Puccini / scrivere / *Tosca*

4. nipoti / comprare / abiti
5. prima guerra mondiale / essere / guerra / lunga
6. (voi) / salutare / amici?
7. (io) / chiudere / finestre / poi / partire
8. Giorgio / condurre / compagne / Teatro Massimo
9. Torino / divenire / centro / moda
10. (loro) / entrare / salotto / Maria
11. Salvatore ed io / rispondere/ telegramma
12. (tu) / prendere / ombrello / e uscire
13. Marco / dovere / restare / casa
14. Gloria e Saverio / decidere / di telefonare / amici
15. (io) / trovare / biglietti / strada

D. Translate the following into English:

1. Carlo Goldoni tradusse molte commedie.
2. Da piccolo, vidi l'opera *Madama Butterfly*.
3. Giuseppe Parini nacque nel 1729.
4. I miei nonni arrivarono a New York nel 1900.
5. Corresti per tre chilometri prima di trovare un tassì?
6. I Turchi rimasero in Grecia per parecchi secoli.
7. Aprimmo quattro bottiglie di vino.
8. I cittadini fuggirono dall'isola.
9. Mi colpisti con un pugno sul naso.
10. Laura non amò mai Petrarca.
11. Finalmente, trovaste la strada per tornare a casa.
12. Misi i libri sulla scrivania prima di uscire.
13. Il poeta Quasimodo produsse diversi capolavori.
14. Molti soldati caddero morti durante la seconda guerra mondiale.
15. Franco aiutò Sandra a scendere le scale.
16. Tu, Gianni ed io ammirammo il panorama di Firenze.
17. Appena finisti il caffè, Luigi entrò nel salotto.
18. Camminaste per le strade di Pompei?
19. Durante il viaggio visitai molte chiese antiche.
20. Annibale punì i traditori.

12. The Present Participle and the Progressive Tenses

REGULAR VERBS

Infinitive	Present Participle
parl*are*, to speak	**parl*ando***, speaking
mett*ere*, to put	**mett*endo***, putting
dorm*ire*, to sleep	**dorm*endo***, sleeping

Note

The present participle of regular verbs is formed by dropping the ending of the infinitive and adding **-ando** to **-are** verbs and **-endo** to **-ere** and **-ire** verbs.

IRREGULAR VERBS

Infinitive	Present Participle
bere, to drink	***bevendo***, drinking
dire, to say	***dicendo***, saying
fare, to do	***facendo***, doing
porre, to place (All **-orre** verbs take **-endo.**)	***ponendo***, placing
tradurre, to translate (All **-urre** verbs take **-cendo.**)	***traducendo***, translating
trarre, to pull	***traendo***, pulling

USES OF THE PRESENT PARTICIPLE

The present participle is used:

1. With **stare** to denote a continuous action in the present (present progressive) or in the past (imperfect progressive).

Sta ***scrivendo***.	He is writing.
Stavo ***leggendo*** un romanzo.	I was reading a novel.

2. To translate the English participle ending in *-ing*.

Sapendo che non ero solo, mi diede due riviste.	*Knowing* that I was not alone, he gave me two magazines.

3. When the present participle is translated by *on*, *upon*, *by*, *while* + a form in *-ing*, or by a clause.

Lo prese, ***dicendo*** grazie.	He took it while *saying* thank you.
Vedendomi se ne andò.	*On seeing me*, he left.

EXERCISES

A. Write the present participle of each of the following verbs:

1. apparire	**6.** bere	**11.** tacere	**16.** comporre
2. vendere	**7.** fornire	**12.** dare	**17.** comprare
3. aprire	**8.** chiedere	**13.** cogliere	**18.** dire
4. prendere	**9.** morire	**14.** andare	**19.** bruciare
5. cercare	**10.** volere	**15.** produrre	**20.** punire

B. Change the following from the present indicative to the present progressive:

Example: *Parla* con Francesca.
Sta parlando con Francesca.

1. *Mangio* degli spaghetti.
2. *Beviamo* una limonata.
3. *Dici* la verità?
4. *Attraversano* una strada grande.
5. *Finite* il lavoro del professore?
6. *Suggerisco* di andare a casa presto.
7. Giorgio non *fa* nulla.
8. *Salgo* le scale di questo palazzo.
9. *Lavori* troppo.
10. *Rispondiamo* al telefono.

C. Change the following from the imperfect to the imperfect progressive:

Example: *Nevicava.*
Stava nevicando.

1. I ragazzi *giravano* per le strade.
2. *Correvo* verso il ponte.
3. Luisa *disegnava* un abito per mia madre.
4. *Ascoltavi* il programma alla radio?
5. *Uscivate* ieri sera quando ho telefonato?
6. *Ballavo* con Sara.
7. Cosa *facevi* ieri alle due?
8. *Davano* dei regali ai ragazzi.
9. Le mie cugine *chiacchieravano* senza fermarsi un attimo.
10. *Aprivamo* la porta quando hanno suonato.

D. Translate the English words into Italian, using the present participle:

Example: (*While*) *speaking*, ho sentito la musica.
Parlando, ho sentito la musica.

1. *Laughing*, portò i fiori alla madre.
2. *Opening the window*, caddi nella neve.
3. *Knowing* che pioveva, rimasi a casa.
4. Mangiamo, *watching* la televisione.
5. Potresti fare molto, *wanting* (*to*).
6. Andarono a scuola, *singing and dancing*.
7. Aiutate la madre, (*by*) *putting* i piatti a posto?
8. Mia madre lavora sempre, *cleaning and washing*.
9. *Drinking* una Coca-Cola, mangiai delle polpette squisite.
10. Colombo trovò il Nuovo Mondo, (*in*) *discovering* l'America.

E. Answer the following questions in complete Italian sentences, using the appropriate form of the present participle:

1. Cosa stai facendo adesso?
2. Con chi stavi chiacchierando stamattina?
3. Di che cosa stava parlando tua madre?
4. Perchè Giovanni non ha studiato?
5. Con chi cenavano le tue zie quando ho telefonato?
6. Sta piovendo ora?
7. Sentite molto mentre state dormendo?
8. Stai pensando a qualche cosa d'importante adesso?
9. Chi sta insegnando la lezione?
10. Cosa stanno facendo i clienti nei negozi?

13. Reflexive Verbs

Reflexive verbs express action that the subject performs upon itself.

Io mi lavo.	I wash myself.
Laura si veste.	Laura dresses herself.

The infinitives of reflexive verbs are generally formed by dropping the final **-e** of regular **-are**, **-ere**, and **-ire** verbs and adding the suffix **-si.**

lavarsi, to wash oneself
sedersi, to sit (to seat oneself)
vestirsi, to dress oneself

PRESENT INDICATIVE

I wash (*am washing, do wash*) *myself,* etc.

io **mi lavo**; tu **ti lavi**; Lei, lui, lei **si lava**; noi **ci laviamo**; voi **vi lavate**; Loro, loro **si lavano**

IMPERFECT

I was washing (*used to wash*) *myself,* etc.

io **mi lavavo**; tu **ti lavavi**; Lei, lui, lei **si lavava**; noi **ci lavavamo**; voi **vi lavavate**; Loro, loro **si lavavano**

FUTURE

I shall (*will*) *wash myself*, etc.

io **mi laverò**; tu **ti laverai**; Lei, lui, lei **si laverà**; noi **ci laveremo**; voi **vi laverete**; Loro, loro **si laveranno**

CONDITIONAL

I would (*should*) *wash myself,* etc.

io **mi laverei**; tu **ti laveresti**; Lei, lui, lei **si laverebbe**; noi **ci laveremmo**; voi **vi lavereste**; Loro, loro **si laverebbero**

PAST ABSOLUTE

I washed myself, etc.

io **mi lavai**; tu **ti lavasti**; Lei, lui, lei **si lavò**; noi **ci lavammo**; voi **vi lavaste**; Loro, loro **si lavarono**

IMPERATIVE

Affirmative	Negative
lavati, wash yourself	**non ti lavare** *Or:* **non lavarti** } don't wash yourself
laviamoci, let's wash ourselves	**non ci laviamo**, let's not wash ourselves
lavatevi, wash yourselves	**non vi lavate**, don't wash yourselves

Note

1. Like the object pronouns, the reflexive pronouns **mi**, **ti**, **si**, **ci**, **vi**, and **si** normally precede the verb.

Mi vesto presto.	I dress quickly.

2. With the affirmative imperative, the reflexive pronouns follow the verb and are attached to it.

Michele, vesti***ti!***	Michael, dress yourself!
Ragazzi, alziamo***ci!***	Boys, let's get up!

3. With the negative imperative of the **tu** form, the reflexive pronoun may precede or follow the verb.

Non metter***ti*** a tavola! *Or:* Non ***ti*** mettere a tavola!	Don't sit at the table!

4. With the present participle, the reflexive pronoun follows the verb.

Lavando***mi,*** sentii un rumore.	While washing myself, I heard a noise.
Mettendo***si*** a tavola, Giovanni cadde a terra.	While placing himself at the table, John fell to the floor.

5. Possessive adjectives are not needed when reflexive verbs are used with parts of the body or with clothing.

Mi lavo le mani.	I wash my hands.
Luisa si pettina i capelli.	Louise combs her hair.
Ci mettiamo le scarpe.	We put on our shoes.
Si mettono i guanti quando fa freddo.	They wear (put on) gloves when it's cold.

6. In compound tenses, all reflexive verbs are conjugated with **essere**. In this case, the reflexive pronoun always precedes the conjugated form of **essere**.

Mi ***sono*** alzato alle sei.	I got up at six o'clock.
Si ***sono*** divertite.	They have enjoyed themselves.

7. With progressive tenses (**stare** + present participle; see Verb Lesson 12), the reflexive pronoun may either precede the conjugated form of **stare** or follow and be attached to the present participle.

Present progressive construction	***Mi*** sto mettendo il cappotto. *Or:* Sto mettendo***mi*** il cappotto.	I am putting on my coat.
Past progressive construction	***Si*** stava lavando quando la vidi. *Or:* Stava lavando***si*** quando la vidi.	She was washing when I saw her.

COMMON REFLEXIVE VERBS

accomodarsi, to make oneself comfortable, to sit down
addormentarsi, to fall asleep
affrettarsi, to hurry up
alzarsi, to get up
annoiarsi, to get bored
appoggiarsi (a), to lean (oneself against)
avvicinarsi (a), to come near
bruciarsi, to burn oneself
chiamarsi, to be called
divertirsi, to enjoy oneself
lavarsi, to wash oneself
mettersi, to wear, to place oneself, to start
pesarsi, to weigh oneself

pettinarsi, to comb oneself
preoccuparsi, to worry (about)
radersi, to shave
raffreddarsi, to catch cold
ricordarsi, to remember
riposarsi, to rest
ritirarsi, to withdraw
sbagliarsi, to be mistaken
sedersi, to sit down
svegliarsi, to wake up
tagliarsi, to cut oneself
trovarsi, to be situated, to find oneself
vestirsi, to dress

EXERCISES

A. Write the correct form of the verb in the present tense:

1. (fermarsi) I viaggiatori _____ davanti al museo.
2. (chiamarsi) Quelle ragazze _____ Anna e Gioconda.
3. (sedersi) (Tu) _____ vicino a Roberto.
4. (divertirsi) (Io) _____ a sentire le canzoni popolari.
5. (mettersi) (Noi) _____ a tavola ogni sera alle sette.
6. (bruciarsi) (Lei) _____ le mani quando accende un fiammifero.
7. (tagliarsi) Bambini, state attenti, altrimenti _____ le dita con quel coltello.
8. (lavarsi) Quei ragazzi _____ attentamente.
9. (vestirsi) Mia sorella _____ da sola.
10. (svegliarsi) Gli studenti _____ presto la mattina.
11. (preoccuparsi) I miei amici _____ dei loro nonni.
12. (annoiarsi) Giorgio ed io _____ mentre quel signore parla.
13. (ritirarsi) Mio zio _____ presto ogni sera.
14. (riposarsi) (Voi) _____ quando tornate a casa?
15. (sdraiarsi) (Tu) _____ per terra quando guardi la televisione?
16. (pettinarsi) Maria _____ ogni minuto.
17. (addormentarsi) I figli di Carlo _____ alle nove di sera.
18. (appoggiarsi) Quando sono stanco _____ alla parete.
19. (pulirsi) La bambina _____ con il tovagliolo.
20. (raffreddarsi) Nostro figlio _____ facilmente.

B. Write the italicized words in the plural:

1. *Ti sedesti* vicino alla finestra.
2. *Mi troverò* davanti alla Basilica di S. Paolo.
3. *Il ragazzo si accomodava* su una poltrona.
4. *Vestiti* presto!
5. *Non ti mettere* quel cappello!
6. Sono sicuro che *mi annoierò* stasera.
7. *La signorina si ricordava* spesso di noi.
8. *Lui si pesò* l'ultima volta dieci anni fa.
9. *Voglio pettinarmi* i capelli.
10. Non *si sentiva* bene.
11. *Ti stavi divertendo* da Luisa?
12. *Mi avvicinerei* volentieri a Sophia Loren!
13. *Mi rado* ogni mattina.
14. *Ti meriteresti* uno schiaffo!
15. Come *si chiama quel signore?*

C. Complete the following sentences in Italian:

1. *Her name is* Giuseppina. _____ Giuseppina.
2. Carlo, *wash yourself!* Carlo, _____!
3. *Don't you feel well,* ragazzi? _____ _____ ragazzi?
4. *Let's not lean* alla finestra! _____ alla finestra!
5. Luisa, *don't wake up* tardi, domani! Luisa _____ tardi, domani!
6. *I wash* le braccia. _____ le braccia.
7. *They don't weigh themselves*, spesso. _____ spesso.
8. Giorgio e Federico, *don't catch cold!* Giorgio e Federico, _____!
9. *You (tu) used to hurry up* quando avevi fame. _____ quando avevi fame.
10. *He was shaving* quando sono entrato. _____ quando sono entrato.
11. *Would you (voi) fall asleep* al cinema? _____ al cinema?
12. Giulio Cesare *wasn't mistaken* spesso. Giulio Cesare _____ spesso.
13. *They could not comb* i capelli. _____ i capelli.
14. *Will she worry about* di arrivare a casa tardi? _____ di arrivare a casa tardi?
15. *You will burn yourself* se non stai attento! _____ se non stai attento!

D. Translate the italicized words into English:

1. *Ci divertivamo* quando eravamo giovani.
2. Gino *si affrettò* a finire il lavoro.

3. *Si laverà la faccia.*
4. *Mi addormenterei volentieri* su questo divano!
5. *Siediti qui*, Marco.
6. *Vi vestirete* prima di mangiare.
7. *Ci sentimmo* troppo male per continuare il viaggio.
8. *Ricordati* di chiudere la porta!
9. *Non ci bruciamo le mani!*
10. *Cora si mise* davanti alla macchina.
11. *Quel ragazzo si chiamava* Cristoforo.
12. *Non dovremmo pettinarci* in pubblico.
13. *Mi annoiavo* a sentire quelle chiacchiere.
14. *Si alzeranno* prima di mezzogiorno.
15. *Ti avvicinasti troppo* al vulcano.

E. Answer the questions in complete Italian sentences:

1. Come ti chiami?
2. A che ora vi alzate la mattina?
3. Cosa ti metti quando piove?
4. Come ti vesti per andare al ballo?
5. Chi si lava la mattina?
6. Come si chiamano i tuoi due amici?
7. Vi annoiate in classe?
8. Dove ti trovi adesso?
9. Chi si rade?
10. Chi si siede davanti al professore?

14. Compound Tenses: Agreement of Past Participles

COMPOUND TENSES

Compound tenses are formed with the auxiliary verb (helping verb) **avere** or **essere** and the past participle. In general, **avere** is used with transitive verbs (verbs that may be followed by a direct object), while **essere** is used with intransitive verbs (verbs that cannot take a direct object).

Present Perfect

(See Verb Lessons 5 and 6.)

(present of the auxiliary + the past participle)

Io ***ho telefonato*** a mio **zio.** (transitive verb: *ho telefonato*; direct object: **zio**)	I telephoned (have telephoned, did telephone) my uncle.
tu hai telefonato, lui ha telefonato, etc.	
Io ***sono arrivato(a)*** **ieri.** (intransitive verb: *sono arrivato(a)*; adverb: **ieri**)	I arrived (have arrived, did arrive) yesterday.
tu sei arrivato(a), lui è arrivato, etc.	

alzarsi, to get up (reflexive form)

(See Verb Lesson 13, Note 6.)

I got up, (I have gotten up, I did get up)

io mi sono alzato(a)	noi ci siamo alzati(e)
tu ti sei alzato (a)	voi vi siete alzati(e)
Lei si è alzato(a)	Loro si sono alzati(e)
lui si è alzato	loro si sono alzati(e)
lei si è alzata	

Pluperfect (Past Perfect)

(imperfect of the auxiliary + the past participle)

I had telephoned

io avevo telefonato	noi avevamo telefonato
tu avevi telefonato	voi avevate telefonato
Lei, lui, lei aveva telefonato	Loro, loro avevano telefonato

I had arrived

io ero arrivato(a)	noi eravamo arrivati(e)
tu eri arrivato(a)	voi eravate arrivati(e)
Lei era arrivato(a)	Loro erano arrivati(e)
lui era arrivato	loro erano arrivati(e)
lei era arrivata	

I had gotten up

io mi ero alzato(a)	noi ci eravamo alzati(e)
tu ti eri alzato(a)	voi vi eravate alzati(e)
Lei si era alzato(a)	Loro si erano alzati(e)
lui si era alzato	loro si erano alzati(e)
lei si era alzata	

Future Perfect

(future of the auxiliary + the past participle)

I shall (will) have telephoned

io avrò telefonato	noi avremo telefonato
tu avrai telefonato	voi avrete telefonato
Lei, lui, lei avrà telefonato	Loro, loro avranno telefonato

I shall (will) have arrived

io sarò arrivato(a)	noi saremo arrivati(e)
tu sarai arrivato(a)	voi sarete arrivati(e)
Lei sarà arrivato(a)	Loro saranno arrivati(e)
lui sarà arrivato	loro saranno arrivati(e)
lei sarà arrivata	

I shall (will) have gotten up

io mi sarò alzato(a)	noi ci saremo alzati(e)
tu ti sarai alzato(a)	voi vi sarete alzati(e)
Lei si sarà alzato(a)	Loro si saranno alzati(e)
lui si sarà alzato	loro si saranno alzati(e)
lei si sarà alzata	

Conditional Perfect

(conditional of the auxiliary + the past participle)

I would (should) have telephoned

io avrei telefonato	noi avremmo telefonato
tu avresti telefonato	voi avreste telefonato
Lei, lui, lei avrebbe telefonato	Loro, loro avrebbero telefonato

I would (should) have arrived

io sarei arrivato(a)	noi saremmo arrivati(e)
tu saresti arrivato(a)	voi sareste arrivati(e)
Lei sarebbe arrivato(a)	Loro sarebbero arrivati(e)
lui sarebbe arrivato	loro sarebbero arrivati(e)
lei sarebbe arrivata	

I would (should) have gotten up

io mi sarei alzato(a)	noi ci saremmo alzati(e)
tu ti saresti alzato(a)	voi vi sareste alzati(e)
Lei si sarebbe alzato(a)	Loro si sarebbero alzati(e)
lui si sarebbe alzato	loro si sarebbero alzati(e)
lei si sarebbe alzata	

Note

In compound tenses, reflexive verbs always have **essere** as the auxiliary verb.

AGREEMENT OF PAST PARTICIPLES

In compound tenses in which **avere** is the auxiliary verb used, the past participle may or may not agree in gender and number with its direct object.

1. The past participle usually does not have to agree when the direct object follows the verb.

Hanno ***venduto*** (*or* ***venduta***) la ***macchina.*** (direct object)	They sold the car.

2. It may agree when the direct object precedes the verb.

La ***macchina*** (direct object) che hanno ***venduta*** (*or* ***venduto***) è vecchia.	The car they sold is old.

3. It always agrees when the object is a direct object pronoun preceding the verb.

Hanno venduto le biciclette? Sì, ***le*** (dir. obj. pron.) hanno ***vendute.***	Have they sold the bikes? Yes, they sold them.

In compound tenses in which **essere** is the auxiliary verb used, the past participle agrees in number and gender with the subject.

Maria è ***venuta.***	Mary came.
Siamo ***partiti(e)***	We left.

In compound tenses involving reflexive verbs, the past participle agrees in gender and number with the subject.

Le ***ragazze*** si sono ***divertite.***	The girls enjoyed themselves.
Carlo si è ***lavato*** le mani.	Charles washed his hands.
I ***bambini*** si sono ***messi*** i calzini.	The children put on their socks.

EXERCISES

A. Write the correct forms of each of the following verbs in the pluperfect, future perfect, and conditional perfect:

1. mettersi (noi)
2. partire (lei)
3. cantare (io)
4. divertirsi (loro, *f.*)
5. perdere (tu)
6. lasciare (voi)
7. cercare (lui)
8. morire (loro, *m.*)
9. uscire (io)
10. sedersi (Lei)
11. mangiare (loro)
12. aprire (noi)
13. stare (lei)
14. fare (tu)
15. tornare (voi)

B. Choose the correct translation of the Italian verb:

1. è rimasto	he stayed, he had stayed, he was staying
2. saranno andati	they went, they had gone, they will have gone
3. ci eravamo divertiti	we have enjoyed ourselves, we had enjoyed ourselves, we will have enjoyed ourselves

4.	avrebbe dimenticato	he did forget, he would have forgotten, he will have forgotten
5.	si sarà vestita	she will have dressed, she would have dressed, she has dressed
6.	sono entrata	I do enter, I had entered, I entered
7.	avevi offerto	you were offering, you had offered, you would have offered
8.	avreste creduto	you would have believed, you used to believe, you have believed
9.	siamo state	we will have been, we have been, we had been
10.	hanno trovato	they do find, they found, they were finding

C. Change the verb tenses in the sentences according to the following pattern:

present indicative to present perfect
future to future perfect
conditional to conditional perfect
imperfect to pluperfect

Example: Parlo con Maria.
Ho parlato con Maria.

1.	*Guadagnerebbe* molto denaro.	_____ molto denaro.
2.	*Capivi* la lezione?	_____ la lezione?
3.	*Suggerisco* di invitare mia zia.	_____ di invitare mia zia.
4.	*Si appoggiano* al muro.	_____ al muro.
5.	*Vi fermerete* dallo zio Antonio.	_____ dallo zio Antonio.
6.	Laura *faceva* molte cose in casa.	Laura _____ molte cose in casa.
7.	*Telefoneresti* alla modista?	_____ alla modista?
8.	*Rispondiamo* prima del 5 settembre.	_____ prima del 5 settembre.
9.	*Traduco* delle lettere per mia sorella.	_____ delle lettere per mia sorella.
10.	Giorgio *si alzerà* prima di noi.	Giorgio _____ prima di noi.
11.	*Cercheremmo* dei posti buoni al concerto.	_____ dei posti buoni al concerto.
12.	*Rompeva* tutto da piccolo.	_____ tutto da piccolo.
13.	*Andrebbero* volentieri con quei giovani.	_____ volentieri con quei giovani.
14.	Cosa *porti* a tua nonna?	Cosa _____ a tua nonna?
15.	*Mangerò* un bel piatto di ravioli.	_____ un bel piatto di ravioli.

D. Write the correct past participial form of the verbs in parentheses:

1. (venire) Susanna è _____.
2. (comprare) Abbiamo _____ due paia di guanti.
3. (trovare) Hanno trovato la macchina? Sì, l'hanno _____.
4. (pettinarsi) Carlo si era _____ bene.
5. (vedere) Chi avrà visto le penne? Luigi le avrà _____.
6. (mettersi) Ci siamo _____ le scarpe.
7. (uscire) Maria, saresti _____ ieri sera?
8. (cantare) Chi ha cantato la canzone? Io l'ho _____.
9. (scegliere) Avrebbe scelto l'abito azzurro Roberto? No, non l'avrebbe _____.
10. (lasciare) Lisa ed Adriana avevano _____ i libri in biblioteca.
11. (cadere) Mia sorella è _____ stamattina.
12. (scrivere) La lettera che hanno _____ è arrivata oggi.
13. (morire) Saremmo _____ di paura!
14. (nascere) Beatrice e Laura erano _____ secoli fa.
15. (studiare) Hai studiato la lezione? No, non l'ho _____.

E. Translate into Italian:

1. I would have seen her.
2. We had corrected the papers.
3. You (tu) will have spent the money.
4. They listened to the opera.
5. She would have dressed herself.
6. He had married her.
7. I had finished them (*m.*).
8. You (Lei) got up at six o'clock.
9. You (voi) would have traveled far.
10. They had sung it (*f.*).

F. In the following sentences, replace the italicized words with pronouns and make all necessary changes, including agreement of past participles:

1. Avresti preso *la polpetta?*
2. Dove avete comprato *il formaggio?*
3. Il medico aveva guarito *Maria?*
4. Tuo padre ha comprato *il cavallo?*
5. Avevi venduto *la macchina sportiva?*

15. Special Uses of the Present and Future

THE PRESENT WITH *DA*

To express an action begun in the past and continuing in the present, **da** (for) and **da quando** or **da quanto tempo** (how long?) are used with the present indicative. This is usually translated in English with the present perfect.

Da quando porti gli occhiali?	How long have you been wearing glasses?
Porto gli occhiali ***da*** un anno.	I have been wearing glasses for a year.
Da quanto tempo aspetti Giorgio?	How long have you been waiting for George?
È ***da*** ieri che aspetto Giorgio.	I have been waiting for George since yesterday.

THE FUTURE AND FUTURE PERFECT OF PROBABILITY

The future is used in Italian to express what is probable, even though the future is not implied. This is expressed in English by "must," "can," "probably," or "I wonder."

Future

Chi sarà?	Who can it be?
Sarà mio fratello.	It must be my brother.

Future Perfect

Dove saranno andati?	Where could they have gone?
Saranno andati all'aeroporto.	They must have gone (probably went) to the airport.

EXERCISES

A. Write the correct form of the verb in parentheses:

1. (suonare) Carlo _____ il violino da dieci anni.
2. (chiacchierare) Le studentesse _____ da tre ore.
3. (essere) (io) _____ in Italia da giugno.
4. (bere) Da quanto tempo (voi) _____ vino?
5. (abitare) Da quando (tu) _____ a Roma?
6. (pregare) Mia nipote _____ da mattina a sera.
7. (pulire) È da una settimana che voi non _____ questa camera!
8. (avere) (noi) _____ questa rivista dal mese scorso.
9. (conoscere) Lidia _____ Paolo da sei mesi.
10. (dormire) Da quando _____ questi bambini?

B. Translate the following sentences into Italian, using the future or future perfect of probability.

1. What time can it be?
2. John must have watched television.
3. It's probably too late.
4. You (tu) probably enjoyed yourself.
5. She probably knows that I have arrived.
6. Could it be cold?
7. They must have danced a *tarantella*.
8. I wonder if we can eat in this restaurant.
9. The boy probably did not see the film.
10. She must be tired.

C. Translate the following into English:

1. Maria sarà tornata alle otto.
2. Il libro starà sul tavolo.
3. Da quanto tempo abitate in questa casa?
4. Lui crederà quella storia.
5. È da quattro anni che frequento l'università.
6. Avranno ragione.
7. Da quando non vedi i tuoi genitori?
8. La lezione comincerà fra poco.
9. I miei compagni saranno già partiti.
10. È da gennaio che non ci sentiamo bene.

D. Answer the following questions in complete sentences in Italian:

Example: What can the weather be like?
Farà caldo.

1. Where can she have gone?
2. How long has he been home?
3. What month can it be?
4. Who can those young men be?
5. How long has your father been ill?
6. With whom can she be speaking?
7. How long has she been speaking on the phone?
8. What can there be to drink?
9. How long have you (Lei) been drinking coffee?
10. Could Paul have married Susan?

Una delle statue più famose di *Leonardo da Vinci*, situata in Piazza del Duomo, a Milano, dirimpetto alla basilica.

16. Review of Verb Lessons 10–15

A. Write in the singular:

1. noi cercheremmo
2. loro visitarono
3. voi sarete andati
4. loro si divertono
5. lavatevi
6. noi ci vestimmo
7. loro stavano parlando
8. voi avevate telefonato
9. loro si saranno svegliati
10. voi finiste

B. Write in the plural:

1. tu perderesti
2. io mi alzai
3. lui sta parlando
4. pulisciti
5. lei sarà partita
6. lui era morto
7. io avrei parlato
8. tu stavi dormendo
9. tu decidesti
10. io mi misi

C. Choose the correct translation:

1. you will have been: saresti stato, sarai stato, sei stato
2. he would take: prenderà, prende, prenderebbe
3. we danced: ballammo, balleremo, balleremmo
4. they would have gone: saranno andati, sono andati, sarebbero andati
5. wash yourselves: lavati, lavatevi, laviamoci
6. he was walking: sta camminando, stava camminando, cammina
7. singing: cantando, canto, cantare
8. we had gone out: siamo usciti, saremo usciti, eravamo usciti
9. they wrote: scrivono, scrissero, scriverebbero
10. don't dress yourself: non ti vestire, non ti sei vestito, non ti sarai vestito
11. avranno mangiato: they ate, they must have eaten, they would have eaten
12. abitò: he resides, he resided, he will reside
13. avrebbe cantato: she sang, she would sing, she would have sung
14. stavamo studiando: studying, we are studying, we were studying
15. da un anno: for a year, a year ago, next year

D. Translate into English:

1. saranno tornati
2. morì
3. studia da tre mesi
4. mangiando
5. si era svegliata
6. l'ho vista ieri

7. stava scrivendo
8. avresti venduto
9. saranno le due
10. mangereste tutto
11. perdette
12. alziamoci presto
13. non li avevano trovati
14. si è pettinata i capelli
15. capii la lezione

E. Translate into Italian:

1. while buying
2. he will have sold
3. we lost
4. they would find
5. I would have washed myself
6. he is here since yesterday
7. it is probably cold
8. we were doing
9. I had drunk
10. the pens that I have seen
11. he would have arrived
12. you burned yourself (tu)
13. her name is Louise
14. she combs her hair
15. they weighed themselves

F. Complete the sentences in Italian:

1. He began to read. _____ a leggere.
2. We spent the night laughing and singing.
   _____ la serata _____ e _____ .
3. How long have you been studying French?
   _____ quando studi il francese?
4. They will have phoned at midnight. _____ a mezzanotte.
5. I fell, running through the streets.
   _____ , _____ per le strade.
6. You (tu) would eat everything. _____ tutto.
7. The ladies were chatting while they were eating.
   Le signore _____ mentre _____ .
8. You (tu) will place yourself next to Maria.
   _____ vicino a Maria.
9. Boys, lean on the shelf!
   Ragazzi, _____ allo scaffale!
10. The Greeks came to Italy and taught the people.
    I Greci _____ in Italia e _____ la gente.

G. Translate the italicized words into Italian:

1. *He chose* due fiori gialli.
2. *She would have watched* la televisione ogni giorno.

3. *They have been reading* quel romanzo da sabato.
4. Dante Alighieri *wrote* "La Divina Commedia."
5. *I will have finished* prima delle cinque.
6. *Opening the door, he left* senza dire una parola.
7. *I had seen her* con suo marito.
8. Roberto e Pietro, *don't cut yourselves!*
9. Gianni *had sat down* al banco.
10. *It must be* Pietro alla porta.

La Scala Regia e una guardia svizzera **in uniforme e arma tradizionali. La Scala Regia è l'entrata principale del Vaticano; la guardia fa parte del corpo militare svizzero che protegge lo Stato Vaticano.**

17. Polite Commands With *Lei* and *Loro*

The polite command is formed from the first person singular of the present indicative. The final **-o** is changed as follows:

-are verbs: to **-i** (Lei) and **-ino** (Loro)
-ere and **-ire** verbs: to **-a** (Lei) and **-ano** (Loro)

REGULAR VERBS

	ordinare, to order	**prendere,** to take	**sentire,** to hear	**finire,** to finish
Lei (*sing.*)	**ordini** (order)	**prenda** (take)	**senta** (hear)	**finisca** (finish)
Loro (*pl.*)	**ordinino** (order)	**prendano** (take)	**sentano** (hear)	**finiscano** (finish)

IRREGULAR VERBS

1. The following verbs form their polite commands by changing the **-o** of the present indicative, first person singular, to **-a** (Lei) and **-ano** (Loro):

INFINITIVE	PRES. IND. FIRST PER. SING.	COMMANDS	
		Lei	Loro
dire, to say	dico	dica	dicano
uscire, to go out	esco	esca	escano
andare, to go	vado	vada	vadano
fare, to do, to make	faccio	faccia	facciano
venire, to come	vengo	venga	vengano
cogliere, to gather	colgo	colga	colgano
rimanere, to stay	rimango	rimanga	rimangano
scegliere, to choose	scelgo	scelga	scelgano

porre, to place (All other **-orre** verbs follow the same pattern.)	pongo	ponga	pongano
salire, to ascend	salgo	salga	salgano
tradurre, to translate (All other **-urre** verbs follow the same pattern.)	traduco	traduca	traducano
bere, to drink	bevo	beva	bevano

2. The following verbs have irregular polite command forms:

Infinitive	Commands	
	Lei	Loro
avere, to have	abbia	abbiano
dare, to give	dia	diano
essere, to be	sia	siano
sapere, to know	sappia	sappiano
stare, to be	stia	stiano

Note

1. The forms of the polite commands are the same as the corresponding forms of the present subjunctive (see Lesson 18), except for the omission of the subject pronouns **Lei** and **Loro.**

2. The negative is formed by putting **non** before the appropriate form of the command.

3. Reflexive pronouns, direct object pronouns, and indirect object pronouns all precede the polite command form.

***Si* lavi** le mani.	Wash your hands.
***Lo* faccia** con attenzione.	Do it with attention.
***Le* diano** questo romanzo.	Give her this novel.

EXERCISES

A. Write the two forms of the polite commands (**Lei** and **Loro**) for each verb:

1. leggere
2. mangiare
3. aprire
4. rispondere
5. lasciare
6. correggere
7. pagare
8. punire
9. mettere
10. bere

B. Change the following sentences from the present indicative to the polite commands:

Example: La signorina telefona a casa.
Signorina, telefoni a casa!

1. I signori *portano* i libri alla biblioteca.
2. Signorina, Lei *dice* la verità.
3. Signor Tulli, Lei *guarda* un programma interessante.
4. Signori, Loro *fanno* tutto bene.
5. La signora Mola non *agisce* male.
6. Il maestro mi *manda* una pagella buona.
7. Signore, Lei mi *sveglia* alle otto.
8. Le signorine *scendono* alla prossima fermata.
9. La signorina mi *dà* il suo numero di telefono.
10. Signora, Lei *viene* con me.

C. Tell Miss Bongiorno to:

1. pensarci bene
2. svegliarsi presto domattina
3. scrivere una lettera
4. bere un'aranciata
5. non prendere un caffè

Tell Mr. and Mrs. Sicilia to:

6. non ridere troppo
7. fare un buon viaggio
8. andare al concerto
9. non perdere la chiave
10. scegliere una rosa rossa

D. Match each English meaning in Column II with the correct command in Column I:

Column I	*Column* II
1. parli	*a.* clean
2. cerchino	*b.* sell
3. venda	*c.* send
4. pulisca	*d.* look for
5. si lavino	*e.* see
6. vedano	*f.* speak
7. sia	*g.* be
8. scenda	*h.* dress yourselves
9. si vestano	*i.* wash yourselves
10. spedisca	*j.* climb down

Il ritrovo invernale di *Cortina d'Ampezzo*, che ha una fama internazionale per lo sport dello sci.

18. Formation of the Subjunctive

PRESENT SUBJUNCTIVE

The present subjunctive is formed from the stem of the present indicative, first person singular. The final **-o** is changed as follows:

-are verbs: to **-i, -i, -i, -iamo, -iate, -ino**
-ere and **-ire** verbs: to **-a, -a, -a, -iamo, -iate, -ano**

REGULAR VERBS

	parlare, to speak	**rispondere,** to answer	**aprire,** to open	**capire,** to understand
io	parl***i***	rispond***a***	apr***a***	capisc***a***
tu	parl***i***	rispond***a***	apr***a***	capisc***a***
Lei, lui, lei	parl***i***	rispond***a***	apr***a***	capisc***a***
noi	parl***iamo***	rispond***iamo***	apr***iamo***	cap***iamo***
voi	parl***iate***	rispond***iate***	apr***iate***	cap***iate***
Loro, loro	parl***ino***	rispond***ano***	apr***ano***	capisc***ano***

Note

1. As in the present indicative, verbs like **capire** and **finire** add **-isc** to the stem in the first, second, and third persons singular and in the third person plural.

2. **-care** and **-gare** verbs add an **-h** to the stem before ending.

   cercare: cerc***hi***, cerc***hi***, cerc***hi***, cerc***hiamo***, cerc***hiate***, cerc***hino***
   pagare: pag***hi***, pag***hi***, pag***hi***, pag***hiamo***, pag***hiate***, pag***hino***

3. **-sciare**, **-ciare**, and **-giare** verbs do not double the **-i** of the stem.

   lasciare: lasc***i***, lasc***i***, lasc***i***, lasc***iamo***, lasc***iate***, lasc***ino***
   cominciare: cominc***i***, cominc***i***, etc.
   mangiare: mang***i***, mang***i***, etc.

IRREGULAR VERBS

andare, to go — vada, vada, vada, andiamo, andiate, vadano
avere, to have — abbia, abbia, abbia, abbiamo, abbiate, abbiano

cogliere, to gather	colga, colga, colga, cogliamo, cogliate, colgano
dare, to give	dia, dia, dia, diamo, diate, diano
dire, to say	dica, dica, dica, diciamo, diciate, dicano
dovere, to have to, must	debba, debba, debba, dobbiamo, dobbiate, debbano
essere, to be	sia, sia, sia, siamo, siate, siano
fare, to do, to make	faccia, faccia, faccia, facciamo, facciate, facciano
porre, to place	ponga, ponga, ponga, poniamo, poniate, pongano
(All other **-orre** verbs follow the same pattern.)	
rimanere, to stay	rimanga, rimanga, rimanga, rimaniamo, rimaniate, rimangano
salire, to ascend	salga, salga, salga, saliamo, saliate, salgano
sapere, to know	sappia, sappia, sappia, sappiamo, sappiate, sappiano
scegliere, to choose	scelga, scelga, scelga, scegliamo, scegliate, scelgano
sedere, to sit	sieda, sieda, sieda, sediamo, sediate, siedano
stare, to be	stia, stia, stia, stiamo, stiate, stiano
udire, to hear	oda, oda, oda, udiamo, udiate, odano
uscire, to go out	esca, esca, esca, usciamo, usciate, escano
venire, to come	venga, venga, venga, veniamo, veniate, vengano

Note

Regardless of conjugation class **(-are, -ere, -ire)**, the endings for the irregular verbs are the same: **-a, -a, -a, -iamo, -iate, -ano.**

PRESENT PERFECT SUBJUNCTIVE

The present perfect subjunctive is formed by combining the present subjunctive of **avere** or **essere** and the past participle of the verb.

comprare, to buy	
io ***abbia*** compr***ato***	noi ***abbiamo*** compr***ato***
tu ***abbia*** compr***ato***	voi ***abbiate*** compr***ato***
Lei, lui, lei ***abbia*** compr***ato***	Loro, loro ***abbiano*** compr***ato***

arrivare, to arrive	
io ***sia*** arriv***ato(a)***	noi ***siamo*** arriv***ati(e)***
tu ***sia*** arriv***ato(a)***	voi ***siate*** arriv***ati(e)***
Lei ***sia*** arriv***ato(a)***	Loro ***siano*** arriv***ati(e)***
lui ***sia*** arriv***ato***	loro ***siano*** arriv***ati(e)***
lei ***sia*** arriv***ata***	

vestirsi, to dress oneself	
io mi ***sia*** vest***ito(a)***	noi ci ***siamo*** vest***iti(e)***
tu ti ***sia*** vest***ito(a)***	voi vi ***siate*** vest***iti(e)***
Lei si ***sia*** vest***ito(a)***	Loro si ***siano*** vest***iti(e)***
lei si ***sia*** vest***ita***	loro si ***siano*** vest***iti(e)***

EXERCISES

A. Change each infinitive to the following forms: (1) first person singular, present indicative; (2) first person singular, present subjunctive; (3) third person plural, present subjunctive.

Example: domandare — domando (1st person sing. pres. ind.)
domandi (1st person sing. pres. subj.)
domandino (3rd person pl. pres. subj.)

1. potere
2. mangiare
3. leggere
4. ascoltare
5. produrre
6. dormire
7. proibire
8. volere
9. udire
10. telefonare
11. correre
12. porre
13. scrivere
14. trasportare
15. spendere
16. suggerire
17. credere
18. rimanere
19. entrare
20. ricevere
21. coprire
22. avere
23. essere
24. amare
25. mettere

B. Write the form of the present subjunctive of each verb according to the subject in parentheses.

1. preferire: (io) (noi) (voi) (loro)
2. volare: (tu) (Giorgio) (Lei) (Loro)
3. divertirsi: (Carlo) (io) (i signori) (voi)
4. scegliere: (tu) (tu e Carlo) (Susanna ed io) (lui)
5. nascere: (loro) (Lei) (io) (tu)
6. negare: (mio fratello) (Loro) (voi) (noi)
7. sapere: (tu) (io) (tu ed io) (loro)
8. lavarsi: (Maria) (tu) (voi) (noi)
9. vendere: (Paolo) (i giovani) (la signora) (io)
10. avere: (tu) (lei) (lui e lei) (voi)
11. accogliere: (io) (mia madre) (loro) (noi)
12. conoscere: (tu) (lui) (voi) (Loro)
13. stare: (loro) (Lei) (noi) (io)
14. soffrire: (tu, Anna) (tu e Anna) (Laura ed io) (Laura e Gina)
15. giocare: (io) (voi) (Luisa) (tu)

C. Change each infinitive to the following forms: (1) first person singular, imperfect indicative; (2) third person singular, present perfect indicative; (3) third person plural, present perfect subjunctive.

Example: spendere spendevo ha speso abbiano speso

1. partire
2. cercare
3. dimenticare
4. alzarsi
5. promettere
6. soffrire
7. tenere
8. dovere
9. venire
10. suonare
11. chiamare
12. svegliarsi
13. morire
14. prendere
15. conoscere
16. salire
17. pescare
18. fare
19. baciare
20. vincere
21. abitare
22. decidere
23. dormire
24. vendere
25. vedere
26. guidare
27. mettersi
28. uscire
29. andare
30. cadere

19. The Subjunctive After Certain Verbs

The subjunctive is used in a dependent clause when the verb in the main clause expresses:

1. a wish: **volere**, to wish, to want; **desiderare**, to desire, to wish; **preferire**, to prefer

Voglio che tu ***venga*** con Maria. main clause — dependent clause	I want you to come (that you come) with Mary.

2. a command or advice: **insistere**, to insist; **ordinare**, to order; **suggerire**, to suggest

Insiste che io lo ***accompagni.*** main clause — dependent clause	He insists that I accompany him.
Suggerisco che tu e Lisa ***andiate*** a casa presto stasera. main clause — dependent clause	I suggest that you and Lisa go home early this evening.

3. emotion: **sperare**, to hope; **temere**, to fear; **essere contento**, to be happy; **dispiacere**, to feel sorry; **dolersi**, to be sorry

Spero che ***stiate*** bene. main clause — dependent clause	I hope that you feel well.

4. doubt, disbelief, uncertainty: **dubitare**, to doubt; **credere**, to believe; **negare**, to deny; **pensare**, to think

Dubito che Giacomo ***arrivi*** in tempo. main clause — dependent clause	I doubt that James will arrive in time.
Penso che ***abbia speso*** troppo. main clause — dependent clause	I think (believe) that he has spent too much.

Credere and **pensare** normally take the subjunctive. These same verbs, however, take the indicative when expressing strong belief such as faith or when the future is intended.

Credo che ***è*** un giovane molto buono. main clause — dependent clause (pres. ind.)	I believe that he is a fine young man.

Penso che ***arriverà*** alle due. — I think he will arrive at two o'clock.

main clause — dependent clause (future)

Note

In each of the preceding sentences, the subject of the main verb is different from the subject of the dependent verb. If the subjects are the same, **che** is omitted and the infinitive form of the dependent verb is used.

Voglio ***mangiare*** adesso.	I want to eat now.
Teme di non ***trovare*** dei posti buoni.	He is afraid that he will not find any good seats.

SEQUENCE OF TENSES

If the verb in the main clause is in the present indicative, future, imperative, or polite command, the present subjunctive or present perfect subjunctive is generally used in the dependent clause.

Dubita (Dubiterà) che io ***sia caduto.*** — He doubts (will doubt) that I have fallen.

pres. ind. — future — pres. perf. subj.

Signore, dica a Giorgio che ***compri*** delle mele. — Sir, tell George to buy (that he buy) some apples.

dica: pol. command — compri: pres. subj.

EXERCISES

A. Choose the correct form of the verbs in parentheses:

1. Spero che io (trovi, trova) una giacca nuova.
2. Non credo che Giovanni (abbia fatto, ha fatto) le valige.
3. Vogliono che loro (abbiano, hanno) molta pazienza.
4. Dite a mia sorella che (porta, porti) un golf.
5. Vorrà che loro (chiamino, chiamarono) il macellaio.
6. Dubita che io (cerchi, cercare) dei fiori.
7. Desidero che Carla (mandi, manda) una cartolina ad Andrea.
8. Ci dispiace che voi (siate, siete) rimasti a casa.
9. Spera di (vedere, veda) quel film nuovo.

10. Sono contento che tu (sia, essere) venuto a trovarmi.
11. Non so se loro (abbiano comprato, hanno comprato) una macchina nuova.
12. Carlo, ordina alle ragazze che (pagare, paghino) il conto!
13. Temo che tu (pulisci, pulisca) pochissimo.
14. Dirò ad Annabella che (esca, esce) al più presto possibile.
15. Vuole che noi (parliamo, parlino) a bassa voce.

B. Rewrite the following sentences, adding the cues and making the necessary changes:

Example: Il treno *parte* alle due.
Dubito che _____.
Dubito che il treno *parta* alle due.

1. Fate un buon viaggio.
   Speriamo che _____.
2. Puoi sciare.
   Sono contento che _____.
3. Spedisce le lettere al nonno.
   Vogliamo che _____.
4. Riceviamo molti regali a Natale.
   Dubito che _____.
5. Giorgio è avvocato?
   Ti dispiace che _____.
6. Prendo un gelato al cinema.
   Lui insiste che _____.
7. Non è bello.
   Mi dispiace che _____.
8. Leggi troppo.
   Temo che _____.
9. Parlate italiano.
   Ci sembra che _____.
10. Piango quando mi faccio male.
    Temono che _____.

C. Write the correct form of the verb in parentheses:

1. (ascoltare) Ci dispiace che tu _____ quelle chiacchiere!
2. (rispondere) Temiamo che loro non _____ bene alle domande.
3. (suonare) Giorgio insisterà che io _____ questo clarinetto!

4.	(dire)	Voglio che tu _____ la verità!
5.	(divertirsi)	Siete contenti che loro _____ tanto?
6.	(cantare)	Desideriamo che tu _____ con loro.
7.	(riuscire)	Credi che Lucio _____ a fare a tempo?
8.	(porre)	Dubito che lei _____ gli abiti sul tavolo.
9.	(chiudere)	Speriamo che Gianni _____ le finestre.
10.	(partire)	I carabinieri vogliono che io _____ immediatamente!
11.	(venire)	Vuoi che noi _____ a pranzare con voi?
12.	(avere)	Susanna è contenta che voi _____ tanta pazienza.
13.	(essere)	Preferisco che loro _____ qui e non da Raffaele.
14.	(dare)	Maria insiste che io _____ un regalo a Tommaso.
15.	(arrivare)	Credo che Pietro _____ stasera alle otto.

D. Translate the following sentences into Italian:

1. They are afraid that I haven't paid the bill.
2. I am happy that my sister has answered.
3. We hope that you (voi) have understood the novel.
4. I do not think that she was here.
5. She insists that I bought this newspaper.
6. Francesco thinks that you (tu) saw Florence.
7. He does not believe that we sold the furniture.
8. I doubt that you (Lei) did it.
9. I am afraid that he took the pen.
10. We are happy that they celebrated their birthday.

E. Answer the following questions in complete sentences in Italian:

1. Lei è contento che faccia bel tempo oggi?
2. Suo padre vuole che Lei compri una macchina sportiva?
3. Desidera che il maestro non dia degli esami?
4. Chi vuole che Lei venga a scuola oggi?
5. Chi dubita che Lei studi in questa classe?
6. Lei pensa che tutti i suoi compagni dicano la verità?
7. A casa Sua chi spera che Lei pulisca la Sua camera?
8. Sua madre insiste che Lei e Suo fratello scrivano bene?
9. Chi sperava di venire con Lei al cinema?
10. Cosa desidera comprare Sua madre quando va al supermercato?

20. The Subjunctive After Impersonal Expressions

The subjunctive is used after certain impersonal expressions if the verb that follows the expressions has an expressed subject.

è **necessario**, **occorre**, **bisogna** — it is necessary	è **improbabile**, it is improbable
è **possibile**, it is possible	è **giusto**, it is right
può darsi, it is possible	è **bene**, it is well
è **impossibile**, it is impossible	è **meglio**, it is better
è **probabile**, it is probable	**peccato**, it is a pity
	è **importante**, it is important

È necessario che **tu** ***arrivi*** presto.	It is necessary that you arrive early.
Peccato che **Maria** ***stia*** male.	It is too bad that Maria is not well.
Bisogna che **loro** ***finiscano*** tutto.	It is necessary that they finish everything.
But:	
È meglio studiare. (*no expressed subject*)	It is better to study.

Note

The subjunctive is not used after impersonal expressions that indicate certainty.

è **certo**, it is certain
è **vero**, it is true
è **sicuro**, it is certain
è **evidente**, it is evident

È certo che **parla** sempre.	It is certain that he always talks.
È vero che Maria è alta.	It is true that Mary is tall.
È evidente che **hai mangiato** bene.	It is evident that you have eaten well.

EXERCISES

A. Write the correct form of the verbs in parentheses:

1. (alzarsi) È importante che Luisa _____ presto ogni mattina.
2. (aspettare) È vero che io ti _____ davanti al portone.
3. (partire) Bisogna che noi _____ per Roma.
4. (vendere) È probabile che lui _____ la macchina da scrivere.
5. (finire) È bene che voi _____ queste discussioni!
6. (mettersi) È meglio che quei signori _____ a tavola ora.
7. (dovere) Peccato che tu _____ rimanere solo.
8. (venire) È sicuro che Gianni _____ con noi.
9. (avere) È possibile che voi _____ ragione questa volta.
10. (essere) Peccato che loro non _____ qui a godersi questo spettacolo.
11. (capire) È necessario che io _____ questa lezione!
12. (spendere) Può darsi che noi _____ troppo.
13. (vestirsi) Occorre che voi _____ elegantemente per il ballo.
14. (telefonare) È improbabile che Luisa _____ a Susanna stasera.
15. (fare) È certo che loro _____ tutto con precisione.

B. Add to each sentence the impersonal expressions shown and make any necessary changes:

Example: *Fa* il lavoro bene.
È necessario che _____.
È necessario che *faccia* il lavoro bene.

1. So il nome di quel signore.
   Bisogna che _____.
2. Dici la verità.
   È vero che _____.
3. Siamo allegri.
   È importante che _____.
4. Non pulisce i piatti bene.
   È certo che _____.
5. Vengono da noi stasera.
   È improbabile che _____.
6. Quell'abito non ti sta bene.
   Peccato che _____.
7. Carlo non si sente tanto bene.
   Può darsi che _____.

8. Scelgo questo invece di quello.
   È meglio che _____ .
9. Uscite prima delle sei.
   È possible che _____ .
10. Dai un regalo ad Anna.
    È giusto che _____ .
11. Maria piange.
    Peccato che _____ .
12. Andiamo al lago con Marco.
    È sicuro che _____ .
13. Cerchi la valigia.
    Occorre che _____ .
14. Non puniscono i loro figli.
    È giusto che _____ .
15. Vi divertite all'opera.
    È bene che _____ .

C. Translate the following into Italian:

1. It is necessary that they choose this meat.
2. It is impossible for us to send the package.
3. It is a pity that you (voi) talk so much!
4. It is important that I eat very little.
5. It is a pity that Paul can't come.
6. It is certain that you (tu) will go to Italy.
7. It is true that he plays the piano well.
8. He must listen to this program.
9. It is possible that she doesn't wash herself very often.
10. They must stay here.

D. Complete the following answers according to the cue given:

Example: Vai dalla nonna stasera?
Sì, bisogna che io _____ .
Sì, bisogna che io vada dalla nonna stasera.

1. A che ora partite per Genova?
   È necessario che noi _____ .
2. Dove sono le ragazze?
   È probabile che loro _____ .
3. Leonardo arriva domani?
   Sì, è certo che lui _____ .

4. Traduci questa lettera per Piero?
   Sì, occorre che io _____ .
5. Quando torna Mariella?
   È possibile che lei _____ .
6. Possiamo finire tutto prima delle nove?
   È sicuro che noi _____ .
7. Porterai un cappello nuovo alla festa?
   Sì, è meglio che io _____ .
8. Come sta Adolfo?
   Può darsi che lui _____ .
9. Dovete studiare per l'esame?
   Sì, è bene che noi _____ .
10. I professori hanno pazienza?
    Sì, occorre che loro _____ .

E. Answer the following questions in complete sentences:

1. È probabile che Lei visiti Suo zio oggi?
2. È vero che Lei ha una sorella minore?
3. Bisogna che Loro facciano i compiti per la classe d'italiano?
4. È giusto che il professore parli tanto?
5. È importante che i ragazzi vadano a casa dopo le lezioni?
6. È sicuro che domani è venerdì?
7. È possibile che piova durante l'estate?
8. È necessario che i bambini bevano molto latte?
9. Occorre dire sempre la verità?
10. È probabile che gli astronauti arrivino sulla luna un'altra volta?

21. Other Uses of the Subjunctive

1. The subjunctive is always used after the following conjunctions:

benchè, although, even though
purchè, provided that
prima che, before
in caso che, in the event that
a meno che . . . non, unless
sebbene, although
nonostante che, although
dato che, since
affinchè, so that, in order that
in modo che, in such a way as
senza che, without
quantunque, although
finchè, until

Telefonerò **prima che** tu ***parta.***	I will phone before you leave.
Non studia **benchè** ***abbia*** il tempo.	He doesn't study even though he has time.

2. The subjunctive is also used after the relative superlative or after adjectives such as **unico** and **solo** when the dependent clause is introduced by **che.**

È **il** romanzo **più importante che** io ***abbia letto.***	It is the most important novel that I have read.
È **l'unica** attrice russa **che** io ***conosca.***	She is the only Russian actress that I know.

EXERCISES

A. Choose the correct form of the verbs in parentheses:

1. È la borsa più piccola che Maria (ha, abbia) comprato.
2. Non andrò a meno che lei mi (accompagna, accompagni).
3. Giorgio è il solo giovane che (porti, porta) una giacca così sporca.
4. Scriverò una cartolina prima che (telefono, telefoni) a Paolo.
5. Andavo alla mostra prima di (visitare, visiti) mia zia.
6. Il maestro insegna purchè gli studenti (imparano, imparino).
7. Questo è il migliore libro che Hemingway (ha, abbia) scritto.
8. Siamo usciti senza che nessuno ci (ha, abbia) visti.
9. Prendete questa carta purchè non la (perdete, perdiate).
10. Anna è l'unica ragazza che (sappia, sa) la risposta.
11. Scriverò la lettera prima che tu (parta, parti).
12. Quantunque non (sia, è) giovane, è molto simpatico.

13. Nel caso che tu (decidi, decida) di non andarci, fammi una telefonata.
14. Il film è troppo lungo benchè (sia, è) interessante.
15. Silvia è la peggiore studentessa che il professore (abbia, ha) mai visto.

B. Change the infinitives in the following sentences to the correct form of the subjunctive:

1. Partiranno purchè non (piovere) più.
2. È la macchina più piccola che mio padre (comprare) in vita sua.
3. Sono l'unico studente che (finire) il lavoro.
4. Abbiamo preparato una bella cena benchè voi (mangiare) già.
5. La torre pendente è l'unica che (stare) per cadere.
6. È il migliore programma che io (vedere).
7. Parlate lentamente perchè tutti vi (capire).
8. Leggo ad alta voce affinchè tu mi (sentire) bene.
9. Susanna non rientra presto benchè i suoi genitori non (essere) a casa.
10. Non spendete troppo a meno che non (trovare) degli abiti buoni.

C. Translate the following sentences into Italian:

1. We shall wait until three o'clock in case Gino calls.
2. Mario will arrive before we leave.
3. Florence and Turin are the only cities which they will visit.
4. We must study in order to succeed.
5. I will buy it although it costs too much.
6. I am speaking loudly so that they may hear me.
7. Don't take the newspaper unless you (tu) want to read it!
8. Gina is the only young lady who reads Italian magazines.
9. It is the most important drama that I have seen.
10. She will leave provided it doesn't snow.
11. He will not buy the necktie until he sees it.
12. Don't (tu) leave before I return.
13. The professor teaches so that the students will learn.
14. John is the tallest boy that I know.
15. His sister will not go to Pisa unless Maria goes, too.

22. Review of Verb Lessons 17–21

A. Choose the correct form of the verb in parentheses:

1. È possibile che (voglia, vuole, voleva) venire.
2. Occorre che voi (faccia, facciate, fate) tutto bene.
3. È vero che Giovanni (studia, studiare, studi) troppo.
4. Signore, (guardi, guarda, guardate) questo.
5. Sono gli unici attori che io (conosco, conosca, conoscere).
6. Dubita che noi (uscire, siamo usciti, saremmo usciti).
7. Signorina, per favore, (pulisce, pulire, pulisca) questa camera.
8. Mia madre vuole che loro (mandino, mandarono, mandano) il pacco a Marta.
9. È certo che non (posso, potere, possa) partire per Roma.
10. Peccato che Laura non (stia, era, è) qui con noi.
11. Bisogna (trovare, trovi, trova) l'indirizzo di Francia.
12. Siamo contenti che tu (abbia scelto, scegli, scegliere) questa gonna verde.
13. Non verrà a meno che loro lo (invitino, invitarono, invitano).
14. È la più grande opera che lui (abbia scritto, scrive, scriverebbe).
15. Voglio (pescare, peschi, pesco) in quel lago.

B. Write the plural:

1. lui stia
2. io trovi
3. tu abbia
4. lei sia venuta
5. tu abbia fatto
6. io risponda
7. tu oda
8. lei salga
9. io finisca
10. lui dia
11. tu sia tornata
12. lei pensi
13. io giuochi
14. tu esca
15. lui sia arrivato

C. Translate the italicized words into Italian:

1. Il carabiniere vuole che *we wait.*
2. Scusi, signore, ma è necessario che Lei *gather* le Sue scarpe.
3. Insiste che io *go* con lui.
4. È contento che Tina *has come* alla festa.
5. Sono i migliori studenti che *I have known.*
6. Siamo sicuri che oggi *is* giovedì.

7. Ti dispiace che loro *have prepared* la colazione?
8. È meglio che tu *give* i garofani a Liliana.
9. Bisogna *to arrive* sulla luna prima di gennaio.
10. Desidero *to see* gli astronauti nella sfilata.
11. Signora, *eat* i cannelloni invece dei ravioli.
12. Insiste che noi *sing* un'aria di Puccini.
13. È probabile che Lucio *will bring* le caramelle a Diana.
14. Gli studenti imparano purchè il maestro *teaches* male.
15. È la più famosa poesia che Petrarca *has written.*

D. Translate into Italian:

1. I doubt that it will snow tomorrow.
2. He is the best president that we have had.
3. Sir, please sit in that chair.
4. We are glad that his mother is well.
5. It's necessary to eat much fruit.
6. He wants us to watch the film.
7. Martha wants to buy that dress.
8. It is possible for us to enter the theatre.
9. They will go unless they are ill.
10. The soldiers will leave before I arrive.
11. She hopes to read the novel.
12. Do you (tu) believe that she is intelligent?
13. Mr. Bianchi, open the door.
14. Young ladies, tell the truth.
15. We prefer that you (Lei) translate this story.

23. Mastery Exercises

A. Write each of the following verbs in the present subjunctive and the present perfect subjunctive:

Example: io (mangiare) mangi (pres. subj.)
abbia mangiato (pres. perf. subj.)

1. tu (andare)
2. noi (piangere)
3. loro (sentire)
4. io (finire)
5. Loro (pagare)
6. lui (mettere)
7. lei (telefonare)
8. voi (dare)
9. io (essere)
10. Maria (avere)
11. tu (fare)
12. chi (dormire)
13. Paolo (salire)
14. noi (venire)
15. le amiche (chiedere)
16. Loro (mettersi)
17. Lei (tenere)
18. io (sperare)
19. loro (volere)
20. voi (spedire)
21. tu (aprire)
22. Nicola (conoscere)
23. noi (sapere)
24. lui (svegliarsi)
25. tu ed io (nascondersi)

B. Complete the paragraph by placing the correct person and/or tense of each of the infinitives listed below in the appropriate blanks:

andare	comprare	preparare	mangiare	portare
cambiare	prendere	fare	ritornare	invitare

Giovanni deve andare in città. Bisogna che __1__ il treno delle otto e che __2__ un biglietto di andata e ritorno alla stazione. Per andare alla stazione, occorre che suo padre lo __3__ con la macchina perchè in periferia non ci sono mezzi pubblici. Una volta in città, occorre che Giovanni __4__ ad un autobus perchè sua madre vuole che lui __5__ a visitare la zia che abita in città. Giovanni spera che la zia lo __6__ restare a pranzo perchè non ha molto denaro in tasca per poter __7__ in un ristorante. Spera anche che la zia gli __8__ il suo piatto preferito e che, come ha già fatto altre volte, la zia __9__ a pranzo alcuni dei suoi amici. In tutti i modi, Giovanni spera di __10__ a casa con il treno delle undici.

C. Write paragraphs in Italian based on each of the following settings:

1. *Setting:* You will be going on a trip to Italy next summer. In no fewer than eight (8) sentences, describe the preparations that you will be making. Make certain that you use at least five (5) of the Italian expressions listed: biglietto, bagagli, negozi, agenzia di viaggi, linea aerea, treno, aeroporto, itinerario, indumenti estivi, medicinali.

2. *Setting:* You went to the doctor because you did not feel well. In no fewer than eight (8) sentences, write about the activities involved with this setting. Make certain that you use at least five (5) of the Italian expressions listed: dormire, bere, mangiare, farsi male, mal di testa, mal di stomaco, riposarsi, scrivere la ricetta, prendere la medicina, sentirsi bene.

D. *Reading stimulus dialogues:* After reading the settings in English, respond in writing in complete Italian sentences to each of the questions or statements:

1. *Setting:* You are calling your friend Giacomo on the phone.
   Giacomo: Pronto. Chi parla?
   Tu: -----
   Giacomo: Ti senti bene adesso?
   Tu: -----
   Giacomo: Perchè non vieni a casa mia stasera?
   Tu: -----
   Giacomo: Ti assicuro che ci divertiremo molto.
   Tu: -----

2. *Setting:* You and Teresa are discussing plans for the evening.
   Teresa: Perchè non c'incontriamo al Caffè Roma stasera?
   Tu: -----
   Teresa: Possiamo prendere un gelato ed ascoltare la musica.
   Tu: -----
   Teresa: Ci sarà anche un cantante popolare.
   Tu: -----
   Teresa: Possiamo invitare anche altri amici, vero?
   Tu: -----
   Teresa: Ottima idea! A che ora ci riuniremo?
   Tu: -----

24. Formation of the Imperfect Subjunctive and Pluperfect (Past Perfect) Subjunctive (Optional)

IMPERFECT SUBJUNCTIVE OF REGULAR VERBS

The imperfect subjunctive of most verbs is formed by dropping the **-re** from the infinitive and adding the endings: **-ssi, -ssi, -sse, -ssimo, -ste, -ssero.**

Infinitive:	**trovare**	**vendere**	**finire**
Stem:	trova-	vende-	fini-
Imperfect Subjunctive:	io trova***ssi***	vende***ssi***	fini***ssi***
	tu trova***ssi***	vende***ssi***	fini***ssi***
	Lei, lui, lei trova***sse***	vende***sse***	fini***sse***
	noi trova***ssimo***	vende***ssimo***	fini***ssimo***
	voi trova***ste***	vende***ste***	fini***ste***
	Loro, loro trova***ssero***	vende***ssero***	fini***ssero***

Note

1. Most verbs that are irregular in the present indicative (see Lesson 3) are usually regular in the imperfect subjunctive. To form the imperfect subjunctive of such verbs, add the endings to the imperfect indicative stem after dropping the **-vo** ending.

	Imperfect Indicative	Imperfect Subjunctive
bere	beve*vo*	beve***ssi***
fare	face*vo*	face***ssi***
uscire	usci*vo*	usci***ssi***

2. The following verbs are irregular in the imperfect subjunctive:

dare, to give	***dessi, dessi, desse, dessimo, deste, dessero***
essere, to be	***fossi, fossi, fosse, fossimo, foste, fossero***
stare, to be	***stessi, stessi, stesse, stessimo, steste, stessero***

PLUPERFECT (PAST PERFECT) SUBJUNCTIVE

The pluperfect subjunctive is formed by the imperfect subjunctive of **avere** or **essere** followed by the past participle of the verb.

cercare, to seek, to look for	
io ***avessi cercato***	noi ***avessimo cercato***
tu ***avessi cercato***	voi ***aveste cercato***
Lei, lui, lei ***avesse cercato***	Loro, loro ***avessero cercato***

tornare, to return	
io ***fossi tornato(a)***	noi ***fossimo tornati(e)***
tu ***fossi tornato(a)***	voi ***foste tornati(e)***
Lei ***fosse tornato(a)***	Loro ***fossero tornati(e)***
lui ***fosse tornato***	loro ***fossero tornati(e)***
lei ***fosse tornata***	

alzarsi, to get up	
io mi ***fossi alzato(a)***	noi ci ***fossimo alzati(e)***
tu ti ***fossi alzato(a)***	voi vi ***foste alzati(e)***
Lei si ***fosse alzato(a)***	Loro si ***fossero alzati(e)***
lui si ***fosse alzato***	loro si ***fossero alzati(e)***
lei si ***fosse alzata***	

EXERCISES

A. Change the infinitives to the following forms: (1) first person singular, imperfect indicative (2) third person singular, imperfect subjunctive (3) first person plural, pluperfect subjunctive:

Example: chiedere chiedevo chiedesse avessimo chiesto

1. volere
2. perdere
3. sentire
4. sedersi
5. condurre
6. rimanere
7. trovare
8. pensare
9. potere
10. pulire
11. lavorare
12. svegliarsi
13. essere
14. aprire
15. guardare
16. dare
17. dire
18. desiderare
19. rispondere
20. imparare
21. morire
22. avere
23. distruggere
24. visitare
25. portare

B. Write the infinitive of the following verbs:

1. facessimo
2. bevessi
3. decideste
4. fosse
5. cantassero
6. stesse
7. appariste
8. dessero
9. avessi
10. mangiassimo
11. leggesse
12. sceglieste
13. comprassimo
14. vi divertiste
15. si alzassero
16. prendesse
17. valessimo
18. ti preoccupassi
19. capissimo
20. correggessero

C. Change the following verbs to the imperfect subjunctive:

Example: vedrà vedesse

1. produrrebbe
2. portai
3. sorprendete
4. hanno alzato
5. possa
6. eravate
7. vedemmo
8. dava
9. fioriscono
10. guardai
11. laverà
12. è passato
13. giocheremmo
14. abbia perso
15. siate usciti
16. correvi
17. avevano ascoltato
18. dovetti
19. muovevamo
20. trovereste
21. mangino
22. abbia messo
23. ricordò
24. lascerà
25. pagherei

Part II—Grammatical Structures

1. Forms of the Articles: Definite and Indefinite

DEFINITE ARTICLES

MASCULINE	FEMININE
Singular	Singular
il ragazzo, the boy *lo* studente, the student (*m.*) *lo* zio, the uncle *l'*amico, the friend (*m.*)	*la* ragazza, the girl *la* studentessa, the student (*f.*) *la* zia, the aunt *l'*amica, the friend (*f.*)
Plural	Plural
i ragazzi, the boys *gli* studenti, the students *gli* zii, the uncles *gli* amici, the friends	*le* ragazze, the girls *le* studentesse, the students *le* zie, the aunts *le* amiche, the friends

Note

1. **Il** is used with masculine singular nouns beginning with a consonant other than **z**, **s** + a consonant, or **gn**. The plural of **il** is **i**.
2. **Lo** is used with masculine singular nouns beginning with **z**, **s** + a consonant, or **gn**: *lo* zio, *lo* studente, *lo* gnocco.
   The plural of **lo** is **gli**: *gli* zii, *gli* studenti, *gli* gnocchi.
3. **La** is used before all feminine singular nouns beginning with a consonant: *la* ragazza, *la* zia, *la* studentessa.
4. **L'** is used for masculine and feminine singular nouns beginning with a vowel: *l'*amico, *l'*amica.
   The plural of **l'** (*m.*) is **gli**: *gli* amici. The plural of **l'** (*f.*) is **le**: *le* amiche.

5. Masculine plural definite articles are used when referring to both male and female members of a group.

***Gli* amici** sono arrivati.	The friends (male and female) have arrived.
Come si chiamano ***i* figli** di Rosa?	What are the names of Rose's children?
***I* nonni** di Susanna sono giovani.	Susan's grandparents are young.

INDEFINITE ARTICLES

Masculine	Feminine
un ragazzo, a boy	***una*** ragazza, a girl
un amico, a friend (*m.*)	***un'*** amica, a friend (*f.*)
uno zio, an uncle	***una*** zia, an aunt
uno studente, a student (*m.*)	***una*** studentessa, a student (*f.*)

Note

1. **Un** is used before all masculine singular nouns beginning with a consonant, other than **z**, **s** + a consonant, or **gn**, or beginning with a vowel.
2. **Uno** is used before all masculine singular nouns beginning with **z**, **s** + a consonant, or **gn**.
3. **Una** is used before all feminine singular nouns beginning with a consonant.
4. **Un'** is used before all feminine singular nouns beginning with a vowel.

REPETITION OF ARTICLES

The articles, definite or indefinite, are generally repeated before each noun.

La sedia e ***la*** tavola sono nuove.	The chair and (the) table are new.
Ho comprato ***una*** penna e ***una*** matita.	I bought a pen and (a) pencil.

EXERCISES

A. Change the following definite articles to the plural:

1. l'amico _____ amici
2. lo specchio _____ specchi
3. l'amica _____ amiche
4. la slitta _____ slitte
5. il libro _____ libri
6. la scimmia _____ scimmie
7. il ristorante _____ ristoranti
8. lo studio _____ studi
9. l'album _____ album
10. l'artista _____ artiste

B. Complete the following with the correct form of **un, uno, una,** or **un'**:

1. È _____ famiglia grande.
2. Ho trovato _____ museo interessante.
3. Giovanni è _____ architetto importante.
4. C'è _____ zio di Maria qui.
5. Abbiamo visto _____ automobile rossa oggi.
6. Tutti gli studenti hanno fatto _____ sbaglio.
7. Prendiamo _____ caffè in questo bar.
8. Cercano _____ farmacia in città.
9. Mettiamoci sotto _____ albero qui vicino.
10. Abitate in _____ strada lontana da noi?

C. Write the definite article for each noun:

1. Preferisci _____ pioggia o _____ neve?
2. _____ inverno e _____ estate sono due stagioni dell'anno.
3. Uso _____ penna e _____ inchiostro per scrivere.
4. _____ foglie cadono sopra _____ erba.
5. _____ denti e _____ lingua sono nella bocca.
6. _____ aviogetto parte quando _____ piloti sono pronti.
7. _____ giovani e _____ signorine si divertivano al cinema.
8. _____ zio di Emma e _____ zia di Marco sono cugini.
9. Mi piacciono _____ polpette e _____ ravioli.
10. _____ professore è davanti alla classe.
11. _____ domanda è facile ma _____ risposta è difficile.

12. _____ zingari arrivarono con _____ cavalli.
13. _____ albergo e _____ pensione appartengono a mio cugino.
14. _____ cattedrale e _____ battistero sono dietro _____ fiume.
15. È _____ ora del pranzo ma _____ studentesse non sono arrivate.

D. Translate the English words into Italian:

1. *The* moglie di Carlo è bellissima.
2. È *a* bella giornata di maggio.
3. *The* uomini stanno mangiando del tonno.
4. Sta parlando di *a* torre pendente.
5. *A* cane può essere *a* amico.
6. Preferisco mangiare *the* banana.
7. *A* minuto non è *an* ora.
8. *The* parco di Palermo ha *a* teatro grande.
9. Metto *the* zucchero e *the* latte nel caffè.
10. Hai fatto *a* sbaglio con la penna.
11. *The* acqua è calda.
12. Roberto ha fatto *a* scherzo a sua sorella.
13. *The* autostrada è grande ma *the* macchine sono piccole.
14. Non lavare *the* piattino e *the* tazze.
15. Per Luisa ho comprato *a* orologio e *a* gonna.
16. Mi piace vedere *the* partite alla televisione.
17. Prende *a* gelato quando cammina per *the* strade.
18. *The* pizza di Carmela è squisita.
19. Non rompere nè *the* finestra nè *the* scaffale.
20. Ma questa è *a* mela o *an* arancia?

2. Contractions of Definite Articles and Prepositions; Possession With *Di*

CONTRACTIONS WITH THE DEFINITE ARTICLES

The prepositions **a, da, di, in,** and **su** are contracted with all definite articles.

DEFINITE ARTICLE	PREPOSITION				
	a (to, at)	**da** (from, by, at the house of)	**di** (of)	**in** (in)	**su** (on)
il	al	dal	del	nel	sul
i	ai	dai	dei	nei	sui
la	alla	dalla	della	nella	sulla
le	alle	dalle	delle	nelle	sulle
gli	agli	dagli	degli	negli	sugli
lo	allo	dallo	dello	nello	sullo
l'	all'	dall'	dell'	nell'	sull'

Mio fratello va ***al*** negozio.	My brother goes *to the* store.
Parlo ***del*** ragazzo.	I'm speaking *of the* boy.

Note

1. The definite articles are rarely combined with the prepositions **con** (with) and **per** (through).

2. **Da** usually means *from*. It may also mean *by*, *at* (*to*) *someone's place* or *house* when followed by a person indicating possession on that person's part.

Andiamo ***dallo*** zio oggi.	We are going to our uncle's (house) today.
Carla è andata ***dal*** macellaio.	Carla went to the butcher's (shop).

With a proper name, including cities, or with pronouns, no article is used.

Vanno *da* Giovanni.	They are going to John's (house).
Torna *da* Pisa.	He is returning from Pisa.

POSSESSION WITH *DI*

1. Possession is expressed in Italian by **di** or **di** + the article before the possessor. There is no apostrophe *s* in Italian to denote possession.

È il libro ***di*** Peppe.	It's Joe's book. (the book of Joe)
È il libro ***del*** ragazzo.	It's the boy's book.
È il libro ***della*** ragazza.	It's the girl's book.
Sono i libri ***degli*** amici.	They are the friends' books.

2. The preposition **di** may take an apostrophe before words beginning with vowels other than *i*.

il libro ***d'***Enrico
Or:
il libro ***di*** Enrico
} Henry's book

Before words beginning with *i*, **di** must take an apostrophe.

la città ***d'***Italia	the city of Italy
il quaderno ***d'***Ida	Ida's notebook

EXERCISES

A. Complete the sentences with the correct form of the preposition in parentheses + the definite article where necessary:

Example: (di) La lingua _____ tedeschi è il tedesco.
La lingua *dei* tedeschi è il tedesco.

1. (di) La moglie _____ avvocato è alta.
2. (in) Ci sono nove figli _____ famiglia di Gemma.
3. (da) Mia zia è tornata ora _____ modista.
4. (a) La maestra dà il libro _____ studente.
5. (su) Mettete i quaderni _____ tavoli, per favore.
6. (di) Questo posto è _____ Giovanna.
7. (di) Questi documenti sono _____ avvocato.
8. (a) Chi insegna la matematica _____ studenti?

9. (da) Verrà _____ stazione fra cinque minuti.
10. (in) Luigina cade sempre _____ neve.
11. (su) Ho lasciato i libri _____ scaffale laggiù.
12. (di) Parlano sempre _____ viaggi fatti in Italia.
13. (in) Dobbiamo entrare _____ albergo in Via Marconi.
14. (da) È uscita _____ porta a sinistra.
15. (a) Il nonno ha regalato un gettone _____ bambino.
16. (di) Giorgio è il fratello _____ Roberto.
17. (in) Marta si guarda sempre _____ specchio.
18. (su) C'è del fango _____ stivali.
19. (da) Ho ricevuto una cartolina _____ amiche di Canio.
20. (a) A Firenze avete mangiato _____ aperto?

B. Replace the words in italics with the words in parentheses, making all necessary changes:

Example: (posta) Va al *teatro*.
Va alla posta.

1. (cantante) È il padre dell'*artista*.
2. (Tommaso) Dà il giocattolo al *ragazzo*.
3. (zia) Sei andato dal *macellaio*?
4. (trattoria) Ho mangiato bene al *ristorante russo*.
5. (museo) (albergo) Sono andati alla *scuola* vicino al *parco*.
6. (edificio) La pioggia cade sul *tetto*.
7. (università) Torneranno fra poco dall'*opera*.
8. (Roma) Non vorranno andare al *centro* con me.
9. (bambina) È il cane del *ragazzino*.
10. (occhi) Ha qualche cosa nella *bocca*.
11. (finestrino) Non buttare niente dalla *finestra*.
12. (scatola) Signore, metta la cenere nel *portacenere*.
13. (zii) È arrivato un pacco da *Milano*.
14. (nostre amiche) Facciamo una telefonata alla *signorina*.
15. (nonni) È il denaro del *cuoco*.

C. Complete the sentences in Italian by translating the words in parentheses:

1. (at the) Prendiamo un gelato _____ negozio.
2. (from) Luisa torna _____ vacanza stasera.
3. (of) Le strade _____ Firenze sono strette.

4. (on the) Una pietra è caduta _____ piede di Caterina.
5. (to) Andiamo invece _____ Maria.
6. (to the) Diamo questa valigia _____ figli di Lola.
7. (in the) Fa molto caldo _____ aeroporto di Milano.
8. (of the) È quella la giacca _____ signore?
9. (at the) Hanno comprato del merluzzo squisito _____ pescivendolo.
10. (from) Vengo _____ Parigi per stare con te.

D. Translate the italicized words into Italian:

1. Vai *to the bank*?
2. *The boy's ties* sono troppo lunghe.
3. Ti piacciono le cotolette *of the cook?*
4. Cerchiamo *Peter's pen*.
5. Ricevette un regalo *from the students*.
6. Ci sono dieci persone *in Tom's family*.
7. Metta i giornali *on the desk*.
8. Non metto zucchero *in the coffee*.
9. *The door of the room* è chiusa.
10. L'annunziatore diede un premio *to the actress*.
11. Oggi è il primo giorno *of the week*.
12. *John's book* non è qui.
13. *The girl's mother* non è arrivata.
14. Ci sono molti fiori *in the vase*.
15. C'erano dei quadri costosi *at the museum*.
16. La mela è caduta *from the tree*.
17. *The family's maid* si chiama Anita.
18. Il treno arrivò *from* Foggia.
19. L'autobus parte *from the stop* numero sette.
20. Non gli piace parlare *on* (*at*) *the telephone*.

3. Uses of the Definite Article

The definite article is generally used before:

1. Nouns used in a general sense.

Ti piacciono ***le polpette***?	Do you like meatballs?
Il latte è buono.	Milk is good.
Mi piace ***la matematica***.	I like mathematics.
L'argento è prezioso.	Silver is precious.

Note

The context indicates whether or not the definite article is to be translated into English.

Ti piacciono le polpette?	Do you like meatballs (in general)?
Ti piacciono le polpette che la mamma ha servito?	Do you like the meatballs that mother has served?

2. Names of languages and other subjects of study, except immediately after **parlare**, **di**, or **in**.

Il tedesco è una lingua importante.	German is an important language.
Studiano ***lo spagnolo*** in classe.	They study Spanish in class.
Non gli piace ***la chimica***.	He doesn't like chemistry.

But:

Parla italiano.	She speaks Italian.
Questa è la classe d'inglese.	This is the English class.
Bisogna scrivere in italiano.	It is necessary to write in Italian.

3. Parts of the body or articles of clothing instead of the possessive adjective.

Si lava ***le mani***.	He washes his hands.
Mi metto ***la camicia***.	I put on my shirt.

4. Titles, except in direct address.

Il signor Bianchi parla bene.	Mr. Bianchi speaks well.
Il Generale Washington non era troppo alto.	General Washington was not too tall.
Il professor Boni insegna bene.	Professor Boni teaches well.

But:

Buon giorno, signor Luni.	Good morning, Mr. Luni.

5. Proper names preceded by an adjective, except in exclamations.

Il piccolo Alfredo è malato.	Little Alfred is ill.
But:	
Povero Alfredo!	Poor Alfred!
La cara Maria ha scritto.	Dear Mary has written.
But:	
Cara Maria!	Dear Mary!

6. Days of the week in a plural sense, to express "on."

Vado a scuola ***il lunedì*** e ***il venerdì.***	I go to school on Mondays and Fridays.
Vengono da noi ***la domenica.***	They come to our house on Sundays.

Note: If the day mentioned is a specific day, the article is omitted.

Parto per Venezia martedì.	I leave for Venice on Tuesday.
L'ho visto giovedì.	I saw him on Thursday.

7. Seasons, expressions of time, and dates.

Vi piace ***la primavera***?	Do you like spring?
Sono ***le quattro***.	It is four o'clock.
Arriverà ***il mese*** prossimo.	She will arrive next month.
È partita ***la settimana*** scorsa.	She left last week.
Oggi è ***il 3 settembre***.	Today is September 3.
Sono stato in Italia ***dal 1960 al 1965***.	I was in Italy from 1960 to 1965.

8. Nouns of measure or weight instead of the English indefinite article.

Costano 500 lire ***il chilo***.	They cost 500 lire a kilo.

9. Names of countries, continents, regions, states, rivers, large islands, except with unmodified feminine names of countries after **di** or **in.**

L'Italia è bella.	Italy is beautiful.
Voglio visitare ***la Toscana.***	I want to visit Tuscany.
Il Texas è grande.	Texas is large.
La Sardegna è un'isola italiana.	Sardinia is an Italian island.
But:	
Le strade d'Italia sono buone.	The roads of Italy are good.
La Francia è in Europa.	France is in Europe.
Palermo è in Sicilia.	Palermo is in Sicily.

Note: Masculine countries and regions and modified feminine countries and regions take the definite article.

Montreal è ***nel Canadà.***	Montreal is in Canada.
L'Umbria è ***nell'Italia*** centrale.	Umbria is in Central Italy.

10. Surnames (not preceded by a given name) and before given names of women, when referring to a person well known to the speaker and to the listener.

Il Petrarca visse molti secoli fa.	Petrarch lived many centuries ago.
La Ginzburg è ben conosciuta.	(Miss) Ginzburg is well known.
La Caterina verrà fra poco.	Catherine will come soon.

11. Possessives, but not in direct address or before a singular, unmodified noun denoting family relationship, except for **loro.**

La mia amica Anna sta male.	My friend Ann is not well.
È ***il mio coltello.***	It's my knife.
La giacca è ***la sua*** e non ***la mia.***	The jacket is his and not mine.
But:	
Mia cara Anna, come stai?	My dear Ann, how are you?
Sua sorella canta male.	His sister sings badly.
Il loro fratello è malato.	Their brother is ill.

12. Infinitives used as nouns when beginning a sentence. These are always masculine and are usually expressed in English by the present participle.

Il mangiare è necessario.	Eating is necessary.
Il parlare troppo non piace a nessuno.	No one likes talking too much.

EXERCISES

A. Complete the sentences with the correct form of a definite article, if it is needed:

1. Gianna partirà per Torino _____ sabato prossimo.
2. Sandra si mette _____ guanti gialli.
3. In classe parliamo _____ italiano.
4. _____ signor Messina prenderà l'aviogetto delle sei.
5. Quei signori vanno in chiesa tutte _____ domeniche.

6. Buona sera, _____ Dottor Sonora.
7. _____ bere non fa bene a tutti.
8. Cosa fai durante _____ estate?
9. Vorrebbe visitare _____ Belgio qualche volta.
10. Mia nonna è venuta in _____ America _____ 1923.
11. Queste ciliege costano un dollaro _____ libbra.
12. Bari è una città di _____ Italia meridionale.
13. _____ Germania e _____ Svizzera sono in _____ Europa.
14. Lavati _____ braccio, Pietro!
15. Vi piacciono ____ spaghetti?
16. Armstrong è andato sulla luna _____ anno scorso.
17. _____ mangiare e _____ lavorare fanno bene alla salute.
18. Questa signorina è _____ mia sorella.
19. _____ Lombardia si trova in _____ Italia.
20. L'attrice italiana vorrebbe abitare in _____ Messico.
21. Per la festa di stasera mi metterò _____ smoking nuovo.
22. Desiderano altro, _____ signori?
23. Bisogna leggere in _____ francese.
24. Il telegramma è arrivato a _____ cinque.
25. _____ Corsica appartiene alla Francia.

B. Translate the English expressions into Italian:

1. Roma è la capitale *of* Italia.
2. *Mr.* Palermo non è a casa.
3. Buona notte, *Miss* Riviera.
4. *Next year*, frequenterò l'università.
5. *On Mondays*, visito i miei cugini.
6. *Her pen* è come la mia.
7. Mi piace *ice cream* ma non *cake*.
8. *Spring* e *summer* sono le mie stagioni preferite.
9. *Gold* è un metallo prezioso.
10. Il signor Gambi parla *German*.
11. *Traveling* è meraviglioso.
12. *General* Battista ha vinto un'altra battaglia.
13. *Little Susan* è sua cugina.
14. *My uncle* voleva andare alla spiaggia.
15. Gli fa male *his* mano.
16. Gloria ci scrisse *last year*.
17. *Spanish* è facile per loro.

18. Reggio Calabria è una città *in* Calabria.
19. Lui ha sempre un libro sotto *his* braccio.
20. Le uova costano 3000 lire *a* dozzina.

C. Translate into English:

1. Lei ha le mani sporche.
2. Il calcio è uno sport italiano.
3. Traducete questa lettera in francese.
4. Ho perso il passaporto.
5. La signora Mattei è caduta la settimana scorsa.
6. Il Pirandello scrisse dei drammi interessanti.
7. Queste camicie costano cinque dollari il paio.
8. Parigi è nella Francia del nord.
9. Le attrici svedesi sono molto alte.
10. I libri sono utili.
11. La domenica mi diverto a casa.
12. Lucio si è messo i miei pantaloni.
13. A Roma, i gatti si trovano dappertutto.
14. Andremo alla spiaggia giovedì.
15. Il capitano Smith non sposò l'indiana.
16. Gli piacevano gli spinaci.
17. Tokio è la capitale del Giappone.
18. Ti piace il formaggio?
19. Mangiano il pesce ma preferiscono la carne.
20. Lei parla inglese, dottore?

D. Translate into Italian:

1. The president visited France.
2. Does she have your (*fam. sing.*) Italian book?
3. Today is March 12.
4. Yesterday was Monday.
5. Put butter on your bread. (*fam. sing.*)
6. Bonn is a city in Germany.
7. His feet hurt him.
8. Winter is the season of snow.
9. I used to take the train on Wednesdays.
10. New York is in the United States.

4. Omission of the Articles

OMISSION OF THE DEFINITE ARTICLE

The definite article is omitted:

1. Before a noun in apposition.

Londra, ***capitale*** d'Inghilterra, è molto grande.	London, the capital of England, is very large.

2. Before ordinal numbers used after names of rulers and popes.

Vittorio Emanuele ***II*** fu re d'Italia.	Victor Emmanuel the Second was king of Italy.
Papa Giovanni ***XXIII*** era sempre allegro.	Pope John the Twenty-third was always happy.

3. In a number of common expressions following prepositions: **a, in, per, da,** etc.

a casa, at home
in casa, at home
da casa, from home
per via aerea, by air
in treno, by train
in chiesa, in (to) church
in città, in (to) town
in campagna, in (to) the country
in montagna, at (to) the mountains
in piazza, in (to) the square
in giardino, in (to) the garden
in cucina, in (to) the kitchen
in cantina, in (to) the basement, cellar
in (a) teatro, in (to) the theater
in biblioteca, in (to) the library
a tavola, at (the) table
in aereo, by plane
in aviogetto, by jet

Note: When reference is made to a particular place, the article is often added.

Andiamo ***alla*** biblioteca in Via Alessandria.	Let's go to the library on Alessandria St.

4. Before lists of nouns.

Ha comprato ***fagioli, spinaci, pomodori,*** e ***lattuga.***	She bought beans, spinach, tomatoes, and lettuce.

OMISSION OF THE INDEFINITE ARTICLE

The indefinite article is omitted:

1. Before unmodified predicate nouns expressing nationality, religion, rank, or occupation.

È ***italiana.***	She's Italian (an Italian).
Sono ***cattolico.***	I am a Catholic.
È ***generale.***	He is a general.
Antonio è ***medico.***	Anthony is a doctor.
But:	
Antonio è ***un buon medico.***	Anthony is a good doctor.

2. Before **cento** and **mille**.

Vale ***cento*** dollari.	It is worth one hundred dollars.
Ho speso ***mille*** lire.	I spent one thousand lire.

3. After **che** and **quale** in exclamations.

Che peccato!	What a pity!
Quale sorpresa!	What a surprise!

4. Before a noun in apposition.

Boccaccio, noto ***autore,*** scrisse il *Decamerone.*	Boccaccio, a noted author, wrote the *Decameron.*

5. After the preposition **da** meaning *as*, *like*, or *in the manner of.*

Visse *da* principe.	He lived like a prince.

EXERCISES

A. Complete the sentences in English:

1. Lisa era a casa alle sette ogni sera.
   Lisa was _____ at seven o'clock every evening.
2. Mio cugino è architetto.
   My cousin is _____.
3. Anita, moglie di Garibaldi, era molto gentile.
   Anita, _____ of Garibaldi, was very gentle.

4. È un buon maestro.
   He is _____ .
5. Ho trovato carta, inchiostro, penne, e matite.
   I found _____, _____, _____, and _____ .
6. C'erano mille soldati in piazza.
   There were _____ soldiers _____ square.
7. Che bella sorpresa!
   _____ surprise!
8. Quel signore è un ministro protestante.
   That man is _____ minister.
9. L'avvocato non è italiano; è svedese.
   The lawyer is not _____; he's _____ .
10. I soldati americani morirono da eroi.
    The American soldiers died _____ .
11. Andranno in città stasera?
    Will they go _____ this evening?
12. Papa Paolo VI è milanese.
    Pope Paul VI _____ Milanese.
13. Cristoforo Colombo, famoso navigatore, nacque a Genova.
    Christopher Columbus, _____, was born in Genoa.
14. Lo zio di Marco è colonnello.
    Mark's uncle is _____ .
15. Quest'abito costa cento dollari.
    This suit costs _____ .

B. Supply appropriate missing words in the following sentences:

Example: Giulio cura gli ammalati.
Allora è _____ .
Allora è *dottore.*

1. Mario difende il suo cliente in corte. Allora è _____ .
2. Cinquanta più cinquanta fanno _____ .
3. Maria è nata in Francia. Allora è _____ .
4. Pietro scrive molti romanzi. Allora è _____ .
5. Giacomo è stato battezzato nella chiesa cattolica. Allora è _____ .
6. Insegno all'università. Perciò sono _____ .
7. Al mercato compriamo sempre patate, mele, _____, _____, e _____ .
8. Parigi, _____ della Francia, ha molti teatri.
9. Mi piace disegnare; perciò, voglio diventare _____ .
10. La Deledda era _____ famosa scrittrice.

C. Translate into English:

1. Mio nipote è meccanico.
2. Vittorio Emanuele III fu re d'Italia.
3. Piero è partito con cento carabinieri.
4. Le ragazze erano andate in chiesa a pregare.
5. Paolo, marito di Anna, è molto simpatico.
6. Non è una buona infermiera.
7. Agisce sempre da buon cristiano.
8. Papa Giulio II conosceva Michelangelo molto bene.
9. Che fame che hanno!
10. Non andare in montagna da solo.
11. C'erano mille donne e mille uomini all'aeroporto.
12. Peppe, noto pescatore, non prese niente.
13. Che sorriso piacevole!
14. Siamo andati in treno da Padova a Verona.
15. Quella poetessa è indiana.

D. Translate into Italian:

1. We are Americans but they are Russians.
2. Tom is a good butcher.
3. What a novel!
4. Young people drink milk, water, wine, coffee, and tea.
5. Genoa, the principal port of Italy, has a large cathedral.
6. Excuse me, sir, are you a tailor?
7. They speak Japanese.
8. He has a memory like an elephant.
9. Let's go home now!
10. This town has a thousand inhabitants.
11. They used to go to the country often.
12. General Lee was an American.
13. My mother is always in the kitchen!
14. He's a rich lawyer.
15. Yesterday we went to the Church of St. Paul.

5. Nouns

GENDER

All nouns are either masculine or feminine in gender.

1. Singular nouns ending in **-o** are generally masculine:

   il libro, the book   **il ragazzo**, the boy

2. Singular nouns ending in **-a** are generally feminine.

   la lampada, the lamp   **la ragazza**, the girl

3. Singular nouns ending in **-e** may be masculine or feminine.

   il pane, the bread   **la lezione**, the lesson

PLURAL OF NOUNS

1. Nouns ending in **-o** or **-e** change the **-o** or **-e** to **-i** in the plural.

il tavolo, the table	**i tavoli**, the tables
il giovane, the young man	**i giovani**, the young men
la lezione, the lesson	**le lezioni**, the lessons

2. Nouns ending in **-a** change the **-a** to **-e** in the plural.

   la matita, the pencil   **le matite**, the pencils

Note

The masculine plural form of a noun may refer to both the male and female members of a group.

i figli, the son and daughter, the children
i bambini, the little boy and girl, the children
i re, the king and queen, the kings (rulers)
i nonni, the grandfather and grandmother, the grandparents
gli zii, the uncle and aunt, the uncles
i ragazzi, the boys, the boys and girls
gli amici, the friends (*m.*), the friends (*m.* and *f.*)
i nipoti, the nephew and the niece, the nephews
i signori Levi, Mr. and Mrs. Levi

NOUNS IRREGULAR IN GENDER

1. Some nouns that end in **-o** are feminine.

la mano, the hand	**le mani**, the hands
la dinamo, the dynamo	**le dinamo**, the dynamos
la radio, the radio	**le radio**, the radios

The nouns **dinamo** and **radio** do not change in the plural.

2. Some nouns that end in **-a** are masculine.

il dramma, the drama	**i drammi**, the dramas
il panorama, the panorama	**i panorami**, the panoramas
il poeta, the poet	**i poeti**, the poets

These nouns form the plural by changing **-a** to **-i**.

3. Some nouns that end in **-ca** or **-ga** are masculine. These nouns form the plural by changing **-ca** to **-chi** or **-ga** to **-ghi**.

il duca, the duke	**i duchi**, the dukes
il collega, the colleague	**i colleghi**, the colleagues

4. Nouns ending in **-ista** or **-cida** may be either masculine or feminine. Masculine nouns change **-a** to **-i** in the plural, and feminine nouns change **-a** to **-e**.

il turista, the tourist (*m.*)	**i turisti**, the tourists
la turista, the tourist (*f.*)	**le turiste**, the tourists
l'artista, the artist (*m.*)	**gli artisti**, the artists
l'artista, the artist (*f.*)	**le artiste**, the artists
il suicida, the suicide (*m.*)	**i suicidi**, the suicides
la suicida, the suicide (*f.*)	**le suicide**, the suicides

NOUNS WITH IRREGULAR PLURALS

I. Masculine Nouns

1*a*. Nouns ending in **-co** change **-co** to **-chi** in the plural if the stress falls on the syllable before the last.

il tabacco, the tobacco	**i tabacchi**, the tobaccos
il giuoco, the game	**i giuochi**, the games

The following nouns are exceptions to this rule:

l'amico, the friend	**gli amici**, the friends

il nemico, the enemy — **i nemici**, the enemies
il porco, the pig — **i porci**, the pigs
il Greco, the Greek — **i Greci**, the Greeks

b. When the stress falls on any other syllable, the plural is formed by changing **-co** to **-ci**.

il monaco, the monk — **i monaci**, the monks

The following noun is an exception to this rule:

lo stomaco, the stomach — **gli stomachi**, the stomachs

2. Nouns ending in **-go** change **-go** to **-ghi** in the plural.

il lago, the lake — **i laghi**, the lakes
il dialogo, the dialogue — **i dialoghi**, the dialogues

Nouns ending in **-logo**, which refer to professions, and those ending in **fago**, change **-logo** to **-logi** and **-fago** to **-fagi** in the plural.

il teologo, the theologian — **i teologi**, the theologians
il sarcofago, the sarcophagus — **i sarcofagi**, the sarcophagi

3. Nouns ending in **-io** change **-io** to **-i** in the plural unless the **-i** is stressed in the singular.

lo studio, the study — **gli studi**, the studies
il figlio, the son — **i figli**, the sons
But:
lo zio, the uncle — **gli zii**, the uncles
il calpestio, the trampling — **i calpestii**, the tramplings
il ronzio, the buzzing — **i ronzii**, the buzzings

II. Feminine Nouns

1. Nouns ending in **-ca** or **-ga** change **-ca** to **-che** and **-ga** to **-ghe** in the plural.

l'amica, the friend — **le amiche**, the friends
la bottega, the shop — **le botteghe**, the shops

2. Nouns ending in **-cia** or **-gia** change **-cia** to **-ce** and **-gia** to **-ge** in the plural unless the **-i** is stressed in the singular.

la faccia, the face — **le facce**, the faces
la valigia, the suitcase — **le valige**, the suitcases

But:

la farmacia, the drugstore	**le farmacie**, the drugstores
la bugia, the lie	**le bugie**, the lies

III. Nouns ending in a consonant, an accented vowel, or in **-i** or **-ie**, and nouns having one syllable, do not change in the plural.

l'autobus, the bus	**gli autobus**, the buses
la città, the city	**le città**, the cities
la crisi, the crisis	**le crisi**, the crises
la serie, the series	**le serie**, the series
il re, the king	**i re**, the kings

IV. Some nouns are masculine in the singular and feminine in the plural.

Masculine Singular	Feminine Plural
il braccio, the arm	**le braccia**, the arms
il centinaio, the hundred	**le centinaia**, hundreds
il dito, the finger	**le dita**, the fingers
il frutto, the fruit	**la frutta**, the fruit (of a tree)
il ginocchio, the knee	**le ginocchia**, the knees
il labbro, the lip	**le labbra**, the lips (of a person)
il miglio, the mile	**le miglia**, the miles
l'osso, the bone	**le ossa**, the bones (of the body)
il paio, the pair	**le paia**, the pairs
l'uovo, the egg	**le uova**, the eggs

Note

A noun of nationality is written with a capital letter, while an adjective of nationality is written with a small letter.

Gli *Italiani* sono allegri.	The Italians are happy.
Preferisco il cibo *americano*.	I prefer American food.

EXERCISES

A. Write the correct form of the definite article:

1. _____ problema
2. _____ mano
3. _____ latte
4. _____ braccia
5. _____ bugie
6. _____ autisti
7. _____ poeta
8. _____ dito
9. _____ penna
10. _____ quadro
11. _____ dramma
12. _____ ginocchio
13. _____ dolce
14. _____ figli
15. _____ collega

B. Change the following to the plural:

1. la radio
2. il re
3. il programma
4. la colazione
5. lo studente
6. il nipote
7. il labbro
8. la suicida
9. la magia
10. la minaccia
11. il filologo
12. il borgo
13. l'amico
14. l'amica
15. la barca

C. Change the following to the singular:

1. le ginocchia
2. i re
3. le autiste
4. gli astrologi
5. i dischi
6. i panorami
7. i pianisti
8. i monaci
9. gli zii
10. le biblioteche
11. le facce
12. le ossa
13. le paia
14. le città
15. i filobus

D. Rewrite the following sentences, changing all italicized words to the plural:

1. *Si lava la mano.*
2. Ecco *il dialogo.*
3. *L'amica* di Giovanni *arriva* ora.
4. *La ragazza viaggia un miglio* ogni giorno.
5. *La dinamo* non *funziona* più.
6. *Il collega* di mio zio *è vecchio.*
7. *Il fuoco si vede* da qui.
8. *Il Greco è arrivato* con la nave.
9. Ascolto sempre *il dramma alla radio.*
10. *Mi piace l'uovo fritto.*

E. Write the feminine equivalent of the words in italics:

1. *Il turista* passa ora per la dogana.
2. Il giornale parlava *del suicida.*

3. *L'amico* di Giorgio sta molto bene.
4. Sono *il nipote* di Maria.
5. Ecco *i figli* di mia zia.
6. Ci sono *molti autisti* per la strada.
7. *Il tavolo* non è grande abbastanza.
8. *Mio cugino* va all'università.
9. *I compagni* si divertono al cinema.
10. Ho *parecchi colleghi* all'ufficio.

F. Translate the following into Italian:

1. the dynamo
2. the aunt and uncle
3. the friend
4. the shirt
5. the lies
6. the pigs
7. the grandparents
8. the father
9. the mother
10. the driver
11. the bus
12. Mr. and Mrs. Cari
13. the poet (*m.*)
14. the wine
15. the cities
16. the virtues
17. the studies
18. the lakes
19. the fruit (*sing.*)
20. the lips
21. the variety
22. the arms
23. the stomach
24. the enemies
25. the monks
26. the astrologer
27. the children
28. the male cousin and the female cousin
29. the water
30. the king and queen

6. Adjectives: Forms, Agreement, Position

FORMS OF ADJECTIVES

SINGULAR		PLURAL		MEANING
Masculine	Feminine	Masculine	Feminine	
nuov*o*	nuov*a*	nuov*i*	nuov*e*	new
alt*o*	alt*a*	alt*i*	alt*e*	tall
grand*e*	grand*e*	grand*i*	grand*i*	large, big
importante*e*	importante*e*	importanti*i*	importanti*i*	important

Note

1. Masculine singular adjectives ending in **-o** have four forms. Masculine singular adjectives ending in **-e** have two forms.
2. Feminine adjectives ending in **-ca**, **-ga**, **-cia**, or **-gia** and masculine adjectives ending in **-co**, **-go**, or **-io** form their plurals according to the rules given for nouns having similar endings in Grammar Lesson 5.

AGREEMENT OF ADJECTIVES

Italian adjectives agree in gender and number with the nouns or pronouns they modify.

Il **pane** di oggi è ***buono***.	Today's bread is good.
La **ragazza** è ***allegra***.	The girl is happy.
Questi **bambini** sono ***cattivi***.	These children are bad.
Sono ***simpatici***.	They are nice.

An adjective modifying two or more nouns of *different* genders is always in the masculine plural.

Alberto ed **Anna** sono ***contenti***.	Albert and Anne are happy.

Past participles used as adjectives must agree with the words modified.

Il **libro** è ***aperto*** o ***chiuso***?	Is the book open or closed?
Le **finestre** sono ***rotte***.	The windows are broken.

POSITION OF ADJECTIVES

Most descriptive adjectives in Italian denoting nationality, religion, color, etc. follow the nouns they modify and agree with them in gender and number.

un signore ***italiano***	an Italian gentleman
una chiesa ***cattolica***	a Catholic church
una bandiera ***rossa***	a red flag

Adjectives of number and quantity precede the nouns they modify.

Ho ***due*** scarpe.	I have two shoes.
Maria ha ***molti*** libri.	Mary has many books.

Common adjectives of quantity are:

molto(a), much	**molti(e)**, many
poco(a), little	**pochi(e)**, few
certo(a), certain	**certi(e)**, certain
qualche, some, any	**alcuni(e)**, some, any
parecchio(a), quite a bit of	**parecchi(ie)**, several
stesso(a), same	**stessi(e)**, same
ogni, each, every	

Note

1. **Qualche** and **alcuni(e)** always have a plural meaning, although **qualche** precedes singular nouns only.

qualche studente	some students
alcuni studenti	some students

2. **Ogni** is invariable.

ogni settimana	every week
ogni tre giorni	every three days

The following descriptive adjectives may also precede the nouns they modify: **bello, bravo, brutto, buono, caro, cattivo, giovane, grande, lungo, nuovo, piccolo, vecchio.**

Sei un *cattivo* **bambino!**	You are a bad child!
Che *bel* **quadro!**	What a beautiful picture!
Piero è un ***buon ragazzo.***	Peter is a good boy.

Note

1. When **bello** precedes the noun, it takes the same endings as the definite article.

	MASCULINE					FEMININE		
	Singular			Plural		Singular		Plural
Def. Art. **bello**	il bel	lo bello	l' bell'	i bei	gli begli	la bella	l' bell'	le belle

2. When **buono** precedes the noun, it takes the same endings as the indefinite article.

	Masculine		Feminine	
Indef. Art. **buono**	un buon	uno buono	una buona	un' buon'

3. When **bello** and **buono** follow the nouns they modify, they have the same endings as adjectives ending in **-o.**

È un **film** ***buono.***	It is a good film.
È uno **zaino** ***bello.***	It is a fine knapsack.

EXERCISES

A. Replace the italicized adjectives with the correct form of each of the three adjectives in parentheses:

1. Sono romanzi *interessanti*. (importante, facile, tedesco)
2. Mia zia è una signora *gentile*. (simpatico, alto, cortese)
3. È una biblioteca *nuova*. (bianco, grande, costoso)
4. Ho trovato dei pantaloni *gialli*. (verde, caro, largo)

5. Le strade in Italia sono *strette*. (piccolo, lungo, pulito)
6. Carla è *americana*. (francese, russo, snello)
7. Hai visto quel film *giapponese*? (turco, inglese, messicano)
8. Ho *sei* matite. (alcuno, parecchio, poco)
9. Che *povere* ragazze! (bravo, caro, bello)
10. Mia sorella compra *troppe* banane. (molto, poco, alcuno)

B. Write the correct form of the adjective in parentheses:

1. (fresco) i pomodori _____ ; l'insalata _____
2. (facile) la lezione _____ ; il lavoro _____
3. (interessante) il programma _____ ; le città _____
4. (vecchio) la _____ famiglia; i _____ castelli
5. (alcuno) _____ signore; _____ signori
6. (poco) _____ studenti; _____ carne
7. (vecchio) un _____ tavolo; una _____ amica
8. (francese) la bandiera _____ ; i soldati _____
9. (stesso) gli _____ bicchieri; le _____ pagine
10. (allegro) i fanciulli _____ ; le compagne _____

C. Choose the correct word in each of the following sentences:

1. Ci sono (qualche, alcuni, troppe) fiori in questo vaso.
2. C'è sempre (qualche, alcune, troppi) programma interessante alla televisione.
3. Hai mandato (alcuni, qualche, poca) regalo a Gloria?
4. (Alcuni, Ogni, Molti) giorno arrivano a casa con ritardo.
5. (Le altre, Lo stesso, Alcuni) studentesse non studiano mai.
6. Hanno venduto (alcune, qualche, poco) slitta ieri.
7. Gianni ha mangiato (qualche, parecchie, poco) mele.
8. Sulla carne si mette (poco, alcune, molta) sale.
9. Marco e Lucia sono dei (buono, buoni, buone) studenti.
10. (La povera, Il povero, Le povere) torre sta per cadere.

D. Change the following to the feminine:

1. alcuni nonni vecchi
2. i fratelli tedeschi
3. qualche nipote simpatico
4. il marito gentile
5. parecchi cugini alti
6. il compagno intelligente
7. lo stesso studente
8. ogni padre francese
9. un povero amico inglese
10. l'attore infelice

E. Complete the following sentences by using the words supplied and making all necessary changes:

1. L'astronauta è stanco.
   Gli astronauti _____ .
   Le maestre _____ .
   Il professore e la maestra _____ .
2. Ho trovato un buon pittore.
   Ho trovato _____ studente.
   Ho trovato _____ amica.
   Ho trovato _____ penna.
3. Fotografiamo le belle attrici!
   Fotografiamo _____ palazzo!
   Fotografiamo _____ torre!
   Fotografiamo _____ studi!
4. Laura era sempre scontenta.
   Lui _____ .
   Lidia e Giacomo _____ .
   Noi _____ .
5. Mia madre portava una bella gonna azzurra.
   Mia madre portava _____ abito _____ .
   Mia madre portava _____ scarpe _____ .
   Mia madre portava _____ guanti _____ .

F. Translate into Italian:

1. I saw some tall mountains.
2. He arrives early every week.
3. They were born in the same year.
4. Did you (*pol. sing.*) buy much butter?
5. He sold six green automobiles.
6. John told several lies.
7. Several trees fell during the storm.
8. I don't like difficult operas.
9. There are a few books on the shelf.
10. She is a poor (needy) old lady.
11. Take this sweet bread to Susan. (*fam. sing.*)
12. He is an old uncle.
13. Her happy sister lives in Rome.
14. That was a terrible program.
15. It was a small bus.

7. Adverbs

Adverbs are generally formed from adjectives by adding **-mente** to the feminine singular of the adjective.

Adjective	Adverb
rapido(*a*), rapid, fast	**rapid*a*mente**, rapidly
franco(*a*), frank	**franc*a*mente**, frankly
intelligente, intelligent	**intelligent*e*mente**, intelligently

If the last syllable of the feminine adjective is **-le** or **-re** and it is preceded by a vowel, the final **-e** is dropped before **-mente.**

Adjective	Adverb
difficile, difficult	**difficilmente**, difficultly (with difficulty)
regolare, regular	**regolarmente**, regularly
But:	
acre, acrid, harsh	**acremente**, acridly, harshly
folle, foolish, insane	**follemente**, foolishly, madly

Some adverbs have special forms.

bene, well
male, badly
molto, very
troppo, too much
poco, little
assai, much

più, more
meno, less
affatto, at all
abbastanza, enough
quasi, almost

Many adverbs are formed by **con** + a noun.

	One-Word Form of Adverb
con allegria, happily	**allegramente**
con affetto, affectionately	**affezionatamente**
con attenzione, attentively	**attentamente**
con cortesia, courteously	**cortesemente**
con intelligenza, intelligently	**intelligentemente**
con pazienza, patiently	**pazientemente**
con sincerità, sincerely	**sinceramente**

COMMON ADVERBS OF PLACE

qui, here
qua, here
là, there
lì, there
su, up
giù, down
quassù, up here
quaggiù, down here
sotto, under
sopra, on, over
dentro, in, inside
fuori, out, outside
vicino, near
lontano, far

COMMON ADVERBS OF TIME

ieri, yesterday
oggi, today
domani, tomorrow
ora, now
adesso, now
dopo, after
prima, before
poi, later
presto, quickly, early
subito, quickly
tardi, later
spesso, often
sempre, always
mai, never

COMMON ADVERBS OF AFFIRMATION OR NEGATION

sì, yes
no, no
certo, certainly
certamente, certainly
sicuro, of course, surely
sicuramente, surely, certainly
veramente, really
naturalmente, naturally
davvero, really
appunto, exactly

EXERCISES

A. Change the following adjectives to adverbs:

1. cortese
2. probabile
3. tipico
4. possibile
5. crudele
6. perfetto
7. amabile
8. triste
9. distinto
10. frequente
11. sincero
12. allegro
13. generale
14. attento
15. folle
16. certo
17. reale
18. nuovo
19. musicale
20. acre

B. Change the following phrases to adverbs:

Example: con allegria
allegramente

1. con ansia
2. con felicità
3. con cortesia
4. con attenzione
5. con tristezza
6. con frequenza
7. con gentilezza
8. con sincerità
9. con rapidità
10. con intelligenza

C. Write the opposite of the following:

1. bene
2. quassù
3. rapidamente
4. sì
5. presto
6. prima
7. tristemente
8. qui
9. poco
10. oggi
11. sempre
12. facilmente
13. più
14. regolarmente
15. probabilmente

D. Translate the italicized words into Italian:

1. Non mangiare *too much*!
2. *Generally* andava dalla nonna ogni domenica.
3. Suonava il pianoforte *softly*.
4. Giacomo non si sentiva *well*.
5. Volete che veniamo *up* o *down*?
6. Non sapeva se andare *outside* o *inside*.
7. Cantava *almost* da soprano.
8. Ne hai mangiati *too many* ieri sera.
9. La bambina ha abbracciato la mamma *affectionately*.
10. Parti *today* o *tomorrow*?
11. Venite *quickly*, bambini!
12. Chi va piano va sano e va *far*.
13. Peppe portava *often* dei panini a scuola.
14. Il marito le parlava *gently*.
15. I nostri compagni arrivano *late* ogni mattina.

E. Write sentences using the items in the order given and adding suitable words:

Example: ieri / mostra / amici
Ieri sono andato alla mostra con alcuni amici.

1. sorella / leggere / lentamente / a casa
2. libro / su / tavolo
3. domani / partire / Francia
4. non / fare / esercizi / ora
5. parlare / sinceramente / genitori
6. Giorgio / sentirsi / male / ieri sera
7. io / mangiare / assai / banchetto
8. essere / quasi / due / pomeriggio
9. noi / scrivere / correttamente / classe
10. signori / guidare / velocemente / qui / Roma

8. Possessives: Adjectives and Pronouns

ADJECTIVE	MASCULINE		FEMININE		PRONOUN
	Singular	Plural	Singular	Plural	
my	il mio	i miei	la mia	le mie	mine
your (*fam.*)	il tuo	i tuoi	la tua	le tue	yours
your (*pol.*)	il Suo	i Suoi	la Sua	le Sue	yours
his, her, its	il suo	i suoi	la sua	le sue	his, hers, its
our	il nostro	i nostri	la nostra	le nostre	ours
your	il vostro	i vostri	la vostra	le vostre	yours
your (*pol.*)	il Loro	i Loro	la Loro	le Loro	yours
their	il loro	i loro	la loro	le loro	theirs

Note

1. The forms of the possessive adjectives and pronouns are identical, except that possessive adjectives agree in number and gender with the nouns they modify, while possessive pronouns agree in number and gender with the nouns they replace.

   Possessive Adjective

È *il mio* gatto.	It's my cat.

   Possessive Pronoun

Di chi è questo **gatto**? **È *il mio*.**	Whose cat is this? It's mine.

2. The definite article usually precedes possessive adjectives and pronouns and must be repeated before each adjective or pronoun.

Ecco ***la*** mia matita e ***il*** mio libro.	Here are my pencil and book.
È ***la*** mia e non ***la*** tua.	It's mine and not yours.

3. With the possessive, the definite article is omitted:

   a. before a singular, unmodified noun denoting family relationship, except for **babbo, mamma, nonno, nonna.**

Mio padre è alto.	My father is tall.
But:	
Il mio fratellino ha sei anni.	My little brother is six years old.
La sua nonna è vecchia.	Her grandmother is old.

   b. in direct address, when the adjective may follow the noun:

È facile, amico mio.	It's easy, my friend.

   c. When the possessive adjective follows the noun and is used for emphasis.

Vado a casa sua.	I go to *his* house.
È un compagno mio, non tuọ.	It's a friend of mine, not yours.

4. The definite article is never omitted with **Loro, loro** since these forms are invariable.

Ho visto ***la*** loro sorella.	I saw their sister.

5. Possessives agree with the object possessed and *not* with the possessor, as in English.

La ragazza ha perso i ***suoi*** **guanti.**	The girl lost her gloves.
Mario ha venduto la ***sua*** **macchina.**	Mario sold his car.
La signora ha trovato il ***suo*** **cappotto**?	Did the lady find her coat?
No, ma ha trovato il ***mio***.	No, but she found mine.

6. The definite article often replaces the possessive adjective when referring to parts of the body and articles of clothing, especially when used with reflexive verbs.

Si lava ***le*** mani.	He washes his hands.
Mi metto ***il*** cappello.	I am putting on my hat.

7. Since **suo, suoi, sua, sue** have several meanings, the intended meaning may be clarified by replacing these possessives with the definite article and by adding **di lui** (his) or **di lei** (her) after the noun.

la borsa ***di lei***	her pocketbook
la sedia ***di lui***	his chair

EXERCISES

A. Choose the correct form of the possessives in parentheses:

1. _____ padre è andato in Francia. (Suo, Il suo)
2. Sono andato a visitare _____ zii. (il loro, i loro)
3. Questa poltrona non è la sua; è _____ . (il tuo, la tua, i tuoi, le tue)
4. Ho dato _____ fiore a Carla. (mio, mia, il mio, la mia)
5. Si lava le mani ma non _____ . (i miei, il mio, le mie)
6. Carlo è _____ amico. (il mio, mio)
7. Hai venduto _____ biciclette? (la tua, le tue, il tuo, i tuoi)
8. La mia macchina è nuova. _____ è vecchia. (La sua, Il suo, Le sue)
9. _____ cucina non era grande. (Il nostro, La nostra, Nostra)
10. _____ sorelline hanno troppi giocattoli. (Le sue, Sue, La sua, I suoi)
11. Il portacenere non appartiene a Franco. Allora non è _____ . (il suo, il loro, la vostra)
12. Dovrò visitare _____ zio. (mio, il mio, miei, i miei)
13. _____ cravatte sono brutte. (Vostre, Vostri, I vostri, Le vostre)
14. _____ cugini sono arrivati poco fa. (Nostra, Nostre, I nostri, Le nostre)
15. Questi fogli sono _____ . (la mia, i miei, le mie, il mio)

B. Write the following sentences in the plural:

1. Mia cugina è bella.
2. Il vostro amico è simpatico.
3. La Loro casa è grande.
4. Questa è la sua.
5. Tua sorella mangia troppo.
6. Non è il nostro sbaglio; è il loro.
7. Suo figlio lavora bene.
8. Si mette la scarpa.
9. Hai il tuo giradischi?
10. Cerchi il mio cane o il suo?

C. Change the following sentences to the singular where applicable:

1. Avete pulito i vostre asciugamani?
2. Le nostre amiche tornano presto.
3. Sono le mie calze e non le tue.
4. I miei zii partiranno fra poco.

5. Ma perchè usano i miei dischi e non i loro?
6. Miei cari amici, bevete il latte!
7. Preferiscono le nostre bambole e non le loro.
8. Giorgio vuole i tuoi regali invece dei suoi.
9. Lavatevi i piedi!
10. I nostri parenti dormono tardi.

D. Translate the italicized words into Italian:

1. *Our* scuola è molto vecchia.
2. Prestatemi *your* piatti per le feste.
3. Preferisce la tovaglia di Maria invece della *ours*.
4. *Their* porta è sempre aperta.
5. Signori, *your* città sono tutte belle.
6. I tuoi professori lavorano molto. Proprio come *his*.
7. *Their* madre è all'ospedale.
8. Ogni paese ha *its* cittadini patriottici.
9. La tua carne è più tenera della *mine*.
10. *Her* zie abitano tutte in Germania.
11. Michele non mi aiuta mai con *my* compito.
12. Invece della tua carta prendo *his*.
13. *My dear* signorina, ecco un bel garofano!
14. *Your* (*fam. pl.*) camera non è grande abbastanza.
15. Mi sono lavato *my* capelli.
16. Sono amici *of his* ma non amici *of mine*.
17. Ha perduto *his* scatola e *ours*.
18. Comprammo *our* scarpe mentre lei comprò *hers*.
19. *Your* abito, signorina, è grazioso.
20. Mettetevi *your* cappelli e non *theirs*.

E. Translate into Italian:

1. his cat and ours
2. your (*pol. sing.*) children and his
3. a sister of theirs
4. her cousin (*f.*) and mine
5. our sofa and hers
6. their aunt
7. their uncles
8. my ideas and yours (*fam. sing.*)
9. his picture and ours
10. your (*fam. sing.*) watch and theirs
11. my friends and yours (*fam. pl.*)
12. her ticket and his
13. your (*pol. sing.*) letters and mine
14. your (*fam. sing.*) horse and hers
15. their family and ours

F. Answer the following questions in complete Italian sentences:

1. Hai visto le mie calze?
2. È grande o piccola la tua scuola?
3. Chi alza la mano in classe?
4. Dopo le lezioni chi si lava le braccia?
5. La tua macchina è più grande della mia?
6. Dai un abbraccio a tua madre ogni mattina?
7. Tuo padre lavora tardi ogni sera?
8. Abbiamo perso le nostre penne in classe?
9. I tuoi amici hanno i loro libri per le lezioni?
10. Abiti vicino ai tuoi compagni?

Il celebre tenore *Enrico Caruso* vestito in costume tradizionale dell'opera "I Pagliacci," che lui rese famosa in tutto il mondo.

9. Demonstrative Adjectives

Adjective	Masculine	Feminine
this these	*questo* quaderno *questi* quaderni	*questa* lampada *queste* lampade
that those	*quel* quaderno *quei* quaderni	*quella* lampada *quelle* lampade
that those	*quell'*amico *quegli* amici	*quell'*amica *quelle* amiche
that those	*quello* studente *quegli* studenti	

Note

1. **Questo** and **questa** become **quest'** before singular words beginning with a vowel.

   ***quest'*uomo** this man ***quest'*alunna** this pupil

2. **Quello** conforms to the forms of the definite article.
3. The demonstrative adjective **codesto(i, a, e)**, meaning *that* (near you), is rarely used today in conversation.
4. The demonstrative adjective must be repeated before each noun.

   Voglio ***questo*** salame e ***questa*** salsiccia. I want this salami and sausage.

EXERCISES

A. Choose the correct form of the adjectives in parentheses:

1. ----- cappello è troppo grande. (Quegli, Quel, Questa)
2. ----- amici sono sempre lì. (Quegli, Quei, Queste)
3. ----- signorine vanno spesso a Venezia. (Questi, Quelle, Quei)
4. ----- zio di Mario è vecchio. (Questo, Quel, Quegli)

5. _____ scarpe mi vanno strette. (Quei, Queste, Quegli)
6. _____ soldati sono un po'giovani. (Questi, Quegli, Quest')
7. _____ ultimo esame era difficile. (Questa, Quest', Quello)
8. _____ fiori hanno un profumo incantevole. (Quelle, Questo, Quei)
9. _____ alberi danno un'ombra rinfrescante. (Quest', Questi, Quei)
10. _____ casa è piccola ma bella. (Quel, Queste, Quella)

B. Rewrite the following sentences by replacing the definite article with the correct form of the demonstrative adjective in parentheses:

Example: Ho preso *il* libro. (questo)
Ho preso *questo* libro.

1. L'uomo è simpatico. (Quello)
2. Mi piacciono i ravioli. (questo)
3. I pantaloni sono un po' lunghi. (Quello)
4. I negozi di Roma sono economici. (Questo)
5. Lo zucchero non è troppo dolce. (Quello)
6. Gli altri amici di Daniela sono arrivati. (Quello)
7. Chi ha fatto la domanda? (questo)
8. Andiamo all'albergo. (quello)
9. Comprarono le mele la settimana scorsa. (quello)
10. Mia madre ha invitato i vicini di casa a pranzo. (questo)

C. Translate the English words into Italian:

1. Chi ha scritto *that* frase?
2. *That* canzone è molto triste.
3. Ho pescato *those* pesci.
4. Abbiamo ricevuto *this* valigia per Natale.
5. *That* frutta non è matura abbastanza.
6. *This* bibita è piacevole.
7. *Those* anelli sono costosissimi.
8. Non mettete i libri su *these* sedie.
9. *That* latte ti farà più bene che male.
10. Mi piace *this* albergo fiorentino.
11. *This* piatto è pulito ma *that* forchetta è sporca.
12. Mangia *that* pera; non mangiare *these* banane.
13. *This* nave parte per l'Italia; *those* navi partono per la Francia.
14. Dove hai trovato *these* sigari profumati?
15. Carlo ha spedito *those* cartoline e Maria ha mandato *this* lettera.

D. Translate into Italian:

1. Mary, take these glasses!
2. Let's eat these manicotti.
3. I want these apples but not those melons.
4. This year John will visit many museums.
5. These shoes are new.
6. That girl was beautiful.
7. I will read this week.
8. Who gave you (*fam. sing.*) those watches?
9. That church is very old.
10. This air is fresh.
11. Those men work all day.
12. These bridges were built many years ago.
13. Do you (*fam. sing.*) want that photograph?
14. Take this cake to your mother! (*fam. sing.*)
15. These students are all lazy!

Quattro colonne del tempio greco detto di *Castore e Polluce* situato nella città di Agrigento (Sicilia).

10. Demonstrative Pronouns

Pronoun	Masculine	Feminine
this (one)	questo	questa
these	questi	queste
that (one)	quello	quella
those	quelli	quelle

Note

1. Demonstrative pronouns must agree in number and gender with the nouns they replace.

   questo **posto** e ***quello*** — this seat and that one
   quelle **scarpe** e ***queste*** — those shoes and these

2. Two masculine demonstrative pronouns, **quegli** and **questi**, are used to translate the *former* and the *latter.* Italians usually place **questi** before **quegli** in a sentence, referring to "*the latter . . . the former*," instead of "*the former . . . the latter*," as in English.

   Gino ed Aldo sono due ragazzi diversi; ***questi*** è studioso e ***quegli*** è pigro. — Gino and Aldo are two different boys; the latter is studious and the former is lazy.

3. The same rule applies in the feminine, except that the pronouns are **questa** and **quella.**

   Lisa ed Anita sono due sorelle; ***questa*** è alta, ***quella*** è bassa. — Lisa and Anita are two sisters; the latter is tall, the former is short.

EXERCISES

A. Choose the correct form of the pronouns in parentheses:

1. Non capiamo *this.* (quella, questi, questo)
2. Chi ha scritto *that?* (questo, quello, quelle)
3. Mi piacciono queste rose ma non *those.* (quelle, quelli, questa)

4. Quel fiume è lungo ma *this one* è corto. (questi, questo, quello)
5. Preferisco quella cravatta a *these.* (quelle, questa, queste)
6. Cosa significa *this?* (quello, questi, questo)
7. Non aprire queste finestre; apri *those.* (quelle, quella, queste)
8. Quest'uomo è simpatico ma *that one* no. (questo, questi, quello)
9. Quella città è più grande di *this one.* (questo, quella, questa)
10. Quei drammi sono più interessanti di *these.* (questi, queste, questo)

B. Replace the italicized words with a demonstrative pronoun:

Example: Ti piace *questa carne?*
Ti piace *questa?*

1. Comprerò *questo quadro.* Comprerò _____.
2. Vuol vedere *quegli stivali.* Vuol vedere _____.
3. *Quell'albero* è bellissimo. _____ è bellissimo.
4. *Queste montagne* sono maestose. _____ sono maestose.
5. *Questa bibita* è molto dolce. _____ è molto dolce.
6. Non ha scelto *questi abiti.* Non ha scelto _____.
7. *Quel viaggio* era stanchevole. _____ era stanchevole.
8. *Quei fichi* sono un po' duri. _____ sono un po' duri.
9. Vogliono cantare con *quell'amica.* Vogliono cantare con _____.
10. Qualcuno ha trovato *quegli anelli.* Qualcuno ha trovato _____.
11. *Quella regina* veste bene. _____ veste bene.
12. Non ho visto *quel turista.* Non ho visto _____.
13. *Quest'autista* è abbastanza vecchia. _____ è abbastanza vecchia.
14. Non parlare con *questo studente.* Non parlare con _____.
15. È da un mese che vivono in *quelle camere.* È da un mese che vivono in _____.

C. Supply the appropriate demonstrative pronoun:

1. Questi pesci sono più squisiti di _____.
2. Questa strada porta a Roma; _____ porta a Firenze.
3. Quelle sedie sono più comode di _____.
4. Ci sono due catene sulla tavola; la mia e _____ di Roberto.
5. Che giovani strani; _____ è snello e _____ è grasso.
6. Di tutte le fotografie nell'album, preferisco _____ di mia madre.
7. Anna ed Angela sono amiche; _____ è inglese; _____ è americana.
8. Eleonora ha il suo ombrello e _____ di mia zia.
9. Quel cane è più feroce di _____.

10. Questa cattedrale è gotica ma _____ sono romane.
11. Preferisco queste pizze a _____.
12. Ecco due problemi di matematica; _____ è facile; _____ è difficile.
13. Gli alberghi di Napoli sono più grandi di _____ di Palermo.
14. Non possono trovare nè la scimmia di Caterina nè _____ di Tommaso.
15. Queste pietre sono preziose ma _____ non valgono molto.

D. Translate into Italian:

1. that store and these
2. these armchairs and the one there
3. her hat and those of her friend
4. that suit or the one on the bed
5. the French class or the Italian one
6. this door and those
7. two sofas: the former is red; the latter is green
8. This pocket is larger than that one.
9. Take those plates, not these. (*fam. sing.*)
10. This is Juliet's balcony, not that one.

Due *Carabinieri* (corpo di polizia nazionale che fa anche parte delle Forze Armate) in alta uniforme [in full uniform], che camminano lungo la strada.

11. Comparison of Adjectives

Positive	Comparative	Superlative
alto, tall	***più alto,*** taller ***più alti*** ***più alta*** ***più alte***	***il più alto,*** (the) tallest ***i più alti*** ***la più alta*** ***le più alte***
intelligente, intelligent	***meno intelligente*** (*m., f.*), less intelligent ***meno intelligenti*** (*m., f.*), less intelligent	***il meno intelligente,*** (the) least intelligent ***i meno intelligenti*** ***la meno intelligente*** ***le meno intelligenti***

Note

1. The regular comparative of an adjective is formed by placing **più** (*more*) or **meno** (*less*) before the adjective. The superlative is formed by placing the proper form of the definite article before the comparative.

2. Comparative and superlative adjectives agree in number and gender with the nouns they modify. A noun modified by the superlative form of the adjective usually follows the definite article and precedes **più** or **meno.**

l'**artista** più noto	the most famous artist
la **stagione** meno interessante	the least interesting season

3. After the superlative, *in* is translated by **di.**

È il ragazzo più alto della classe.	He is the tallest boy in the class.

TRANSLATION OF *THAN*

Than is generally translated by **di** or **che:**

I. By **di:**

a. before a noun.

Gennaio è più lungo *di* **febbraio.**	January is longer than February.
Carlo è meno simpatico *di* **Susanna.**	Charles is less nice than Susan.

b. before a pronoun.

Giovanni canta più ***di* me**.	John sings more than I.

c. before numerals.

Ho letto più ***di* cinque** novelle.	I read more than five short stories.

II. By **che**:

1. *a*. before an adjective.

Sono più snello ***che* grasso**.	I'm thinner than I am fatter.

b. before an adverb.

Scrive meno attentamente ***che* rapidamente**.	She writes less attentively than rapidly.

c. before an infinitive.

Dormire è più facile ***che* lavorare.**	It's easier to sleep than to work.

d. before a participle (gerund).

Si fa di più lavorando ***che* giocando**.	One accomplishes more by working than by playing.

2. In comparisons of quantity, usually with two nouns.

Mangiano più **carne *che* pesce**.	They eat more meat than (they do) fish.
In questa salsa c'è più **sale *che* pepe**.	There's more salt than pepper in this sauce.

3. In comparisons followed by a preposition.

L'inverno è più bello **in** campagna ***che* in** città.	Winter is more beautiful in the country than in the city.
Il cielo è più sereno **a** Bari ***che* a** Torino.	The sky is clearer in Bari than in Turin.

4. In comparisons between verbs.

Parlare è più facile ***che* cantare**.	Speaking is easier than singing.
È meno difficile **pescare *che* studiare**.	It's less difficult to fish than to study.

ADJECTIVES COMPARED IRREGULARLY

Positive	Comparative	Superlative
buono (i, a, e), good	***migliore*** (*sing.*), better ***migliori*** (*pl.*), better	***il*** (***la***) ***migliore*** (*sing.*), (the) best ***i*** (***le***) ***migliori*** (*pl.*), (the) best
cattivo, bad	***peggiore,*** worse	***il*** (***la***) ***peggiore,*** worst
grande, big (old)	***maggiore,*** bigger (older)	***il*** (***la***) ***maggiore,*** (the) biggest (oldest)
piccolo, small (young)	***minore,*** smaller (younger)	***il*** (***la***) ***minore,*** (the) smallest (youngest)

Note

1. The preceding adjectives are also compared regularly.

Positive	Comparative	Superlative
buono, good	***più buono,*** better	***il più buono,*** the best
cattivo, bad	***più cattivo,*** worse	***il più cattivo,*** the worst
grande, big	***più grande,*** bigger	***il più grande,*** the biggest
piccolo, small	***più piccolo,*** smaller	***il più piccolo,*** the smallest

2. **Migliore** and **peggiore** usually precede the nouns they modify.

il miglior(e) **libro**	the best book
la peggior(e) **lezione**	the worst lesson

3. The irregular forms of **buono** and **cattivo** are more commonly used than the regular forms of the comparative and superlative. However, they are interchangeable.

4. **Più grande** and **più piccolo** are used when referring to size. **Maggiore** and **minore** are used when referring to age.

Giorgio è ***più grande*** di Pietro.	George is *bigger* than Peter.
Giorgio è ***il maggiore*** della famiglia.	George is *the oldest* in the family.

EXERCISES

A. Complete the following sentences by changing the adjectives in parentheses to the comparative:

Example: (simpatico) Carla è _____ Luisa.
Carla è *più simpatica di* Luisa.

1. (buono) Questi libri sono _____ quelli.
2. (grande) La tua macchina è _____ mia.
3. (grande) Tonio è _____ Lucio.
4. (bello) La primavera è _____ in campagna che in città.
5. (triste) Mia zia è _____ che allegra.
6. (difficile) Per noi è _____ cantare che lavorare.
7. (forte) I tuoi cugini sono _____ te.
8. (caldo) Il tè è _____ caffè.
9. (cattivo) Nella nostra classe Maria è _____ Peppe.
10. (alto) Di queste due torri, quella è _____.

B. Complete the following sentences by changing the adjectives in parentheses to the superlative:

Example: romanzo (interessante) Questo è _____ che io abbia letto.
Questo è *il romanzo più interessante* che io abbia letto.
amico (buono) Giovanni è _____ mio.
Giovanni è *il migliore amico* mio.

1. maestro (peggiore) Adesso abbiamo _____ della scuola.
2. pranzo (squisito) La nonna ha preparato _____ di tutti.
3. (migliore) Siamo _____ della squadra.
4. (peggiore) Questa qualità è _____ di tutte.
5. (minore) Roberto è _____ della famiglia.
6. studente (pigro) Io sono _____ della classe d'italiano.
7. abito (caro) Ho comprato _____ del negozio.
8. lettera (breve) Mi hanno scritto _____ possibile.
9. donna (scontento) La signora Gemma è _____ del gruppo.
10. (peggiore) Mi dispiace ma questa carta è _____ che abbiamo visto.

C. Complete each sentence by using the correct form of *than* (**di** or **che**):

1. Patrizia è più debole _____ lui.
2. Il poeta aveva scritto più _____ dieci poesie.

3. Marzo è più lungo _____ febbraio.
4. Questa scatola è più larga _____ lunga.
5. Fa più freddo nell'inverno _____ nell'estate.
6. È meno semplice dipingere _____ scrivere.
7. Preferiamo abitare più in città _____ in campagna.
8. Ci sono più musei a Roma _____ a Palermo.
9. Qui si vendono meno broccoli _____ spinaci.
10. Mia nipote ha mangiato più _____ sette banane.
11. Quella finestra è meno grande _____ questa.
12. Enrico è minore _____ Paolo.
13. Ho speso meno _____ cinquanta dollari.
14. Scusi, signore, Lei è arrivato prima _____ loro?
15. Pietro mi sembra più affamato _____ studioso!

D. Complete the following by translating the English words into Italian:

1. Ecco *the smallest* delle porte.
2. Ho letto *the least important novel* dell'anno.
3. Debora è *the oldest* della famiglia.
4. Come si chiama *your* (*fam. sing.*) *best* amico?
5. I miei compagni sono *more courteous* dei suoi.
6. Roma è *the largest city* d'Italia.
7. Avevano pescato *more than* trenta pesci.
8. Le Alpi sono *the highest mountains* d'Europa.
9. Lidia è *the most popular girl* della scuola.
10. Questi pantaloni erano *cheaper* di quelli di Enrico.
11. La lezione era *harder than easier.*
12. Chi è *the worst* cantante qui?
13. Il film di ieri non era *more interesting?*
14. I pacchi di Natale sono *heavier than* quelli di Pasqua.
15. Gli astronauti russi sono *older than* quelli americani.

E. Translate into Italian:

1. Our car is lighter than theirs.
2. My sister is taller than Ada.
3. She is the worst actress in the film.
4. I lost more than seven pens.
5. These handkerchiefs are less costly than those.
6. He is the most courageous man in the world.
7. The sun is brighter in Pisa than in New York.

8. This apartment is the least expensive.
9. Michael is more intelligent than you.
10. She is my best teacher.

F. Answer the following questions in complete sentences:

1. Chi è il minore della tua famiglia?
2. Qual' è il mese più corto dell'anno?
3. Qual' è la stagione più calda dell'anno?
4. Chi è più studioso di te in classe?
5. Chi è più pigro di te in classe?
6. Chi è il ragazzo più alto della classe?
7. Il gatto è più grande o più piccolo del cavallo?
8. Qual' è il fiume più lungo d'Italia?
9. Sei più famoso o meno famoso di Guglielmo Marconi?
10. Chi è più cortese, tuo cugino o tua cugina?

***Il ponte del Rialto*, visto dal Canal Grande. Questo famoso ponte chiuso risale ai tempi gloriosi della storia di Venezia.**

12. Comparisons of Equality

Comparisons of equality are expressed by:

1. **Tanto** + adjective (or adverb) + **quanto** = as . . . as.

   Or:

   Così + adjective (or adverb) + **come** = as . . . as.

Claudio è ***tanto*** buono ***quanto*** Giorgio.	Claude is as good as George.
Lidia canta ***così*** bene ***come*** Rosa.	Lydia sings as well as Rose.

Note

In either case, **tanto** or **così** may be omitted.

Claudio è buono quanto Giorgio.
Lidia canta bene come Rosa.

2. **Tanto(a, i, e),** + noun (or pronoun) + **quanto** = as much (as many) . . . as.

Ho ***tanti*** gatti ***quanti*** cani.	I have as many cats as dogs.
Aveva ***tanta*** carne ***quanto*** pesce.	He had as much meat as fish.
Giovanni ha ***tanti*** di questi ***quanto*** di quelli.	John has as many of these as of those.

3. When definite articles or demonstrative adjectives precede the noun, however, only **tanto . . . quanto** are used, and no agreement is made.

Mi piacciono ***tanto*** **i** ravioli ***quanto*** **i** manicotti.	I like ravioli as much as manicotti.
Gli piace ***tanto*** **l'**acqua ***quanto*** **la** Coca-Cola.	He likes water as much as Coca-Cola.
Amo ***tanto*** **questa** mobilia ***quanto*** **quella.**	I like this furniture as much as that one.

4. **Tanto(a, i, e)** + **quanto** = as much (as many) as.

Quante mele hai? Ne ho ***tante*** ***quanto*** te.	How many apples do you have? I have as many as you do.

Hai molto denaro? Ne ho ***tanto quanto*** te.	Do you have much money? I have as much as you do.
Lei non ha ***tanto quanto*** lui.	She does not have as much as he.

EXERCISES

A. Complete the sentences by using **così . . . come** or **tanto . . . quanto** with the correct form of the adjectives in parentheses:

1. (alto) Maddalena è _____ Arturo.
2. (antipatico) I tuoi amici sono _____ le tue amiche.
3. (nuovo) Lo stadio di Siracusa era _____ quello di Messina.
4. (azzurro) Gli occhi di Pasquale sono _____ quelli di Ida.
5. (allegro) Dante non era _____ Beatrice.
6. (giovane) Mia madre è _____ mio padre.
7. (vecchio) Il loro cavallo è _____ la vacca di Giovanna.
8. (povero) Siamo _____ vostra zia.
9. (felice) I miei genitori sono _____ i tuoi.
10. (artistico) Michelangelo era _____ Leonardo.

B. Complete the following by using the correct form of **tanto . . . quanto**:

1. Insiste sempre a mangiare _____ carne _____ pane.
2. Ha lasciato _____ scarpe _____ calze.
3. Marzo ha _____ giorni _____ maggio.
4. Compravano _____ vino _____ loro.
5. Ho _____ amici _____ te.
6. Gli piace _____ questa casa _____ quella.
7. Nel parco ci sono _____ fiori _____ alberi.
8. Leggi _____ libri _____ tuo fratello?
9. Ha mangiato _____ oggi _____ ieri.
10. Preferiscono _____ i romanzi _____ le novelle.

C. Translate the English expressions into Italian:

1. Lavora *as much as* te.
2. Queste strade sono *as dirty as* quelle.
3. Ha *as many lamps as* lampadine.
4. Siete *as attentive as* possibile?
5. Fa *as cold in December as in* gennaio.

6. Nella chiesa ci sono *as many priests as* monaci.
7. Non fare *as much as* me.
8. Gli Egiziani erano *as sad as* i Francesi.
9. L'erba qui non è *as green as* quella del giardino botanico.
10. Mi vuoi dare *as much ink as* carta?
11. Mi piacciono le opere di Verdi *as much as* quelle di Puccini.
12. Ti piace questa *as much as* quella?
13. Carmine ha comprato *as many stamps as* buste.
14. Amiamo l'Italia *as much as* gli Stati Uniti.
15. Cantano *as rapidly as* parlano.

D. Answer the following questions in complete sentences:

1. La bandiera americana ha tante stelle quanto il cielo?
2. Hai tante penne quanta carta?
3. Sei tanto intelligente quanto i tuoi compagni?
4. Fa così freddo in ottobre come in dicembre?
5. Sei forte come tuo fratello?
6. Mangi tanto quanto tuo fratello (o sorella)?
7. Febbraio è tanto lungo quanto agosto?
8. Sai tanto quanto il professore?
9. Tua madre spende tanto denaro quanto tuo padre?
10. Ti piace l'italiano tanto quanto la matematica?

E. Translate into Italian:

1. Laura is as beautiful as Viola.
2. He drinks as much as I.
3. I bought as many shoes as socks.
4. We study as much as possible.
5. This lesson is as hard as that one.
6. His uncles are as poor as ours.
7. They have as many sisters as brothers.
8. Angela is as nice as her friend.
9. I read as many books as you (*fam. sing.*).
10. John's house is as large as mine.

13. The Absolute Superlative

The absolute superlative, in which the subject is not compared with anything else, is formed:

1. By using **molto** before an adjective or adverb.

Ecco un grattacielo ***molto*** alto. (adj.)	Here is a very tall skyscraper.
Elena canta ***molto*** bene. (adv.)	Helen sings very well.

2. By dropping the final vowel of the adjective and attaching **-issimo(a, i, e).**

Ecco un grattacielo ***altissimo.***	Here is a very tall skyscraper.
Quel bambino è ***piccolissimo.***	That child is very small.

Note

Words that end in **-ci**, **-chi**, or **-ghi** in the masculine plural retain those endings before adding the **-ssimo(a, i, e).**

Singular	Plural	Absolute Superlative
simpatico	simpati***ci***	simpati***ci***ssimo simpati***ci***ssima simpati***ci***ssimi simpati***ci***ssime
ricco	ric***chi***	ric***chi***ssimo ric***chi***ssima ric***chi***ssimi ric***chi***ssime
largo	lar***ghi***	lar***ghi***ssimo lar***ghi***ssima lar***ghi***ssimi lar***ghi***ssime

Very much or *very many* is expressed by **moltissimo(a, i, e).**

Mangia ***moltissimo.***	He eats very much.
Scrive ***moltissime*** poesie.	He writes many poems.

EXERCISES

A. Complete the following sentences by changing the adjectives in parentheses to the **-issimo** form or to the irregular form, where applicable:

Example: (felice) Luigi è _____.
Luigi è *felicissimo*.

1. (piccolo)	Questo ragazzo è _____ .
2. (lungo)	L'Autostrada del Sole è _____ .
3. (poco)	Tu bevi _____.
4. (caro)	Le bambole in questo negozio sono _____.
5. (dolce)	Ho provato delle caramelle _____.
6. (simpatico)	Giorgio è un giovane _____.
7. (cattivo)	Quell'alunna è _____ .
8. (grazioso)	Beatrice era _____.
9. (importante)	La lezione di oggi era _____.
10. (difficile)	I verbi italiani sono _____.

B. In each sentence change the italicized words to another form of the absolute superlative:

1. Questo tacchino è *molto buono.*
2. Abbiamo visto un leone *molto feroce.*
3. Le paste della Pasticceria Lambiase sono *squisite*.
4. Alla fine della giornata i professori sono *molto stanchi.*
5. La nonna di Lola è *molto vecchia.*
6. Come poeta, Dante era *molto grande.*
7. Ho trovato una giacca *molto pesante.*
8. Il Viale Amendola a Firenze è *molto lungo.*
9. I genitori di Sandra si sentivano *molto male.*
10. La qualità di questa cioccolata è *molto buona.*
11. Non c'è dubbio che Patrizia è *molto ricca.*
12. Giovanni sarà un pittore *molto esperto.*
13. La carne che hai comprato è *molto cattiva.*
14. Tutte le nostre compagne sono *molto intelligenti.*
15. Questa orchestra è *molto nuova.*

C. Translate the following English expressions into Italian:

1. Le macchine di quest'anno sono *very small.*
2. Tua sorella non è *very nice.*
3. L'erba di quel prato era *very green.*
4. Mia madre mi ha regalato una lampada *very large.*
5. Ma questo tetto è *very old.*
6. Nel giornale c'è una fotografia *very good.*
7. Ho dovuto leggere un romanzo *very curious.*
8. Non hanno *very many* amiche.
9. L'orologio di Tina è *very new.*
10. L'Italia ha la forma di uno stivale *very long.*
11. I giocatori della nostra squadra di calcio sono *very fast.*
12. Il monaco pregava *very silently.*
13. Non mangiare quelle pere perchè sono *very sweet!*
14. Nel Giardino Boboli ci sono dei fiori *very beautiful.*
15. Ma quel pavimento è *very dirty.*

Veduta tipica di *una partita di calcio*. Il calcio è lo sport più popolare dell'Italia.

14. Personal Pronouns After Prepositions (Disjunctive Pronouns)

Singular	Plural
con ***me***, with me da ***te***, from you (*fam.*) per ***lui***, ***esso***, for him, it (*m.*) di ***lei***, ***essa***, of her, it (*f.*) da ***sè***, by himself, herself, itself, yourself a ***Lei***, to you (*pol.*)	prima di ***noi***, before us senza (di) ***voi***, without you (*fam.*) per ***loro***, ***essi***, for them (*m.*) per ***loro***, ***esse***, for them (*f.*) da ***sè***, by themselves, yourselves tra ***Loro***, between you (*pol.*)

USES OF DISJUNCTIVE PRONOUNS

1. After prepositions.

Cosa vuole da ***lei?***	What does he want from her?
Vogliono venire con ***noi.***	They want to come with us.

2. In exclamations.

Povero ***me!***	Poor me!
Beati ***loro!***	Lucky them!

3. As direct objects when the emphasis is on the pronoun rather than on the verb.

Chiama ***me***, non ***te.***	He is calling me, not you.
Vedo ***lui***, non ***lei.***	I see him, not her.

4. When **lui, lei,** and **loro** are used as predicate nominatives after **essere.**

È ***lei.***	It is she.
Sono ***loro*** che parlano.	It is they who speak.

5. With comparisons.

Sono più vecchio di ***lui.***	I am older than he.
Maria è più alta di ***me.***	Mary is taller than I.

EXERCISES

A. Change the italicized words to disjunctive pronouns:

Example: Cammino con *Carlo.*
Cammino con *lui.*

1. Parlo di *Giorgio* e di *Lisa.*
2. Non parlare con *i bambini!*
3. Lo studente fa il compito da *se stesso.*
4. Beata *Gloria!*
5. Fanno tutto per (*io*).
6. Dividiamo questa torta con *quelle signorine.*
7. Piero non sa fare niente senza di (*tu ed io*).
8. Sono entrato nella classe prima di *Anna e Viola.*
9. Abito con *mia zia.*
10. Vorrei andare con *te e con tua sorella.*

B. Choose the correct word in parentheses:

1. Lisa sta vicino a (io, te, tu).
2. Quegli uomini fabbricano la casa da (lui, sè, egli).
3. Compriamo questo regalo per (loro, suo, tu).
4. Gianni scrisse una lettera per (vostro, voi, io).
5. Sta seduto tra (tu e Maria, te e lei, io e Maria).
6. È il libro di (vostro, lei, suo) non di lui.
7. Vogliamo farlo da (il loro, tu, noi).
8. La signora ha piantato i fiori da (lui, sè, sua).
9. Desidera lavorare con (me, egli, io e Marco).
10. Siediti di fronte a (tu, lui, egli).

C. Answer each of the following questions, replacing the italicized words with a disjunctive pronoun:

Example: Hai comprato queste calze per *tua sorella?*
Sì, ho comprato queste calze per *lei.*

1. Vai a scuola con *i tuoi fratelli?*
2. È vero che hai telefonato *ai signori Pompa?*
3. Chi ha viaggiato con *Anita?*
4. Hai messo il libro tra *il banco e la sedia?*
5. Avete ricevuto una lettera *dai vostri compagni?*
6. Hai parlato con *il professore* stamattina?

7. Puoi studiare senza *tua sorella* (or *tuo fratello*)?
8. Devi scrivere con *la penna?*
9. Ti puoi sedere tra *i tuoi amici?*
10. Chi ha messo le scarpe *sui tavoli?*

D. Translate the English words into Italian:

1. Povero *you!* (*fam. pl.*)
2. Parla sempre di *you* (*fam. sing.*) e non di *me.*
3. Venite vicino a *us.*
4. È *she* alla porta, non *they.*
5. Sara fa tutto da *herself.*
6. Volete venire con *us* o con *her?*
7. Ecco un piatto per *you*, Signorina Lelia.
8. Non sono lontani da *you*, ragazzi.
9. Vanno con *you* (*fam. sing.*), Aldo.
10. Il pacco è per *him.*
11. Ho portato delle caramelle con *me.*
12. Cosa facevi per *them?*
13. Peppe ha prenotato una macchina per *himself.*
14. La cravatta è per *me*, non per *you* (*fam. sing.*).
15. Cosa sai di *us?*

***I trulli*, tipiche casette pugliesi con tetti a forma di cono, che si trovano per lo più nel paesetto di Alberobello.**

15. Single Object Pronouns

DIRECT OBJECT PRONOUNS

Pietro ***mi*** conosce.	Peter knows *me.*
Pietro ***ti*** conosce.	Peter knows *you.* (*fam.*)
Pietro ***lo*** conosce.	Peter knows *him.*
Pietro ***la*** conosce.	Peter knows *her.*
Pietro ***La*** conosce.	Peter knows *you.* (*pol. m. and f.*)
Pietro ***ci*** conosce.	Peter knows *us.*
Pietro ***vi*** conosce.	Peter knows *you.* (*fam. pl.*)
Pietro ***li*** conosce.	Peter knows *them.* (*m. pl.*)
Pietro ***le*** conosce.	Peter knows *them.* (*f. pl.*)
Pietro ***Li*** conosce.	Peter knows *you.* (*pol. m. pl.*)
Pietro ***Le*** conosce.	Peter knows *you.* (*pol. f. pl.*)

Note

The direct object pronoun **La** is used for masculine and feminine polite address in the singular. For the plural, **Li** is used for masculine polite address and **Le** is used for feminine polite address.

INDIRECT OBJECT PRONOUNS

Pietro ***mi*** parla spesso.	Peter often speaks *to me.*
Pietro ***ti*** parla spesso.	Peter often speaks *to you.* (*fam.*)
Pietro ***gli*** parla spesso.	Peter often speaks *to him.*
Pietro ***le*** parla spesso.	Peter often speaks *to her.*
Pietro ***Le*** parla spesso.	Peter often speaks *to you.* (*pol. m. and f.*)
Pietro ***ci*** parla spesso.	Peter often speaks *to us.*
Pietro ***vi*** parla spesso.	Peter often speaks *to you.* (*fam. pl.*)
Pietro parla ***loro*** spesso.	Peter often speaks *to them.* (*m. and f. pl.*)
Pietro parla ***Loro*** spesso.	Peter often speaks *to you.* (*pol. m. and f. pl.*)

POSITION OF OBJECT PRONOUNS

1. Object pronouns generally precede verbs, except **loro** and **Loro**, which follow them.

Gina ***le*** compra.	Gina buys them. (*f.*)
Mando ***loro*** un pacco per Natale.	I send them a package for Christmas.

2. Other than **loro** and **Loro**, all object pronouns generally follow the verb and are attached to it in the following instances:

   a. With the affirmative imperative of the **tu**, **noi**, and **voi** forms, but not with **Lei** and **Loro** forms.

Anna, porta***mi*** quel libro.	Anna, bring me that book.
Ragazzi, compriamo***lo*** ora.	Boys, let's buy it now.
Bambini, telefonate***ci*** alle tre.	Children, call us at 3 o'clock.
But:	
Signorina, ***lo*** faccia, per favore.	Miss, do it, please.
Signori, ***li*** comprino oggi.	Gentlemen, buy them today.

Note

With the negative imperative of **tu**, **noi**, and **voi** forms, the pronouns usually precede the verb. With the **tu** form, there is an option.

Non ***le*** comprare. *Or:* Non comprar***le***.	Don't buy them. (*f.*)
Non ***lo*** ascoltiamo.	Let's not listen to him.
Non ***gli*** telefonate.	Don't telephone him.

   b. With the infinitive, when the infinitive depends on auxiliary verbs such as **dovere, potere, volere**, or **sapere**. The object pronoun may either be attached to the infinitive or come before the conjugated verb.

Voglio veder***lo***. *Or:* ***Lo*** voglio vedere.	I want to see it.

If the infinitive depends on **fare**, **lasciare**, **vedere**, **sentire**, or **udire**, the pronouns *must* be placed *before* the conjugated verb.

Lo sento parlare.	I hear him speak.
La fa andare al cinema.	He makes her go to the movies.

   c. With the present participle (gerund).

Gli ho scritto, mandando***gli*** i tuoi saluti.	I wrote to him, sending him your regards.
Aiutando***la***, le diedi la mano.	In helping her, I gave her my hand.

d. With the past participle used alone.

Detto***gli*** tutto, me ne andai.	Having told him all, I went away.
Trovate***le***, si mise a piangere.	Having found them, she started to cry.

e. With **ecco** (here is, here are).

Ecco***lo*** che arriva.	Here he comes now.
Ecco***mi*** qui.	Here I am.

Note

1. When an imperative consists of a single syllable or is stressed on the final syllable, the consonant of the pronoun attached to the verb is doubled, except with **gli.**

Da***mmi*** il libro.	Give me the book.
Di***lle*** tutto.	Tell her everything.
But:	
Fa***gli*** quel favore.	Do him that favor.

2. In compound tenses, the past participle agrees in number and gender with the direct object pronoun.

Le lettere? ***Le*** ho scritt***e*** oggi.	The letters? I wrote them today.

3. The indirect object pronoun is used, at times, to replace the possessive adjective, especially in regard to clothing or parts of the body.

Le fa male la testa.	Her head hurts her.
Gli fa male la mano.	His hand hurts him.
Gli ho lavato le mani.	I washed his hands for him.

EXERCISES

A. Rewrite the following sentences, replacing the italicized words with pronouns and making all necessary changes in position:

Example: Vidi *i giovani.*
Li vidi.

1. Metto *i piatti* sul tavolo.
2. Non capisco *la lezione.*

3. Parlo *con le signorine.*
4. Chi ascolta *la radio?*
5. Ho scritto una lettera *a mia sorella.*
6. Ecco *i cani.*
7. Signore, mangi *la pasta asciutta.*
8. Amici, chiamiamo *i nostri compagni!*
9. Non dimenticare *le scarpe!*
10. Scrivendo *la cartolina*, si mise a ridere.
11. Aprite *la porta!*
12. Carlo, porta il giornale *a papà!*
13. Ecco *la mia carta.*
14. Non facciamo *quel lavoro!*
15. Da' la matita *a Giovanni!*

B. Rewrite the following sentences and translate the italicized English words into Italian, making all necessary changes:

1. Lola spiega il problema *to him.*
2. Non mettiamo *them* (*f.*) nel vaso!
3. Lidia telefona *to me* ogni giorno.
4. Signora, non disturbi *her!*
5. Roberto, di' qualche cosa *to us!*
6. Carmela invita *them* (*m.*) spesso.
7. Non possiamo fare *it* (*f.*).
8. Mandiamo un pacco *to them!*
9. Sento cantare *you* (*fam. sing.*).
10. Non parlare *to her!*
11. Leggi *it!* (*m.*)
12. Sara vende le candele *to you.* (*fam. pl.*)
13. Aiutate *them!* (*m.*)
14. Fa' un favore *to me!*
15. Aspettano *you.* (*pol. sing.*)

C. Change the following sentences to the negative:

1. Telefonagli!
2. Voglio comprarlo.
3. Ci guardi, per favore!
4. Compratelo!
5. Offriamogli una caramella!
6. Vi vedono giocare.
7. Potete cucinarli adesso.
8. Stammi vicino!
9. Visitiamola!
10. Scrivi loro una cartolina!

D. Answer in Italian, replacing the italicized words by a direct or indirect object pronoun:

Example: Vuoi vendere *il tuo orologio?*
Sì, voglio venderlo.

1. Visiti *i tuoi nonni* spesso?
2. Senti *l'altoparlante?*
3. Avete invitato *Maria* alla festa?
4. A che ora telefoni *al tuo amico* (*alla tua amica*)?
5. Capisci *l'italiano?*
6. Il professore sta leggendo *una novella.*
7. Parli *con le ragazze* nei negozi?
8. Spieghi molte cose *a tuo padre?*
9. Conosci *le signorine Petrella?*
10. Aiuti *i tuoi genitori* ogni settimana?
11. Dove hai trovato *quelle scarpe?*
12. Chi ha rotto *il magnetofono?*
13. Puoi vedere *gli aviogetti* da casa tua?
14. Scrivi spesso *ai tuoi cugini?*
15. Usate *l'inchiostro* in classe?

E. Translate into Italian:

1. Don't speak with her, Mario!
2. Here it is. (*f.*)
3. Having seen them (*m.*), I bought them.
4. Anna, tell her everything!
5. We sent them a postcard.
6. I don't know him.
7. They hear us sing every day.
8. Sir, give me the bill.
9. Mother, phone us at three o'clock.
10. They won't send her a letter.
11. We spoke to him, telling him everything.
12. Will you (*fam. sing.*) teach me?
13. I want to listen to them. (*f.*)
14. They see us study.
15. You (*fam. pl.*) have to do it (*m.*) now!

16. Double Object Pronouns

FORMS OF THE DOUBLE OBJECT PRONOUNS

When a verb has two object pronouns, the indirect object (usually the pronoun referring to a person), except for **loro** and **Loro**, precedes the direct object pronoun (usually the object pronoun referring to a thing).

Maria *me* *lo* (*la*) vende. (*me* = ind. obj.; *lo* = dir. obj.; *la* = dir. obj.)	Maria sells it to me. (it = dir. obj.; me = ind. obj.)
Maria *me li* (*le*) vende.	Maria sells them to me.
Maria *te lo* (*la*) vende.	Maria sells it to you. (*fam.*)
Maria *te li* (*le*) vende.	Maria sells them to you.
Maria *glielo* vende.	Maria sells it to him (to her).
Maria *Glielo* (*Gliela*) vende.	Maria sells it to you (*pol. m. and f.*)
Maria *se la* vende.	Maria sells it to herself.
Maria *ce lo* (*la*) vende.	Maria sells it to us.
Maria *ve lo* (*la*) vende.	Maria sells it to you. (*fam. pl.*)
Maria *lo* (*la*) vende *loro.*	Maria sells it to them. (*m. and f.*)
Maria *li* (*le*) vende *Loro.*	Maria sells them to you. (*pol. m. and f.*)

Note

1. The pronouns **mi, ti, si, ci,** and **vi** become **me, te, se, ce,** and **ve** before the direct object pronoun.

Te **lo** mandano.	They send it to you.
Me **lo** metto.	I put it on (myself).

2. The pronouns **gli** and **le** become **glie- (Glie-)**, which combine into one word with the direct object pronouns: **lo, la, La, li, le, Li, Le,** and **ne.**

Glielo spediamo.	We send it to him (to her).

3. The pronouns **loro** and **Loro** follow the verb and are written as separate words.

Lo dico ***loro.***	I tell them about it.

POSITION OF THE DOUBLE OBJECT PRONOUNS

Double object pronouns, like single object pronouns, generally precede the verb, except for **loro** and **Loro.**

Non ***te lo*** lascio.	I won't leave it to you.

Exceptions:

1. With the affirmative imperative of **tu**, **noi**, and **voi** forms (as in Grammar Lesson 15).

Manda*glielo*(*la*)!	Send it to him (to her)!
Vendiamo*glieli!*	Let's sell them to him (to her)!
But:	
Signore, *me la* mandi!	Sir, please send it to me!

Note

With the negative imperative of the **tu** form, the double object pronouns may be attached to the infinitive or placed before the infinitive.

Non *me li* spedire! *Or:* Non spedir*meli!*	Don't send them to me!

2. With infinitives.

Puoi portar*melo?* *Or:* *Me lo* puoi portare?	Can you bring it to me?
Ce li fa preparare.	He makes us prepare them.

Note

With the auxiliary verbs **potere**, **volere**, **dovere**, and **sapere**, the two pronouns may be attached to the infinitive or placed before the conjugated verb. With the auxiliary verbs **fare**, **lasciare**, **vedere**, **sentire**, and **udire**, the pronouns must be placed before the conjugated verb. In either case, the indirect pronouns precede the direct object pronouns, except for **loro** and **Loro**.

3. With the present participle (gerund).

Dando*tela*, uscì dalla stanza.	Giving it to you, he left the room.

4. With the past participle.

Detto*glielo*, me ne andai.	Having told it to him, I went away.

5. With **ecco** (here is, here are).

Ecco*veli.*	Here you are. (Meaning: "Here, take them, they are for you.")

6. With single-syllable imperatives.

Fa***mmelo.***	Do it for me.
Di***glielo.***	Tell it to him.

The consonant of the pronoun attached to the verb is doubled, except with **gli.** (See Grammar Lesson 15, Note 1.)

EXERCISES

A. Choose the expression in parentheses that best translates the English words:

1. Giorgio *sends it to me.*	(me la manda, mandamelo, me li manda)
2. Signora, *show it to him!*	(glieli mostri, mostriamoglielo, glielo mostri)
3. Il professore *teaches them to us.*	(ce lo insegna, ce li insegna, insegnacelo)
4. Mamma, non *prepare it for us!*	(prepariamolo, ce lo preparare, preparaci)
5. Nessuno *explains it to you.*	(te lo spiega, spiegatelo, glielo spiega)
6. *Give it to me!*	(Dallo, Daccelo, Dammelo)
7. *We write it to her.*	(Scriviamola, La scriviamo loro, Gliela scriviamo)
8. *I lend it to him.*	(Glielo presto, Me lo presta, Lo presto loro)
9. Ragazzi, *pay it to me!*	(pagamelo, pagatemelo, pagateglielo)
10. Scusi, signorina, ma *I'll do it for you.*	(me lo faccia, Glielo faccio, ce lo faccio)

B. Rewrite the following sentences, replacing the italicized words with a pronoun and making all necessary changes:

Example: Gli vende *la casa.*
Gliela vende.

1. Le manda *il pacco.*
2. Mi metto *il cappello.*
3. Inviamo loro *le sigarette.*
4. Chi ti ha dato *le penne?*
5. Descrivigli *il quadro!*
6. Mi racconti *la storia*, per favore, signorina!
7. Lavatevi *le mani!*

8. Non mi regalano mai *il giradischi.*
9. È sicuro che ti dicono *la verità?*
10. Promettiamogli *il regalo!*
11. Signore, le dia *i bottoni!*
12. Scrivendoti *la lettera*, mi misi a cantare.
13. Vendetemi *la macchina!*
14. Si asciuga *la faccia* bene.
15. Comprati *il giornale!*

C. Rewrite the following sentences, replacing the italicized words with double object pronouns and making all necessary changes:

Example: Vende *la giacca a Giovanni.*
Gliela vende.

1. Anna, prepara *la colazione per me!*
2. Non promette *la Vespa a Luigi.*
3. Signor Pace, dipinga *il quadro per noi!*
4. Accendiamo *la lampada per te.*
5. Le maestre insegnano *le regole agli studenti.*
6. Faccio *il lavoro per Loro*, signori.
7. Porta *le pantofole a lui!*
8. Spedite *la cartolina a vostra sorella!*
9. Non chiedere *il denaro a noi!*
10. Fa *la domanda a suo fratello.*

D. Complete the translation in English:

1. Te l'ho detto.	I told _____.
2. Glielo farò domani.	I'll do _____ tomorrow.
3. Lo regaliamo loro ogni anno.	We give _____ each year.
4. Descrivetemelo, per favore!	_____, please!
5. Pietro non ce lo spiega mai.	Peter never explains _____.
6. Dategliele!	Give _____!
7. Signora, non me li spedisca prima di gennaio!	Madam, don't send _____ before January!
8. Ve li ha già portati?	Has he already brought _____?
9. Mandagliela subito!	Send _____ right away!
10. Il professore lo sta dicendo loro.	The professor is telling _____.
11. Vuoi mostrarcelo?	Do you want to show _____?
12. Non se lo può fare.	He cannot do _____.
13. Prestameli!	Lend _____!
14. Glielo hai pagato?	Have you paid _____?
15. Compratelі loro!	Buy _____!

E. Answer the following questions in complete sentences, replacing the italicized words with direct and indirect object pronouns:

1. Dai *un bacio a tua madre* ogni giorno?
2. Compri *la chitarra per tuo fratello?*
3. Sai spiegare *la lezione ai tuoi amici?*
4. Il professore deve dare *il denaro a te e ai tuoi compagni?*
5. Tuo padre paga *le tasse al governo?*
6. Mostri *le fotografie a Cora?*
7. Giacomo ha mandato *la cartolina a te?*
8. Tua sorella prepara *la colazione per tua madre?*
9. Hai descritto *la nave ai tuoi cugini?*
10. Chi ha pagato *il conto al cameriere?*

F. Rewrite the following sentences, translating the English words in parentheses and placing them in the correct position in the sentences:

1. Giorgio scrive (it to us).
2. Vogliamo spiegare (them to you) (*fam. pl.*).
3. Hanno insegnato (it to him).
4. Non comprare (them for me)!
5. Vendiamo (it to her)!
6. Dia (it to them)!
7. Promise (them to us)!
8. Confessava (it to you) (*fam. sing.*).
9. Dipingi (them for us)!
10. Presta (them to her)!

G. Translate into Italian:

1. They want to bring it (*m.*) to you (*fam. pl.*).
2. Read (*fam. sing.*) it (*f.*) to me.
3. Carry (*pol. sing.*) them (*f.*) for him.
4. He gave them (*m.*) to me.
5. Throw (*fam. pl.*) it (*m.*) to us.
6. Mail (*pol. pl.*) them (*f.*) to them.
7. Show (*pol. sing.*) it (*m.*) to her.
8. I'll teach them (*m.*) to you (*fam. sing.*).
9. Prepare (*fam. pl.*) it (*f.*) for me.
10. I must explain them (*f.*) to you (*pol. pl.*).

17. Phrase Replacements: *Ci, Vi,* and *Ne*

USES OF CI AND VI

Ci and **vi**, besides being object pronouns, are unemphatic adverbial pronouns of place, both meaning *here* or *there.*

Chi va a Roma?	Who is going to Rome?
Mario *ci* va.	Mario is going (there).
Cosa hai messo su questo tavolo?	What did you put on this table?
Vi ho messo una pentola.	I put a pot (here).

Ci and **vi** are also used at the beginning of a sentence in the same way that the word *there* is used in English.

*C'*è un giovane alto alla porta.	There's a tall young man at the door.
Vi sono troppe automobili a New York.	There are too many cars in New York.

Ci and **vi** replace prepositional phrases introduced by **a.**

Credi a quelle storie?	Do you believe those stories?
Sì, *ci* credo.	Yes, I believe them.
Pensi a noi?	Do you think of us?
Sì, *vi* penso.	Yes, I think of (about) them.

Note

1. **Ci** and **vi** are interchangeable, although **ci** is used more commonly. The use of **ci** or **vi** often depends upon sound.

Ci viene spesso.	He comes here often.
Not:	
*Vi v*iene spesso.	

2. **Ci** and **vi** cannot be used when there is any emphasis on the place mentioned. **Lì** or **là** should be used instead.

Dove hai messo il libro?	Where did you put the book?
L'ho messo *lì.*	I put it there.
Il pacco è *lì.*	The package is (over) there.

Ci and **vi** replace prepositional phrases introduced by **da** when it means *to* or *at*.

Vai da tuo zio?	Are you going to your uncle's (house)?
Sì, ***ci*** vado più tardi.	Yes, I will go later.
Maria è dal macellaio?	Mary is at the butcher's (shop)?
No, ***ci*** andrà fra poco.	No, she will go in a little while.

USES OF NE

Ne replaces a partitive construction and prepositional phrases introduced by **di.**

Raccoglie dei fiori per Maria.	He picks some flowers for Mary.
Ne raccoglie per Maria.	He picks some for Mary.
Parla di Paolo.	She speaks of Paul.
Ne parla.	She speaks (of him).

Ne also replaces prepositional phrases introduced by **da** when it means *from there*.

Vieni da Firenze?	Are you coming from Florence?
Sì, ***ne*** torno ora.	Yes, I am returning now (from there).

Ne is always used with numerals and adjectives of quantity, even though it is not translated in English.

Quante scarpe hai?	How many shoes do you have?
Ne ho dieci.	I have ten (of them).
Ci sono venti studenti in questa classe.	There are twenty students in this class.
Ce ***ne*** sono venti.	There are twenty (of them).

Ne precedes the verb in compound tenses. As a direct object pronoun, **ne** generally requires agreement of the past participle.

Quante sardine hai pescato?	How many sardines did you catch?
Ne ho pescat***e*** quindici.	I caught fifteen (of them).
Avete preso delle riviste?	Have you taken any magazines?
Sì, ***ne*** abbiamo pres***e*** tre.	Yes, we took three (of them).

POSITION OF **CI, VI,** AND **NE**

The rules for the position of **ci, vi,** and **ne** in a sentence are the same as the rules for object pronouns (see Grammar Lesson 15). When **ci** and **ne** or **vi** and **ne** are used together in a sentence, **ne** follows **ci** or **vi**, which change to **ce** and **ve** (see Grammar Lesson 16).

Quante frasi ci sono nel libro?	How many sentences are there in the book?
Ce ne sono cento. / *Or:* / ***Ve ne*** sono cento.	There are one hundred (of them).

Note

Ci, vi, and **ne** become **c', v',** and **n'** before words beginning with **e-**.

*C'*erano / *Or:* / *V'*erano — delle attrici giapponesi.	There were some Japanese actresses.
Ve ***n'***erano molte.	There were many (of them).

EXERCISES

A. Rewrite the following sentences, replacing the italicized words with **ci (vi)** or **ne**:

1. Sono andati *al museo.*
2. Siamo tornati *da Genova* poco fa.
3. Non fate *degli sbagli.*
4. Giuocano *nella piazza.*
5. Vogliono *delle acciughe.*
6. Viene spesso *a casa mia.*
7. L'astronauta è tornato *dalla luna*.
8. Date *del latte* al bambino.
9. Quando vai *a trovarlo?*
10. Penso *ai miei compagni.*
11. Non credo *a quelle chiacchiere.*
12. Quando ritornerai *da Perugia?*
13. Fanno *delle lunghe passeggiate.*
14. Facciamo *dei ravioli!*
15. Ho passato la mia vacanza *in Italia.*

B. Use **ci (vi)** or **ne** to complete the following sentences:

1. Mangio della frutta. Tu _____ mangi?
2. Quanti stivali hai comprato? _____ ho comprati quattro.
3. Quanti ragazzi vedi? _____ sono almeno venti.
4. Dobbiamo comprare dei giornali. _____ dobbiamo comprare dieci.
5. Chi è andato a casa? Francesco _____ è andato.
6. Ci sono molti teatri a Parigi. Ce _____ sono molti a Parigi.
7. Pensano spesso alle lezioni. _____ pensano spesso.
8. Hai fatto delle compere? No, non _____ ho fatte.
9. Hanno bisogno di sigarette? Sì, _____ hanno bisogno.
10. Chi è alla porta? _____ è una signorina triste.

C. Translate the following into Italian:

1. They buy some.
2. There are two pencils.
3. I have nine.
4. Let's give him some!
5. She comes here often.
6. Go there, not here. (*pol. pl.*)
7. Buy four. (*pol. sing.*)
8. Sir, speak of it.
9. George thinks about it.
10. There is a gift for you (*pol. sing.*).
11. Didn't they send any?
12. Did you (*fam. sing.*) break the glasses? Yes, I broke seven.
13. Is Mary home? No, she's not.
14. We are going to the movies. Don't stay there too long. (*fam. pl.*)
15. How many cousins do you (*fam. sing.*) have? I have thirty.
16. Don't buy any. (*pol. pl.*)
17. There are six.
18. At what time did he return (from there)?
19. I don't believe that story.
20. You (*fam. pl.*) do not live there any longer.

D. Answer the following questions using **ci (vi)** or **ne** in the answer:

1. Vai dal dottore quando non ti senti bene?
2. A che ora torni dal teatro la sera?
3. Mangi troppi spaghetti?

4. Compri dei sigari per tuo nonno?
5. Quante cartoline mandi per Natale?
6. Vai spesso a visitare i tuoi parenti?
7. Quanti compiti hai fatto quest'anno?
8. Quando hai bisogno di un ombrello?
9. Resterai in classe dopo le tre?
10. Quanti libri hai comprato quest'anno?

E. Translate the following into English:

1. C'è un topo nella camera di Marco!
2. Il gatto si è nascosto lì.
3. Non portargliene.
4. Ce n'erano troppe in casa mia.
5. Datemene almeno cinque.
6. Ci andava spesso da bambino.
7. Ne parlò frequentemente a noi.
8. Vedi gli uccelli? Ce ne saranno duecento.
9. Se ne andò alle sette.
10. Volete andare al parco? Andateci!
11. Se hai tante matite, prestamene una.
12. Le piacciono gli abiti e ne sceglie tre.
13. Ecco i romanzi. Quanti ve ne sono?
14. Ho il tuo giradischi. Ne hai bisogno?
15. Se vogliono visitare la torre perchè non ci vanno?

18. The Partitive

The partitive *some* or *any* is formed in Italian by combining the preposition **di** and the definite article. It may be used in the singular or in the plural. It is used to express an indefinite quantity.

Beviamo ***del*** vino rosso.	We drink some red wine.
Ha comprato ***dei*** panini?	Did you buy any rolls?
Ho ***delle*** cravatte verdi.	I have some green ties.

Note

1. The partitive is normally not used in negative sentences.

Non voglio pasta àsciutta.	I do not want (any) macaroni.
Non ho fratelli.	I do not have any brothers.

2. In the negative singular only, the partitive may be replaced by the adjective **nessuno**, which takes the endings of the indefinite article **(nessun, nessuno, nessuna, nessun'). Non** precedes the verb.

Non ha ***nessun*** libro.	He doesn't have any books. (He has no books).
Non avevano ***nessuna*** sedia.	They had no chairs.

3. The partitive may be dropped:

a. When a list of things is given.

Vendevano calze, scarpe, e fazzoletti.	They sold stockings, shoes, and handkerchiefs.

b. When a contrast is made.

Leggo novelle, non romanzi.	I read short stories, not novels.

c. When used in an indefinite and general manner.

Avete libri interessanti in casa?	Do you have any interesting books at home?
Compra sempre arance molto piccole.	She always buys very small oranges.

d. In interrogatives.

Cercano libri? *Or:* Cercano dei libri?	Are they looking for some books?
Ha (degli) amici?	Does he have (any) friends?

The partitive may also be expressed by:

a. **Alcuni(e)** (always in the plural).

Compratemi ***alcuni*** pacchetti di caramelle!	Buy me some packages of candy.
Ci sono ***alcuni*** violini quassù.	There are some violins up here.

b. **Qualche**, which is invariable and is followed by a singular noun even though it expresses a plural idea.

Dipinge sempre ***qualche*** bella ragazza.	He always paints some beautiful girls.
Lasciamo ***qualche*** biscotto a Paolo!	Let's leave some biscuits for Paul!

c. **Un po' di** in the affirmative when the partitive means *a little*, *a bit of*, usually with food, materials, or uncountable things.

Mettici ***un po' di*** sale.	Put some salt (on it).
Mi presti ***un po' di*** carta?	Will you lend me some paper?
But:	
Non mangio pane.	I do not eat (any) bread.

Note

1. When *some of it*, *some of them*, *any of it*, *any of them* are implied, **ne** is used (see Grammar Lesson 17).

Non ***ne*** compro perchè costano troppo.	I do not buy any because they cost too much.
Non ***ne*** mangiare. *Or:* Non mangiar***ne***.	Don't eat any (of it).

2. **Alcuni(e)** and **qualche** may be used only when *some* or *any* means *several* or *a few*, but not when *some* or *any* stands for *a little*.

3. **Un po' di** and **alcuni(e)** may be used as pronouns.

Ti piacciono gli spaghetti, allora mangiane ***un po'***.	You like spaghetti, so eat some.
Di tanti spettatori, soltanto ***alcuni*** se ne andarono.	Of the many spectators, only a few left.

EXERCISES

A. Choose the correct form of the partitive in each sentence:

1. Marco, dammi (alcuni, qualche, un po' di) pepe, per favore.
2. Non avevano (nessuna, alcune, del) carta.
3. Sulla spiaggia ci sono (nessuno, alcuni, qualche) ombrelloni.
4. Mia sorella ha bevuto (dell', alcune, parecchie) acqua minerale.
5. Nell'album c'era (alcune, un po' di, qualche) fotografia.
6. Trovarono (dei, un po' di, alcune) bottoni sul tavolo.
7. Non comprate (un po' di, alcuni, nessun) giornale.
8. Giovanni ha (un po' di, qualche, alcuni) amici dappertutto.
9. Nel caffè ci mettiamo sempre (un po' di, qualche, alcuni) zucchero.
10. Se ti piacciono quelle mele, comprane (delle, alcune, qualche).
11. Non hanno preso (degli, nessun, qualche) pesce.
12. Mi puoi dare (alcuni, del, nessun) denaro?
13. Ci sono (alcune, della, qualche) forchette con (alcuni, un po' di, nessun) cucchiai.
14. Vedemmo (delle, qualche, alcuni) cattedrali magnifiche in Francia.
15. Ha scritto (alcune, qualche, un po' di) lettera ieri.

B. Change the following sentences to the affirmative:

1. Non voglio spaghetti.
2. Non hanno bevuto acqua.
3. Non aveva sedie in casa.
4. Non desideriamo caffè.
5. Non portarmi mele oggi!
6. Non c'era nessun ragazzo a scuola.
7. Non volevano l'inchiostro azzurro.
8. Sono arrivati senza valige.
9. Non ci sono caramelle in questa scatola.
10. Mia madre non ha vestiti nuovi.

C. Change the following sentences to the negative:

1. Vogliono dell'insalata mista.
2. Ho letto dei romanzi tristi.
3. Aveva rotto qualche piatto.
4. C'erano delle automobili per la strada.
5. Ha mandato alcuni fiori a Sara.
6. C'è un po' di neve fuori.
7. Volevo del salame.
8. Giorgio ha venduto qualche televisore.
9. Nunzio ha alcune sorelle.
10. Comprateci delle calze!

D. Translate into Italian:

1. I eat spaghetti, not ravioli.
2. I sold books, pens, pencils, and magazines.
3. He always buys fresh tomatoes.
4. Put (*fam. sing.*) some salt on the broccoli.
5. We saw some paintings at the museum.
6. There weren't any horses in the country.
7. I didn't write any (of them).
8. Do you (*fam. pl.*) want any biscuits?
9. I always drink coffee.
10. For Christmas, my father received cigars, cigarettes, and tobacco.
11. Send some to Laura. (*fam. sing.*)
12. Bring us some lean meat. (*fam. pl.*)
13. We sent some postcards to our friends.
14. Have you (*fam. sing.*) seen any jets?
15. They didn't wear any gloves.

E. Answer the following questions in complete sentences in Italian:

1. Cosa vende il fruttivendolo?
2. A casa tua si beve latte?
3. Prendi del pesce o della carne?
4. Ci sono degli Australiani nella tua classe?
5. Dove si vende del gelato fresco?
6. Ricevi dei bei regali per il tuo compleanno?
7. Quali animali mangiano erba?
8. In classe chi fa dei compiti completi?
9. Ci sono dei bei film da vedere?
10. C'è neve d'estate?

19. Interrogatives: Adjectives, Pronouns, Adverbs

ADJECTIVES

che?, what?, what kind of?
quale?, **quali?** (*m.* and *f.*), which?
quanto(a)?, how much?
quanti(e)?, how many?
di chi?, whose?

Che romanzo è questo?	What (what kind of) novel is this?
Quale signore è partito?	Which gentleman departed?
Quanta pasta hai comprato?	How much macaroni did you buy?
Quanti scaffali ci sono?	How many shelves are there?
Di chi sono queste tovaglie?	Whose tablecloths are these?

Note

1. **Che** is used both for singular and plural.
2. **Quale, quali** agree in number and gender with the nouns they modify.
3. **Di chi**, when used to mean *whose*, always takes the verb **essere**.

PRONOUNS

che cosa? / **che?** / **cosa?** } what?	**con chi?**, with whom?
chi?, who, whom?	**da chi?**, from whom?
quale?, **quali?**, which one(s)?	**per chi?**, for whom?
quanto(a)?, how much?	**a chi?**, to whom?
quanti(e)?, how many?	

Che cosa / *Che* / *Cosa* } hai fatto?	What did you do?

Chi parla?	Who is speaking?
Quale hai perso?	Which one did you lose?
Quanto ne hai mangiato?	How much did you eat?
Quante ne sono cadute?	How many fell?
Con chi esci?	With whom are you going out?

ADVERBS

Quando?, When?
Dove?, Where?
Come?, How?
Perchè?, Why?

Quando siete venuti?	When did you come?
Dove è andato Gino?	Where did Gino go?
Come ti sei vestito?	How did you dress yourself?
Perchè non hanno risposto?	Why didn't they answer?

EXERCISES

A. Choose the word or expression in parentheses that best completes the sentence:

1. (Che, Chi) compri?
2. (Quante, Quale) torte hai preparato?
3. (Quando, Quanti) vai al museo?
4. (Di chi, Per chi) comprate la macchina?
5. (Quale, Chi) cappello preferisci?
6. (Cosa, Quanto) è la biologia?
7. (Quando, Quante) ne abbiamo vendute?
8. Con (chi, come) giuochi ogni sabato?
9. (Perchè, Quanto) non visiti più tua zia?
10. (Qual, Chi) è la ragione di questo discorso?
11. A (quali, che) dei miei amici rispondete?
12. (Che, Quando) tempo fa oggi?
13. (Cosa, Quale) cravatta ha scelto?
14. (Chi, Di chi) cerchi?
15. (Quanta, Quando) volete andare da Lucia?

B. Translate the English words into Italian:

1. *Whose* è questo cappotto?
2. *Whom* volevano visitare alla festa?
3. *How* sta sua madre?
4. *Which* sedie avete rotto?
5. *When* verranno da noi?
6. *With whom* sono usciti ieri sera?
7. In *which* paese abitate?
8. *Who* ha trovato le scarpe di Maria?
9. *How many* candele sono sulla torta?
10. *How much* costa quel pane?
11. *What kind of* frutta ti piace?
12. *Which* ragazza è la più bella della classe?
13. *From whom* hai ricevuto questa cartolina?
14. *What* ora è?
15. *How much* ne vuoi di questa banana?

C. Complete each question by replacing the italicized word or expression with an interrogative expression:

Example: Scrivono *una lettera.*
Cosa scrivono?

1. *Carlo* è caduto. _____ è caduto?
2. Andiamo *alla spiaggia.* _____ andiamo?
3. Preferisci *quest'abito.* _____ abito preferisci?
4. Non viene *perchè è stanco.* _____ non viene?
5. Mangiano *molto* pesce. _____ pesce mangiano?
6. Ha venduto *quella* casa. _____ casa ha venduto?
7. *Tutti* vi saranno stasera. _____ vi sarà stasera?
8. Lavora con *suo fratello.* _____ lavora?
9. Ricevette *una cartolina.* _____ ricevette?
10. *Giovanni* parla bene. _____ parla bene?
11. Ha preparato una cena *per Luigi.* _____ ha preparato una cena?
12. Hanno *tre* figli. _____ figli hanno?
13. Andranno *lunedì.* _____ andranno?
14. Parliamo *di Carlo ed Anna.* _____ parliamo?
15. La giacca appartiene *a loro.* _____ appartiene la giacca?

D. Write the correct interrogative adjective, pronoun, or adverb:

1. _____ ha telefonato? — Peppe ha telefonato.
2. _____ vuole tuo fratello? — Vuole un quaderno.
3. _____ anni ha Liliana? — Ha diciassette anni.
4. _____ andate dal macellaio? — Andremo alle undici.
5. _____ film danno all'Arena? — Danno un film musicale.
6. _____ fai adesso? — Sto completando il mio lavoro.
7. _____ parlavi con Antonio? — Parlavo di Marta.
8. _____ ti senti, Gigi? — Non mi sento bene.
9. _____ non mangi quella carne? — È troppo grassa.
10. _____ ne hanno scritte? — Ne hanno scritte una dozzina.
11. _____ costa quel salame? — Costa poco, signora.
12. _____ abbiamo lasciato da Michele? — Abbiamo lasciato l'ombrello.
13. _____ chiamavi? — Chiamavo mio suocero.
14. _____ ti sei vestito così elegantemente? — Vado al ballo in maschera.
15. _____ hanno scelto da bere? — Hanno scelto un buon vino bianco.

E. Translate into Italian:

1. Which cathedral do you (*fam. sing.*) prefer?
2. Where are they?
3. With whom is she speaking?
4. Whose son is he?
5. When are you (*pol. sing.*) leaving for England?
6. Which shoes are more comfortable?
7. Why are you (*fam. sing.*) tired?
8. What have they bought?
9. How much of it (*f.*) did you (*fam. pl.*) eat?
10. What time is it?
11. Who was that?
12. To whom did you (*pol. sing.*) speak?
13. Which of these books is yours (*fam. pl.*)?
14. For whom does he work?
15. How much do they weigh?

20. Relative Pronouns

The most common relative pronouns are:

1. **che** (*who, whom, that, which*), used both as subject and direct object for people and things. **Che** is never used with prepositions.

Il ragazzo ***che*** conosci è molto triste.	The boy whom you know is very unhappy.
La tazza ***che*** è sul tavolo è rotta.	The cup that is on the table is broken.

2. **cui** (*who, which*), used as the object of the preposition.

Il maestro **per *cui*** scrivo è molto severo.	The teacher for whom I am writing is very severe.
La signorina **a *cui*** ho dato il numero è simpatica.	The girl to whom I gave the number is nice.

3. **il cui, la cui, i cui, le cui** (*whose* or *of which*).

Ecco il giardino ***i cui*** fiori sono bellissimi.	Here is the garden whose flowers are very beautiful.
La ragazza ***il cui*** fratello è partito è francese.	The girl whose brother has left is French.

Note that the relative pronoun *whose* agrees in gender and number with the noun it modifies, not with the possessor.

4. **quale (il quale, la quale, i quali, le quali)**, used instead of **che** or **cui** for emphasis or to avoid ambiguity or repetition.

Il libro, ***il quale*** è sul tavolo, è molto interessante.	The book, which is on the table, is very interesting.
Il maestro, per ***il quale*** scrivo, è molto severo.	The teacher, for whom I am writing, is very severe.
Ecco le finestre ***dalle quali*** vediamo l'oceano.	Here are the windows from which we see the ocean.

Note that the article in front of **quale** contracts with the preposition in front of it (if there is one).

5. **chi** (*he who, the one who, whom, someone,* etc.).

Chi cerca trova.	He who seeks finds.
Non credo mai a ***chi*** parla troppo.	I never believe someone who speaks too much.

Note

Chi . . . chi may be used to mean *some . . . others* or *some.*

Chi va, chi viene.	Some go, some come.

6. **ciò che, quel che, quello che** (*what, that which*).

Ciò che dice è una bugia.	What he is saying is a lie.
Quel che (***Quello che***) mangio è buono.	That which (What) I am eating is good.

EXERCISES

A. Choose the correct word or expression in parentheses:

1. Questa è la casa (in cui, quale) abito.
2. Le persone (cui, che) parlano troppo non sono simpatiche.
3. Ecco il giovane (la quale, la cui) macchina è stata rubata.
4. La signora (dalla quale, che) riceve molti regali è mia zia.
5. I soldati (che, di cui) vi ho parlato sono arrivati.
6. Vuole tutto (quale, ciò che) vede.
7. (Cui, Quella che) mi piace di più è l'opera di Verdi.
8. Quello è il signore (al quale, che) abbiamo telefonato.
9. (Che, Chi) beve troppo non dovrebbe guidare la macchina!
10. È un ragazzo (che, i cui) abiti sono sempre puliti.
11. Gli spaghetti, (i quali, chi) erano squisiti, non costavano molto.
12. Teresa è la signorina (alla quale, che) ho dato il nastro.
13. Era il giradischi (il quale, di cui) ti abbiamo parlato.
14. Ecco il televisore (cui, che) mio padre mi ha regalato.
15. Ho spolverato (il quale, quello che) era nella camera.

B. Translate the English word or expression into Italian:

1. Ci sono molti alberi *that* sono caduti.
2. Quello è l'uomo *of whom* hanno scritto una poesia.
3. Ecco il libro *whose* pagine si sono ingiallite.
4. Mostrateci i pantaloni *that* avete comprato.
5. *He who* perde tempo non guadagna niente.
6. Lucio e Carmine sono i ragazzi *with whom* giuocano spesso.
7. Non dite *that which* ha fatto!
8. Ecco la camera *in which* dormirete.
9. Voglio vedere il film *that* danno all'Arena.

10. Hanno capito *what* ha detto il professore?
11. Michele è il compagno *to whom* ho scritto.
12. Romeo era la persona *of whom* Giulietta parlava sempre.
13. È la quarta lezione *that* ha studiato.
14. Vi sono alcuni studenti *whose* sorelle sono belle.
15. La casa *in which* abitavano era piccola.

C. Supply the appropriate relative pronoun:

1. La moglie è la persona _____ prepara la cena.
2. Ecco mio cognato _____ è dottore.
3. Vedete _____ è sulla scrivania?
4. Questa è la bottiglia _____ ho messo del vino.
5. I signori _____ parlavo sono spagnuoli.
6. È la sedia _____ mi ero seduto ieri.
7. La chiesa _____ siamo entrati è molto antica.
8. Dov'è l'orologio _____ è caduto?
9. L'amica a _____ scrivo si trova in Europa.
10. Il macellaio è l'uomo _____ vende la carne.

D. Translate into Italian:

1. the child whose arm is broken
2. what I studied
3. the drama of which he spoke
4. the mineral water that we drank
5. the women to whom we phone
6. the man whose son is young
7. the ties whose price is expensive
8. what is on the shelf
9. the pencil with which we write
10. the astronauts who left
11. the ballerina whose legs are long
12. the dog whose eyes are green
13. what we sold
14. the windows from which we watch
15. the records to which we listen

21. Negatives

NEGATIVE EXPRESSIONS

non, not	**non . . . più**, no more, no longer
non . . . mai, never, not ever	**non . . . neanche** } not even
non . . . niente (nulla), nothing	**non . . . nemmeno** } not even
non . . . nessuno, no one, nobody	**non . . . neppure** } not even
non . . . affatto, not at all, by no means	**non . . . che**, only
non . . . nè . . . nè, neither . . . nor	**non . . . ancora**, not yet
non . . . mica, not really	

Note

1. A verb is usually made negative by placing **non** before it.

Non viene stasera.	She is not coming this evening.

2. When one or more pronouns precede the verb, **non** is placed before the pronoun or pronouns.

Non gliel'ho dato.	I didn't give it to him.

3. Unlike English, a sentence in Italian may have two negative words. In such cases, **non** must precede the verb and the other negative must follow the verb.

Non hanno trovato ***nessuno*** a casa.	They didn't find anyone at home.
Non parliamo ***mai*** in classe.	We never speak in class.

4. For emphasis, negative words, such as **mai, niente, nulla, nessuno**, etc. may precede the verb. In such cases, **non** is omitted.

Nessuno partirà stasera. *Or:* ***Non*** partirà ***nessuno*** stasera.	No one will leave tonight.
Nulla è possibile in questa classe. *Or:* ***Non*** è possibile ***nulla*** in questa classe.	Nothing is possible in this class.

5. **Affatto, che,** and **più** may never precede the verb for emphasis.
6. **Mai, niente, nulla, nessuno**, etc. may also be used in responses that contain no verb.

Cosa hai fatto ieri? ***Nulla.*** (***Niente.***)	What did you do yesterday? Nothing.

7. In an affirmative question, **mai** means *ever.*

Sei ***mai*** stato a Capri?	Have you ever been to Capri?

8. Before a noun, **nessuno** agrees in number and gender with the noun and observes the ending of the indefinite article: **nessun, nessuno, nessuna, nessun'**.

IDIOMATIC NEGATIVE EXPRESSIONS

niente affatto, nothing at all
senza far niente, without doing anything
niente pane (burro, etc.), no bread (butter, etc.) (as an adjective)
in nessuna maniera, by no means

EXERCISES

A. Complete the sentences in Italian:

1. We cannot eat at all.	Non possiamo mangiare _____ .
2. He can neither read nor write.	Non può _____ leggere _____ scrivere.
3. She never spoke to him.	Non gli ha parlato _____ .
4. I do not want to see anything.	Non voglio vedere _____ .
5. Not even John drinks wine.	_____ Giovanni beve vino.
6. Nothing is difficult for us.	_____ è difficile per noi.
7. Why don't you (*fam. sing.*) study any longer?	Perchè non studi _____ ?
8. Mary saw only two bears.	Maria non ha visto _____ due orsi.
9. We really didn't sleep too long.	Non abbiamo dormito _____ .
10. He does nothing.	Non fa _____ .
11. The singers do not dance.	I cantanti _____ ballano.
12. By no means.	_____ affatto.

13. Has she ever been to France?	È _____ stata in Francia?
14. They left without saying anything.	Uscirono _____ dire _____.
15. No salt, please.	_____ sale, per favore.
16. Paul had no desire to eat.	Paolo non aveva _____ voglia di mangiare.
17. We no longer travel together.	Non viaggiamo _____ insieme.
18. No one entered.	_____ è entrato.
19. Neither he nor I walked.	_____ lui _____ io camminammo.
20. He hasn't awakened yet.	Non si è svegliato _____.

B. Rewrite the following sentences by using the alternate form of the negative:

Example: Non ho libri.
Libri non ne ho.

1. Non è arrivato nessuno.
2. Gianni non dice neanche una bugia.
3. Neppure Lisa è venuta.
4. Non abbiamo nè cantato nè ballato.
5. Non lo credo mai.
6. Non ha pagato nulla per la radio.
7. Non avevo niente.
8. Non c'è neppure un leone.
9. Nessuno ci parlerà.
10. Non devi guardare nemmeno la televisione.

C. Rewrite the following sentences in the negative:

1. Arriverò oggi o domani.
2. Ha qualche amico.
3. Vanno sempre a caccia.
4. Patrizia fa tutto.
5. Qualcuno dorme ancora.
6. Vengono a casa mia o a casa tua.
7. Tutti mi vedranno.
8. La posta è arrivata.
9. Anche Gloria ha risposto bene.
10. Volevano parlare ancora.

D. Translate the following sentences into Italian:

1. He neither smokes nor drinks.
2. They do not write at all.
3. Did you (*fam. sing.*) ever go to the theater?
4. What would you (*pol. sing.*) like? Nothing.
5. We do not sew any longer.

6. She explains only one thing.
7. He never forgets to write.
8. None of them returned.
9. Not even she phoned!
10. Have you (*fam. sing.*) eaten? Not yet.
11. Do you (*fam. sing.*) ever wash? Never.
12. There wasn't even one boy there.
13. His beard was not really long.
14. I did not feel any pain.
15. We are not tired at all.

E. Answer the questions with negative sentences in Italian:

1. Cosa avete fatto oggi in classe?
2. Vai al museo o alla biblioteca?
3. La tua amica ha qualche libro interessante?
4. Cosa beve Tommaso?
5. A chi hai telefonato ieri?
6. Cosa c'è sulla scrivania?
7. Sei stato mai in California?
8. Ci sono lezioni la domenica?
9. Tina ha dei fratelli o delle sorelle?
10. È caduto qualche cosa?

22. Cardinal and Ordinal Numbers

CARDINAL NUMBERS

0–19

0 **zero**	6 **sei**	13 **tredici**
1 **uno**	7 **sette**	14 **quattordici**
2 **due**	8 **otto**	15 **quindici**
3 **tre**	9 **nove**	16 **sedici**
4 **quattro**	10 **dieci**	17 **diciassette**
5 **cinque**	11 **undici**	18 **diciotto**
	12 **dodici**	19 **diciannove**

20–99

20 **venti**	28 **ventotto**	50 **cinquanta**
21 **ventuno**	29 **ventinove**	60 **sessanta**
22 **ventidue**	30 **trenta**	70 **settanta**
23 **ventitrè**	31 **trentuno**	80 **ottanta**
24 **ventiquattro**	40 **quaranta**	90 **novanta**
25 **venticinque**	41 **quarantuno**	99 **novantanove**
26 **ventisei**	48 **quarantotto**	
27 **ventisette**		

100–900

100 **cento**	400 **quattrocento**
101 **cent(o)uno**	500 **cinquecento**
110 **centodieci**	600 **seicento**
200 **duecento**	700 **settecento**
300 **trecento**	800 **ottocento**
	900 **novecento**

1,000–1,000,000,000

1,000 **mille**	100,000 **centomila**
1,001 **milleuno**	1,000,000 **un milione**
2,000 **duemila**	2,000,000 **due milioni**
	1,000,000,000 **un miliardo**

Note

1. **Uno** is the only cardinal number to agree in gender with the singular noun it modifies. It has the same forms as the indefinite article.

Ho ***una*** matit*a*.	I have one (a) pencil.

As a pronoun, **uno** is always used for the masculine singular and **una** for the feminine singular.

Amici? Ne ho ***uno*** soltanto.	Friends? I have only one.
Non ho due penne; ne ho ***una***.	I do not have two pens; I have one (of them).

Uno is often used in the shortened form **un** after **venti, trenta,** etc., when the number is followed by a noun. Otherwise, it remains **uno**.

Ho ***ventun*** **anni**.	I am twenty years old.
Quanti anni hai? Ne ho ***ventuno***.	How old are you? I am twenty.

2. **Venti, trenta, quaranta . . . novanta** drop the final vowel before combining with **uno** and **otto**. When they combine with **tre**, the final **-e** takes an accent.

ventuno	twenty-one
trentatrè	thirty-three

3. **Mille** (one thousand) becomes **mila** in the plural.

duemila	two thousand

4. When **milione** and **miliardo** are used as nouns, they are joined to the following noun by the preposition **di**.

tre ***milioni di*** abitanti	three million inhabitants

If other numbers follow them, **di** is omitted.

due ***milioni trecentomila*** lire	two million three hundred thousand liras

5. **Cento** and **mille** are never preceded by **un**.

Ho ***cento*** lettere.	I have one hundred letters.
Ci sono ***mille*** persone.	There are one thousand persons.

6. Multiple numbers are very often written as one word.

nel ***millenovecentosettantasette***	in 1977

7. Arithmetic expressions:

due più due fa (fanno) quattro	2 + 2 = 4
cinque meno tre fa (fanno) due	5 - 3 = 2
sei per sei fa (fanno) trentasei	6 X 6 = 36
nove diviso per tre fa (fanno) tre	9 ÷ 3 = 3

ORDINAL NUMBERS

1st	**primo (a, i, e)**	12th	**dodicesimo**
2nd	**secondo (a, i, e)**		**decimo secondo**
3rd	**terzo**	13th	**tredicesimo**
4th	**quarto**		**decimo terzo**
5th	**quinto**	14th	**quattordicesimo**
6th	**sesto**		**decimo quarto**
7th	**settimo**	20th	**ventesimo**
8th	**ottavo**	21st	**ventunesimo**
9th	**nono**	23rd	**ventitreesimo**
10th	**decimo**	30th	**trentesimo**
11th	**undicesimo**	100th	**centesimo**
	undecimo	1000th	**millesimo**
	decimo primo		

Note

1. All ordinal numbers are adjectives and agree in number and gender with nouns they modify.

Sono i ***primi*** giorni dell'anno.	These are the first days of the year.
È la ***centesima*** volta.	It is the one hundredth time.

2. Each ordinal number, except for the first ten, can be formed by dropping the final vowel of the cardinal number and adding **-esimo(a)**.

venti	20
ventesimo	20th

3. The -e is doubled in **ventitreesimo, trentatreesimo,** etc.

4. Ordinal numbers are used as in English, but the article is omitted before the number denoting succession with rulers and popes.

Enrico Quinto	Henry the Fifth
Papa Paolo Sesto	Pope Paul the Sixth

5. Beginning with **terzo,** masculine forms of the ordinal numbers are used for the second part (denominator) of a fraction.

due terzi	2/3
tre ottavi	3/8
un terzo	1/3

6. The adjective **mezzo(a),** meaning *half*, agrees with the noun when it precedes the noun but not necessarily when it follows the noun.

una *mezz'*ora	a half hour, half an hour
But:	
un'ora e ***mezzo*** (or ***mezza***)	an hour and a half

The noun for *half* is **la metà,** used at times as an adjective.

Mi diede ***la metà.***	He gave me half.
But:	
Era ***a metà*** strada.	He was half way there.

7. The following forms are often used instead of numbers, especially with literature and art, to refer to centuries from the 13th on:

il ***Duecento***	the 13th century (the twelve hundreds)
il ***Trecento***	the 14th century (the thirteen hundreds)
il ***Quattrocento***	the 15th century
il ***Cinquecento***	the 16th century
il ***Seicento***	the 17th century
il ***Settecento***	the 18th century
l'***Ottocento***	the 19th century
il ***Novecento***	the 20th century

COLLECTIVE NUMBERS

Approximate numbers are rendered in Italian by the suffix **-ina.**

una ***diecina*** di donne	about ten women
una ***ventina***	about twenty
una ***trentina***	about thirty

Una dozzina may mean *about twelve* or *exactly twelve.*

Centinaio and **migliaio** mean *about a hundred* and *about a thousand.* They are masculine in the singular but feminine in the plural, with the ending of **-aia**.

un ***centinaio*** di barche	about one hundred boats
parecchie ***migliaia***	several thousands

EXERCISES

A. Write as numbers:

1. quattordici
2. trentadue
3. cinquantuno
4. mille
5. undici
6. un milione
7. ottantasei
8. centomila
9. diciassette
10. quarantatrè
11. duemilatrecento
12. cinquemila
13. sessantuno
14. novantanove
15. sedici
16. sei
17. due
18. tre milioni seicentomila
19. seicentonovanta
20. diciannove

B. Choose the correct word in parentheses:

1. Venne a scuola per la (prima, una, primo) volta.
2. Papa Pio (Dodici, Dodicesimo, Dodicesima) morì parecchi anni fa.
3. Aprile è il (quarta, quattro, quarto) mese dell'anno.
4. Siamo nel (venti, ventesimo, ventesima) secolo.
5. Celebrò il suo (decimo, decima, dieci) compleanno.
6. Ci sono (trenta, trentunesimo, trentunesima) giorni nel mese di giugno.
7. Sette più due fa (nove, nono, nona).
8. Ho due biglietti per la (sei, sesto, sesta) fila a teatro.
9. È solo il (due, secondo, seconda) libro che ho comprato.
10. Dieci diviso per due fa (quinto, cinque, quinta).

C. Write in Italian:

1. 33
2. 2/3
3. 11th
4. 1,001
5. 100,000
6. 2,000,000
7. 5/7
8. 0
9. 94
10. 100
11. 210
12. 50th
13. 18
14. 32nd
15. 6/9
16. 648
17. 7,000
18. 69
19. 9th
20. 3rd

D. Answer in complete sentences in Italian:

1. Qual' è il primo mese dell'anno?
2. Quanto fa dieci meno otto?
3. Quale secolo precede il ventesimo secolo?
4. Quanti anni ci sono in un secolo?
5. Quanti giorni ci sono nel mese di febbraio?
6. Quale strada viene prima della sesta?
7. Quante domande ci sono in questo esercizio?
8. Qual' è il decimo mese dell'anno?
9. In quale anno celebrerai il tuo ventunesimo compleanno?
10. Quante stagioni ci sono in un anno?
11. Quante ore ci sono in un giorno?
12. Qual' è il primo giorno della settimana?
13. Quale capitolo segue il dodicesimo?
14. Quanto fa dodici più tredici?
15. Chi è la prima della classe?

E. Translate into English:

1. un milione di soldati
2. Papa Giovanni XXIII
3. mille dollari
4. ottantanove donne
5. tre ottavi
6. una quindicina
7. cinquanta foglie
8. la seconda montagna
9. centinaia di cavalli
10. centotrè scarpe
11. cinquecento biglietti
12. una quarantina di mele
13. il quarto astronauta
14. una novantina di anni
15. quindici meno quattro fa undici
16. il nono nonno
17. una dozzina di uova
18. otto sedie
19. pagina duecentotrè
20. duemila case

F. Translate into Italian:

1. a dozen magazines
2. $3 \times 3 = 9$
3. the ninth month
4. $7 \div 7 = 1$
5. four million inhabitants
6. George the Second
7. four fifths
8. the one hundredth day
9. twelve months
10. tenth year
11. the fifth row
12. eighty words
13. $8 + 8 = 16$
14. the first class
15. about one thousand horses
16. fifteen bottles
17. Francis the Third
18. seventy-fifth anniversary
19. about one hundred students
20. 1973

23. Dates

DAYS OF THE WEEK

lunedì, Monday	**venerdì**, Friday
martedì, Tuesday	**sabato**, Saturday
mercoledì, Wednesday	**domenica**, Sunday
giovedì, Thursday	

MONTHS OF THE YEAR

gennaio, January	**maggio**, May	**settembre**, September
febbraio, February	**giugno**, June	**ottobre**, October
marzo, March	**luglio**, July	**novembre**, November
aprile, April	**agosto**, August	**dicembre**, December

SEASONS OF THE YEAR

la primavera, spring	**l'autunno**, autumn (fall)
l'estate (*f.*), summer	**l'inverno**, winter

Note

1. The Italian words for days of the week, except **domenica,** and all months are masculine. They are all written in small letters unless they occur at the beginning of a sentence.
2. **In** or **di** may be used with the seasons as with the months:

Siamo ***in*** primavera.	It is spring.
Siamo ***in*** settembre.	It is September.
Era ***in*** estate.	It was summer.
Eravamo ***di*** giugno. Eravamo ***in*** giugno.	It was June.

In seems to be used more often by Italians at present.

COMMON DATE EXPRESSIONS

Che giorno della settimana è oggi?	What day of the week is it?
Oggi è mercoledì.	Today is Wednesday.
Qual' è la data di oggi? **Quanti ne abbiamo oggi?**	What is today's date?
Che giorno è oggi?	What day is it today?
Oggi è il primo marzo.	Today is March 1st.
Oggi è il tre aprile.	Today is April 3rd.
Or:	
Oggi ne abbiamo tre.	Today is the third (of the month).
Partiranno il quattro novembre.	They will depart on November 4.
Sono nato il sei luglio.	I was born on July 6.
il mille ottocento-quaranta	(the year) 1840
il sei luglio, millesette-centoottanta	July 6, 1780
nel millenovecento-cinquanta	in 1950

Note

1. In dates, cardinal numbers, preceded by the definite article, are used instead of ordinal numbers, except for the first day of the month.

È ***il primo*** maggio.	It is May 1st.
È ***il tre*** marzo.	It is March 3rd.

2. The definite article may or may not be omitted if the day of the week precedes the date.

domenica, otto agosto 1962 *Or:* domenica, ***l'***otto agosto 1962	Sunday, August 8, 1962

3. When one is referring to a single year, the definite article is used.

il 1832	1832

When both the year and the month but not the exact date are intended, the definite article and preposition are used.

nel maggio ***del*** 1940	in May of 1940

4. The English words *on* and *of* are omitted in Italian dates. Instead, the definite article is used.

Arrivò ***il*** due settembre.	He arrived on September 2nd.

5. English expressions such as *on Mondays*, *on Tuesdays*, etc., are translated in Italian by the singular name of the day preceded by the definite article.

Vado a chiesa ***la domenica.***	I go to church on Sundays.

When only one day in particular is intended (*on Monday*, *on Tuesday*), the day of the week is used without the article.

Parto per Milano domenica.	I will leave for Milan on Sunday.

6. The year is expressed in Italian by thousands and hundreds and not by hundreds as in English. In Italian, the year is preceded by the definite article.

il millenovecentosettanta	1970
nel milletrecento	in 1300

EXERCISES

A. Write the dates which follow each of the phrases below:

Example: Monday, August 5
Tuesday, August 6

1. venerdì, ventun marzo
2. lunedì, trenta aprile
3. mercoledì, ventisette settembre
4. sabato, quattro luglio
5. martedì, diciotto maggio
6. domenica, ventotto febbraio
7. giovedì, sedici gennaio
8. lunedì, nove ottobre
9. venerdì, trentun agosto
10. domenica, ventiquattro dicembre

B. Complete the following sentences:

1. Il giorno prima di domenica è _____ .
2. La primavera comincia nel mese di _____ .
3. _____ ha ventotto o ventinove giorni.
4. _____ è il sesto mese dell'anno.
5. La festa dell'Indipendenza Americana si celebra il _____ luglio.
6. Fa molto caldo durante l'_____ .
7. Natale si celebra nel mese di _____ .
8. I mesi che hanno trenta giorni sono _____ , giugno, _____ , e _____ .
9. Il primo giorno di scuola è _____ .
10. Non ci sono classi nè _____ nè _____ .
11. Vado alla spiaggia nel mese di _____ .
12. Il mio compleanno è nel mese di _____ .
13. La mia stagione preferita è _____ .
14. Il giorno dopo il trentun maggio è _____ .
15. Il compleanno di George Washington si celebra nel mese di _____ .

C. Answer the following questions:

1. Quanti ne abbiamo oggi?
2. Quanti ne avremo mercoledì prossimo?
3. Qual' è la data del tuo compleanno?
4. In quale anno sei nato(a)?
5. In che anno siamo ora?
6. Qual' è il tuo giorno preferito e perchè?
7. Quando si celebra la scoperta dell'America?
8. Quale mese segue agosto?
9. Oggi è venerdì?
10. Quando si celebra il Capodanno?

D. Translate the following into Italian:

1. February 12, 1902
2. October 4, 1952
3. in April
4. January 13, 1956
5. 1972
6. March 8, 1960
7. in winter
8. August 11, 1953
9. November 1, 1938
10. in 1840
11. December 7, 1941
12. on Sundays
13. Thursday
14. It's September.
15. Thursday, May 8, 1969

E. Translate into Italian:

1. What is today's date?
2. It is March 1, 1994.
3. Dante was born in 1265 and died in 1321.
4. Yesterday was February 29th.
5. It was in August of 1965.
6. Today is April 1st.
7. I left for Rome on June 8, 1971.
8. Venice was very important from 1200 to 1492.
9. Tomorrow will be Saturday, November 28.
10. What day of the week is it today?
11. I was born on March 2, 1958.
12. We were in Rome from April 5, 1963 until May 9, 1964.
13. Michelangelo died on February 18, 1564.
14. He won the award in 1956.
15. They came from Florence on Sunday.

Veduta dei piani superiori del *Palazzo Vecchio* con la sua famosa torre. Questo palazzo è usato ancora oggi come sede del municipio di Firenze.

24. Time Expressions

In time expressions, *it is* is expressed by **è** for *one o'clock* and **sono** for *two o'clock*, *three o'clock*, etc.

Che ora è? Che ore sono?	What time is it?
È l'una.	It is one o'clock.
Sono le due (le tre).	It is two o'clock (three o'clock).

In Italian, the hour is given first, then the minutes.

Sono le due e dieci.	It is ten after two.
Sono le cinque meno venti.	It is twenty to five.
Sono le sette e un quarto.	It is a quarter after seven.
Sono le nove e mezzo (mezza).	It is half past nine.
Sono le nove e trenta.	It is nine thirty.
È l'una meno un quarto. *Or:* Sono le dodici e quarantacinque.	It is a quarter to one.

Note

1. *After* or *past* is expressed by **e**; *to* or *of* by **meno**; *a quarter* by **un quarto**, and *half past* by **e mezzo (mezza)** or **e trenta.**
2. After *half past*, minutes are expressed with the following hour minus **(meno)** the minutes.

alle sei meno cinque	at 5:55
le undici meno dieci	10:50 or ten to eleven

COMMON TIME EXPRESSIONS

È mezzogiorno.	It is noon.
È mezzanotte.	It is midnight.
a che ora?	at what time?
all'una precisa **all'una in punto**	at one o'clock sharp
le sette del mattino **(di mattina)**	seven o'clock in the morning

le quattro del pomeriggio	4 P.M.
le nove di sera	9 P.M.
verso le dieci	about 10 o'clock
un quarto d'ora	a quarter hour, a quarter of an hour
una mezz'ora	a half hour

Italians also use the 24-hour system for telling time, particularly for schedules: trains, airlines, buses, concerts, etc. Italians also use it to avoid confusion. In the 24-hour system, one P.M. is 13 o'clock, 12 P.M. (midnight) is 24 o'clock, etc.

Il treno parte alle ***tredici***.	The train leaves at 1 P.M.
l'aereo arriverà alle ***diciannove***.	The plane will arrive at 7 P.M.
Il concerto incominciò alle ***venti***.	The concert began at 8 P.M.
Perchè non c'incontriamo alle ***ventidue***?	Why don't we meet at 10 P.M.?

EXERCISES

A. Complete the sentences in Italian:

1. What time is it?	Che _____ sono?
2. It is 3:20.	Sono le _____ .
3. It is 7:40 A.M.	Sono le _____ .
4. It is midnight.	È _____ .
5. He left at half past twelve.	È uscito alle _____ .
6. It is 3 P.M.	Sono le _____ .
7. It is exactly ten o'clock.	Sono le _____ .
8. It is twenty-five of five.	Sono le _____ .
9. She returned at 9:30 P.M.	È tornata alle _____ .
10. I saw him about eight o'clock.	L'ho visto _____ .
11. There is still a quarter of an hour.	C'è ancora _____ .
12. Come at 6:15.	Venite alle _____ .
13. It is exactly midnight.	È _____ .
14. It was nine o'clock in the morning.	Erano le _____ .
15. It must be a quarter to eight in the evening.	Saranno le _____ .

B. Write the time in Italian:

1. at 2:30 P.M.
2. about seven o'clock
3. ten minutes to one
4. noon
5. 3:00 sharp
6. 10:45 A.M.
7. half past eleven
8. 7:05
9. at midnight
10. 1:00 sharp
11. 6:57
12. a quarter to ten
13. 5:05 A.M.
14. 1:30
15. 2:20

C. Answer the following questions:

1. Che ora è?
2. A che ora ti alzi la mattina?
3. A che ora incomincia la classe d'italiano?
4. A che ora cenate a casa tua?
5. A che ora guardi la televisione?
6. A che ora ritorna tuo padre a casa ogni sera?
7. Quando mangi la colazione a scuola?
8. A che ora incominciano le classi la mattina?
9. Quando vai a letto la sera?
10. A che ora finiscono le classi?

D. Translate into English:

1. Sono le due precise di mattina.
2. È mezzanotte e mezza.
3. Carla è tornata verso le cinque.
4. Ho scritto per mezz'ora.
5. Si sono svegliati alle sei.
6. C'è più di un quarto d'ora.
7. È l'una e tredici del pomeriggio.
8. Partirà stasera alle diciannove e quaranta.
9. Lavora fino alle sette di sera.
10. Sono le undici meno un quarto.
11. Sono le tredici o le quattordici?
12. Erano le tre meno quindici.
13. È andata al cinema dalle due alle cinque del pomeriggio.
14. Saranno quasi le dieci.
15. Ha risposto al telefono alle tre precise.

E. Translate into Italian:

1. It ends at four o'clock in the afternoon.
2. We stayed until 2:40 A.M.
3. They arrived on the moon at about one o'clock.
4. It is five minutes to four.
5. At what time did you (*fam. pl.*) eat?
6. The President spoke at 10 P.M. sharp.
7. The train arrived at 2 A.M.
8. It will be eight o'clock soon.
9. I will be in Florence in a half hour.
10. Lisa phoned at noon.
11. We met Laura at a quarter past noon.
12. I'll take the 10 o'clock train.
13. The program began at 9 P.M.
14. Dante met Beatrice at 8 A.M. sharp.
15. Come (*fam. pl.*) at about 5:30 P.M.

Veduta di *una spiaggia dell'isola d'Ischia*, la quale, d'estate, è visitata da molti turisti. Ci sono centinaia di queste piccole spiagge lungo le coste della penisola.

25. Prepositions With Infinitives

1. Some verbs require the preposition **di** before an infinitive. Verbs denoting *belief*, *opinion*, *command*, *request*, *completion*, *emotion*, *fear*, or *endeavor* take **di.** The most common verbs are:

accettare, to accept
accorgersi, to notice
assicurare, to assure
aver paura, to be afraid
cercare, to try, to strive to
cessare, to stop
chiedere, to ask
comandare, to order
credere, to believe
decidere, to decide
dimenticare, to forget
dire, to say
domandare, to ask (of)
finire, to finish
godere, to enjoy
impedire, to prevent
mancare, to fail
meravigliarsi, to be amazed
offrire, to offer
parere, to seem
pensare, to think
permettere, to permit
pregare, to pray, to ask
preoccuparsi, to worry
proibire, to forbid
promettere, to promise
ricordarsi, to remember
scrivere, to write
smettere, to stop
sperare, to hope
temere, to fear

Cerca *di* fare troppo.	He tries to do too much.
Dimentica *di* mangiare.	She forgets to eat.
Ho **promesso** *di* scrivere.	I promised to write.
Mi **assicura** *di* essere presente.	He assures me he would be present.
Ho **finito** *di* scrivere.	I finished writing.

2. Some verbs require the preposition **a** before an infinitive. Verbs denoting *motion*, *beginning*, *teaching*, or *learning*, and a few other verbs, require the preposition **a** before the infinitive. The most common verbs are:

abituarsi, to accustom oneself
aiutare, to help
andare, to go
arrivare, to arrive
cominciare, to begin
consentire, to consent
continuare, to continue
esitare, to hesitate
imparare, to learn
insegnare, to teach
invitare, to invite
mandare, to send
mettersi, to set about, to begin to
persuadere, to persuade
prepararsi, to prepare
rinunciare, to give up
riuscire, to succeed
stare, to be, to stand
tornare, to do again
uscire, to go out

Pietro **impara** ***a*** leggere.	Peter learns to read.
Ci **aiuta** ***a*** preparare le valige.	He helps us to prepare our suitcases.
Vanno ***a*** cantare.	They are going to sing.
Cominciano ***a*** camminare.	They are beginning to walk.

3. Some verbs do not require a preposition before an infinitive. The most common verbs are:

bastare, to suffice	**preferire**, to prefer
bisognare, to need	**sapere**, to know
desiderare, to desire	**sentire**, to feel, to hear
dovere, to owe, to have to, must	**toccare**, to be one's turn to
fare, to do, to make	**udire**, to hear
lasciare, to leave, to allow	**vedere**, to see
potere, to be able	**volere**, to want, to wish

Bisogna pulire tutto.	It's necessary to clean everything.
Devo suonare il violino.	I have to play the violin.
Potevano andare al museo.	They could have gone to the museum.
Sa preparare molte cose.	She knows how to prepare many things.

4. Impersonal expressions with **essere** do not require a preposition before a dependent infinitive.

È difficile dirlo.	It is hard to say it.
È un piacere sentirlo.	It is a pleasure to hear it.
È necessario studiare.	It is necessary to study.
È meglio andare presto.	It is better to go early.
È importante scrivere bene.	It is important to write well.

5. The infinitive in Italian is used as an object of the preposition when the present participle is used in English.

Gli telefonai ***prima di partire.***	I phoned him *before departing.*
Oltre a cantare, sa ballare e recitare.	*Besides singing*, she can dance and act.
Senza parlare, se ne andò.	*Without speaking*, he went away.

6. **Da** is also used before an infinitive that follows **qualcosa, niente, nulla, altro, molto**, or **poco.**

Hai **qualcosa** ***da*** fare?	Do you have anything to do?
Non ho **niente** ***da*** fare.	I have nothing to do.

7. The preposition **per** is used before an infinitive when *to* or *in order to* is indicated in English.

Studiamo ***per*** imparare.	We study to (in order to) learn.

8. **Stare + per +** infinitive means *to be about to.*

Stanno per partire.	They are about to leave.
Stava per finire.	He was about to finish.

9. Most adjectives and nouns require **di** before an infinitive.

Adjectives	Nouns
certo di, certain of	**il bisogno di**, the need to
contento di, happy to	**l'intenzione di**, the intention to
degno di, worthy of	**la paura di**, the fear of
geloso di, jealous of	**il tempo di**, the time to
impaziente di, impatient to	
lieto di, happy to	
sicuro di, sure to	

Ero ***contento di*** stare a casa.	I was happy to stay home.
Sei ***sicuro di*** te stesso?	Are you sure of yourself?
Carlo è ***geloso della*** moglie.	Charles is jealous of his wife.
Susanna ha ***l'intenzione di*** tornare in Italia.	Susan intends to return (has the intention of returning) to Italy.
Non hanno ***il tempo di*** riposarsi.	They don't have time to rest.

10. After **dopo, dopo di,** and **per** (meaning *because*, *on account of*), the past infinitive is usually used.

Dopo aver mangiato troppo, mi addormentai.	*After having eaten* too much, I fell asleep.
Partirono per l'Africa ***dopo essersi sposati.***	They left for Africa *after getting married*.
Ero irritato ***per aver lavorato*** tanto.	I was angry *for having worked* so much.

11. Some common prepositions **(con, da, di, fra, tra, in)** take a definite article before the infinitive. The infinitive, in this case, usually functions as a noun. The English is rendered by the present participle.

Non gli piace il pesce, ma finisce ***col* mangiarlo**.	He does not like fish, but he ends *by eating it.*
Ci proibì ***di* dirlo**.	He prohibited us *from saying it.*
Parlammo ***del* venire** di Paolo.	We spoke *of Paul's coming* (as a noun).
Non si sa decidere ***tra il* dire** e ***il* fare.**	She cannot decide *between saying and doing.*
Piansi ***nel* dirlo**.	I cried *on saying it.*

12. The preposition **da** is also used before an infinitive to express:

a. Purpose

Ho una Vespa ***da* vendere.**	I have a Vespa for sale. *Or:* I have a Vespa to sell.

b. Use

È la nostra macchina ***da* scrivere.**	It is our typewriter.
C'è della carta ***da* scrivere.**	There is some writing paper.

c. Manner or necessity

Non ho nulla ***da* fare**.	I have nothing to do.
C'è ***da* dire** molto.	There is much to say (that has to be said).

13. Some adjectives are followed by **a** before an infinitive.

adatto a, suitable for	**lento a**, slow to
buono a, good for	**pericoloso a,** dangerous to
disposto a, disposed to	**pronto a,** ready to
facile a, easy to	**utile a**, useful to
inutile a, useless to	

Non siete **buoni *a*** farlo.	You are not good (enough) to do it.
È sempre **pronto *a*** parlare.	She is always ready to speak.
Siamo **lenti *a*** lavorare.	We are slow to work.

EXERCISES

A. Choose the correct expression in parentheses:

1. Sanno (fare, da fare, a fare) tutto.
2. Eri contento (di, a, per) volare in aviogetto?
3. Ho cominciato (a studiare, studiare, di studiare) il latino.
4. Desideravano (di leggere, leggere, per leggere) un romanzo di Manzoni.
5. Dopo (visitare, aver visitato, per visitare) il museo andò da Luisa.
6. Occorre (a vendere, da vendere, vendere) tutte queste scatole.
7. È meglio (cantato, cantare, per cantare) a bassa voce.
8. Ha paura (di andarci, andarci, esserci andato).
9. Senza (poteva, di poter, poter) ballare andai (a sedermi, sedermi, di sedermi).
10. Si diverte (a giocare, giocare, da giocare) con i bambini.
11. Chi vorrebbe (per uscire, di uscire, uscire) stasera?
12. Sono qui (per pulire, pulire, di pulire) la camera.
13. Avete qualcosa (dirmi, a dirmi, da dirmi)?
14. Luigi deve (scrivere, di scrivere, a scrivere) a sua cugina.
15. È importante (di ascoltare, ascoltare, ad ascoltare) bene.

B. Complete the following by inserting a preposition when necessary:

1. Cominciò _____ dirlo.
2. Non voleva _____ andare dal dottore.
3. Bisognava _____ uscire prima delle sette.
4. Si erano dimenticati _____ comprare il pane.
5. Cercherò _____ telefonarti alle nove.
6. Era difficile _____ parlare in quella classe.
7. Preferite _____ bere acqua o latte?
8. Oltre _____ scrivere poesie sa _____ scrivere della prosa magnifica.
9. Peppe è impaziente _____ incominciare il viaggio.
10. Era contento _____ viaggiare da solo.
11. Non esitate mai _____ dire la verità.
12. Dopo _____ aver dormito mangiò un bel piatto di maccheroni.
13. Rifiutammo _____ andarci.
14. Mangio _____ vivere.
15. Prima _____ lavarvi, prendete un asciugamano.
16. Aveva promesso _____ portarci una lampada.
17. Sai _____ sciare bene?

18. Riescono _____ pescare sempre molti pesci.
19. Occorreva _____ lavorare rapidamente.
20. Senza _____ piangere, il bambino si alzò dal pavimento.

C. Translate the English expressions into Italian:

1. *After having worked*, ritornò a casa.
2. *Before buying* la tavola, domanda il prezzo!
3. *They hope to* scrivere giovedì prossimo.
4. *I want to* godere questa passeggiata.
5. *We are about to* prendere il treno per Roma.
6. *It is necessary to* frequentare la classe di tedesco.
7. Ogni sera abbiamo qualcosa *to do.*
8. *Are you (fam. pl.) sure of* poter venire con noi?
9. Maria è sempre *happy to* visitare i suoi amici.
10. Finì di *writing without speaking.*
11. Lo vedemmo *swimming.*
12. Lola non ha *nothing to say.*
13. Ho finito proprio ora di *paying* il conto.
14. *It is better to* camminare che prendere il filobus.
15. Non è difficile *looking for it.*

D. Answer the following questions in complete sentences:

1. Cosa puoi fare dopo le lezioni?
2. Hai dimenticato di portare i libri in classe?
3. Cosa fai dopo aver guardato la televisione?
4. Prima di venire a scuola dove vai?
5. Provi a parlare italiano con i tuoi amici?
6. Ti piace vedere il film alla televisione?
7. Preferisci studiare o giocare?
8. Sei contento (a) di essere americano(a)?
9. È necessario avere molti amici?
10. Chi vuole uscire ogni sera?
11. Si può mangiare senza bere?
12. È necessario comprare un biglietto per viaggiare in treno?
13. Sai ballare?
14. È necessario aprire la porta per entrare in classe?
15. Vuoi leggere un giornale o una rivista?

E. Translate the following into Italian:

1. It is necessary to speak Italian.
2. He left the theater without saying a word.
3. Do you (*fam. sing.*) know how to write?
4. He finished laughing.
5. Those children have little to eat.
6. I am about to swim with Anne.
7. She helped me to clean the table.
8. It is better to eat at home.
9. They are leaving to visit Germany.
10. We are about to watch a film.
11. John took a walk after having slept.
12. She kissed me before going out.
13. They are teaching me to dance.
14. Will you (*fam. sing.*) have much to do?
15. I told him to walk slowly.

Ciclisti in corsa che partecipano al famoso *Giro d'Italia*. Il ciclismo è il secondo sport d'importanza in Italia.

26. Mastery Exercises

A. Translate the italicized expressions into Italian (see Grammar Lessons 1-5):

1. Perchè non mangi *apples?*
2. *French* è una lingua interessante.
3. *Mr. Perla* non parla mai con quei ragazzi.
4. *Germany and Spain* sono due nazioni *European.*
5. Carlo non è *a doctor*; è *a lawyer.*
6. Ho ordinato *paper*, *books*, *notebooks*, *magazines*, *and pens.*
7. Sofia è *a rich actress.*
8. *Henry IV* era un buon re.
9. Questa è *Paul's* giacca.
10. *On Wednesdays* andiamo sempre in un ristorante italiano.
11. C'erano dei garofani bellissimi *in the garden.*
12. Vanno *to France* per le vacanze di Pasqua.
13. Non fa altro che guardare *automobiles* da mattina a sera.
14. Ho ricevuto un regalo *from the friends* (*f.*) di Giulio.
15. *Poor Martha*, non sta bene affatto!
16. *Poor little* Anita è all'ospedale.
17. *Eating* fa bene a tutti.
18. Napoli è una città *in* Italia meridionale.
19. Mio nonno è sempre *at home* alle sette.
20. Si è lavato *his hands.*
21. Quello era *a drama* interessante.
22. Avevano trovato molti *pigs* nel mercato.
23. La chiesa ha molti *theologians* che sono americani.
24. Si è bruciato *his fingers.*
25. A Firenze ci sono molte *drugstores.*

B. Choose the expression in parentheses that best translates the English (see Grammar Lessons 6-10):

1. *My* cugino è un giovane molto intelligente. (Mio, Il mio)
2. *That* scaffale è troppo alto. (Quello, Quel)
3. Ci sono *some* bicchieri sporchi sul tavolo. (qualche, alcuni)
4. Non avete trovato *any* rivista? (nessuna, niente)
5. È *my old aunt* che vive in California. (la mia zia vecchia, mia zia vecchia)

6. Ha perso i miei guanti invece dei *hers.* (sue, suoi)
7. *Their* fratello è molto alto. (Loro, Il loro)
8. Sono amiche *of theirs* non *of ours.* (loro, i loro) (le nostre, nostre)
9. *This* frutta è un po' amara. (Quest', Questa)
10. Non fa altro che pettinarsi *her* capelli. (i suoi, i)
11. Preferisco questi banchi e non *those.* (quei, quelli)
12. Lui la ama *sincerely.* (sincera, sinceramente)
13. Tutto il giorno i bambini vanno *up and down.* (sopra, su e giù)
14. Lavora abbastanza *all day long.* (tutti i giorni, tutto il giorno)
15. Anna e Federico sono *sad.* (triste, tristi)
16. Ha pulito *some* finestra. (delle, qualche)
17. Il mio santo preferito è *Saint* Ambrogio. (San, Sant')
18. Il signor Cuto si sente *well.* (buono, bene)
19. Luisa arriva in ritardo *almost* sempre. (quasi, mai)
20. *This* autista è molto scortese! (Quell', Quest')

C. Translate the following English expressions into Italian (see Grammar Lessons 11-13):

1. Susanna è *the prettiest in the* classe.
2. Volare *is easier than* camminare.
3. Quei broccoli *are better than* questi.
4. Luigi è *the youngest in the* famiglia.
5. Questo vino è *very good.* (one word)
6. C'è più gente a Palermo *than in* Firenze.
7. Arturo è *as small as* Caterina.
8. Hanno comprato *as much* pane *as* biscotti.
9. Petrarca era *very important* (one word) come poeta.
10. L'uva di quest'anno *is better than* quella dell'anno scorso.
11. Si fa *less* scherzando *than* lavorando.
12. Maria scrisse *more than* sette lettere.
13. La neve è *whiter* in campagna *than* in città.
14. Era *the worst* lezione di tutte.
15. Non avevamo *as many* pomodori *as* loro.
16. Sciava *as much as I.*
17. Lidia è *very nice.*
18. La signora Cara è *more beautiful than ugly.*
19. Mangiate *more* rapidamente *than* cortesemente.
20. Quante penne hai? Ne ho *as many as* lui.

D. Rewrite the following sentences replacing the italicized words with pronouns (see Grammar Lessons 14–16):

1. Portate *i libri a lei!*
2. Da' *il piatto a me!*
3. Andate al museo con *i vostri zii?*
4. Vuole venire con *Gino e Sara.*
5. Ascolta *la radio* ogni sera.
6. Lascia andare *Violetta* al negozio.
7. Il maestro spiega il problema *a lui.*
8. Vogliono vendere *la motocicletta.*
9. Non ha potuto rivelare *il suo amore al signore.*
10. Vedo *Lisa* non *Franco.*
11. Signore, mi dia *il sale e il pepe.*
12. Baciando *i ragazzi*, la madre se ne andò.
13. Non ti lavare *le dita!*
14. Dai *i fiori a Teresa?*
15. Povera *Annalisa!*

E. Choose the correct expression in parentheses:

1. Mi dia *some* zucchero. (un po' di, del, alcuno)
2. Li ho messi *there.* (ci, lì, ne)
3. C'era *some* ragazza sulla spiaggia. (alcune, qualche, un po' di)
4. *Which* senatori sono repubblicani? (Chi, Quali, Cosa)
5. *What* hanno trovato? (Chi, Cosa, Da chi)
6. *How* siete venuti? (Quando, Come, Chi)
7. La ragazza *whose* zio è ricco, si chiama Rita. (il cui, che, cui)
8. La sedia *that* è rotta è verde. (chi, il che, che)
9. *Nothing* è impossibile per Marco. (nessuno, nemmeno, niente)
10. L'autobus *never* parte in orario. (non . . . mai, non . . . neanche, non . . . più)
11. *There* è un signore alla porta. (C', N', Li)
12. *There are* sei. (Vi sono, Ve ne sono, Ne sono)
13. Nelle vetrine c'erano *some* vasi fiorentini. (alcuni, qualche, delle)
14. *He who* studia trionfa. (Che, Chi, Cui)
15. Voleva *some* insalata verde. (alcune, dell', degli)
16. *What* mangio è squisito. (Chi, Ciò che, Quel)
17. *How much* ne hai bevuto? (Quando, Quanto, Che)
18. Questa è la nave *with which* parto. (con, con cui, con quale)
19. *Who* canta? (Che, Quale, Chi)
20. Ci sono molti negozi *that* sono aperti. (perchè, che, quale)

F. Translate the English expressions into Italian:

1. È passata *a half hour.*
2. Ho visto *about one hundred* barche.
3. Avevano portato un quadro *to us.*
4. È il loro *fiftieth* anniversario.
5. Era triste *for having* perso il treno.
6. Le sue gambe sono più lunghe *than mine.*
7. Oggi è *November 1.*
8. Non volevano *go to school.*
9. La guerra finì *in 1945.*
10. Lavoro anche *on Sundays.*
11. *Two thirds* della classe è assente.
12. Ho paura *to walk* da solo di notte.
13. *After having* cantato, parlai con Lucio.
14. Laura *him* visita ogni sera.
15. Non vuole *to work.*
16. *Cats* sono animali domestici.
17. Carlo sta *showing it* (*f.*) *to her.*
18. Sono *four-thirty in the morning.*
19. È necessario *to speak* bene.
20. *They are about to* cantare.
21. Susanna non va *neither* al parco *nor* alla biblioteca.
22. *In the morning*, vado al mercato.
23. Non raccontare *it* (*m.*) *to me!*
24. Ci sono *two million* di abitanti a Roma.
25. Era nato *on June 7.*
26. *What* film noioso!
27. Non ho *any coffee.*
28. Abitiamo *in the United States.*
29. Avevo cinque *of them.*
30. È il mio cappello, non *hers.*
31. *What* è la capitale d'Italia?
32. *I know how to* farlo.
33. Dov'è *Michael's bread?*
34. Ecco *one hundred* francobolli.
35. Siamo *in winter.*
36. Pierina è *the ugliest in the* gruppo.
37. Ho visto *a sad little boy.*
38. Non avete *nothing to do?*
39. Pulitevi *your arms!*

40. È sicuro *of doing* il lavoro.
41. Questa carne è *the worst that* abbia mai mangiato.
42. *We never promised* di andarci.
43. *No* attrice mi piace.
44. So ballare *as well as* Maria.
45. Vengono *from Austria.*
46. *Did you* (*fam. pl.*) *drink well* a quel ristorante?
47. Ecco *some sweet pears.*
48. *Her father* è molto giovane.
49. Viaggiano *frequently* in treno.
50. Giampiero fu *the first* ad arrivare sulla luna.

G. Complete the following sentences:

1. Siamo _____ primavera.
2. Dante nacque _____ 1265.
3. Prendi i libri _____ sono caduti!
4. Trenta più sette fa _____.
5. Sono le sette _____ sera.
6. È la migliore _____ coro.
7. Ecco il ragazzo _____ ti parlo spesso.
8. Vuole andare a Parigi _____ visitare lo zio.
9. Andremo _____ Inghilterra l'anno prossimo.
10. Quaranta meno dodici fa _____.
11. _____ è un mese che ha trentuno giorni.
12. Mi dia _____ zucchero, per favore.
13. Vuoi della frutta? No, grazie, non voglio _____.
14. Gli hai mandato il pacco? Sì, _____ mandato.
15. Lavori più di Peppe? No, lavoro _____ di Peppe.
16. Ho rotto una dozzina _____ uova.
17. Di solito quando andate in chiesa? Di solito ci andiamo _____ domenica.
18. Vai spesso al cinema? Sì, _____ vado ogni settimana.
19. Quante sedie hai comprato? _____ ho comprate due.
20. Sette per cinque fa _____.
21. È più alto _____ bello.
22. La neve cadeva _____ campo.
23. _____ romanzo hai letto recentemente?
24. Hai sentito gli uccelli? Sì, _____ sentiti.
25. Lisa era la signorina con _____ ero andato alla scampagnata.
26. Se Giovanni è più giovane di Pietro, allora è _____.

27. Nove diviso per tre fa _____.
28. La classe inizia sempre _____ nove precise.
29. Cominciarono _____ preparare la cena.
30. Oltre _____ studiare bene bisogna scrivere bene.
31. Caterina è gelosa _____ suo fratello.
32. Erano tornate _____ modista.
33. Scrisse la lettera _____ inglese.
34. Assisi è _____ Italia centrale.
35. _____ cantare bene è una cosa bella.
36. Perchè non vai _____ casa adesso?
37. Tonio è _____ buon falegname.
38. Ti fanno male _____ braccia?
39. Si è lavato _____ capelli.
40. La mia santa preferita è _____ Lucia.
41. È _____ stesso cane che ho visto ieri.
42. _____ sono _____ fiori bellissimi in Olanda.
43. Se vai nell'ascensore non andare su e _____.
44. Invece di partire oggi, partirò _____.
45. Mia cugina non si sente molto _____.
46. Ci dispiace, ma questa penna non è la tua; è _____.
47. Questa carta è buona ma _____ è usata.
48. Teresa è _____ alta _____ Gino.
49. Ci sono più torri a San Gimignano _____ a Pisa.
50. Hanno bisogno d'inchiostro? No, non _____ hanno bisogno.

Part III—Idioms

1. Idioms With *Avere*

1. **aver caldo**, to be warm (of person)
   Ho caldo perchè le finestre sono chiuse.
   I am warm because the windows are closed.

2. **aver freddo**, to be cold
   Hai freddo senza la giacca?
   Are you cold without your jacket?

3. **avere appetito** / **aver fame** } to be hungry
   Avevo una ***fame*** da lupo.
   I was as hungry as a wolf.

4. **aver sete**, to be thirsty
   Abbiamo una ***sete*** enorme.
   We are enormously thirsty.

5. **aver sonno**, to be sleepy
   La bambina ***ha sonno.***
   The child is sleepy.

6. **aver ragione**, to be right
   Sono sicuro che ***hanno ragione.***
   I am certain that they are right.

7. **aver torto**, to be wrong
   Ho sempre ***torto*** in classe!
   I'm always wrong in class!

8. **aver fretta**, to be in a hurry
   Non ***avete*** mai ***fretta?***
   Aren't you ever in a hurry?

9. **aver paura (di),** to be afraid (of)
   Non ***ha paura di*** niente.
   He (she) is not afraid of anything.

10. **aver bisogno (di),** to need (to)
    Hanno sempre ***bisogno di*** noi.
    They always need us.

11. **aver voglia (di),** to feel like
    Non ***avevano voglia di*** mangiare.
    They didn't feel like eating.

12. **aver tempo (di),** to have time
    Avrà tempo di studiare.
    He (she) will have time to study.

13. **avere intenzione di,** to intend to
    Hai intenzione di lavorare?
    Do you intend to work?

14. **aver l'aria (di),** to seem (to), to look (as if)
    Ha l'aria triste.
    He (she) seems unhappy.

15. **avere . . . anni,** to be . . . years old
    Tina ***ha*** sedici ***anni.***
    Tina is sixteen years old.

16. **aver luogo,** to take place
    Il concerto ***avrà luogo*** martedì sera.
    The concert will take place on Tuesday evening.

17. **aver mal di . . . ,** to have a . . . ache
    Aveva (un) ***mal di*** testa.
    He (she) had a headache.

18. **aver da . . . ,** to have to
    Cosa ***hai da*** scrivere?
    What do you have to write?
    Non ***avevo*** niente ***da*** dire.
    I had nothing to say. (I didn't have anything to say.)
    Hanno molto ***da*** fare.
    They have much to do.

19. **aver pazienza,** to be patient
    Il professore deve ***avere*** molta ***pazienza.***
    The teacher must have much patience.

20. **aver la bontà di** + infinitive, to be kind enough to, please
    Abbi la bontà di aiutarci.
    Be kind enough to help us. Please help us.

EXERCISES

A. *Progressive Substitution.* The drill begins with a complete Italian sentence. Complete each of the following sentences, substituting the new word or words given and using as much of the preceding sentence as possible. For example, begin with this sentence: Io ho caldo.

INCOMPLETE SENTENCES	COMPLETED SENTENCES
Noi _____.	Noi *abbiamo caldo.*
_____ freddo.	*Noi abbiamo* freddo.
_____ hanno _____.	*Loro* hanno *freddo.*

Lui ha fame.

1. _____ ragione.
2. _____ torto.
3. Tina e Mario _____ sedici anni.
4. Noi _____.
5. _____ caldo.
6. Le bimbe _____ sonno.
7. _____ fretta.
8. _____ tempo per studiare.
9. _____ non _____ paura di niente.
10. Tu _____.

B. Complete each sentence by writing the appropriate form of an idiom with **avere**:

1. Il marito _____ di lavorare per fare soldi.
2. Il concerto _____ martedì sera.
3. Gino deve _____ perchè è andato a dormire presto.
4. Si deve _____ per bere.
5. Deve essere scontento, perchè _____ sempre _____ triste.

6. Tu _____ scrivere una lettera a tua madre.
7. Stanno sempre seduti perchè non _____ niente _____ fare.
8. Il professore deve _____ molta _____.
9. Vado dal dottore perchè _____ gola.
10. Dovete _____ la bontà _____ venire a casa.

C. Translate into English:

1. Lo studente non avrà tempo di studiare prima degli esami.
2. Il carabiniere non ha mai paura di fare il suo dovere.
3. Ho sempre tempo di parlare con te.
4. Uno dei miei figli ha sedici anni; l'altro ne ha tredici.
5. Non avete voglia di giocare a carte?
6. Ho sempre freddo d'inverno se non mi metto il cappotto.
7. Nella vita bisogna aver pazienza.
8. Mia moglie ha mal di testa quasi tutti i giorni.
9. Abbi la bontà di non disturbarmi quando studio.
10. La partita di calcio avrà luogo giovedì alle 14:00.

D. Translate into Italian:

1. I'm not hungry, only thirsty.
2. He doesn't have time to play.
3. The comedy will take place at six o'clock.
4. Mary has a toothache.
5. They weren't afraid of anything.
6. Do you (*fam. sing.*) need us?
7. The boys will have much to do this evening.
8. He's always right and I'm always wrong!
9. Susan was cold last night.
10. My grandfather had nothing to do.

2. Idioms With *Fare*

1. **fare** (used with expressions of weather)

Che tempo fa?	How's the weather?
Fa bel tempo.	The weather is fine (good).
Fa cattivo tempo.	The weather is bad.
Fa caldo d'estate.	It's warm in the summer.
Fa freddo d'inverno.	It's cold in the winter.
Fa fresco stasera.	It's cool tonight.

2. **fare a meno di,** to do without
   Faremo a meno di queste buste.
   We will do without these envelopes.

3. **fare amiciza,** to make friends
   Fa amicizia con tutti.
   He makes friends with everyone.

4. **fare attenzione (a),** to pay attention (to)
   Non *fanno* mai *attenzione a* quello che dico.
   They never pay attention to what is said.

5. **farsi il bagno,** to take a bath, to swim.
   Si *fa il bagno* soltanto il sabato sera.
   He takes a bath only on Saturday evenings.

6. **fare (una) brutta figura,** to make a bad showing
   fare (una) bella figura, to make a good showing
   Ho *fatto bella figura* al ballo ieri sera.
   I made a good showing at the dance last night.

7. **farsi la barba,** to shave
   Gino *si fa la barba* ogni mattina.
   Gino shaves every morning.

8. **fare la prima colazione,** to have breakfast
   fare colazione, to have lunch
   Avete fatto la prima colazione stamattina?
   Did you have breakfast this morning?

9. **fare una conferenza,** to give a lecture
   Il professore *farà una conferenza* giovedì.
   The professor will give a lecture on Thursday.

10. **farsi coraggio**, to take heart, to have courage
    Facciamoci coraggio e andiamo a scuola.
    Let's take heart and go to school.

11. **fare la conoscenza di,** to make the acquaintance of
    Hanno fatto la conoscenza di quella ragazza svedese.
    They made the acquaintance of that Swedish girl.

12. **fare una domanda (a),** to ask (a question)
    Fa troppe ***domande.***
    She asks too many questions.

13. **fare una fotografia**, to take a picture
    Feci molte ***fotografie*** quando ero in Italia.
    I took many pictures when I was in Italy.

14. **fare male a,** to hurt
    farsi male, to hurt oneself
    Hai ***fatto male a*** Carla?
    Did you hurt Carla?
    Ti ***sei fatto male?***
    Did you hurt yourself?

15. **fare una partita (a),** to play a game (of)
    Voglio ***fare una partita a*** carte.
    I want to play cards.

16. **fare una passeggiata,** to take a walk
    fare una gita, to take a ride, to take a trip
    fare un viaggio, to take a trip
    Facciamo una passeggiata in piazza.
    Let's take a walk in the square.
    Faranno una gita a Pisa.
    They will take a trip to Pisa.

17. **fare paura (a),** to frighten
    Questo romanzo mi ***fa paura.***
    This novel frightens me.

18. **fare presto,** to hurry up
    Fa' presto, Giacomo.
    Hurry up, James.

19. **fare una telefonata (a)**, to make a telephone call (to)
    Ho fatto una telefonata al carabiniere.
    I made a phone call to the carabiniere.

20. **fare uno scherzo (a)**, to play a trick (on)
    Gli studenti ***fanno uno scherzo*** al professore ogni lunedì.
    The students play a trick on the teacher every Monday.

21. **fare tardi**, to be late
    farsi tardi, to get late
    Maria, non ***fare tardi!***
    Mary, don't be late!
    Si sta facendo tardi.
    It's getting late.

22. **fare torto (a)**, to do wrong (to)
    Non volevo ***fare torto a*** nessuno.
    I did not want to do wrong to anyone.

23. **strada facendo**, on the way
    Strada facendo, vidi uno scoiattolo.
    On the way, I saw a squirrel.

24. **faccia Lei**, you do it, you decide
    Signora, ***faccia Lei***, se vuole.
    Madam, you do it, if you like.

25. **non fa niente**, it doesn't matter
    Non fa niente se non viene.
    It doesn't matter if he doesn't come.

26. **faccia pure**, go right ahead, please do
    Faccia pure, signorina.
    Go right ahead, Miss.

27. **due giorni fa**, two days ago
    tre anni fa, three years ago
    Tornò in Italia ***tre anni fa.***
    He returned to Italy three years ago.

28. **fare il medico, l'avvocato**, to be a doctor, a lawyer
    Michele ***vuole fare*** il medico.
    Michael wants to be a doctor.

29. **fare una visita (a),** to visit
    Abbiamo fatto una visita a mia nonna.
    We visited my grandmother.

30. **fare un regalo,** to give a gift
    Mi ***hanno fatto un*** bel ***regalo.***
    They gave me a nice gift.

31. **fare le valige,** to pack (suitcases)
    Faremo le valige più tardi.
    We will pack later.

32. **fare il meglio** / **fare del proprio meglio** } to do one's best
    Fa' questo lavoro ***il meglio*** possibile.
    Do this work in the best way possible.
    Faccio del mio meglio.
    I do the best I can.

EXERCISES

A. Match each Italian expression in column I with the corresponding English expression in column II:

Column I	*Column* II
1. farsi la barba	*a.* on the way
2. fare freddo	*b.* to pack
3. fa cattivo tempo	*c.* to shave
4. strada facendo	*d.* to do without
5. fare le valige	*e.* to take a trip
6. tre giorni fa	*f.* to be cold
7. fare a meno di	*g.* to make the acquaintance of
8. fare brutta figura	*h.* the weather's bad
9. fare la conoscenza di	*i.* to make a bad showing
10. fare una gita	*j.* three days ago

B. Complete each sentence by writing the appropriate word or expression, using idioms with **fare**:

1. Marta vuole _____ un viaggio in Francia.
2. Carlo è caduto e si è _____ male.
3. In classe, bisogna fare _____.

4. La mattina, prima di andare a scuola, Paolo si fa _____.
5. Con la macchina fotografica, Giovanni _____ molte fotografie.
6. Nel mese di dicembre fa sempre _____.
7. Giorgio è caduto mentre ballava; allora ha fatto _____ figura.
8. D'estate fa molto _____.
9. Subito, non voglio _____ tardi.
10. Prima di partire, _____ le valige.

C. Translate the English words into Italian:

1. Luisa *takes a bath* soltanto il venerdì sera.
2. *It's hot* stasera.
3. A Perugia, i turisti *take a walk* ogni sera.
4. *Hurry up*, Michele. È tardi.
5. Nella nostra classe, *we do our best.*
6. I signori *shaved this morning.*
7. *Will you* (*fam. pl.*) *have breakfast* domani?
8. I film alla televisione mi *frighten.*
9. *I'll phone* a mia sorella più tardi.
10. Marco *played a trick* ai suoi amici ieri.
11. Bambini, *don't hurt* Maria!
12. *We made a bad showing* alla partita.
13. Gli studenti *ask too many questions.*
14. Signora, *it's getting late.*
15. Per Natale, *we give them a gift.*

D. Answer the questions in complete sentences:

1. In quale stagione fa molto freddo?
2. Quando ti fai il bagno?
3. A chi fate una telefonata ogni sera?
4. Cosa vuoi fare quando finisci di studiare?
5. Quando cadono, i tuoi amici si fanno male?
6. Chi non fa attenzione in classe?
7. Quando gli studenti non rispondono bene in classe, che figura fanno?
8. A che ora ti fai la barba la mattina?
9. Hai fatto la conoscenza di qualche ragazzo (ragazza) in questa classe?
10. Quando fate colazione a casa vostra?

3. The Verb *Piacere*

1. ***Mi*** ***piace*** la polpetta. (to me) (is pleasing)	I like the meatball.
2. ***Mi*** ***piacciono*** le polpette. (to me) (are pleasing)	I like the meatballs.
3. ***Gli*** ***piace*** il romanzo. (to him) (is pleasing)	He likes the novel.
4. ***Le*** ***piace*** il romanzo. (to her) (is pleasing)	She likes the novel.
5. ***Gli*** ***piacciono*** i romanzi. (to him) (are pleasing)	He likes novels. (See *Note*, page 101.)
6. ***Le*** ***piacciono*** i romanzi. (to her) (are pleasing)	She likes novels.
7. ***Ci*** ***piace*** la rosa. (to us) (is pleasing)	We like the rose.
8. ***Ci*** ***piacciono*** le rose. (to us) (are pleasing)	We like roses.
9. ***Ti*** (Vi) ***piace*** ballare. (to you) (is pleasing)	You like to dance.
10. Il libro ***piace*** a Tommaso.	Thomas likes the book. (The book is pleasing to Thomas.)
11. I libri ***piacciono*** a Tommaso.	Thomas likes the books. (The books are pleasing to Thomas.)
12. ***Piace*** Loro l'automobile?	Do you like the car? (Is the car pleasing to you?)
13. ***Piacciono*** loro i fiori?	Do they like flowers? (Are flowers pleasing to them?)

Note

1. The verb **piacere** (to be pleasing) is used to express the English verb "to like." "I like the meatball" is rendered in Italian by "The meatball is pleasing to me." "He likes the novel," by "The novel is pleasing to him."

2. The verb **piacere** is generally used in the third person singular or the third person plural.

3. The thing liked is the object in English but becomes the subject in Italian. Since the verb must agree with the subject, **piacere** must be in the singular if the subject is in the singular; **piacere** must be in the plural if the subject is in the plural.

4. The indirect object pronouns **(mi, ti, gli, Le, le, ci, vi, Loro, loro)** must always be used with **piacere.** Note that **Loro** and **loro** follow the verb.

Piace ***Loro*** l'automobile?	Do you like the car?
Piace ***loro*** la pasta.	They like the macaroni.

5. **Piacere** is conjugated with **essere** in the perfect tenses. The past participle then agrees in gender and number with the subject.

Mi sono **piaciut*e* le zie** di Maria.	I liked Mary's aunts.
Ci sono **piaciut*i* i ravioli.**	We liked the ravioli.

EXERCISES

A. *Progressive Substitution.* The drill begins with a complete Italian sentence. Complete each of the following sentences, substituting the new word or words given and using as much of the preceding sentence as possible. For example, begin with this sentence: Io ho caldo.

INCOMPLETE SENTENCES	COMPLETED SENTENCES
Noi _____.	Noi *abbiamo caldo.*
_____ freddo.	*Noi abbiamo* freddo.
_____ hanno _____.	*Loro* hanno *freddo.*

Mi piacciono le polpette.

1. _____ romanzi.
2. _____ il _____.
3. Ti _____.
4. _____ piacciono _____.
5. _____ scarpe rosse.
6. _____ rossa.
7. Gli _____.
8. _____ mele _____.
9. _____ verde.
10. Ci _____.

B. Translate the English words into Italian:

1. Ci piacciono *roses.*
2. Mi piace *bread.*
3. Perchè ti piacciono *Italian cars?*
4. Gli piacciono *soccer games?*
5. Piace loro *the red hat.*
6. A Pietro piacciono *lamps.*
7. A Teresa piace *to sing.*
8. Signora, Le piace *to dance?*
9. Mi piace *to read* il giornale.
10. A te piacciono *cigarettes?*

C. Translate into Italian:

1. Viola likes to drive.
2. They like Italian songs.
3. Do you (*pol. sing.*) like tomatoes?
4. I like a beautiful movie.
5. We like to watch television.
6. The children like toys.
7. Louis likes to visit Florence.
8. She likes Mario's letters.
9. John likes to tell the truth.
10. Miss, do you like these dishes?

D. Answer the questions in complete sentences:

1. Ti piace venire alla classe d'italiano?
2. A Maria (Paolo, etc.) piacciono le acciughe?
3. Perchè ti piace ascoltare i dischi?
4. Vi piacciono i romanzi americani?
5. Ai professori piacciono gli studenti pigri?
6. Cosa ti piace più di qualsiasi altra cosa?
7. A tua madre piace cucinare?
8. Quando ti piace andare al cinema?
9. Quali programmi ti piacciono alla televisione?
10. Agli studenti piacciono i compiti?

4. Idioms With *A*

1. **a** (with means of transportation), on, by

   a cavallo, on horseback
   a piedi, on foot, to walk

   Invece di andare ***a piedi,*** voglio andare ***a cavallo.***
   Instead of walking, I want to go on horseback.

2. **a** (with time expressions), goodbye, until . . .

   arrivederci, see you soon, so long
   a domani, until tomorrow
   a martedì (mercoledì, etc.), until Tuesday (Wednesday, etc.)
   a stasera, see you tonight

   Ci vedremo in classe. ***A domani,*** allora.
   We'll meet in class. See you tomorrow, then.

3. **a causa (di),** because of, on account of

   È arrivato in ritardo ***a causa della*** pioggia.
   He arrived late because of the rain.

4. **a proposito (di),** about, concerning, by the way

   Gli parlerò ***a proposito di*** quella macchina.
   I'll talk to him about that car.

5. **a destra,** on (to) the right

   a sinistra, on (to) the left

   Il Colosseo è ***a destra,*** signora, non ***a sinistra.***
   The Colosseum is on the right, madam, not on the left.

6. **a voce alta, ad alta voce,** in a loud voice, aloud

   a voce bassa, a bassa voce, in a soft (low) voice

   Non parlare ***a voce alta.***
   Don't talk in a loud voice.

7. **a casa,** at home

   Vado **a casa** adesso.
   I'm going home now.

8. **a scuola,** in (at, to) school

   Quando andate ***a scuola?***
   When are you going to school?

9. **a quest'ora,** at (by) this time

   Sarà arrivato ***a quest'ora.***
   He must have arrived at this time (by this time.)

10. **allo stesso tempo,** at the same time

    Può mangiare e bere ***allo stesso tempo.***
    He can eat and drink at the same time.

11. **a tempo,** in time

    Venni ***a tempo*** per cantare.
    I came in time to sing.

12. **a pagina . . . ,** on page . . .

    Il romanzo finisce ***a pagina*** trecento.
    The novel ends on page 300.

13. **all'estero,** abroad

    Viaggio ***all'estero*** ogni estate.
    I travel abroad every summer.

14. **al piede di,** at the foot of

    Il villaggio è ***ai piedi delle*** Alpi.
    The village is at the foot of the Alps.

15. **all'aperto,** in the open air, outdoors, out of doors

    Ci piace pranzare ***all'aperto.***
    We like to dine outdoors (out of doors).

16. **al di sopra,** on top, above
    al di sotto, beneath, under
    Le scarpe sono ***al di sotto*** di tutti quei libri.
    The shoes are under all those books.

17. **al contrario,** on the contrary

    Non ti piacciono? ***Al contrario,*** mi piacciono molto.
    Don't you like them? On the contrary, I like them very much.

18. **almeno**, at least

Spenderò ***almeno*** cento dollari.
I'll spend at least one hundred dollars.

19. **a poco a poco**, little by little, a little at a time

Finì tutta la pasta ***a poco a poco.***
He finished all the macaroni a little at a time.

EXERCISES

A. Match each Italian expression in column I with the corresponding English expression in column II:

Column I	*Column* II
1. a voce alta	*a.* at home
2. a causa di	*b.* at this time
3. a casa	*c.* until tomorrow
4. a piedi	*d.* on the contrary
5. a quest'ora	*e.* at least
6. al contrario	*f.* in a loud voice
7. almeno	*g.* on foot
8. a poco a poco	*h.* outdoors
9. all'aperto	*i.* because of
10. a domani	*j.* little by little

B. Translate into English:

1. A giovedì.
2. Arriverà allo stesso tempo.
3. Arrivederci.
4. Il treno è a sinistra.
5. al di sopra
6. a pagina novanta
7. Va a piedi.
8. La strada è a destra.
9. Parla a bassa voce.
10. Sono a casa.

C. Translate the English words into Italian:

1. Non parlare *in a loud voice!*
2. *By the way,* dove sei andata ieri sera?
3. Via Roma è *on the left.*
4. Maria e Peppe sono arrivati *at the same time.*
5. Rimango *at home* il sabato.

6. Ci piace mangiare *outdoors.*
7. Conta i suoi denari *little by little.*
8. Le signorine vanno *on horseback* per il parco.
9. Aprite i libri *to page* sessantadue.
10. Ci sono *at least* trecento persone nel teatro.

D. Complete the sentences with an appropriate idiom:

Example: Ballavano e cantavano _____.
Ballavano e cantavano allo stesso tempo.

1. Per andare al Colosseo, prenda la strada _____.
2. I giovani parlano _____ in classe.
3. Invece di prendere il tassì, andiamo _____.
4. _____, come sta tua madre?
5. Non rimanere _____ stasera.
6. Abbiamo trovato un bel ristorante _____.
7. Il romanzo che cerchi è _____ di tutti quei giornali.
8. Mio zio abita _____.
9. Dove vai _____?
10. Non possono venire _____ della neve.
11. Non dimenticare di arrivare _____.
12. Arrivederci _____.
13. Piazza di Spagna è _____, e Via del Corso è _____.
14. A che ora vai _____?
15. Bisogna fare tutto _____.

E. Answer the questions in complete sentences:

1. Vieni a scuola a piedi?
2. Siete mai andati a cavallo?
3. Quando rimani a casa?
4. Puoi scrivere e parlare allo stesso tempo?
5. Il professore arriva in classe allo stesso tempo ogni giorno?
6. Siete mai andati ad un ristorante all'aperto?
7. Quando sali le scale, sali a destra o a sinistra?
8. Quale parte del corpo è al di sotto delle gambe?
9. Tuo padre è all'estero?
10. Chi fa il lavoro a poco a poco in classe?

5. Idioms With *Di*

1. **di buon'ora**, early

   Sara viene ***di buon'ora*** ogni giorno.
   Sara comes early every morning.

2. **di buona voglia**, willingly
   di mala voglia, unwillingly

   Lo fa sempre ***di mala voglia.***
   He always does it unwillingly.

3. **di giorno in giorno**, from day to day.

   Il tempo cambia ***di giorno in giorno.***
   The weather changes from day to day.

4. **di mattina**, by day
   di giorno, in the daytime
   di sera, in the evening
   di notte, in the night, at night, by night

   Arriverà ***di notte*** col treno delle dodici.
   He will arrive at night with the twelve o'clock train.

5. **di tanto in tanto** } now and then
   di quando in quando } now and then

   Nevica in Sicilia ***di tanto in tanto.***
   It snows in Sicily now and then.

6. **di nuovo**, again

   È caduto ***di nuovo.***
   He fell again.

7. **di che colore . . .?**, what color . . .?

   Di che colore è il garofano?
   What color is the carnation?

8. **di moda**, in style, in fashion

   Le cravatte sono sempre ***di moda.***
   Ties are always in fashion.

9. **di questo modo**, in this way, in this fashion

    Fatelo ***di questo modo.***
    Do it this way.

10. **d'improvviso**, suddenly

    Uscì ***d'improvviso.***
    He left suddenly.

11. **di dove**, where . . . from?

    Di dove sei?
    Where are you from?

12. **d'estate**, in the summer
    d'autunno, in the autumn
    d'inverno, in the winter

    D'estate fa sempre bel tempo.
    The weather is always fine in the summer.

Note

Primavera (spring) may also take the preposition **in.**

Fa fresco ***in primavera.***
Fa fresco ***di primavera.***
It's cool in spring.

13. **di . . . anni**, years old

    È un giovane ***di*** venti ***anni.***
    He is a young man twenty years old.

14. **di male in peggio**, from bad to worse

    Le cose vanno ***di male in peggio.***
    Things are going from bad to worse.

15. **di fretta**, in haste, in a hurry

    Ma perchè vai sempre ***di fretta?***
    But why are you always in a hurry?

16. **di buon appetito**, with a good appetite, heartily

    Mangiai quella sera ***di buon appetito.***
    I ate heartily that night.

17. **di fronte a,** opposite

La chiesa è ***di fronte alla*** biblioteca.
The church is opposite the library.

18. **di andata e ritorno,** round-trip fare

Un biglietto ***di andata e ritorno,*** per favore.
One round-trip ticket, please.

19. **di ritardo,** late

Marta è arrivata con due ore ***di ritardo.***
Martha arrived two hours late.

20. **di tanto in tanto,** from time to time

Da bambino, andavo da mio nonno ***di tanto in tanto.***
As a child, I used to go to my grandfather's from time to time.

EXERCISES

A. Translate the English words into Italian:

1. *Suddenly,* Carlo venne a trovarci.
2. Ci piace andare a Napoli *now and then.*
3. Faceva tutto *unwillingly.*
4. Un biglietto *round-trip*, per favore.
5. Mio cugino va sempre *in a hurry*.
6. La Scala è *opposite the* statua di Leonardo da Vinci.
7. Tutto va *from bad to worse.*
8. *What color* è la macchina di Gino?
9. Va a trovare la nonna *in the autumn.*
10. Scusi, signore, *where are you from?*
11. È un signore *sixty years old.*
12. Arriveranno *in the evening* a Fiesole.
13. Non lo fa mai *willingly.*
14. Cantate l'inno *again.*
15. Quelle gonne sono *in fashion.*

B. Translate into English:

1. Lavoro di notte.
2. Di dove sono quei signori?

3. La situazione politica va di male in peggio.
4. Luisa ci visita di tanto in tanto.
5. La casa di Anna è di fronte alla cattedrale.
6. I giorni sono più lunghi d'estate.
7. Le giacche larghe non sono di moda.
8. Comprerò due biglietti d'andata e ritorno.
9. È caduto d'improvviso.
10. Il treno arriverà con un'ora di ritardo.

C. Translate into Italian:

1. Do it in this fashion. (*fam. sing.*)
2. It rains often in the spring.
3. Suddenly, George knocked on the door.
4. She always walks in a hurry.
5. Long skirts are in fashion.
6. The bus leaves on time now and then.
7. Let's leave at midnight.
8. He wrote the letter willingly.
9. We will have to get up early tomorrow.
10. It's cold in winter.

D. Answer the questions in complete sentences:

1. Quali scarpe sono di moda ora?
2. Dove vai d'inverno?
3. Fa caldo d'inverno o d'estate?
4. La classe d'italiano va di male in peggio o no?
5. Di dov'è tuo padre?
6. Fate il vostro lavoro di buona o di mala voglia?
7. Venite a scuola di giorno o di notte?
8. Chi arriva di buon'ora in classe?
9. Di che colore è la tua camicia (cravatta, gonna, etc.)?
10. Esci dall'aula di fretta ogni giorno?

6. Other Prepositional Idioms

1. **dapprima,** at first, first of all

   Dapprima, faremo una telefonata allo zio Pietro.
   First of all, let's phone Uncle Peter.

2. **dal mattino alla sera,** from morning to night

   Non fa nulla ***dal mattino alla sera.***
   He does nothing from morning to night.

3. **da un lato,** on one side, from one side, aside

   Mettiamo queste riviste ***da un lato.***
   Let's put these magazines aside.

4. **da dove?,** where? from where?

   Da dove vieni?
   Where are you coming from?

5. **da,** at someone's home or place of business

   Luisa è andata ***da*** Michele.
   Louise went to Michael's (home).

6. **da un giorno (un mese, un anno),** for a day (a month, a year)

   Studio il francese ***da tre anni.***
   I have been studying French for three years.

7. **da** (scope, use)

   Ho della carta ***da scrivere.***
   I have some writing paper.
   Dov'è la macchina ***da scrivere?***
   Where is the typewriter?

8. **in casa,** at home

   Liliana è ***in casa.***
   Lillian is at home.

9. **in** (with means of transportation), by
   in auto, by car
   in treno, by train
   in piroscafo, by ship

in aereo, by plane
in aviogetto, by jet
in autobus, by bus

Andrò in Italia ***in aereo.***
I'll go to Italy by plane.

10. **in quanto a**, as for, as regards

In quanto a suo fratello, era un giovane intelligente.
As for his brother, he was an intelligent young man.

11. **invece di**, instead of

Mangiò ***invece di*** lavorare.
He ate instead of working.

12. **in italiano** (or other languages), in Italian

Scrive ***in italiano*** o ***in inglese?***
Does she write in Italian or in English?

13. **in alto**, high
in basso, below, low

Quel pilota vola troppo ***in alto*** per me.
That pilot flies too high for me.

14. **in ritardo**, late

Non so perchè arriva sempre ***in ritardo.***
I don't know why he always arrives late.

15. **in anticipo**, early, in advance (as a deposit)

Venne ***in anticipo*** per l'appuntamento.
He came early for the appointment.
Mi diede venti dollari ***in anticipo.***
He gave me twenty dollars as a deposit.

16. **in città**, to (into) town

Vogliamo andare ***in città*** più tardi.
We want to go into town later.

17. **invano**, in vain

Scriveva a lei ***invano.***
He wrote to her in vain.

18. **in seguito**, later, following, following upon, after

    Partiremo ***in seguito*** al concerto.
    We will leave after the concert.

19. **in punto**, exactly, sharp

    Sono le tre ***in punto.***
    It is three o'clock sharp.

20. **per caso**, by chance

    Ha visto la penna, ***per caso?***
    Have you seen the pen, by chance?

21. **per conseguenza**, therefore, consequently

    Non ho studiato. ***Per conseguenza,*** sono stato bocciato.
    I didn't study. Consequently, I failed.

22. **per esempio**, for example

    Per esempio, "ragazzi" è maschile.
    For example, "boys" is masculine.

23. **perciò**, therefore, so

    È tardi; ***perciò,*** torniamo a casa.
    It's late; therefore, let's go home.

24. **per favore**, please

    Mi dia il burro, ***per favore.***
    Give me the butter, please.

25. **giorno per giorno**, day by day
    mese per mese, month by month

    Perde peso ***giorno per giorno.***
    She is losing weight day by day.

26. **per lo meno**, at least

    Dammi un panino ***per lo meno.***
    Give me a roll at least.

27. **su e giù**, up and down

    Smettiamo di andare ***su e giù***.
    Let's stop going up and down.

28. **su per giù**, more or less

    Vale cento dollari ***su per giù.***
    It's worth one hundred dollars, more or less.

29. **sul far della sera**, about dusk
    sul mezzogiorno, about noon

    I colori sono belli ***sul far della sera.***
    The colors are beautiful about dusk.

30. **su . . .** , come on

    Su, bambini, alzatevi!
    Come on, children, get up.

EXERCISES

A. Use each expression below in the sentences that follow. Each expression may be used only once:

in casa	**in ritardo**
in aereo	**in alto**
invece	**in punto**
da un anno	**giorno per giorno**
da	**su per giù**

1. Ma perchè arriva sempre _____ ?
2. Antonio vuole rimanere _____ .
3. La classe di biologia comincia sempre alle tre _____ .
4. Vogliamo andare a teatro _____ di andare al cinema.
5. Non vedo Luigi _____ .
6. Le sorelle di Marco sono andate _____ Rosa.
7. Le piace viaggiare _____ quando va in Italia.
8. Studia di più _____ .
9. Ci sono trenta ragazze, _____ , in questa classe.
10. Durante la partita, la palla è andata troppo _____ .

B. Translate into English:

1. Andiamo in città!
2. Ogni giorno arrivano in anticipo.
3. Su, signorine, coraggio!
4. Da dove venite, amici?
5. Faremo una gita in auto domenica.

6. In quanto a Marialena, devo dire che è pigra.
7. Perchè non scrive invece di telefonare continuamente?
8. È da un mese che non fumo.
9. Metti i libri da un lato, per piacere.
10. Dapprima, guardiamo questo programma!
11. È invano parlare.
12. Questa, per esempio, è una scatola.
13. Il soldato cammina su e giù per le strade.
14. È giovedì, perciò bisogna preparare la torta.
15. Fate il compito, per lo meno.

C. Translate the English words into Italian:

1. Come sei venuto? *By train.*
2. *From where* è venuto Lei?
3. Ho speso venti dollari, *more or less.*
4. Non voglio far niente, *from morning to night.*
5. Quell' aviogetto vola troppo *high.*
6. *At first* mi sembrava un cavallo bianco.
7. Cammina dritto *instead of* scherzare!
8. Sai dire questo *in Spanish?*
9. Alzatevi alle sette *sharp.*
10. Pulisce quella macchina *month by month.*
11. Abbiamo comprato tutti i regali *as regards* Natale.
12. Quando sono andati *to Marisena's?*
13. Non si pulisce le scarpe *for a year now.*
14. Hanno dormito tardi. *Consequently*, hanno perso il treno.
15. La nonna è *at home* col nonno.

D. Answer the questions in complete sentences:

1. Da dove vieni ora?
2. Ti piace guardare la televisione invece di uscire?
3. Tuo padre arriva al lavoro in ritardo o in anticipo?
4. Siete andati da Paolo (Maria, etc.) ieri?
5. È vero che fai il tuo lavoro dal mattino alla sera?
6. Hai una macchina da scrivere?
7. Su per giù, quanto denaro hai in tasca (o nella borsa)?
8. Da quanto tempo non mangi ravioli?
9. Con chi andate in città?
10. È invano studiare?

7. Miscellaneous Idioms and Expressions

1. **andare a passeggio**, to go for a walk
   Andranno a passeggio alle cinque.
   They will go for a walk at five o'clock.

2. **andare a piedi**, to go on foot, to walk
   Da qui bisogna *andare a piedi.*
   From here it is necessary to go on foot.

3. **andare a teatro**, to go to the theater
   Vai a teatro da solo?
   Are you going to the theater alone?

4. **andare in chiesa (in biblioteca)**, to go to church (to the library)
   Vado in chiesa tutte le domeniche.
   I go to church every Sunday.

5. **andare a cavallo**, to go on horseback
   andare a pescare, to go fishing
   Non *andare a pescare* con Giacomo.
   Don't go fishing with James.

6. **andare in aereo (in auto, in bicicletta, in treno)**, to go by plane (by car, by bicycle, by train)
   Sono *andati* in Francia *in treno.*
   They went to France by train.

7. **chiudere a chiave**, to lock
   Avete *chiuso* la porta *a chiave?*
   Did you lock the door?

8. **dare il benvenuto**, to welcome
   Ci hanno *dato il benvenuto* appena siamo arrivati.
   They welcomed us as soon as we arrived.

9. **sta bene**, all right
   "*Sta bene*," rispose Marco.
   "All right," answered Mark.

10. **stamattina**, this morning
    stasera, this evening
    stanotte, tonight
    Canterà *stasera* al ballo.
    She will sing this evening at the dance.

11. **oggigiorno**, nowadays
    Oggigiorno ci sono molte macchine a Roma.
    Nowadays there are many cars in Rome.

12. **a buon mercato**, cheap (cheaply)
    Il pesce ***si vende a buon mercato.***
    Fish is cheap.

13. **peccato**, too bad
    Si è fatto male. ***Peccato.***
    He hurt himself. Too bad.

14. **domattina** / **domani mattina** } tomorrow morning
    domani sera, tomorrow evening
    La vedremó ***domattina.***
    We will see her tomorrow morning.

15. **d'accordo,** O.K., agreed, all right
    Porta il golf. ***D'accordo.***
    Bring the sweater. All right.

16. **ieri sera**, last night
    L'ho comprato ***ieri sera.***
    I bought it last night.

17. **in otto giorni** / **fra otto giorni** } in a week
    in quindici giorni / **fra quindici giorni** } in two weeks
    Finirà il corso ***in otto giorni.***
    He will finish the course in a week.

18. **ancora una volta**, again, once again
    Ci visiterà ***ancora una volta.***
    She will visit us again.

19. **laggiù**, over there
    La chiesa vecchia è ***laggiù.***
    The old church is over there.

20. **tutti e due**, both
    Li ho visti ***tutti e due.***
    I saw them both.

21. **più tardi,** later
    Mia madre farà i ravioli ***più tardi.***
    My mother will make the ravioli later.

22. **non è vero?**, aren't you?, isn't he?, don't they?, isn't it so?, etc.
    Venite con noi, ***non è vero?***
    You are coming with us, aren't you?

23. **l'anno scorso, la settimana passata,** last year, last week
    Scoprirono un bel lago ***l'anno scorso.***
    They discovered a beautiful lake last year.

24. **l'anno prossimo, il mese prossimo**, next year, next month
    Studierò il cinese ***l'anno prossimo.***
    I'll study Chinese next year.

25. **un po' di,** a little (of), some
    Metteteci ***un po' di*** sale.
    Put some salt on it.

26. **in orario**, on time
    Arrivano sempre ***in orario.***
    They always arrive on time.

EXERCISES

A. Match each Italian expression in column I with the corresponding English expression in column II:

Column I	*Column* II
1. dare il benvenuto	*a.* next month
2. chiudere a chiave	*b.* go on horseback
3. andare a cavallo	*c.* too bad
4. ieri sera	*d.* agreed
5. tutti e due	*e.* some
6. il mese prossimo	*f.* to welcome
7. un po' di	*g.* this evening
8. d'accordo	*h.* last evening
9. stasera	*i.* both
10. peccato	*j.* to lock

B. Use each of the expressions below in the sentences that follow. Each expression may be used only once:

andare a teatro	**andare in chiesa**
in orario	**domattina**
ieri sera	**fra due giorni**
peccato	**ancora una volta**
laggiù	**d'accordo**
chiudere a chiave	**più tardi**
a buon mercato	**l'anno scorso**
non è vero	

1. Non dimenticare di _____ il portone.
2. Verrò a casa tua _____.
3. _____ Giovanna ed io andammo a Roma.
4. Non voglio andare a letto; voglio _____ invece.
5. _____ che tu non ti senta bene!
6. _____, andiamo a prendere una pizza!
7. La domenica devo _____ a pregare.
8. Queste calze non costano molto. Sono _____.
9. Prendiamo un tassì così arriveremo _____ .
10. _____ abbiamo visto un film meraviglioso.
11. Vedi, _____ c'è un tramonto spettacoloso!
12. Non venire stamattina: vieni _____ invece.
13. Ripetete le parole _____.
14. Oggi è giovedì, _____?
15. Incomincerò a dipingere quel quadro _____.

C. Translate into Italian:

1. This morning I feel cold.
2. Nowadays the Americans respect the Italians.
3. All right. Let's go swimming!
4. They went to the library to look for a book.
5. I'll sell the car in eight days.
6. The bus always arrives on time.
7. She spoke to both of them.
8. Mr. and Mrs. Betola go everywhere on foot.
9. Too bad your (*fam. sing.*) cousin couldn't come.
10. It's cold today, isn't it?

D. Answer the questions in complete sentences:

1. A chi dai il benvenuto ogni mattina?
2. Come stai stamattina?
3. Cosa hai letto ieri sera?
4. Venite a scuola in orario ogni giorno?
5. Ti piace andare a passeggio la domenica?
6. Siete mai andati a pescare?
7. I tuoi genitori vanno in bicicletta?
8. Cosa farai stasera?
9. Dove andrete più tardi?
10. L'anno prossimo dove andrete in vacanza?

La chiesa di Sant'Ambrogio a Milano. Questa chiesa è un esempio di architettura romanica, uno stile usato moltissimo in Italia per la costruzione delle chiese.

8. Mastery Exercises

A. Choose the correct expression in parentheses:

1. Pia non sorride mai. Ha (l'aria triste, sete, tempo, bisogno).
2. Marta balla bene. Allora fa (brutta figura, bella figura, il bagno, la conoscenza).
3. Per andare in Francia bisogna fare (le valigie, una passeggiata, torto, tardi).
4. Da qui al palazzo si può andare (i, a, ai, sui) piedi.
5. Per trovare il museo bisogna girare (a scuola, a destra, in treno, in aereo).
6. Le gonne corte non sono (a casa, di moda, in ritardo, d'improvviso).
7. Ci sono molti grattacieli (in campagna, in auto, in città, al teatro).
8. Ci mettiamo dei vestiti leggeri quando (nevica, è caldo, fa freddo, fa caldo).
9. Abitano al di sotto di voi? No, abitano (al di sopra, altamente, dopo, prima) di noi.
10. Alla fine della classe, il professore dice sempre, "(Dapprima, A domani, Al contrario, Incominciamo)."
11. I treni in Germania arrivano sempre (all'estero in orario, al di sotto, in casa).
12. Prima di partire ricordati di chiudere la porta (a chiave, di moda, a cavallo, tutti e due).
13. Ero andato in Italia (la settimana prossima, domani, fra otto giorni, l'anno scorso).
14. È tuo quest'orologio? No, (è più tardi di, ho paura di, è di, avrà luogo) Michele.
15. Mi piacerebbe visitare il Colosseo (l'altro ieri, ancora una volta, sabato scorso, tutti e due).
16. Andiamo al parco? (D'accordo., Laggiù., Ho torto., Diamogli il benvenuto.)
17. Prima di andare al lavoro ogni mattina, Roberto (ha sedici anni, fa amicizia, si fa la barba, fa' pure).
18. Non tornare tardi (ieri mattina, stanotte, a buon mercato, ieri sera).

19. Questi pantaloni non costano molto; sono (a buon mercato, in anticipo, su per giù, in ritardo).

20. Se vuole andare alla villa, signora (sia di moda, faccia pure, si faccia il bagno, faccia uno scherzo).

B. Complete the English sentences:

1.	Non gli piacciono i pomodori.	He _____ tomatoes.
2.	Strada facendo vide tre scimmie.	_____ she saw three monkeys.
3.	Quando fa qualcosa non ha mai fretta.	When he does something _____.
4.	Il ballo ebbe luogo giovedì scorso.	The dance _____ Thursday.
5.	Non andai al cinema perchè avevo mal di testa.	I didn't go to the movies because _____.
6.	Ha fatto a meno di un nuovo paio di scarpe.	She _____ a new pair of shoes.
7.	Prendono un caffè ogni sera all'aperto.	They have coffee _____.
8.	Ho speso su per giù venti dollari.	I spent _____.
9.	Ci diedero un benvenuto molto cordiale.	_____ very cordially.
10.	Siete arrivati proprio ora, non è vero?	You just arrived, _____?
11.	La sorella di Giulio ha ventitrè anni.	Giulio's sister _____.
12.	Su, signora, si prepari per il ballo!	_____, get ready for the dance!
13.	Oggigiorno è raro vedere un buon film.	_____ to see a good film.
14.	Giorgio ha studiato all'estero.	George studied _____.
15.	Tutti e due passeggiavano tranquillamente.	_____ were walking peacefully.
16.	L'anno scorso c'erano troppi turisti a Venezia.	_____ there were too many tourists _____ Venice.
17.	Sono le sette in punto.	It's seven _____.
18.	Gli prepariamo la colazione giorno per giorno.	We _____ for him _____.
19.	Hai ragione. Non ho detto la verità.	_____. I didn't tell the truth.
20.	È andato in California in aereo.	He went _____.

C. Match each Italian expression in column I with the corresponding English expression in column II:

Column I	*Column* II
1. invece di	*a.* to feel like
2. da un lato	*b.* early
3. aver voglia	*c.* it's cold
4. fa freddo	*d.* on the right
5. a sinistra	*e.* instead of
6. dapprima	*f.* it doesn't matter
7. a destra	*g.* at least
8. in anticipo	*h.* on the left
9. non fa niente	*i.* at first
10. per lo meno	*j.* on one side

D. Complete each sentence with one of the following words or expressions. Each word or expression may be used only once:

ad alta voce	allo stesso tempo	su e giù
perciò	a pagina	un po' di
per favore	piace	fra otto giorni
a casa	mese per mese	laggiù
piacciono	a buon mercato	autobus

1. Invece di tornare oggi Liliana tornerà dall'Inghilterra _____.
2. Ho comprato queste cravatte perchè erano _____.
3. Stasera non voglio restare _____ da solo.
4. Il professore ha detto di voltare _____ dieci.
5. Scusi, mi dia _____ pepe, signorina.
6. I ragazzi correvano _____ per le scale.
7. Ci mandano notizie dei parenti _____.
8. Giacomo, _____, mi vuoi dare quel libro?
9. Le polpette fatte in casa mi _____ molto.
10. Chiacchiera e scrive _____.
11. La giacca non è quassù e _____.
12. Vogliono cantare, _____ vanno a scuola per imparare.
13. Ma perchè devi sempre parlare _____?
14. Questa torta non mi _____.
15. Il viaggio da Siena a Firenze si fa in _____.

E. Express in an Italian sentence that:

1. you like red shoes
2. there is a tree on the right
3. your brother is seventeen years old
4. you have a toothache
5. Mary sings from morning to night
6. we will go to town later
7. Louis is always wrong
8. little by little it is getting warmer
9. you have some writing paper
10. at night we go to the theater
11. they are very hungry
12. everyone is always in a hurry
13. we have much to do
14. she takes a bath very often
15. it is getting late
16. it is cold in winter
17. we all studied in vain
18. you eat at about noon
19. Louise will leave in two weeks
20. you're never right

F. Translate into Italian:

1. My sister doesn't like vegetables.
2. A year ago, we went abroad.
3. Those students always speak in a low voice.
4. Are you (*fam. pl.*) cold without your hat?
5. Why don't they pay attention in class?
6. Do it, if you like, sir.
7. Lucy wants to be a teacher.
8. She teaches me every day.
9. Don't say it in that fashion. (*fam. sing.*)
10. They come to our home from time to time.
11. What color is that car?
12. I bought a round-trip ticket.
13. His cold has gone from bad to worse.
14. Where is she coming from?
15. Give him at least a new bicycle. (*fam. sing.*)
16. You (*fam. pl.*) should lock the door by key.
17. I hurt my arm while writing.
18. These shoes are in fashion nowadays.
19. We welcomed the general at the door.
20. Mark saw the two of them at the beach.

Part IV—Vocabulary

1. Synonyms

Synonyms	Meanings
abbastanza, sufficiente	enough, sufficient
abitare, vivere	to live, dwell
accadere, succedere	to happen
accogliere, dare il **benvenuto**	to receive, welcome
accordarsi, mettersi d'accordo	to come to an agreement
l'**affetto**, l'**amore**	affection, love
allegro, felice, contento	happy, content
altrui, degli altri	of others
l'**alunno**, l'**allievo**, lo **studente** (*m.*)	student (*m.*)
alzare, elevare, levare	to raise
ammazzare, uccidere	to kill
andare fuori, uscire	to go out, go away
andare giù, scendere	to go down
andare su, salire	to go up
l'**angoscia**, l'**angustia**	anguish
antico, vecchio	ancient, old
arrivare a, giungere a	to get to, arrive
aspettare, attendere	to wait (for)
attraversare, traversare	to cross
l'**avvenimento**, l'**evento**	happening, event
avverso, contrario	against
avviarsi, incamminarsi	to set out
la **battaglia**, la **lotta**	battle, struggle
buttare, lanciare, tirare	to throw
celebre, famoso, illustre	famous
chiedere, domandare	to ask
comprendere, capire	to understand
il **diavolo**, il **demonio**	devil
differente, diverso, distinto	different
dimenticare, scordare	to forget

il **dottore** (*m.*), il **medico**	doctor
l'**errore** (*m.*), lo **sbaglio**	mistake
l'**est** (*m.*), il **levante** (*m.*), l'**oriente** (*m.*)	east
la **faccia**, il **viso**, il **volto**	face
favorito, preferito	favorite
finire, conchiudere, terminare	to end, finish
la **follia**, la **pazzia**	madness
la **gentilezza**, la **cortesia**	kindness
la **gioia**, la **letizia**	joy, gladness
grave, serio	serious
l'**idea**, il **pensiero**	thought
ignorare, non sapere	to be ignorant of, not know
incominciare, iniziare, mettersi a	to begin (to)
lontano, distante	far away, distant
il **luogo**, il **sito**, il **posto**	place
il **maestro**, il **professore**	teacher, professor
menare, condurre	to lead
mettersi, indossare, portare	to wear
la **nazione**, il **paese**	nation, country
nervoso, irritato	nervous, irritated
il **nord**, il **settentrione**	north
l'**operaio**, il **lavoratore**, il **lavorante**	worker (*m.*)
l'**ovest** (*m.*), il **ponente** (*m.*), l'**occidente** (*m.*)	west
il **palazzo**, l'**edificio**	building
permettere, lasciar fare	to permit, allow
poi, dopo	then, afterward
pregare, supplicare	to beg, implore
la **rabbia**, l'**ira**	rage
raccontare, narrare	to narrate
restare, rimanere	to remain
ricordarsi, rammentarsi	to remember
riflettere, pensare	to reflect, think
ritornare a casa, rientrare, rincasare	to go back home
il **ritratto**, la **fotografia**	picture, photograph
rompere, spezzare	to break
snello, magro	thin, slender
soffice, morbido	soft
soltanto, solamente	only

spedire, mandare, inviare	to send, to mail
splendido, magnifico	wonderful
la **sposa**, la **moglie**	wife
lo **sposo**, il **marito**	husband
la **stanza**, la **sala**	room
subito, rapidamente	quickly, rapidly
il **sud**, il **meridione**	south
il **timore**, la **paura**	fear
triste, scontento	sad, unhappy
uguale, simile	equal, similar
usare, servirsi di	to use
vicino, presso	near
volere, desiderare	to wish, want, desire

EXERCISES

A. Match each word in column I with the synonym in column II:

Column I	*Column* II
1. aspettare	*a*. il viso
2. rimanere	*b*. attendere
3. antico	*c*. la stanza
4. l'alunno	*d*. comprendere
5. la sala	*e*. levare
6. la faccia	*f*. contrario
7. capire	*g*. l'amore
8. avverso	*h*. lo studente
9. l'affetto	*i*. vecchio
10. alzare	*j*. restare

B. Substitute an appropriate synonym for the italicized word or expression in each of the following sentences:

1. C'è una *stanza* da pranzo in casa mia.
2. *Il dottore* verrà più tardi.
3. La crisi internazionale è veramente *grave*.
4. *Voglio* andare al cinema stasera.
5. *La fotografia* di mio padre è sul tavolo.
6. Vogliamo *uscire* insieme sabato sera?
7. Mio fratello è stato sempre un tipo *allegro*.

8. La vita *dell'operaio* è sempre molto dura.
9. *Il settentrione* è la zona industriale dell'Italia.
10. Ti voglio *chiedere* se tu andrai a teatro oggi.
11. *Il professore* presenta la lezione agli studenti.
12. Quella persona è piena di *cortesia*.
13. Mia sorella *abita* a New York.
14. Non so perchè tu sei (sia) sempre *scontento*.
15. Giovanni è *contrario* all'idea.

C. Select the synonym for the italicized word:

1. *l'evento* — il regalo, l'avvenimento, lo sbaglio
2. *l'edificio* — il palazzo, il museo, la chiesa
3. *lanciare* — tirare, lasciare, cantare
4. *terminare* — finire, fare, fingere
5. *giungere* — arrivare, partire, venire
6. *magro* — alto, basso, snello
7. *il marito* — la moglie, lo sposo, il fratello
8. *vicino* — lontano, presso, prima
9. *narrare* — raccontare, dire, negare
10. *celebre* — forte, corto, famoso

D. Select the word that does *not* belong in each group:

1. lo studente, l'allievo, l'alunno, l'alloggio
2. il lavorante, il lavoratore, il libro, l'operaio
3. indossare, vestire, mettersi, portare
4. diverso, differente, distinto, distante
5. inviare, sperare, spedire, mandare
6. il luogo, il posto, il pomodoro, il sito
7. l'est, il levante, l'occidente, l'oriente
8. buttare, pensare, tirare, lanciare
9. felice, allegro, contento, scontento
10. il volto, il voto, il viso, la faccia

E. Write two Italian synonyms for each of the following words:

1. to lead
2. wife
3. fear
4. rage
5. wonderful
6. equal
7. far away
8. to go down
9. anguish
10. afterward

2. Opposites I

accendere, to ignite, light	**spegnere**, to put out, extinguish
accostarsi, to approach	**allontanarsi**, to move away (from)
allegro, happy	**triste**, unhappy
amare, to love	**odiare**, to hate
amaro, bitter	**dolce**, sweet
l'**amico**, friend	il **nemico**, enemy
l'**amore** (*m.*), love	l'**odio**, hate
andare, to go	**venire**, to come
aperto, open	**chiuso**, closed
arrivare, to arrive	**partire**, to depart
assente, absent	**presente**, present
basso, low	**alto**, high
bello, beautiful	**brutto**, ugly
bene, well	**male**, badly
bianco, white	**nero**, black
buono, good	**cattivo**, bad
caldo, warm	**freddo**, cold
caro, expensive	**a buon mercato**, cheap
comprare, to buy	**vendere**, to sell
con, with	**senza**, without
dare, to give	**ricevere**, to receive
davanti, in front of	**dietro**, behind
destra, right	**sinistra**, left
dimenticare, to forget	**ricordare**, to remember
l'**est** (*m.*), east	l'**ovest** (*m.*), west
facile, easy	**difficile**, difficult
forte, strong	**debole**, weak
giocare, to play	**lavorare**, to work
il **giorno**, day	la **notte**, night
la **gioventù**, youth	la **vecchiaia**, old age
grande, large, big	**piccolo**, small
la **guerra**, war	la **pace**, peace
ieri, yesterday	**domani**, tomorrow
l'**inizio**, the beginning	la **fine**, the end
lì, **là**, there	**qui**, **qua**, here
magro, thin	**grasso**, fat
molto, much	**poco**, little
parlare, to speak	**tacere**, to keep quiet

prima, before	**dopo**, after
qualcuno, someone	**nessuno**, no one
il **ragazzo**, boy	la **ragazza**, girl
il **signore**, gentleman	la **signora**, lady
sopra, on	**sotto**, under
su, up	**giù**, down
il **sud**, south	il **nord**, north
svegliarsi, to wake up	**addormentarsi**, to fall asleep
trovare, to find	**perdere**, to lose
l'**uomo**, man	la **donna**, woman
vecchio, old	{ **nuovo**, new { **giovane**, young
vicino, near	**lontano**, far
vincere, to win	**perdere**, to lose

EXERCISES

A. Match each word in column I with the antonym in column II:

Column I	*Column* II
1. caldo	*a*. vendere
2. bello	*b*. presente
3. amare	*c*. lontano
4. vecchio	*d*. a buon mercato
5. molto	*e*. brutto
6. vicino	*f*. piccolo
7. trovare	*g*. perdere
8. dolce	*h*. cattivo
9. sopra	*i*. freddo
10. comprare	*j*. nuovo
11. caro	*k*. sinistra
12. buono	*l*. sotto
13. destra	*m*. amaro
14. grande	*n*. poco
15. assente	*o*. odiare

B. Select the opposite of the italicized word:

1. *perdere* — vincere, vendere, venire
2. *sinistra* — sopra, dritto, destra
3. *vicino* — presso, lontano, qui
4. *basso* — medio, alto, magro
5. *bianco* — bianca, nero, giallo
6. *domani* — pomeriggio, oggi, stasera
7. *triste* — allegro, sporco, meglio
8. *tacere* — lavorare, parlare, nascere
9. *bene* — male, facilmente, difficilmente
10. *verità* — buccia, bugia, burla

C. From the list below, choose the *opposite* word that best suits each sentence:

con	grasso
su	perdere
forte	freddo
pace	entrare
accendere	qua

1. Ti prego di *uscire* dalla porta.
2. Come si chiama quel ragazzo *magro?*
3. Andrai in vacanza *senza* tuo marito?
4. La *guerra* mondiale è una cosa necessaria.
5. Mi fai il favore di *spegnere* la luce?
6. Nell'aula fa un *caldo* da morire!
7. La stanza è *giù*, al primo piano.
8. Non fai altro che *vincere* sempre.
9. Il libro è *là*.
10. Quel ragazzo è *debole*.

D. Complete each of the following sentences by using an opposite word:

1. Lo zucchero non è amaro; è _____ .
2. Il negozio non è all'inizio della strada; è alla _____ .
3. Il cane non è sopra la tavola; è _____ la tavola.
4. La mia casa non è grande; è _____ .
5. Via Napoli è a destra, ma Via Carducci è a _____ .
6. Invece di essere davanti alla scrivania, sono _____ la scrivania.
7. Non voglio tacere; voglio _____ .

8. Quel bicchiere non è bello; è _____ .
9. Il regalo di Nanda non era caro; era _____ .
10. Ti prego di non prendere molto; prendi _____ .

E. Translate the following opposites into Italian:

1. warm, cold
2. beginning, end
3. easy, difficult
4. old age, youth
5. to fall asleep, to wake up
6. fat, thin
7. under, on
8. before, after
9. badly, well
10. to work, to play

Veduta di *Camogli*, tipico paesetto di pescatori, situato lungo "la Riviera ligure."

3. Opposites II

alzarsi, to get up	**sedersi**, to sit down
andare, to go	**venire**, to come
aprire, to open	**chiudere**, to close
avvicinarsi, to come closer	**allontanarsi**, to go farther away
biondo, blond	**bruno**, brunette
chiaro, light	**scuro**, dark
la **città**, city	la **campagna**, country
divertirsi, to enjoy oneself	**annoiarsi**, to be bored
la **domanda**, question	la **risposta**, answer
domandare, to ask	**rispondere**, to answer
entrare, to enter	**uscire**, to leave
l'**estate** (*f.*), summer	l'**inverno**, winter
incominciare, to begin	**finire**, to end
leggero, light	**pesante**, heavy
la **madre**, mother	il **padre**, father
maggiore, older	**minore**, younger
meglio, better (*adv.*)	**peggio**, worse
mettersi, to put on	**togliersi**, to take off
il **mezzogiorno**, noon	la **mezzanotte**, midnight
migliore, better (*adj.*)	**peggiore**, worse
molto(i), much, many	**poco (pochi)**, little, few
morire, to die	{ **nascere**, to be born { **vivere**, to live
obbedire, to obey	**disobbedire**, to disobey
partire, to leave	**arrivare**, to arrive
permettere, to allow	**proibire**, to forbid
piangere, to cry	**ridere**, to laugh
pieno, full	**vuoto**, empty
più, more	**meno**, less
possibile, possible	**impossibile**, impossible
povero, poor	**ricco**, rich
la **primavera**, spring	l'**autunno**, autumn, fall
il **primo**, the first	l'**ultimo**, the last
pulito, clean	**sporco**, dirty
qualche cosa, something	**niente**, nothing
il **re**, king	la **regina**, queen
ricordare, to remember	**dimenticare**, to forget

rimanere, to stay	**andarsene**, to go away
riuscire, to succeed	**fallire**, to fail
salire, to go up	**scendere**, to go down
sempre, always	**mai**, never
sì, yes	**no**, no
il **sole**, sun	la **luna**, moon
la **sorella**, sister	il **fratello**, brother
spesso, often	**raramente**, rarely
tardi, late	**presto**, early
la **terra**, earth, land	{ il **mare**, sea il **cielo**, sky, heaven
uscire, to go out	**entrare**, to enter
utile, useful	**inutile**, useless
la **verità**, truth	la **bugia**, lie
la **vita**, life	la **morte**, death
vivo, alive	**morto**, dead

EXERCISES

A. Match each word in column I with the antonym in column II:

Column I	*Column* II
1. aprire	*a.* bionda
2. la bugia	*b.* scuro
3. il re	*c.* spesso
4. presto	*d.* la verità
5. raramente	*e.* la moglie
6. piangere	*f.* la regina
7. bruna	*g.* andarsene
8. chiaro	*h.* minore
9. morire	*i.* ridere
10. maggiore	*j.* peggio
11. avvicinarsi	*k.* chiudere
12. rimanere	*l.* qualche cosa
13. niente	*m.* vivere
14. meglio	*n.* tardi
15. il marito	*o.* allontanarsi

B. Choose the opposite of the word in italics:

1. *la moglie*	la figlia, il marito, il cugino
2. *partire*	uscire, prendere, arrivare
3. *la primavera*	l'autunno, l'estate, l'inverno
4. *la sorella*	la madre, lo zio, il fratello
5. *amare*	piacere, odiare, stringere
6. *andare*	uscire, partire, venire
7. *aprire*	uscire, chiudere, portare
8. *pulito*	limpido, chiaro, sporco
9. *maggiore*	grande, vecchio, minore
10. *incominciare*	finire, iniziare, mettersi a

C. Write the opposite of each italicized word:

1. Questa camera è molto *pulita.*
2. Oggi lui si sente *peggio.*
3. È *l'ultimo* mese dell'anno.
4. Qual'era *la risposta* di Maria Luisa?
5. Carlo, bisogna *partire* in orario.
6. Al supermercato, abbiamo comprato *più* di due chili di mele.
7. È *inutile* andare a scuola.
8. Il treno è partito a *mezzanotte.*
9. Guarda Giorgio, quel bambino vuole *togliersi* la camicia!
10. Mi dispiace signore, ma il pacco è troppo *leggero.*

D. Translate into Italian:

1. full, empty
2. never, always
3. the lie, the truth
4. to love, to hate
5. to forget, to remember
6. to get up, to sit down
7. to succeed, to fail
8. rarely, often
9. to ask, to answer
10. many, few

E. Complete the following sentences, using words with opposite meanings:

1. Quel vecchio non vuole *morire.* Vuole _____ .
2. Invece di andare in Italia in *primavera*, perchè non andiamo d'_____ ?
3. Quando vedo un film triste, voglio *piangere* invece di _____ .
4. Il signor Bianchi è nato *povero* ma è morto _____ .
5. Noi non andiamo *mai* al cinema. Mia sorella, però, ci va _____ .

6. Ma Rosa, non vedi: la tua risposta non è *utile*, è _____.
7. Nella fotografia c'era il *re* e la _____.
8. Non hanno capito. Ho detto che devo alzarmi *presto*, non _____.
9. In questa classe i ragazzi sono *peggiori* e le ragazze sono _____.
10. Il mio bicchiere è *vuoto*, mentre il tuo è _____.
11. Ieri Luisa era *bionda*; oggi, invece, è _____.
12. La *campagna* è bella, ma preferisco la _____.
13. Paolo non era il *minore* della famiglia; era il _____.
14. Ho visto il *primo* e l'_____ spettacolo.
15. Quando gli astronauti viaggiano, vedono il *sole* e la _____.

Il Canal Grande con alcuni tipici palazzi e case veneziane. Nel disegno [drawing] si vede anche una gondola, unico mezzo di trasporto dell'antica Venezia.

4. At Home I

THE FAMILY

la **famiglia**, family
i **parenti**, relatives
i **genitori**, parents
il **padre**, father
la **madre**, mother
il **marito**, husband
la **moglie**, wife
il **papà**, dad, father
il **babbo**, dad, daddy
la **mamma**, mom, mother
il **neonato**, newborn
il **bambino**, child (*m.*)
la **bambina**, child (*f.*)
il **figlio**, son
la **figlia**, daughter
il **fratello**, brother
la **sorella**, sister
il **nonno**, grandfather
la **nonna**, grandmother
lo **zio**, uncle
la **zia**, aunt
il **nipote**, nephew, grandson
la **nipote**, niece, granddaughter
il **cugino**, cousin (*m.*)
la **cugina**, cousin (*f.*)

THE HOME

la **casa**, home, house
l'**autorimessa**, il **garage** } garage
l'**appartamento**, apartment
il **piano**, floor, story (1st floor, etc.)
il **pianterreno**, ground floor
il **tetto**, roof
il **muro**, outside wall
l'**entrata**, the entrance
la **chiave**, key
la **porta**, door
l'**uscio**, doorway
il **portiere**, il **portinaio** } doorman
la **finestra**, window
il **camino**, chimney
il **giardino**, garden
il **soffitto**, ceiling
la **parete**, wall (of an apartment)
la **stanza**, la **sala**, la **camera** } room
la **camera da letto**, bedroom
la **sala da pranzo**, dining room
la **cucina**, kitchen
la **cuoca**, cook
il **salotto**, living room
lo **studio**, study
la **veranda**, porch, veranda
la **terrazza**, terrace
il **balcone**, balcony
il **soggiorno**, den
la **sala da bagno**, il **bagno** } bathroom
il **termosifone**, radiator

lo **scantinato**, la **cantina** } cellar, basement
l'**ascensore** (*m.*), elevator
le **scale**, stairs
la **scala**, stair(case)
il **pavimento**, floor (of a room)
la **luce**, light
il **fiammifero**, il **cerino** } match
l'aria condizionata, air conditioning
lo scaldabagno, water heater

THE FURNITURE

l'**armadio**, closet
i **mobili**, pieces of furniture
la **mobilia**, furniture
la **sedia**, chair
la **poltrona**, armchair
il **tavolo**, la **tavola** } table
il **letto**, bed
il **comò**, il **cassettone** } chest of drawers
il **tiretto**, drawer
lo **scaffale**, bookcase
la **credenza**, sideboard
il **comodino**, night table
il **baule**, chest
la **cristalliera**, breakfront
il **tavolino**, coffee table
la **lampada**, lamp
la **lampadina**, electric bulb
il **divano**, il **sofà** } sofa
il **pianoforte**, piano
il **tappeto**, rug
i **veli**, curtains
le **tende**, drapes
il **quadro**, picture, painting
il **ritratto**, picture, photograph
lo **specchio**, mirror
l'**orologio**, watch, clock
il **telefono**, telephone
il frigorifero, refrigerator
la **stufa**, stove
la **lavatrice**, washing machine
la **lavastoviglie**, dishwasher
il **forno**, oven
il **lavandino**, sink

EXERCISES

A. Choose the word or expression in parentheses that best completes the sentence:

1. Gli amici si ricevono nel (salotto, bagno, soffitto).
2. Il capo della famiglia italiana è (la madre, il padre, lo zio).
3. La sigaretta si accende con (il portiere, la luce, il cerino).
4. La porta si apre con (la chiave, la finestra, la lampada).
5. Il soggiorno è (un divano, una stanza, una casa).
6. Il neonato è (un bambino, un nonno, una zia).

7. Il pianoforte si usa per (salire, pranzare, suonare).
8. I veli si trovano quasi sempre vicino (alla finestra, al camino, all'appartamento).
9. Il comodino è (un mobile, un fiammifero, un frigorifero).
10. Per parlare si usa (l'orologio, il telefono, il ritratto).

B. Select the item that does *not* belong in each group:

1. la cucina, la camera, la sorella, il bagno
2. il bambino, il cugino, il nipote, il camino
3. il letto, il tiretto, la luce, la sedia
4. la nipote, la sala, la scala, la porta
5. il marito, la lampada, la moglie, la zia
6. i genitori, i veli, i parenti, i cugini
7. lo scantinato, lo specchio, l'orologio, il telefono
8. il cerino, il salotto, la cucina, il garage
9. la sedia, il neonato, la tavola, il pianoforte
10. il letto, il comodino, il tappeto, il babbo

C. If a statement is true, write **vero**. If a statement is false, rewrite the statement to make it true:

1. Il soggiorno è una stanza.
2. Il letto è nella parete.
3. Mia zia è la nipote di mio padre.
4. La scala porta al soffitto.
5. La madre è sempre in cucina.
6. Il frigorifero si trova spesso in giardino.
7. Lo specchio è sulla parete.
8. Il divano si trova quasi sempre nel garage.
9. Mia nonna è una buona cuoca.
10. Mio cugino è il figlio di mio fratello.
11. La sorella di mia madre è mia zia.
12. La famiglia è composta di molti parenti.
13. L'armadio si trova spesso nella camera da letto.
14. Il portinaio accudisce alla cucina.
15. C'è il pavimento in ogni stanza.

5. At Home II

MEALS

il **cibo**, food
il **pasto**, meal
la **prima colazione**, breakfast
la **colazione**, lunch
il **pranzo**, dinner
la **cena**, supper
il **contorno**, side dish
l'**appetito**, appetite
il **vasellame**, dinnerware
il **piatto**, plate
la **scodella**, soup plate
la **zuccheriera**, sugarbowl
la **saliera**, saltshaker
la **pepaiola**, pepper-shaker
il **bicchiere**, drinking glass
la **tazza**, cup
il **piattino**, saucer
l'**argenteria**, silverware
il **coltello**, knife
la **forchetta**, fork
il **cucchiaio**, tablespoon
il **cucchiaino**, teaspoon
la **tovaglia**, tablecloth
il **tovagliolo**, napkin
la **brocca**, pitcher
la **bottiglia**, bottle
la **caraffa**, carafe
la **lista delle vivande** } menu
il **menù** }
il **ristorante**, restaurant
la **trattoria**, family-type restaurant
il **conto**, bill
la **mancia**, tip

FOODS

l'**antipasto**, appetizer
l'**uovo**, egg (le **uova**, eggs)
il **formaggio**, cheese
il **burro**, butter
il **pesce**, fish
il **pollo**, chicken
la **carne**, meat
il **manzo**, beef
il **vitello**, veal
il **maiale**, pork
il **capretto**, goat
l'**agnello**, lamb
la **farina**, flour
il **pane**, bread
il **panino**, bread roll
il **brodo**, broth
la **minestra**, soup (vegetable)
la **verdura**, vegetables (leafy)
i **legumi**, vegetables (peas, potatoes, beans, etc.)
l'**insalata**, salad
l'**aceto**, vinegar
l'**olio**, oil
il **dolce**, dessert
la **frutta**, fruit
la **frutta secca**, dried fruit
le **noci**, nuts
il **gelato**, ice cream
la **torta**, cake
la **pizza**, pizza

il **riso**, rice
la **pasta**, uncooked macaroni
la **pasta asciutta**, cooked macaroni, usually covered with tomato sauce
il **sale**, salt
il **pepe**, pepper
lo **zucchero**, sugar

BEVERAGES

l'**aperitivo**, aperitif
la **bevanda**, beverage
l'**acqua minerale**, mineral water
l'**acqua**, water
l'**aranciata**, orangeade
la **birra**, beer
il **caffè**, coffee
la **cioccolata**, chocolate milk
la **crema**, cream
la **gassosa**, soft drink
il **latte**, milk
la **limonata**, lemonade
il **succo**, juice
il **tè**, tea
il **vino**, wine
il **digestivo**, bitter drink (to help digestion)

FRUITS AND VEGETABLES

l'**arancia**, orange
la **banana**, banana
la **ciliegia**, cherry
il **fico**, fig
la **fragola**, strawberry
il **limone**, lemon
la **mela**, apple
la **pera**, pear
la **pesca**, peach
la **prugna** } plum
la **susina** }
l'**uva**, grapes
i **broccoli**, broccoli
la **carota**, carrot
i **fagioli**, beans
i **fagiolini**, string beans
la **patata**, potato
i **piselli**, peas
il **pomodoro**, tomato
i **ceci**, chick-peas
la **cipolla**, onion

SHOPPING

il **supermercato**, supermarket
il **mercato**, market
il **negozio**, store
la **bottega**, small store, shop
la **macelleria**, butcher shop
il **commesso**, salesman
la **compera**, purchase
il **prezzo**, price
la **scelta**, choice
il **gusto**, taste

la **panetteria**, bake shop, bakery
la **pescheria**, fish market
la **drogheria** / il **negozio di generi alimentari** } grocery store
la **polleria**, chicken market
la **salumeria**, delicatessen
il **gran magazzino**, department store
il **mercante**, merchant
il **cliente**, customer
la **quantità**, quantity

il **chilogrammo**, kilogram (= 2.2 pounds)
la **libbra**, pound
il **metro**, meter (= 39.3 inches)
la **dozzina**, dozen
la **scatola**, box, can
il **denaro** / il **soldi** / la **moneta** } money
gli **spiccioli**, change (money)

EXERCISES

A. Choose the word or expression that best completes the sentence:

1. Per comprare la carne, vado alla (panetteria, polleria, macelleria).
2. Oggi ho mangiato una (drogheria, mela, birra).
3. Cosa c'è da bere? C'è (una fragola, un pranzo, una birra).
4. Ma cosa metti sul pane? Un po' di (ristorante, burro, mancia).
5. Invece della carne, preferisco (il pesce, la tazza, una dozzina).
6. Dopo che ho pagato ho lasciato (il commesso, la mancia, il mercato).
7. Mio nonno beve (susine, limone, vino) con i pasti.
8. Ma cosa usi per tagliare la bistecca? Uso (la forchetta, il coltello, il cucchiaio).
9. Mia madre vuole una dozzina di (uova, cena, crema).
10. Hai visto che bei biscotti vendono in quella (pescheria, polleria, panetteria)?
11. Dopo la cena, mia madre ci serve un bel (menù, pollo, dolce).
12. Con la carne, mi piace (la frutta, l'insalata, il manzo).
13. Se volete mangiare bene dovreste andare in una (drogheria, trattoria, verdura).
14. Si usa (il coltello, la forchetta, il cucchiaino) per mettere lo zucchero nel caffè.
15. Giacomo è un (mercato, commesso, pomodoro) nel negozio d'abbigliamento.

B. Translate into Italian:

1. a bottle of wine
2. a cup of coffee

3. a glass of milk
4. a dozen apples
5. a kilogram of beef
6. a tomato salad
7. five bananas
8. a box of figs
9. a plate of macaroni
10. bread and butter

C. Complete the sentences:

1. Il brodo si prende con _____ .
2. Dopo cena mangio _____ .
3. La mia carne preferita è _____ .
4. Ragazzi, mettete il latte nel _____ .
5. No, Paolo, devi usare il _____ per tagliare il pane.
6. Ho comprato questo pesce nella _____ in Via Formia.
7. Anita, pulisciti le mani con _____ .
8. Scusi, signore, vuol pagare _____ per favore?
9. Il pane si compra in una _____ .
10. Perchè non andiamo a mangiare in quel _____ ?

D. Answer the following questions in complete sentences:

1. Di che colore è il latte?
2. Dove si va per comprare del salame?
3. A che ora fai la prima colazione?
4. Cosa bevi durante i pasti?
5. Cosa si mette sulla tavola prima dei piatti e dei tovaglioli?
6. Quante libbre ci sono in un chilogrammo?
7. Come si chiama il pasto della sera?
8. Qual è la vostra frutta preferita?
9. Preferisci i piselli o le carote?
10. Cosa si lascia al cameriere dopo aver mangiato in un ristorante?

6. Personal Items

THE BODY

il **corpo**, body
la **testa**, head
i **capelli**, hair
il **viso** } face
la **faccia** } face
l'**occhio**, eye
la **fronte**, forehead
la **guancia**, cheek
la **barba**, beard
l'**orecchio**, ear
  le **orecchie** (gli **orecchi**), ears
il **naso**, nose
la **bocca**, mouth
il **labbro**, lip
  le **labbra**, lips
la **lingua**, tongue
il **dente**, tooth
il **mento**, chin
la **gola**, throat
il **collo**, neck

la **spalla**, shoulder
il **braccio**, arm
  le **braccia**, arms
il **gomito**, elbow
il **polso**, wrist
la **mano**, hand
  le **mani**, hands
il **dito**, finger
  le **dita**, fingers
la **gamba**, leg
il **ginocchio**, knee
  le **ginocchia**, knees
la **caviglia**, ankle
il **piede**, foot
il **cuore**, heart
il **dorso** } back
la **schiena** } back
lo **stomaco**, stomach
la **pelle**, skin
il **sangue**, blood

CLOTHING

i **vestiti**, clothes
gli **abiti**, suits, clothes
i **pantaloni**, pants
la **giacca**, jacket
la **camicia**, shirt
il **soprabito**, topcoat
il **cappotto**, overcoat
il **cappello**, hat
la **tasca**, pocket
la **veste**, dress
la **gonna**, skirt

il **mantello**, cape
il **golf**, sweater
il **guanto**, glove
la **scarpa**, shoe
lo **stivale**, boot
la **calza**, stocking
i **calzini**, socks
l'**impermeabile** (*m.*), raincoat
la **cravatta**, tie
la **borsa**, pocketbook
la **cintura**, belt

la **blusa** / la **camicetta**, blouse
la **sottoveste**, slip
il **fazzoletto**, handkerchief
l'**ombrello**, umbrella

HEALTH

la **salute**, health
la **forza**, strength
l'**energia**, energy
la **cura**, cure
l'**abitudine** (*f.*), habit
l'**effetto**, effect
il **sonno**, sleep
il **riposo**, rest
il **sogno**, dream
il **malato**, patient
la **malattia**, illness
il **dolore**, pain
il **raffreddore**, cold
la **febbre**, fever
il **bagno**, bath
la **doccia**, shower
il **sapone**, soap
gli **occhiali**, eyeglasses
l'**ospedale** (*m.*), hospital
la **clinica**, hospital, clinic
l'**infermiera**, nurse
il **dottore** / il **medico**, doctor
il **farmacista**, pharmacist, druggist
la **medicina**, medicine
la **ricetta**, prescription

FEELINGS

l'**allegria**, happiness
la **contentezza**, contentment
la **gioia**, joy
il **piacere**, pleasure
l'**amore** (*f.*), love
la **speranza**, hope
la **bontà**, kindness
l'**odio**, hate
la **tristezza**, sadness
la **vergogna**, shame
la **paura** / il **timore**, fear
l'**interesse** (*m.*), interest
il **dispiacere**, regret

EXERCISES

A. Match each Italian word in column I with its English meaning in column II:

Column I	*Column* II
1. il soprabito	*a.* hands
2. il riposo	*b.* shame
3. l'impermeabile	*c.* health
4. l'odio	*d.* rest
5. la bontà	*e.* shower
6. le mani	*f.* pleasure
7. la cintura	*g.* topcoat
8. la salute	*h.* soap
9. la doccia	*i.* chest
10. la camicetta	*j.* tie
11. la vergogna	*k.* hate
12. il sapone	*l.* belt
13. la cravatta	*m.* raincoat
14. il petto	*n.* blouse
15. il piacere	*o.* kindness

B. Choose the word or expression in parentheses that best completes each sentence:

1. Se fa freddo, mettiti (la cintura, il cappotto, la lingua).
2. Per parlare si deve usare (il dorso, la cravatta, la lingua).
3. Sai che piove? Prendi (l'ombrello, la cravatta, il fazzoletto).
4. Marta ha mal di (sapone, cappello, dente).
5. Questo film mi fa (carità, paura, bontà).
6. Quando è caduto si è fatto male (alle calze, ai guanti, alle braccia).
7. Pulitevi il naso con (il fazzoletto, l'ombrello, la borsa).
8. Bisogna aver fede, carità e (lingua, speranza, cravatta).
9. Invece dell'odio gli dovresti, mostrare (la lingua, l'amore, il timore).
10. Non mi sento bene. Ho (l'abitudine, la febbre, la salute).

C. Complete with appropriate words:

1. Ha mangiato molto. Ha mal di _____.
2. Se fa freddo, mettiti il _____.
3. La giacca è bella, ma i _____ sono orribili.

4. Questa _____ andrebbe bene con quella camicia.
5. Mi devo riposare perchè ho _____.
6. Giacomo, quando ti fai la doccia usa questo _____ deodorante.
7. Povero Luigi. Si è fatto male e lo hanno portato all'_____.
8. Se avete un raffreddore, prendete questa _____.
9. Non vedo tanto bene dall'_____ sinistro.
10. Nell'ospedale l'_____ ha cura dei malati.
11. È un _____ fare la Sua conoscenza.
12. Prima di metterti le scarpe, non dimenticare di metterti _____.
13. Signore, fa cattivo tempo, si metta il _____ in testa.
14. Ho regalato una _____ a mia madre.
15. Se non vuoi perdere i pantaloni, devi usare una _____.

D. Translate into Italian:

1. They do everything with much interest.
2. You (*fam. sing.*) should show her more kindness and love.
3. My neck hurts.
4. Where does he find all that energy?
5. Louise must wear glasses.
6. Michael, don't comb your hair in the kitchen!
7. It will rain later. Let's take an umbrella and a raincoat.
8. I gave my uncle a tie for his birthday.
9. There is no cure for that illness.
10. Take (*fam. pl.*) a bath instead of a shower.

E. Answer the following questions in complete sentences:

1. Cosa fai quando hai un raffreddore?
2. Cosa vi mettete quando nevica?
3. Hai paura di stare al buio?
4. Quando dormi, sogni spesso?
5. Cosa fa un farmacista?
6. Provi mai gioia?
7. Dove sono i malati?
8. Cosa prendi quando hai un dolore?
9. Dove comprate i vostri vestiti?
10. Con quale parte della faccia senti gli odori?

7. Miscellaneous Words I

OCCUPATIONS, TRADES

il **mestiere**, trade, profession
l'**operaio**, worker
il **barbiere**, barber
il **parrucchiere**, hair stylist
la **parrucchiera**, hair stylist, hairdresser
il **falegname**, carpenter
il **commerciante**, businessman
il **macellaio**, butcher
l'**autista**, driver, chauffeur
il **domestico**, butler, valet
la **domestica**, maid
il **commesso**, salesman
la **commessa**, saleswoman
l'**impiegato**, employee, office worker
il **contadino**, farmer
il **meccanico**, mechanic
il **poliziotto**, policeman
il **tipografo**, printer
il **facchino** }
il **portabagagli** } porter
il **cuoco**, chef
la **modista**, milliner, hat designer
il **sarto**, tailor
la **sarta**, dressmaker
il **cameriere**, waiter
la **cameriera**, waitress, maid
il **panettiere**, baker
il **pasticciere**, confectioner
il **calzolaio**, shoemaker
la **dattilografa**, typist
la **segretaria**, secretary
il **venditore**, vendor
il **postino**, mailman
il **muratore**, bricklayer, mason
il **manovale**, construction worker
l'**ebanista**, cabinetmaker
lo **spazzino**, garbage man
il **saldatore**, welder
l'**idraulico**, plumber

PROFESSIONS

il **pittore**, painter (of pictures)
l'**avvocato**, lawyer
il **dottore** }
il **medico** } doctor
il **dentista**, dentist
l'**ingegnere** (*m.*), engineer
il **maestro**, teacher
la **maestra**, teacher
il **professore** }
la **professoressa** } teacher, professor
l'**artista** (*m.* and *f.*), artist
lo **scienziato**, scientist
lo **scrittore**, writer
il **pilota**, pilot
il **poeta** }
la **poetessa** } poet
il **ragioniere**, accountant
il **giornalista**, news reporter
l'**infermiera**, nurse
il **giudice**, judge
il **farmacista**, pharmacist, druggist
l'**attore**, actor
l'**attrice**, actress
l'**architetto**, architect
l'**autore** (*m.*), writer, author
lo **scultore**, sculptor

SOCIAL RELATIONS

la **persona**, person
l'**amico(a)** } friend
il **compagno** } friend
la **conoscenza**, acquaintance
il **vicino**, neighbor
il **signore**, gentleman
la **signora**, lady
l'**invitato(a)**, invited guest
l'**amicizia**, friendship
la **cortesia**, courtesy
il **successo**, success
la **verità**, truth
la **bugia** } lie
la **menzogna** } lie
il **favore**, favor
la **fortuna**, luck, fortune
l'**occasione** (*f.*), opportunity, occasion
il **carattere**, disposition
il **compleanno**, birthday
l'**anniversario**, anniversary
l'**onomastico**, name day
il **regalo**, gift
la **lettera**, letter
la **foto**, photograph
l'**indirizzo**, address
l'**appuntamento**, appointment

EXERCISES

A. Match each Italian word in column I with its English meaning in column II:

Column I	*Column* II
1. l'impiegato	*a.* lie
2. il postino	*b.* courtesy
3. la menzogna	*c.* neighbor
4. l'attore	*d.* shoemaker
5. la commessa	*e.* employee
6. la cortesia	*f.* birthday
7. l'attrice	*g.* actor
8. il calzolaio	*h.* actress
9. il medico	*i.* address
10. il parrucchiere	*j.* scientist
11. il compleanno	*k.* mailman
12. lo scienziato	*l.* accountant
13. l'indirizzo	*m.* hair stylist
14. il ragioniere	*n.* doctor
15. il vicino	*o.* saleswoman

B. Choose the word that best completes the sentence:

1. (Il postino, Il medico, L'avvocato) mi porta le lettere ogni giorno.
2. Via Roma, numero 48, è (la cortesia, l'indirizzo, la verità) di Carlo Mazzi.
3. Invece di dire la verità, lei dice sempre (delle bugie, degli indirizzi, dei favori).
4. Questo quadro è stato dipinto da un famoso (farmacista, ragioniere, artista).
5. Se vuoi la medicina buona devi andare da (quello scrittore, quel farmacista, quell'avvocato).
6. Porta le scarpe dal (macellaio, farmacista, calzolaio).
7. Quando mia madre non si sente bene, va (dall'invitato, dal dottore, dal pilota).
8. Sai che scrivi bene? Potresti essere (scrittore, artista, dottore).
9. Devono chiamare (un macellaio, un contadino, un falegname) per fare costruire un armadio.
10. Maria è una buona (dattilografa, amica, commessa) perchè scrive molto bene a macchina.

C. Complete the sentences:

1. Franco è un mio _____.
2. Per Natale, Pina mi ha dato un bel _____.
3. Questo _____ guida l'aviogetto molto male.
4. Sono andato ad un _____ in Via Cerbino per quest'abito.
5. _____ ha scritto un bell'articolo nel giornale.
6. Marco, non dire una menzogna. Devi dire _____.
7. Quando siamo arrivati a casa di Laura, _____ ha aperto la porta.
8. _____ ci ha tagliati i capelli.
9. _____ ci ha portato questo pane freschissimo e caldo.
10. Il signor Pipa insegna molto bene. È un ottimo _____.

D. Translate into Italian:

1. When my tooth hurts, I go to the dentist.
2. There were ten good actresses in that film.
3. Giampiero is a chauffeur.
4. Tina is a good secretary.
5. They were neighbors of mine.
6. Friendship is the most important thing in the world.

7. We were guests at the party.
8. The nurse gave me some medicine.
9. What is your (*fam. sing.*) address?
10. We have an appointment at 8 o'clock.

E. Answer the following questions in complete sentences:

1. Chi costruisce i ponti nelle città?
2. Chi è il tuo compagno più caro?
3. Che cosa fa il dottore?
4. Il giornalista cosa fa?
5. Cosa vende una commessa?
6. Chi ti porta i bagagli al tassì?
7. Chi porta la posta a casa?
8. Chi mantiene l'ordine pubblico?
9. Come si chiama un operaio che stampa libri?
10. Se devi andare in corte, di chi hai bisogno?

Il classico *carretto siciliano* decorato con scene di avventure di crociati e Saraceni. Oggi si usa quasi esclusivamente come attrazione turistica oppure nelle sfilate.

8. Miscellaneous Words II

MEANS OF TRANSPORTATION

l'**auto** (*f.*), l'**automobile** (*f.*), la **macchina** — automobile, car
l'**aereo**, l'**aeroplano** — plane
l'**aviogetto**, jet plane
il **treno**, train
la **ferrovia**, railroad
la **nave**, ship
il **piroscafo**, steamship
il **tram**, trolley
il **filobus**, trolleybus
l'**autobus** (*m.*), bus
il **tassì**, taxi
la **metropolitana**, subway
la **bicicletta**, bicycle
la **motocicletta**, motorcycle

TRAVEL

la **gita**, il **viaggio**, — trip
la **passeggiata**, walk
l'**arrivo**, arrival
la **partenza**, departure
il **soggiorno**, stay
il **chilometro**, kilometer (=5/8 mile)
il **viaggiante**, il **viaggiatore** — traveler
la **guida**, guide
il **portabagagli**, porter
il **bagaglio**, baggage
il **giro (in macchina)**, car ride
il **baule**, trunk
la **valigia**, suitcase
il **pacco**, package
la **stazione**, station
il **biglietto**, ticket
lo **sportello**, ticket window
la **vettura**, coach (of a train)
il **vagone**, car (of a train)
l'**orario**, timetable
il **molo**, pier, dock

LEISURE, AMUSEMENTS

la **vacanza**, vacation
in **ferie**, on vacation
il **giorno libero**, day off
la **festa**, holiday
Natale (*m.*), Christmas
Pasqua, Easter
il **teatro**, theater
l'**opera**, opera
il **concerto**, concert
il **dramma**, drama, play
l'**orchestra**, orchestra
la **radio**, radio
la **musica**, music
la **canzone**, song
il **violino**, violin
il **giuoco**, game
le **carte**, playing cards
la **palla**, ball
il **giocattolo**, toy
la **bambola**, doll
lo **sport**, sport
la **pesca**, fishing

il **cinema**, movie house
il **film**, film, movie
la **commedia**, comedy, play
la **televisione**, television program
il **televisore**, televison set
il **tennis**, tennis
la **pallacanestro**, basketball
il **calcio**, soccer
il **nuoto**, swimming

TIME

il **momento**, moment
il **secondo**, second
il **minuto**, minute
l'**ora**, hour
il **giorno**, day
la **giornata**, day, daytime
il **mattino** / la **mattina** } morning
il **pomeriggio**, afternoon
la **sera** / la **serata** } evening
la **vigilia**, eve
la **notte**, night
la **settimana**, week
il **fine-settimana**, weekend
il **mese**, month
la **stagione**, season
l'**anno**, year
il **secolo**, century
la **data**, date
oggi, today
ieri, yesterday
domani, tomorrow
dopodomani, day after tomorrow
il **passato**, past
l'**avvenire** (*m.*), future

EXERCISES

A. If a statement is true, write **vero**. If a statement is false, rewrite the statement to make it true:

1. Natale è sempre in novembre.
2. Si può andare in bicicletta da New York a Roma.
3. Ci sono sette giorni in una settimana.
4. Di solito, la metropolitana è sottoterra.
5. Il giocattolo è un pasto.
6. Per prendere il treno, bisogna comprare un biglietto.
7. Il chilometro è più lungo del miglio.
8. Il giorno dopo di oggi è ieri.
9. L'estate è una stagione.
10. Ci sono settanta secondi in un minuto.

B. Choose the word or expression in parentheses that best completes the sentence:

1. Per divertirci, guardiamo (la televisione, il libro, il soggiorno).
2. Quando parto per l'Italia, faccio (il treno, le valigie, la nave).

3. Andremo al concerto (dopodomani, ieri, tre giorni fa).
4. Durante la nostra visita al museo, Filippo era (la partenza, la guida, il tram).
5. Cosa fai per (la vigilia, l'inverno, la vettura) di Natale?
6. Per il suo compleanno, gli hanno regalato (una commedia, un giocattolo, una partenza).
7. Abbiamo cantato (una canzone, un film, un dramma).
8. Pietro sa suonare (il soggiorno, le carte, il violino) molto bene.
9. Ci sono cento anni in (un giorno, un secolo, una settimana).
10. Martedì prossimo è (nell'avvenire, nel passato, nel pomeriggio).

C. Complete the sentences:

1. Il piroscafo sta partendo dal _____.
2. Scusi, signorina, a che ora è la _____ del treno?
3. La migliore parte della _____ è dalle 8 alle 10 di sera.
4. Oggi è domenica, domani è lunedì, _____ è martedì.
5. Questa Ferrari va a 100 _____ all'ora.
6. Mi dispiace, signora, ma senza il _____ non può salire in treno.
7. A teatro abbiamo riso durante l'intera _____.
8. Ogni sera faccio una _____ lungo la piazza.
9. Mi alzo presto la _____.
10. Quanti _____ ci sono in un'ora?
11. Il mio _____ preferito è il tennis.
12. Deve comprare il biglietto allo _____.
13. Se oggi è sabato, _____ era venerdì.
14. Per andare da una parte della città all'altra, si prende un _____.
15. Ho acceso la _____ per ascoltare le notizie.

D. Answer the following questions in complete sentences:

1. Che tipo di musica preferisci?
2. In che mese siamo?
3. Cosa farete dopodomani?
4. Dove si va per comprare i biglietti per il treno?
5. Cosa avete fatto ieri?
6. Vai mai al concerto? Con chi?
7. Quali programmi ti piacciono alla televisione?
8. Che lavoro fanno i portabagagli?
9. Quali sono i mezzi di trasporto della nostra città?
10. A che ora vi addormentate la sera?

9. Miscellaneous Words III

NATION, GOVERNMENT

la **nazione**, il **paese** } country, nation
la **patria**, fatherland
il **popolo**, population, people
lo **stato**, state
la **capitale**, capital
la **società**, society
il **governo**, government
la **lingua**, tongue, language
l'**abitante** (*m.* and *f.*), inhabitant
il **cittadino**, citizen (*m.*)
la **cittadina**, citizen (*f.*)
la **legge**, law
il **diritto**, right
la **libertà**, liberty
la **pace**, peace
la **democrazia**, democracy
la **repubblica**, republic
la **rivoluzione**, revolution
la **bandiera**, flag
il **capo**, leader
il **presidente**, president
il **primo ministro**, prime minister
il **re**, king
la **regina**, queen
la **corte**, court
il **senato**, senate
il **senatore**, senator
il **deputato**, representative

CITY

la **città**, city
l'**isolato**, block
il **quartiere**, section
la **strada**, la **via** } street
il **viale**, avenue
il **marciapiede**, sidewalk
il **ponte**, bridge
il **parco**, park
la **piazza**, plaza, square
la **statua**, statue
il **traffico**, la **circolazione** } traffic
la **polizia**, police
la **velocità**, speed
la **folla**, crowd
il **giornale**, newspaper
l'**industria**, industry
la **ditta**, la **compagnia** } company
l'**elettricità**, la **corrente** } electricity
il **progresso**, progress

BUILDINGS

l'**edificio**, building
il **palazzo**, mansion, palace
la **biblioteca**, library
la **banca**, bank

il **castello**, castle
la **torre**, tower
la **cattedrale**, cathedral
la **chiesa**, church
l'**albergo**, hotel
la **fabbrica**, factory
il **grattacielo**, skyscraper
la **posta** / l'**ufficio postale**, post office
il **muro**, exterior wall, wall of a city
l'**entrata**, entrance
l'**uscita**, exit

MATERIALS

l'**acciaio**, steel
l'**alluminio**, aluminum
l'**argento**, silver
il **carbone**, coal
il **cotone**, cotton
il **cuoio**, leather
il **ferro**, iron
la **gomma**, rubber
la **lana**, wool
il **legno**, wood
il **lino**; linen
il **mattone**, brick
il **merletto**, lace
il **metallo**, metal
il **nailon**, nylon
l'**oro**, gold
l'**ottone** (*m.*), brass
la **pelliccia**, fur
la **pietra**, stone
il **rame**, copper
la **seta**, silk
il **vetro**, glass

COLORS

arancione, orange
azzurro, (sky) blue
bianco, white
blu, blue
giallo, yellow
grigio, gray
marrone, brown
nero, black
rosa, pink
rosso, red
verde, green
viola, violet

Note

Arancione, **marrone**, **blu**, and **viola** are invariable in the singular and the plural.

EXERCISES

A. Match each Italian word in column I with its English meaning in column II:

Column I	*Column* II
1. giallo	*a.* sidewalk
2. il viale	*b.* exit
3. la bandiera	*c.* gray
4. il merletto	*d.* avenue
5. il marciapiede	*e.* crowd
6. la pace	*f.* liberty
7. la folla	*g.* iron
8. grigio	*h.* yellow
9. il ferro	*i.* traffic
10. la lingua	*j.* citizen
11. l'uscita	*k.* tongue
12. viola	*l.* lace
13. la libertà	*m.* peace
14. la cittadina	*n.* violet
15. la circolazione	*o.* flag

B. Translate into Italian:

1. the gray church
2. the blue glass
3. the Italian government
4. the red metal
5. the American citizen
6. the white wool
7. the black coal
8. the narrow streets
9. a quiet city
10. the industrial revolution
11. the pink lace
12. Here's the English prime minister.
13. He's a French senator.
14. liberty and peace
15. the capital of the state

C. Choose the word or expression that best completes the sentence:

1. Vicino al porto di New York, c'è una (ditta, statua, legge) della libertà.
2. Di solito le nuvole sono (azzurre, bianche, verdi).
3. Se abito in un paese sono (un cittadino, una chiesa, un governo).
4. Il marito della regina è il (deputato, senatore, re).
5. Devo depositare del denaro nella (torre, bandiera, banca).
6. Facciamo una passeggiata per la (piazza, posta, torre).

7. L'anello di Rosa è fatto di (lana, oro, merletto).
8. L'Italia è (una città, un'industria, un paese).
9. Il rapido è arrivato alla (stazione, cattedrale, gomma).
10. Che bel cappotto di (marmo, ferro, pelliccia)!
11. Quando andiamo a Torino, abitiamo sempre in (una chiesa, un albergo, una biblioteca).
12. La camicia che ho comprato è fatta di (mattoni, carbone, cotone).
13. Bisogna camminare (sul marciapiede, sull'edificio, sul grattacielo).
14. Il giudice si trova (in corte, nella torre, nella statua).
15. Roma è la (società, capitale, piazza) d'Italia.

D. Use the following words in the sentences below. Each word may be used only once:

corrente	castello
rossa	fabbrica
lana	ponte
lingua	cattedrale
presidente	uscita

1. Dove hai comprato quell'abito di _____ ?
2. Il _____ americano viene eletto per quattro anni.
3. Hai visto che bei mosaici ci sono in quella _____ ?
4. Il duca di Windsor abita in un bellissimo _____ .
5. Signore, esca da questa _____ a sinistra.
6. Mio zio lavora in una _____ di Chicago.
7. Sai che passa molta _____ per questo filo?
8. Bisogna attraversare il _____ per andare dall'altra parte del fiume.
9. Che bella candela _____ !
10. Per me l'italiano è la più bella _____ del mondo.

10. Miscellaneous Words IV

COUNTRYSIDE

la **campagna** } countryside
il **paesaggio** }
il **campo**, field
il **bosco**, woods
la **foresta**, forest
la **sabbia**, sand
l'**albero**, tree
la **foglia**, leaf
la **pianta**, plant
l'**erba**, grass
il **fiore**, flower
la **rosa**, rose
il **garofano**, carnation
il **grano**, wheat
la **pioggia**, rain
la **neve**, snow
il **ghiaccio**, ice
l'**aria**, air
il **vento**, wind
il **cielo**, sky
la **stella**, star
il **sole**, sun
la **luna**, moon
l'**ombra**, shadow
la **fontana**, fountain
la **veduta**, view

ANIMALS

l'**animale** (*m.*), animal
il **cane**, dog
il **gatto**, cat
il **cavallo**, horse
la **vacca** } cow
la **mucca** }
il **bue**, ox
la **capra**, goat
il **porco**, pig
la **pecora**, sheep
l'**agnello**, lamb
il **vitello**, calf
l'**asino**, donkey
l'**uccello**, bird
il **gallo**, rooster
la **gallina**, hen
il **coniglio**, rabbit
il **leone**, lion
la **tigre**, tiger
la **volpe**, fox
il **lupo**, wolf
l'**elefante** (*m.*), elephant
la **coda**, tail
l'**ala**, wing
il **nido**, nest

GEOGRAPHY

la **geografia**, geography
il **mondo**, world
la **terra**, earth, land
la **collina**, hill
la **spiaggia**, beach
il **deserto**, desert

lo **spazio**, space
il **tempo**, time
l'**oceano**, ocean
il **mare**, sea
il **fiume**, river
il **ruscello**, brook
il **lago**, lake
la **montagna**, mountain
la **costa**, coast
la **riva**, shore, bank
l'**isola**, island
la **penisola**, peninsula
la **regione**, region
la **provincia**, province
il **villaggio**, village
il **porto**, port

EXERCISES

A. If a statement is true, write **vero.** If a statement is false, rewrite the statement to make it true:

1. La gallina ci dà le uova.
2. La vacca è un animale ferocissimo.
3. Si vede il sole di notte.
4. Il pane si fa col grano.
5. C'è tanta acqua nel deserto.
6. La Toscana è una regione italiana.
7. La rosa è un'erba.
8. La pecora è la regina della foresta.
9. Gli uccelli dormono nei loro nidi.
10. L'Italia è un'isola.

B. Choose the word or expression that best completes each sentence:

1. Il lupo ha (le ali, la coda, le piume).
2. Il Mediterraneo è un (mare, oceano, fiume).
3. Le stelle sono (nel nido, nel cielo, nel deserto).
4. Durante il mese di aprile, c'è sempre (molta neve, molto ghiaccio, molta pioggia).
5. (Il cane, L'elefante, Il lupo) è un animale domestico.
6. Ci sono molti alberi verdi (nella foresta, nel deserto, nel mare).
7. Il latte viene (dalla mucca, dal coniglio, dalla gallina).
8. Il garofano è (un vaso, una foglia, un fiore).
9. Mi piace nuotare (nello spazio, nell'erba, nel lago).
10. Stanotte non si vede (la luna, la coda, il vento).
11. I nostri amici abitano in un (villaggio, porto, fiume).
12. Da questa montagna c'è una bella (regione, veduta, gallina).

C. Complete the following sentences:

1. Durante il mese di marzo, c'è molto _____ .
2. Marco è caduto sul _____ davanti a casa sua.
3. Che acqua limpida che scende da quella _____ !
4. Il mio animale preferito è _____ .
5. L'Atlantico è un grande _____ .
6. La Sardegna non è una penisola; è un'_____ .
7. Dopo che nuoto, mi sdraio sulla _____ .
8. Vedi quell'_____ come vola fra gli alberi!
9. Abbiamo fatto un picnic in _____ .
10. Sediamoci all' _____ di quest'albero.

D. Answer the following questions in complete sentences:

1. Quando fa cattivo tempo, cosa cade dal cielo?
2. Di giorno, da dove viene la luce?
3. Quali sono quattro animali della foresta?
4. Quali sono alcuni animali che si mangiano?
5. Quali sono cinque regioni italiane?
6. Come si chiamano due grandi isole italiane?
7. Dove preferisci nuotare?

11. Miscellaneous Words V

SCHOOL

la **scuola**, school
il **liceo**, state secondary school
il **cortile**, courtyard
la **campana** } bell
il **campanello** } bell
l'**orologio**, clock
il **direttore**, principal
il **preside**, principal, dean
il **professore**, teacher, professor
il **maestro**, teacher
il **bidello**, custodian
l'**ufficio**, office
la **classe**, class
l'**allievo(a)** } student, pupil
l'**alunno(a)** } student, pupil
lo **studente**, student (*m.*)
la **studentessa**, student (*f.*)

CLASSROOM

l'**aula**, classroom
la **scrivania**, teacher's desk
il **banco**, student's desk
la **lavagna**, chalkboard
la **cimosa**, chalkboard eraser
la **carta geografica**, map
il **cestino**, wastepaper basket
la **riga**, ruler
il **gesso**, chalk
l'**inchiostro**, ink
la **penna**, pen
la **matita**, pencil
la **carta**, paper

LESSON

la **lezione**, lesson
il **lavoro**, work
il **libro**, book
il **quaderno**, notebook
il **dizionario** } dictionary
il **vocabolario** } dictionary
la **spiegazione**, explanation
l'**esercizio**, exercise
il **compito**, homework
la **pagina**, page
la **linea**, line
la **frase**, sentence
la **parola**, word
il **proverbio**, proverb
la **lettura**, reading
il **romanzo**, novel
la **novella**, short story
la **storia**, history, story
la **poesia**, poetry, poem
la **grammatica**, grammar
il **vocabolario**, vocabulary
la **domanda**, question
la **risposta**, answer
l'**esempio**, example
l'**esame** (*m.*), exam
lo **sbaglio**, mistake
il **voto**, grade
la **pagella**, report card

EXERCISES

A. Match each Italian word in column I with its English meaning in column II:

Column I	*Column* II
1. il cestino	*a.* chalkboard eraser
2. l'inchiostro	*b.* explanation
3. la parola	*c.* chalkboard
4. la riga	*d.* wastebasket
5. il preside	*e.* bell
6. la scrivania	*f.* chalk
7. la cimosa	*g.* clock
8. la spiegazione	*h.* pupil
9. l'aula	*i.* principal
10. la lavagna	*j.* word
11. il gesso	*k.* classroom
12. l'orologio	*l.* question
13. il campanello	*m.* desk
14. la domanda	*n.* ink
15. l'alunno	*o.* ruler

B. Choose the word or expression in parentheses that best completes the sentence:

1. Devo scrivere una lettera. Dammi una (riga, penna, cimosa).
2. Aprite i libri (a pagina, alla lavagna, alla pagella) nove.
3. Lo scrittore ha scritto (una carta geografica, una novella, una matita).
4. Hanno suonato (la pagina, il cestino, il campanello).
5. Carlo, metti i tuoi libri (sul banco, sulla lettura, sul gesso).
6. Guarda (il quaderno, l'inchiostro, l'orologio) e dimmi che ore sono.
7. Cancella la lavagna con (la matita, la penna, la cimosa).
8. Si scrive alla lavagna con (il gesso, la riga, l'inchiostro).
9. (L'esame, La cimosa, La carta geografica) di fisica era difficile.
10. Ho letto (un voto, un ufficio, una novella) molto interessante.

C. Use the following words in the sentences below. Each word may be used only once:

sbagli	cortile	storia	parola
studentessa	domanda	carta	riga
frase	pagella	lavagna	orologio

1. Dovete scrivere una _____ completa.
2. Se vuoi disegnare bene devi usare la _____ .
3. Mi dispiace, Michele, ma ci sono troppi _____ su questo foglio.
4. I ragazzi stanno giocando nel _____ .
5. Se non sai la risposta, perchè non fai una _____ in classe?
6. Che ora indica _____ ?
7. Gianna è la migliore _____ di questa classe.
8. Non mi piace studiare la _____ della Francia.
9. I voti su questa _____ sono pessimi.
10. Mi presti un foglio di _____ ?
11. Il professore mi manda alla _____ per scrivere la risposta.
12. Non sanno il significato di questa _____ .

D. Answer the following questions in complete sentences:

1. Qual' è il vostro romanzo preferito?
2. Chi è il preside di questa scuola?
3. Cosa usi per scrivere una lettera ad un amico?
4. Cosa metti nel cestino di solito?
5. Perchè guardate l'orologio quando siete in classe?
6. Come si chiama il vostro professore (la vostra professoressa) d'italiano?
7. Perchè consulti il dizionario?

***Castel Sant'Angelo*, antico castello papale, con il ponte degli Angeli che attraversa il fiume Tevere. Oggi il castello è uno dei musei più importanti della città di Roma.**

12. Mastery Exercises

A. Write an appropriate opposite word for each of the following words:

Example: nuovo, vecchio
caldo, freddo

1. poco
2. debole
3. l'amore
4. grasso
5. la donna
6. alzarsi
7. il re
8. giovane
9. allontanarsi
10. la campagna
11. morire
12. difficile
13. su
14. il sud
15. brutta
16. dare
17. chiuso
18. la notte
19. davanti
20. domani

B. Write an appropriate synonym for each of the following words:

Example: affetto, amore
finire, terminare

1. rientrare
2. la lotta
3. simile
4. presso
5. andare su
6. l'amore
7. antico
8. mettersi a
9. lo sbaglio
10. serio
11. dopo
12. supplicare
13. la rabbia
14. il posto
15. famoso
16. la moglie
17. il demonio
18. uccidere
19. l'avvenimento
20. l'edificio

C. Choose the word that does *not* belong in each group:

1. padre, madre, salotto, cugino
2. tiretto, tappeto, moglie, specchio
3. giardino, scuola, bagno, banane
4. carne, riso, zucchero, divano
5. birra, ciliegia, mela, pesca
6. tè, cioccolata, latte, manzo
7. faccia, gonna, orecchio, ginocchio
8. allegria, odio, bontà, cravatta
9. drogheria, salumeria, paura, macelleria
10. penna, avvocato, medico, dentista
11. aereo, treno, nave, televisore
12. salute, pelle, febbre, dolore
13. pollo, vitello, agnello, pomodoro

14. sorella, divano, letto, comodino
15. insalata, carne, dolce, acqua
16. parco, nazione, governo, legge
17. chiesa, cattedrale, castello, giornale
18. azzurro, giallo, bianco, ferro
19. cane, gatto, carne, cavallo
20. scuola, isola, pagella, gesso
21. montagna, oceano, regione, casa
22. albero, foglia, fiore, elefante
23. gallo, lago, mare, oceano
24. alluminio, ottone, rame, nido
25. appetito, cibo, ristorante, sonno

D. In each group, choose the two words that have the same meaning:

1. stanza, faccia, palazzo, viso, operaio
2. ammazzare, aspettare, andare fuori, uccidere, arrivare
3. scendere, uscire, andare fuori, salire, cominciare
4. sposo, diavolo, marito, maestro, medico
5. illustre, poco, molto, celebre, antico
6. alunna, madre, figlio, studentessa, sedia
7. servirsi di, finire, iniziare, attendere, usare
8. differente, simile, paura, timore, ira
9. ovest, oriente, meridione, settentrione, occidente
10. allegro, scontento, gentile, morbido, triste
11. amico, zio, giovane, compagno, alunno
12. lasciare, andarsene, arrivare, partire, mangiare
13. iniziare, pulire, capire, comprendere, coprire
14. ritratto, paese, fotografia, manzo, frutta
15. operaio, piede, affetto, faccia, amore
16. contento, grave, simpatico, serio, mediocre
17. camminare, passeggiare, rispondere, trovare, svegliarsi
18. pantaloni, camicetta, blusa, giacca, cappello
19. lentamente, rapidamente, bene, subito, cortesemente
20. alzare, mettere, dormire, elevare, nascere

E. Choose the word or expression in parentheses that best completes each sentence:

1. La mattina mi lavo (la stanza, la faccia, i libri).
2. D'estate ci piace andare in (albero, campagna, salone).

3. Si va dal macellaio per comprare (patate, carne, carta).
4. Andranno in California (ieri, dopodomani, l'anno scorso).
5. Giorgio ha depositato del denaro in una (folla, banca, biblioteca).
6. Mi faceva male il dente; allora sono andato (dal panettiere, dal dentista, dall'avvocato).
7. Quando piove, si mette (la tasca, il fazzoletto, l'impermeabile).
8. Tra le bevande preferite c'è (l'arancia, la limonata, il pane).
9. Le galline fanno (il formaggio, l'insalata, le uova).
10. Mia madre mette i vestiti (nel frigorifero, nell'armadio, sulla lampada).
11. Tra una camera e l'altra c'è (la parete, il sole, la verità).
12. Quando fa bel tempo, c'è sempre (la pioggia, il sole, la neve).
13. Sul gelato mettiamo (delle fragole, del pesce, del brodo).
14. Non sente bene perchè gli fanno male (le labbra, le orecchie, le dita).
15. Per farmi tagliare i capelli, vado (dal parrucchiere, dalla modista, dal falegname).

F. Choose the English word that best translates each Italian word:

1. forte	weak, fort, strong, building
2. poltrona	sofa, armchair, den, door
3. pesca	fish, pear, lamb, peach
4. denti	teeth, cup, hat, legs
5. verdura	rice, soup, vegetables, meat
6. carne	dog, meat, dessert, cream
7. gusto	taste, skin, potato, wind
8. cappotto	hat, hair, coat, dress
9. gioventù	old age, boy, girl, youth
10. snello	fat, tall, thin, short
11. senza	on, under, with, without
12. destra	behind, left, in front of, right
13. soffitto	roof, ceiling, floor, wall
14. odio	hate, love, happiness, sadness
15. paura	shame, hope, fear, joy
16. scrittore	actor, writer, lawyer, teacher
17. sarta	designer, dressmaker, tailor, waitress
18. ferie	iron, vacation, game, play
19. valigia	trunk, ship, suitcase, car
20. pomeriggio	noon, morning, evening, afternoon
21. deputato	king, senator, representative, leader
22. albergo	home, hotel, cathedral, tower

23. oro — water, gold, wool, glass
24. foglia — sheet, crowd, leaf, madness
25. lavagna — chalkboard, chalk, eraser, washroom

G. Choose the Italian word that best translates each English word:

1. mistake — orrore, sbaglio, minestra, ora
2. homework — compiti, casa, costo, cavallo
3. happy — celebre, felice, buono, cattivo
4. soft — molto, poco, duro, morbido
5. east — oriente, ponente, settentrione, meridione
6. chair — sito, sedia, sera, serenata
7. bed — lavoro, luce, letto, lotta
8. cry — piovere, piangere, piegare, pregare
9. nothing — nulla, neanche, nessuno, non
10. wine — mela, vino, mucca, velo
11. clean — pepe, patata, parco, pulito
12. love — amico, amore, lana, lampada
13. win — perdere, promettere, venire, vincere
14. under — sopra, su, sotto, sono
15. old — antico, nuovo, giovane, chiuso
16. ugly — simpatico, bello, sincero, brutto
17. worse — meglio, cattivo, peggiore, minore
18. always — sempre, mai, nemmeno, mica
19. restaurant — pensione, lista, trattoria, palazzo
20. shirt — calze, cappello, capello, camicia
21. cheek — palma, dito, guancia, labbro
22. ship — aereo, nave, macchina, ponte
23. nest — nido, neve, cesto, costa
24. grass — grattacielo, erba, fiore, albero
25. word — uomo, palpebra, parola, donna
26. city — campo, campagna, città, cielo
27. sweet — amaro, dolce, bello, brutto
28. break — comprare, mettere, prendere, rompere
29. near — preso, presso, penso, paura
30. easy — dolce, difficile, facile, leggero
31. health — salame, salute, salsa, succo
32. lie — menzogna, luce, mento, lana
33. mailman — mela, posta, postino, monte
34. winter — pioggia, primavera, inverno, neve
35. Christmas — Pasqua, Capodanno, Natale, Epifania

36. doll — bomba, bambola, bambina, bacio
37. hour — oro, giorno, sera, ora
38. year — anno, mese, ora, settimana
39. bridge — pane, ponte, polso, posto
40. sun — sale, sole, solo, sulla
41. lamb — anello, agnello, maiale, gallina
42. egg — vuoto, uva, uovo, uomo
43. tall — corto, alto, magro, snello
44. living room — bagno, soffitto, salotto, cucina
45. wait — ascoltare, aspettare, pesare, misurare
46. ice cream — pane, dolce, gelato, torta
47. expensive — a buon mercato, economico, caro, grande
48. lose — prendere, mettere, trovare, perdere
49. woman — uomo, figlia, donna, dono
50. happening — edificio, evento, angustia, paese

Il Duomo **di Milano. Questa famosa basilica è l'unica chiesa totalmente gotica costruita in Italia.**

Part V—Civilization

1. La Geografia dell'Italia

INTRODUZIONE

L'Italia, chiamata popolarmente "il Paese del Sole" o "il Bel Paese," è una penisola situata al sud dell'Europa. Lo Stivale–così soprannominata (*nick-named*) perchè la sua forma fisica rappresenta un lungo stivale–è situato essenzialmente nel Mar Mediterraneo, bagnato dal Mar Ligure e dal Mar Tirreno lungo la costa occidentale, e dal Mare Adriatico e dal Mare Ionio lungo la costa orientale. Le Alpi, catene di montagne situate al nord, separano l'Italia dal resto dell'Europa.

SUPERFICIE (*AREA*), ABITANTI, CLIMA

L'Italia è un paese relativamente piccolo. Equivale in dimensione agli stati della Georgia e della Florida messi insieme. Ha una superficie totale di 301,054 chilometri quadrati (*square kilometers*) (116,300 miglia quadrate) con una lunghezza di circa 1400 chilometri (760 miglia), e una larghezza di 170 Km. (100 miglia) al punto più largo. L'Italia ha una popolazione di circa 58,000,000 abitanti, un po' troppi per una nazione così piccola.

La penisola è situata nella zona temperata, ma il clima è variabile da nord a sud. Nel nord, il clima è quasi come quello del nord degli Stati Uniti. Quello di Milano, per esempio, è più o meno come quello di New York, mentre il clima del Trentino è come quello dello stato del Colorado. Queste zone nordiche sono pregiatissime (*highly regarded*) per gli sport invernali, specialmente sulle alte cime delle Alpi.

Al centro, il clima è più mite. L'inverno è freddo, ma c'è poca neve. Vi sono invece dei lunghi periodi di pioggia nei mesi di dicembre, gennaio, e febbraio.

Al sud, il clima è prevalentemente mite anche durante l'inverno. La temperatura raramente scende al di sotto dei 7 gradi centigradi (45 gradi Fahrenheit). (In Italia, si usa il sistema centigrado per misurare la temperatura.) L'estate, invece, è caldissima, ma con poca umidità. Il clima dell'Italia del sud si può paragonare a quello della California.

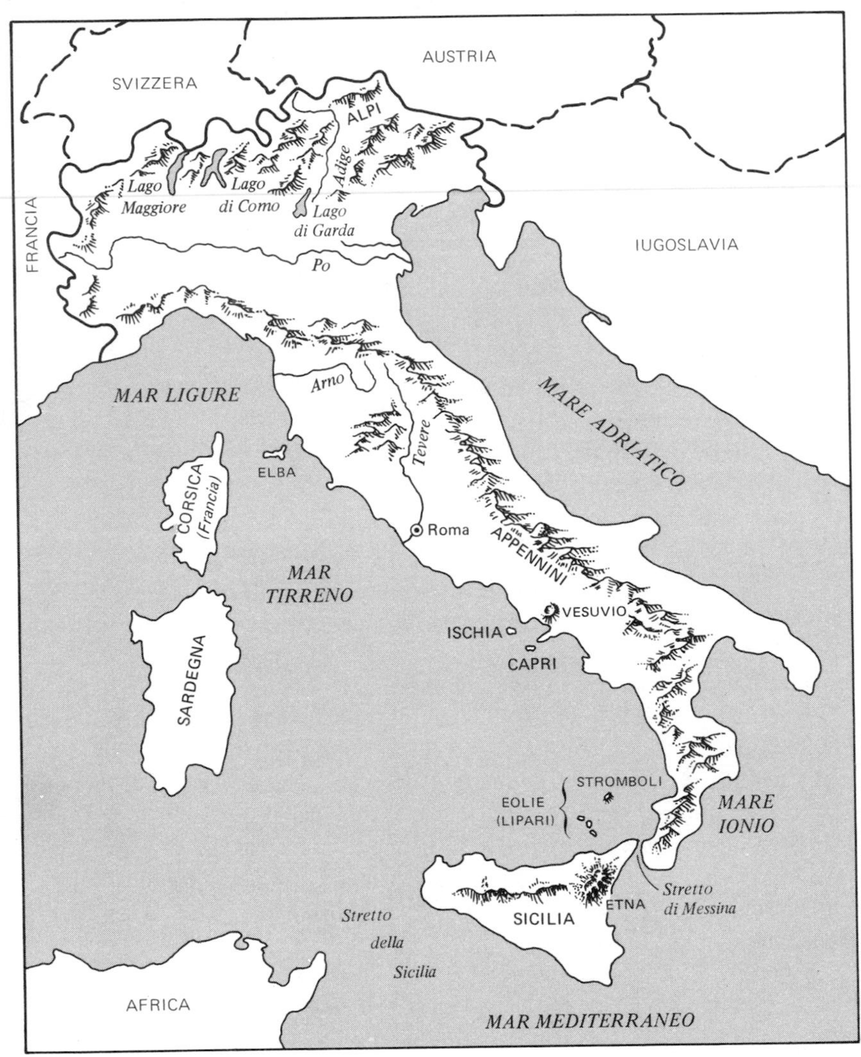

CATENE DI MONTAGNE E CIME PRINCIPALI

L'Italia ha due catene di montagne: **le Alpi**, che servono da frontiera naturale al nord e separano la penisola all'occidente dalla Francia, al nord dalla Svizzera, all'oriente dall'Austria e dalla Iugoslavia; **gli Appennini**, che attraversano l'Italia da nord a sud, a forma di "spina dorsale" (*spinal column*), e finiscono in Sicilia.

1. **Il Monte Rosa**, situato nella Val (Valle) d'Aosta, è alto 4,638 metri (15,000 piedi) ed è la cima più alta delle Alpi italiane.

2. **Il Gran Sasso**, situato nell'Abruzzo, è alto 2,914 metri (9,554 piedi).

3. **Il Monte Bianco**, la cima più alta dell'Europa, è ai confini della Francia con l'Italia.

4. **Il Monte Cervino** (*Matterhorn*), altra montagna altissima, è ai confini tra l'Italia e la Svizzera; si trova, però, in territorio svizzero.

FIUMI E LAGHI

I fiumi principali italiani sono quattro:

1. **Il Po**, che attraversa il Piemonte, la Lombardia, il Veneto, e poi sbocca (*flows*) nel Mare Adriatico, è il fiume più lungo dell'Italia. Si estende per 652 chilometri (420 miglia). Le regioni che vengono bagnate da questo fiume sono fertilissime.

2. **Il Tevere**, che attraversa l'Umbria, il Lazio, passa per Roma, e poi sbocca nel Mar Tirreno, è lungo 405 chilometri (250 miglia).

3. **L'Adige**, che passa per il Trentino e per il Veneto e poi sbocca nel Mare Adriatico, è lungo 410 chilometri (230 miglia).

4. **L'Arno**, che attraversa la Toscana, passa per Pisa e Firenze, e sbocca nel Mar Ligure, è lungo 241 chilometri (150 miglia).

Tre fiumi, meno importanti, formano *i laghi* principali dell'Italia. **Il Ticino** forma **il Lago Maggiore**, situato tra il Piemonte e la Lombardia. **L'Adda** forma **il Lago di Como**, situato nella Lombardia. **Il Mincio-Sarca** forma **il Lago di Garda**. Quest'ultimo è il più grande lago dell'Italia ed è situato tra la Lombardia e il Veneto.

VULCANI

In Italia ci sono tre vulcani che sono ancora attivi:

1. **Il Vesuvio**, che dà sul golfo di Napoli.

2. **Lo Stromboli**, sull'isola Stromboli, la quale fa parte del gruppo delle Isole Eolie (Lipari) che si trovano vicino alla Sicilia.

3. **L'Etna**, in Sicilia, è il più grande e il più attivo.

ISOLE, STRETTI, GOLFI

L'Italia è circondata da molte isole situate specialmente all'ovest e al sud della penisola. Le più grandi sono:

La Sicilia, nel Mediterraneo, e **la Sardegna,** nel Mar Tirreno. Tra le isole più piccole, ma note, ci sono: **l'Isola d'Elba,** nel Mar Tirreno, lungo la costa toscana; **le Isole Eolie (Lipari),** nel Mar Tirreno, vicino alla Sicilia; le isole di **Capri** ed **Ischia,** nel Mar Tirreno, vicino Napoli.

Lo Stretto di Messina separa la Sicilia dal Continente, mentre la Sicilia è separata dal Nord Africa dallo **Stretto della Sicilia,** che fa parte del Mediterraneo.

L'Italia è ricca di golfi. I più importanti sono: **il Golfo di Genova,** con le bellissime spiagge della "Riviera ligure"; **il Golfo di Venezia,** con la città galleggiante di Venezia e le isole di Murano, Burano, e Torcello; **il Golfo di Napoli,** con le spiagge di Sorrento, Positano, ed Amalfi; ed **il Golfo di Taranto,** con le sue bellissime spiagge ioniche.

EXERCISES

A. Match the numbers on the map with each of the following:

1. l'Arno
2. il Lago di Como
3. gli Appennini
4. il Po
5. l'Etna
6. il Tevere
7. l'Adige
8. il Lago di Garda
9. il Vesuvio
10. il Lago Maggiore

B. Match the letters on the map with each of the following:

1. Capri
2. Sicilia
3. Mar Ligure
4. Mar Tirreno
5. Stretto di Messina
6. Elba
7. Mare Adriatico
8. Stromboli
9. Sardegna
10. Mare Ionio

C. Complete the sentences:

1. L'Italia ha la forma di _____.
2. _____ separano l'Italia dal resto dell'Europa.
3. L'Italia ha una superficie di _____ chilometri quadrati.
4. L'Italia ha un clima prevalentemente _____.
5. Gli Appennini attraversano la penisola da _____.

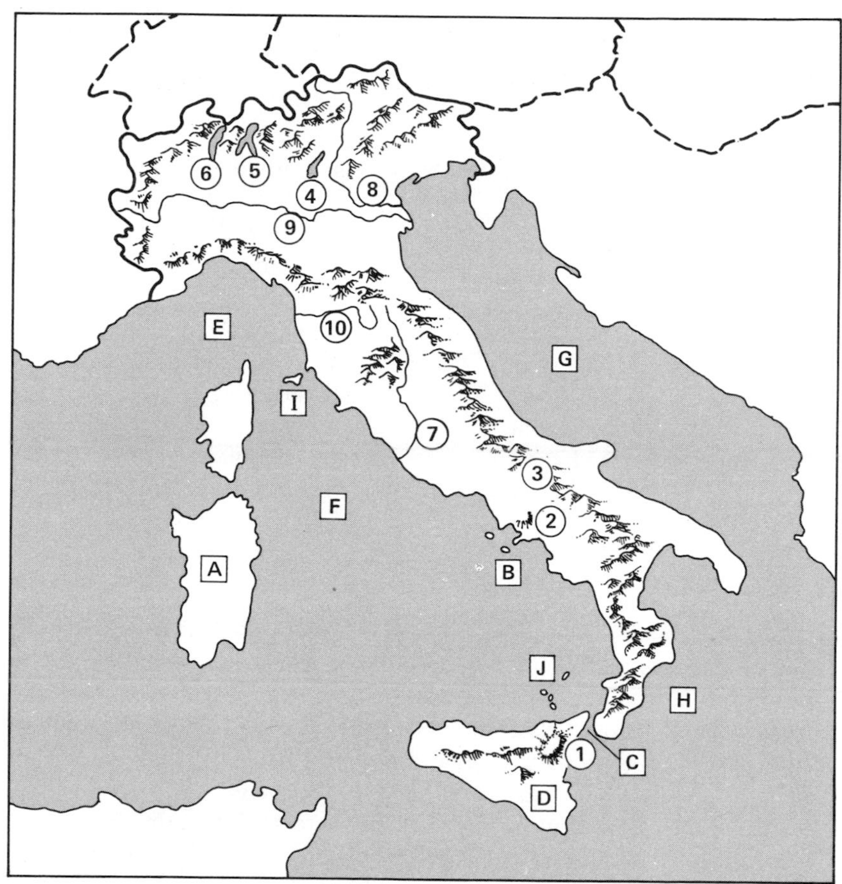

6. L'Italia ha una popolazione di _____ abitanti.
7. La montagna altissima situata negli Abruzzi si chiama _____.
8. Il monte tra la Francia e l'Italia è il _____.
9. L'Italia è chiamata "il Paese del Sole" o _____.
10. Le Isole Eolie sono situate vicino alla _____.
11. Il Monte Etna è _____.
12. Il Tevere passa per la città di _____.
13. L'Italia è circondata dai mari: _____, _____, _____, _____.
14. I tre laghi situati in Lombardia sono: _____, _____, _____.
15. Il fiume più lungo della penisola è _____.
16. L'Arno passa per la città di _____ e sbocca nel Mar _____.
17. Lo stretto che separa la penisola dalla Sicilia si chiama _____.

18. La "Riviera ligure" è sul golfo di _____.
19. La Sardegna è nel Mar _____.
20. L'isola di Murano è situata nel golfo di _____.

D. Match each item in column I with its description in column II:

Column I	*Column* II
1. Mediterraneo	*a.* fiume
2. Sardegna	*b.* isola
3. Maggiore	*c.* porto
4. Ticino	*d.* golfo principale
5. Taranto	*e.* mare
6. Messina	*f.* monte
7. Italia	*g.* penisola
8. Appennini	*h.* stretto
9. Rosa	*i.* montagne
10. Napoli	*j.* lago

E. Complete the following paragraph in Italian:

L'estate prossima farò un viaggio in Europa. Andrò prima in Francia e poi attraverserò la frontiera italiana, passando __1__, le montagne che separano l'Italia dalla Francia. Alla frontiera potrò vedere __2__, la cima più alta dell'Europa. Viaggerò in treno fino a Napoli. Il treno passerà lungo l'altra catena di montagne, __3__, che forma la "spina dorsale" della penisola italiana. Prima di arrivare a Napoli mi fermerò a Firenze per ammirare il fiume __4__ e poi a Roma per vedere il fiume __5__. Una volta giunto a Napoli potrò finalmente visitare __6__, vulcano che dà sul __7__, e le isole di __8__ e __9__, che sono vicine alla città di Napoli.

F. Identify each item with a short sentence in Italian:

1. lo Stivale
2. il Gran Sasso
3. l'Adige
4. l'Etna
5. l'Elba
6. le Eolie
7. lo Stromboli
8. la Sardegna
9. la "Riviera ligure"
10. il Lago Maggiore
11. l'Adriatico
12. il Po
13. l'Adda
14. Murano
15. Sorrento

2. Divisione Geografica e Regioni

L'Italia è divisa in tre parti: (1) **l'Italia settentrionale** o del nord, (2) **l'Italia centrale**, e (3) **l'Italia meridionale** o del sud. L'Italia meridionale è anche conosciuta col nome di "il Mezzogiorno." Politicamente, la penisola è divisa in 20 **regioni** le quali sono poi suddivise (*subdivided*) in **province**. Ogni regione ha il suo capoluogo (*capital or leading city*) che quasi sempre è anche il capoluogo della provincia in cui si trova. Cioè, ogni regione ed ogni provincia ha una città o paese principale.

LE REGIONI

Le regioni dell'Italia settentrionale sono otto:

1. **Il Piemonte**, situato al nord-ovest della penisola, ai confini della Francia, è noto per i suoi ritrovi invernali (*winter resorts*) e per le sue industrie, in particolare quella meccanica che produce: le macchine FIAT, aerei, motori per marina, ecc. L'industria tessile (*textile*) è anche importante in questa regione. Il Piemonte è fertilissimo e produce dei vini squisitissimi, fra cui lo **spumante**, lo "champagne" italiano. Torino, il capoluogo, è una delle più belle città d'Italia ed è anche una delle città importanti per la moda italiana.

2. **La Valle d'Aosta**, anche a nord-ovest, è un paradiso per i tifosi (*fans or followers*) degli sport invernali. Ha numerose centrali idroelettriche (*hydroelectric stations*) che forniscono energia alle fabbriche di acciaio (*steel*). Il capoluogo di questa regione è Aosta.

3. **La Liguria**, situata lungo la costa nord-ovest dell'Italia, forma un arco intorno al Mar Ligure e ci dà la bella "Riviera ligure" o "Riviera italiana" con le sue spiagge bellissime. Questa regione, il cui capoluogo è Genova, primo porto d'Italia, è molto industriale ed è il centro dell'industria marittima italiana con molti cantieri navali (*shipyards*).

4. **La Lombardia**, situata direttamente al nord, ai confini della Svizzera, è la regione più ricca del paese. Milano, il suo capoluogo, ha quasi due milioni di abitanti. La regione è essenzialmente industriale e agricola. I suoi tre laghi (Maggiroe, Como, Garda) sono pregiatissimi posti di villeggiatura sia per gli Italiani che per gli stranieri.

5. **Il Trentino-Alto Adige** è la regione nel nord-est dell'Italia che confina con l'Austria. Famosa per i suoi vini deliziosi e per la sua grande produzione

Questa carta geografica può essere utile per completare alcuni esercizi nelle lezioni 2, 3, 4, 5.

agricola, questa regione una volta apparteneva all'Austria. Il suo capoluogo è Trento dove si parlano due lingue: l'italiano e il tedesco.

6. **Il Veneto** è famoso per il suo capoluogo, Venezia, chiamata la "Serenissima." Ci sono inoltre altre bellissime città medioevali come Padova e Verona. Questa è una regione essenzialmente agricola, che produce anche dei vini molto buoni.

7. La regione più orientale dell'Italia è **il Friuli-Venezia Giulia.** Questa è una zona agricola e industriale. Trieste, il capoluogo, è importante per i suoi cantieri navali. Una grande parte degli elettrodomestici (*small appliances*) italiani sono manifatturati nel Friuli.

8. **L'Emilia-Romagna** è tra le più ricche zone agricole dell'Italia. Produce cereali, frutta, barbabietole da zucchero (*sugar beets*), formaggi, vini eccellenti, e carne saporosissima. Bologna, capoluogo dell'Emilia, è chiamata "dotta" a causa della sua università antica e "grassa" perchè è anche la capitale gastronomica italiana. La regione è al centro dell'Italia settentrionale.

EXERCISES

A. Complete the following sentences:

1. L'Italia è divisa in _____ regioni.
2. _____ è il capoluogo dell'Emilia.
3. Le fabbriche FIAT sono situate nel _____.
4. La "Riviera ligure" si trova nella _____.
5. La "Serenissima" è un altro nome per _____.
6. Oltre all'italiano, si parla il _____ nel Trentino-Alto Adige.
7. La regione più ricca dell'Italia è _____.
8. I laghi italiani più grandi si trovano nella _____.
9. L'Italia meridionale è anche chiamata _____.
10. Il capoluogo della Val d'Aosta è _____.

B. Match each item in column I with the corresponding item in column II:

Column I	*Column* II
1. Torino	*a.* centrali idroelettriche
2. la "Riviera ligure"	*b.* Friuli-Venezia Giulia
3. cereali	*c.* nord
4. Verona	*d.* Lombardia
5. Val d'Aosta	*e.* Piemonte
6. la città "dotta"	*f.* "champagne" italiano
7. l'Italia settentrionale	*g.* Emilia-Romagna
8. il Lago di Garda	*h.* Liguria
9. gli elettrodomestici	*i.* Bologna
10. lo spumante	*j.* Veneto

C. Complete the following paragraph in Italian:

Io studio l'italiano a scuola. La settimana scorsa, il professore ha dato delle lezioni sulla divisione geografica e sulle regioni settentrionali dell'Italia. Abbiamo imparato che l'Italia è divisa in __1__ regioni. Queste regioni si suddividono poi in __2__. Ogni regione e ogni provincia ha il suo centro principale che si chiama __3__. Abbiamo imparato anche che la regione più industriale dell'Italia è __4__. La sua città principale è __5__, che produce le automobili __6__. Questa città è anche la capitale della __7__ italiana, mentre la stessa regione produce anche un vino che è considerato come lo "champagne" italiano. Questo vino si chiama __8__.

D. Identify each item with a short sentence in Italian:

1. il Mezzogiorno
2. l'Italia settentrionale
3. Aosta
4. Genova
5. Lombardia
6. Como
7. Padova
8. Venezia
9. Milano
10. Emilia-Romagna
11. "dotta"
12. Trieste
13. Trento
14. Bologna
15. la "Serenissima"

3. Altre Regioni

Le regioni dell'Italia centrale sono sei:

1. **La Toscana**, da secoli chiamata la "culla (*cradle*) dell'arte" e la "culla del Rinascimento," è situata al centro dell'Italia, sulla costa occidentale. Firenze, il capoluogo, è la città più famosa di questa regione, a causa delle sue bellezze artistiche. Altre città note sono: Pisa, con la sua torre pendente, Siena, Pistoia, Lucca, e Arezzo. La regione è importante anche per l'artigianato (*skilled craftsmanship*), industrie varie, e l'agricoltura, compreso la produzione dei famosi vini **Chianti**.

2. **L'Umbria**, famosa per i suoi santi, è situata proprio nel mezzo della penisola. Perugia, il capoluogo, ha la famosa Università per Stranieri. Fra le altre città della regione ci sono: Assisi, il luogo natio (*birthplace*) di San Francesco; Spoleto, dove ogni estate ha luogo il "Festival dei Due Mondi"; e Orvieto, nota per la sua cattedrale e per il suo vino magnifico.

3. Un'altra regione agricola è **le Marche**, all'est dell'Umbria, sull'Adriatico. Il capoluogo di questa regione è Ancona, un porto abbastanza importante. La regione è anche conosciuta per la sua industria peschereccia (*fishing*) e per le industrie di carta (*paperworks*). Urbino, una delle sue città, è il luogo di nascita del pittore famoso del Rinascimento, Raffaello Sanzio, e dell'architetto Bramante. Nell'angolo nord-orientale delle Marche, c'è la più piccola repubblica del mondo, **San Marino**, che ha una superficie di 40 chilometri quadrati (24 miglia quadrate).

4. Nel **Lazio**, c'è la capitale della Repubblica Italiana, Roma. La regione è al sud della Toscana, sulla costa del Mar Tirreno. Roma ha quasi tre milioni di abitanti ed è il centro delle reliquie (*relics*) e dei monumenti di quattro culture: la latina, l'etrusca, la romana, e la cristiana. Nel mezzo della città di Roma, c'è il più piccolo stato indipendente del mondo, **la Città del Vaticano**, sede della Chiesa Cattolica.

5. **L'Abruzzo**, una regione montuosa, è principalmente agricola. Il capoluogo è L'Aquila, città antica e ricca di monumenti. La città più popolata è Pescara, che dà sull'Adriatico.

6. **Il Molise**, divenuta regione nel 1963, è al sud dell'Abruzzo. Il capoluogo è Campobasso, rinomato (*well known*) per l'industria di coltellerie (*cutlery*).

Le regioni dell'Italia meridionale sono sei:

1. **La Campania**, situata al sud-ovest, lungo il Mar Tirreno, è prevalentemente agricola. Questa è la regione più popolata dell'Italia. Il capoluogo è Napoli, che si trova sul Golfo di Napoli, col suo Vesuvio incantevole. I centri turistici includono: Capri, Ischia, Pompei ed Ercolano—due città sepolte dalle ceneri del Vesuvio nel 79 d.C. (*after Christ*)—Sorrento, Amalfi, e Positano. Tutte queste città o isole sono bellissime.

2. **La Puglia**, il tacco (*heel*) dell'Italia, dipende principalmente dall'agricoltura, specialmente: sul grano (*wheat*, *grain*), sulle viti (*vineyards*), sull'olio, e sul tabacco. Bari, il capoluogo, è la seconda città del Mezzogiorno, dopo Napoli. È una città bellissima che dà sull'Adriatico. Altre città importanti sono Brindisi e Taranto che, con Bari, formano il "triangolo industriale del sud." Alberobello, un paese nella Puglia, è molto noto per i suoi "trulli" (*coneshaped houses*).

3. **La Basilicata** è una regione aspra (*bitter*, *harsh*) e montuosa, prevalentemente agricola. È forse la regione più povera dell'Italia. Il capoluogo è Potenza.

4. **La Calabria** occupa la punta estrema dello "Stivale." Anche questa regione è essenzialmente agricola. Di recente, però, si sta sviluppando come centro turistico, specialmente lungo le spiagge ioniche. Qualche anno fa, Catanzaro è diventata il capoluogo della Calabria. Le altre città importanti sono: Reggio Calabria e Cosenza.

5. **La Sicilia**, la maggiore isola nel Mediterraneo, chiamata anticamente "Trinacria" per la sua forma a triangolo, è ricca di agricoltura. Questa isola è specialmente conosciuta per la produzione degli agrumi (*citrus fruits*), del grano, e dell'uva. Ci sono anche risorse minerarie di zolfo (*sulfur*) e asfalto (*asphalt*). Palermo, il capoluogo, è ricca di monumenti e cattedrali.

6. **La Sardegna**, l'altra grande isola italiana, è diventata molto popolare recentemente per i suoi ritrovi estivi, lungo la nota "Costa Smeralda." Come la Sicilia, è essenzialmente agricola ma anche ricca di metalli e del poco carbone che si trova in Italia. Il capoluogo è Cagliari. Altre città importanti sono Sassari e Nuoro.

EXERCISES

A. Match each item in column I with the corresponding item in column II:

Column I	*Column* II
1. Perugia	*a.* San Francesco
2. Roma	*b.* la Puglia
3. Chianti	*c.* l'Abruzzo
4. Assisi	*d.* il Lazio
5. L'Aquila	*e.* la Campania
6. Bari	*f.* la Sardegna
7. Trinacria	*g.* l'Umbria
8. Ancona	*h.* le Marche
9. Cagliari	*i.* la Sicilia
10. Napoli	*j.* la Toscana

B. Complete the following sentences:

1. La "culla del Rinascimento" è un altro nome per _____.
2. Urbino è una città delle _____.
3. Il più piccolo stato indipendente del mondo è _____.
4. Le città che formano il "triangolo del sud" sono _____, _____, e _____.
5. Il nuovo capoluogo della Calabria è _____.
6. _____ è la regione più povera dell'Italia.
7. Il Lazio è situato sulla costa del Mar _____.
8. Il "Festival dei Due Mondi" viene festeggiato ogni estate a _____.
9. La regione più popolata dell'Italia è _____.
10. _____ forma il tacco dell'Italia.
11. Lo zolfo si trova in abbondanza in _____.
12. _____ è il capoluogo della Basilicata.
13. La "Costa Smeralda" fa parte della _____.
14. Pescara, nell'Abruzzo, è sul Mare _____.
15. Orvieto è nota per la sua _____ e per il suo _____.

C. Complete the following paragraphs in Italian:

Mia zia mi ha scritto una lettera nella quale descrive tutti i luoghi che ha visto mentre viaggiava per l'Italia centrale e meridionale. Mi dice che è andata prima a Roma, che si trova nella regione del __1__. Durante il suo soggiorno nella capitale, ha visitato lo stato indipendente più piccolo del mondo, __2__ e tutte le reliquie __3__, __4__, __5__, __6__, che formano il complesso della civiltà moderna occidentale. Dopo aver visitato Roma, è andata in __7__, regione che è anche chiamata la "culla dell'arte," e si è fermata per primo a __8__, capoluogo di questa regione. Ha visitato anche __9__ per vedere la __10__ che pende. Si è divertita moltissimo ed ha avuto l'opportunità di assaggiare l'originale vino __11__ che è il rinomato vino prodotto in questa regione. È andata poi nell'Umbria ed ha visitato __12__, dov'è situata l'Università per Stranieri e poi ad __13__, la città di nascita di San Francesco. Dopo aver visitato __14__, la repubblica più piccola del mondo, che è situata nell'angolo nord-orientale delle __15__, mia zia è andata poi verso il __16__ per visitare la regione della Campania. Ha visitato per primo il capoluogo di questa regione, __17__, con il suo golfo incantevole e poi è andata a vedere le due città sepolte dalle ceneri del Vesuvio: __18__ ed __19__. Dalla Campania è passata alla __20__, regione che si chiama anche "il tacco dell'Italia," per visitare i __21__ che si trovano nel paese di Alberobello.

Mi scrive che fra qualche giorno andrà anche in Calabria ed in Sicilia per visitare __22__ e __23__, i capoluoghi di queste due regioni meridionali.

D. Identify each item with a short sentence in Italian:

1. Ancona
2. Roma
3. Bramante
4. Campobasso
5. la Campania
6. Brindisi
7. Nuoro
8. Perugia
9. Assisi
10. il Chianti
11. il Molise
12. il Vesuvio
13. il Mezzogiorno
14. Trinacria
15. Cosenza

4. Roma

Roma, la "Città Eterna," è la capitale della Repubblica Italiana ed ha circa tre milioni di abitanti. La città fu fondata, secondo la leggenda, dai fratelli Romolo e Remo, e si estende su sette colli.

Il fiume **Tevere** attraversa questa bella città che è il centro politico e religioso della penisola. Roma è colma (*full*) di magnifici monumenti, edifici, musei, e chiese, molti dei quali risalgono (*date back*) ai tempi dell'Impero Romano.

ROMA ANTICA

1. **Il Colosseo,** costruito nel 72 d.C. (dopo Cristo), è un'arena che fu usata per giuochi fra gladiatori, fra uomini e animali feroci, e per finte (*mock*) battaglie marittime. Il Colosseo attrae ancora molti turisti ogni anno.

2. **Le Terme di Caracalla** furono costruite anticamente come bagni (*baths*) e per convegni pubblici. Nella Roma moderna, però, sono state convertite a teatro d'opera dove ogni estate vengono presentate le più grandi opere italiane.

3. **Il Foro Romano** è il luogo più celebre dell'Antica Roma. Qui ci sono i resti (*remains*) dei monumenti dell'Impero Romano.

4. **Il Panteon** era il tempio consacrato a tutti gli dei (*gods*) ed è uno dei capolavori (*masterpieces*) architettonici (*architectural*) di Roma antica. Adesso è una chiesa cattolica dove sono sepolti (*interred*) alcuni grandi italiani, fra i quali Raffaello Sanzio, famoso pittore del Rinascimento.

CHIESE

1. **La Basilica di San (S.) Pietro,** capolavoro attribuito in gran parte a: Michelangelo, Raffaello, Bramante, e Bernini. Questa basilica è la più grande del mondo e fra le sue bellezze artistiche c'è la famosa *Pietà* di Michelangelo. La Basilica di San Pietro è anche la chiesa più importante del mondo perchè rappresenta la sede del Cattolicesimo.

2. **Trinità dei Monti** è situata al di sopra di Piazza di Spagna e contiene molte opere d'arte.

3. **San Paolo fuori le Mura,** una delle più belle chiese di Roma, fu eretta sopra la tomba di S. Paolo.

4. **San Giovanni in Laterano** è la prima chiesa patriarcale dell'Occidente nella Chiesa Cattolica. È anche la sede del Vescovo di Roma. Il titolo di Vescovo di Roma viene automaticamente assunto dal Papa.

5. **Santa Maria Maggiore**, una delle basiliche di Roma, ha un interno adorno di ricchissimi marmi.

PIAZZE

1. **Piazza Venezia** è il luogo dove si radunavano (*met*) migliaia di persone per sentire i discorsi di Benito Mussolini, che parlava dal balcone di Palazzo Venezia. Dirimpetto c'è il grandissimo Altare alla Patria, monumento a Vittorio Emanuele II, che contiene la tomba del Milite Ignoto (*Unknown Soldier*).

2. **Piazza Navona** è celebre per la colossale fontana scolpita dal Bernini.

3. **Piazza di Spagna** è forse la piazza più visitata del mondo con la sua lunga scalinata, ornata di fiori vivaci in primavera.

4. **Piazza Colonna** è situata vicino al centro di Roma. È il luogo più attivo della città.

5. **Piazza del Popolo** è una delle piazze più belle della Città Eterna. È situata sotto il Pincio, un parco ben conosciuto per i suoi fiori e i suoi viali.

6. **Piazza Esedra**, adesso chiamata Piazza della Repubblica, è a pochi passi dalla Stazione Termini, la principale stazione ferroviaria di Roma.

7. **Piazza San Pietro** è la piazza più grande di Roma. Questa piazza ha un grandissimo colonnato, a forma di semicerchio. Ognuna delle colonne fu scolpita dal Bernini insieme alle statue che si trovano al sommo del colonnato. Nel centro della piazza vi è situato un grande obelisco che risale ai tempi antichi, mentre dirimpetto all'obelisco, c'è la scalinata principale per entrare nella Basilica di San Pietro.

FONTANE

1. **La Fontana di Trevi** è famosa dappertutto per la sua bellezza. Secondo la leggenda, ogni persona che vi butta un soldino (*penny*) tornerà a Roma un'altra volta.

2. **La Fontana dei Dioscuri** è vicina al Quirinale, residenza del Presidente della Repubblica.

3. **La Fontana dell'Esedra**, in Piazza della Repubblica, ha delle statue di bronzo scolpite dallo scultore Rutelli.
4. **La Fontana delle Tartarughe** è una delle fontane più attraenti di Roma. È opera di Giacomo Della Porta e di Taddeo Landini.

PARCHI E VILLE

1. **Villa Borghese** è il parco principale di Roma. I suoi giardini, oltre a bellissimi viali, contengono il giardino zoologico e il Museo Borghese.
2. **Villa Ada** era la vecchia dimora (*residence*) dei re italiani.
3. **Villa Gloria**, ricca di pini, è stata dedicata ai caduti italiani (*Italian war dead*).
4. **Villa Medici** è uno dei parchi caratteristici di Roma.
5. **Il Pincio** è un parco situato sulla collina dello stesso nome. Dal Pincio si vede un panorama stupendo della città con i suoi tramonti meravigliosi.
6. **Villa Sciarra**, sul Gianicolo (*Janiculum Hill*), ha una fontana famosa e molte piante rare.

STRADE

1. **La Via Appia Antica** era la strada principale dell'Impero Romano che continua tuttora fino a Brindisi nella Puglia, ed è usata ancora oggi.
2. **Via Margutta** si visita per ammirare pittori e scultori da tutte le parti del mondo, che vengono qui per vivere e per lavorare.
3. **Via (Vittorio) Veneto**, chiamata la via più lussuosa (*luxurious*) dell'Italia, è piena di grandi alberghi e di caffè dove si vedono molti "astri" (*stars*) del cinema.
4. **Via Condotti**, dove le vetrine sono piene (*filled*) di modelli e di prodotti dell'artigianato (*skilled craftsmanship*) italiano. Ci sono molti negozi pieni dei più recenti modelli della moda italiana.

ALTRI LUOGHI IMPORTANTI

1. **La Cappella Sistina** è una cappella vaticana di grande importanza artistica. Contiene il noto soffitto (*ceiling*) di Michelangelo ed anche il suo *Giudizio Universale* (*Last Judgment*).

2. **Le Catacombe** sono una rete di passaggi sotterranei (*underground passageways*) usate dai cristiani per evitare le persecuzioni romane.

3. **La Stazione Termini** è la stazione ferroviaria principale di Roma.

4. **Castel Sant'Angelo**, antica fortezza papale, è oggi un museo di grande importanza.

5. **La Città Universitaria** è un complesso di edifici che forma l'università di Roma.

6. **Lo Stadio dei Centomila** è il campo sportivo principale di Roma.

7. **Il Foro Italico** è un complesso di stadi sportivi costruito per le Olimpiadi del 1960.

8. **E.U.R. (Esposizione Universale Roma)** è anche un complesso di palazzi modernissimi che doveva essere la nuova sede del governo italiano, secondo Benito Mussolini. Oggi è una delle zone residenziali più pregiate di Roma, che si chiama popolarmente l'E.U.R.

EXERCISES

A. Match each item in column I with the corresponding item in column II:

Column I	*Column* II
1. Panteon	*a.* Bernini
2. "Città Eterna"	*b.* 72 d.C.
3. Piazza Navona	*c.* strada romana
4. la *Pietà*	*d.* tempio antico
5. Terme di Caracalla	*e.* fontana
6. Appia Antica	*f.* il Milite Ignoto
7. S. Giovanni in Laterano	*g.* Roma
8. Trevi	*h.* bagni pubblici
9. Monumento a Vittorio Emanuele II	*i.* prima basilica patriarcale
10. Colosseo	*j.* San Pietro

B. Complete each of the following sentences:

1. Il fiume _____ attraversa la città di Roma.
2. Le Olimpiadi del 1960 ebbero luogo nel _____.

3. Le Catacombe venivano usate dai _____.
4. E.U.R. significa _____.
5. Una grande basilica romana, nota per i suoi ricchissimi marmi, è _____.
6. Il Museo Borghese si trova nella Villa _____.
7. Per trovare scrittori e pittori, bisogna andare in Via _____.
8. La più lussuosa strada dell'Italia è _____.
9. _____ è la stazione principale di Roma.
10. Il complesso di edifici che forma l'Università di Roma è chiamato _____.
11. Trinità dei Monti è situata al di sopra di Piazza _____.
12. Il soffitto della Cappella Sistina fu dipinto da _____.
13. Secondo la leggenda, per tornare a Roma, bisogna buttare un _____ nella Fontana di Trevi.
14. Bernini scolpì una grande fontana per Piazza _____.
15. La sede del Vescovo di Roma è _____.
16. I prodotti dell'artigianato italiano si possono ammirare nelle vetrine di Via _____.
17. La Via _____ va fino a Brindisi.
18. La tomba di San Paolo è sotto la Basilica di _____.
19. La *Pietà* si trova nella Basilica di _____.
20. Secondo la leggenda, Roma fu fondata dai fratelli _____ e _____.

C. Identify each of the following items:

1. antico tempio degli dei
2. luogo più celebre dell'antica Roma
3. stadio sportivo usato per le Olimpiadi
4. strada dove si vedono molti pittori
5. passaggi sotterranei usati molti secoli fa
6. luogo dov' è dipinto il *Giudizio Universale*
7. dove si gode l'opera d'estate
8. la basilica più grande del mondo
9. fondata dai fratelli Romolo e Remo
10. costruito nel 72 d.C.

D. Complete the following paragraph in Italian:

La settimana scorsa ho fatto un giro per la "Città __1__," Roma. Prima, ho visitato la Basilica di __2__, la più grande del mondo. Poi sono entrato nella Cappella __3__, dove ho visto il *Giudizio Universale* di __4__. A pochi passi da lì, ho visitato l'antica fortezza dei Papi, __5__. Da lì, sono andato al Foro __6__, vicino al Monumento a Vittorio Emanuele II, che contiene la tomba del __7__. Continuando il mio giro, sono entrato nel __8__, dove i gladiatori di duemila anni fa combattevano. Essendo stanco dopo tante visite, ho deciso di fermarmi per prendere un caffè espresso in Via __9__, forse la strada più famosa d'Italia.

E. Identify each item with a short sentence in Italian:

1. Palazzo Venezia
2. "Città Eterna"
3. Foro Romano
4. Trinità dei Monti
5. Altare alla Patria
6. Via Condotti
7. Stazione Termini
8. Castel Sant'Angelo
9. Stadio dei Centomila
10. Colosseo
11. Cappella Sistina
12. Piazza Navona
13. Museo Borghese
14. Via Margutta
15. E.U.R.

La famosa *scalinata di Piazza di Spagna* con la veduta di *Trinità dei Monti*, una delle chiese più famose di Roma.

5. Altre Città Italiane

Le città italiane più popolate (con più di 500,000 abitanti) sono: Roma, Milano, Napoli, Torino, Genova, Palermo, e Bologna.

PORTI

1. **Genova**, chiamata la "Superba," si trova sul Mar Ligure, ed è il porto più grande dell'Italia. Con Milano e Torino, forma il "triangolo industriale del nord." I suoi cantieri navali sono molto importanti.
2. **Napoli**, sul Mar Tirreno, è il secondo porto d'Italia. La bellezza del suo porto è rinomata in tutto il mondo. Navi da tutte le parti del mondo arrivano in questo porto.
3. **Livorno (Leghorn)**, altro porto importantissimo dell'Italia, è situata in Toscana, sul Mar Ligure.
4. **Palermo**, capoluogo della Sicilia, che dà sul Mar Tirreno, è un grande centro commerciale. Fra i suoi monumenti ci sono la Cattedrale, il Palazzo Reale, e il Teatro Massimo. La bellissima Cattedrale di Monreale è a pochi chilometri da Palermo.
5. **Trieste**, sul Mar Adriatico, ha degli ottimi cantieri navali. Tra le sue industrie più importanti ci sono quelle idroelettriche, tessili (*textiles*), e chimiche.
6. **Venezia**, la "Serenissima" o la "Regina dell'Adriatico," era il porto più importante dell'Italia prima della scoperta del Nuovo Mondo nel 1492. Milioni di turisti vengono ad ammirare questa città incantevole di più di 100 isole, 160 canali, e 400 ponti. È nota per il Canal Grande, il Ponte dei Sospiri, il Ponte del Rialto, la Basilica di Piazza San Marco, e il Palazzo dei Dogi.

CITTÀ INDUSTRIALI E STORICHE

1. **Milano**, capoluogo della Lombardia, chiamata la "New York" dell'Italia, è la capitale industriale e commerciale della penisola. Milano è anche ricca di monumenti ed edifici importantissimi:

   a. **Il Teatro della Scala**, il teatro d'opera più importante del mondo.
   b. **Il Duomo**, l'unica vera cattedrale gotica in Italia.
   c. **La Chiesa di Santa Maria delle Grazie**, che ospita *il Cenacolo*, o *l'Ultima Cena*, di Leonardo da Vinci.

d. **Il Castello Sforzesco**, dimora degli antichi signori di Milano, adesso un museo.
e. **La Pinacoteca di Brera**, importante galleria d'arte che contiene opere della "Scuola Veneta e Lombarda."

2. **Torino**, il capoluogo del Piemonte, è la terza città del "triangolo del nord." Una volta era la sede della Casa Reale italiana. Situata sul Po, è uno dei centri scientifici e industriali più importanti dell'Italia. È il centro delle automobili FIAT ed è anche uno dei centri della moda italiana.

3. **Firenze**, capoluogo della Toscana, è un vero gioiello d'arte e di storia, la vera "culla del Rinascimento."

Chiese:

a. **Il Duomo**, o la Cattedrale di Santa Maria del Fiore, con la grandissima cupola disegnata da Brunelleschi.
b. **Santa Maria Novella**, di stile arabo, possiede opere di Ghirlandaio.
c. **Santa Croce**, la "Westminster Abbey" dell'Italia, contiene le tombe di molti famosi italiani: Machiavelli, Rossini, Michelangelo, Galileo.
d. **San Lorenzo**, chiesa in cui si trovano **le Cappelle Medicee** con le *Tombe di Giuliano e Cosimo dei Medici* scolpite da Michelangelo.

Gallerie e Musei:

a. **La Galleria degli Uffizi**, una delle più note d'Italia.
b. **Il Bargello**, museo situato nell'antico palazzo del Podestà.
c. **Il Palazzo Pitti**, il più grande palazzo di Firenze, contiene una delle migliori raccolte (*collections*) di pittura nel mondo.
d. **L'Accademia di Belle Arti**, dove è esposto l'originale *Davide* di Michelangelo.

Piazze:

a. **Piazza del Duomo**, che include il Duomo, il Battistero, e il Campanile di Giotto. Le porte di bronzo, scolpite da Ghiberti, e chiamate "le Porte del Paradiso," fanno parte del Battistero.
b. **Piazza della Signoria**, davanti al Palazzo Vecchio, il quale è ancora oggi il palazzo comunale di Firenze. Ad un lato della piazza, c'è la Loggia dei Lanzi, con molte statue di artisti celebri.
c. **Piazza Santa Croce**, con le sue botteghe di cuoio.
d. **Piazzale Michelangelo**, che offre una veduta magnifica di Firenze e dei suoi dintorni (*surroundings*).

Ponte Vecchio è il ponte più antico che attraversa l'Arno. Ha molte piccole botteghe di orefici (*goldsmiths*) visitate da milioni di turisti ogni anno.

4. **Bologna,** con le sue torri famose Asinelli e Garisenda, è la capitale dell'Emilia-Romagna. È una città medioevale, nota per la sua scuola di medicina e per la sua università, fondata nel 1152, che è la più antica del mondo. Bologna è anche considerata la capitale della gastronomia italiana.
5. **Pisa,** in Toscana, è una città rinomata per la Torre Pendente, per il suo Battistero, e per la bellissima Cattedrale in Piazza dei Miracoli.
6. **Siena,** città toscana, è famosa per il rito annuale del "Palio," corsa che ha luogo il 2 luglio e il 16 agosto nella piazza principale.
7. **Perugia,** capoluogo dell'Umbria, è la sede della **Perugina,** cioccolato rinomato in tutto il mondo. La sua **Università per Stranieri** è frequentata da studenti che vengono da tutte le parti del mondo.
8. **Bari,** capoluogo della Puglia, è chiamata la "Torino del Sud." È il luogo della **Fiera del Levante,** una fiera (*fair*) commerciale che ha luogo ogni anno.
9. **Padova,** antica città universitaria nel Veneto, è nota per la basilica del suo santo, Sant'Antonio.
10. **Assisi** è una città medioevale umbra, resa famosa dal suo santo natio, San Francesco.
11. **Ravenna,** città antica della Romagna, è celebre per i suoi mosaici e per la la tomba di Dante Alighieri.

ALTRE CITTÀ

1. **Bolzano,** città vicino all'Austria, è importante per gli sport invernali.
2. **Cortina d'Ampezzo,** nelle montagne Dolomiti, è nota per gli sport invernali.
3. **Carrara** è famosa per le sue montagne di marmo.
4. **San Remo** è il centro dove si celebra il **Festival della Canzone Italiana.**
5. **Parma,** luogo di nascita di Arturo Toscanini, direttore d'orchestra, e di Giuseppe Verdi, è nota anche per il suo formaggio chiamato **parmigiano.**
6. **Modena** è la città dove si costruiscono le macchine da corsa, Ferrari e Maserati.
7. **Rimini** è visitata ogni anno da migliaia di turisti per le sue belle spiagge.

EXERCISES

A. Match each item in column I with the corresponding item in column II:

Column I	*Column* II
1. la "New York" dell'Italia	*a.* Genova
2. il primo porto italiano	*b.* Torino
3. il Palazzo dei Dogi	*c.* Siena
4. la "culla del Rinascimento"	*d.* Bari
5. il capoluogo del Piemonte	*e.* Palermo
6. la Torre degli Asinelli	*f.* Firenze
7. città nota per il "Palio"	*g.* Milano
8. la "Torino del Sud"	*h.* Pisa
9. il Teatro Massimo	*i.* Bologna
10. la Torre Pendente	*j.* Venezia

B. Complete the following sentences:

1. _____ è il secondo porto dell'Italia.
2. Il Duomo, l'unica vera cattedrale gotica italiana, è a _____.
3. Venezia è anche chiamata la _____ o la _____.
4. Il Campanile di Giotto si trova a _____.
5. L'università più vecchia del mondo è situata a _____.
6. Studenti stranieri possono frequentare l'Università per Stranieri a _____.
7. I turisti che vogliono visitare la tomba di Dante devono andare a _____.
8. _____ è famosa per le sue montagne di marmo.
9. La Ferrari viene costruita nella città di _____.
10. Il Ponte _____ è a Firenze.
11. La chiesa _____ è considerata la "Westminster Abbey" italiana.
12. Venezia ha più di _____ canali e più di _____ ponti.
13. Per sentire l'opera a Milano, bisogna andare al Teatro _____.
14. Il *Davide* di Michelangelo è nell'Accademia _____.
15. La capitale gastronomica italiana è _____.

C. Write the name of the city:

1. la Piazza dei Miracoli
2. la Basilica di San Marco
3. la Pinacoteca di Brera
4. il Festival della Canzone
5. luogo di nascita di Toscanini

6. la città di Sant'Antonio
7. il capoluogo dell'Umbria
8. Piazzale Michelangelo
9. la Fiera del Levante
10. centro invernale nelle Dolomiti
11. città dove si fabbricano le Maserati
12. centro delle automobili FIAT
13. le "porte di bronzo" di Ghiberti
14. la città di San Francesco
15. città nota per le sue spiagge

D. Complete the following paragraph in Italian:

Oggi, nella nostra classe d'italiano, abbiamo visto un film sulla città di Firenze. Questa città è considerata la __1__ perchè è un vero gioiello d'arte e di storia. Il film comincia con una veduta panoramica della città e dei dintorni vista dal __2__. Poi la cinepresa (*camera*) si ferma in Piazza del Duomo per mostrarci il __3__ e il __4__ di Giotto. Il narratore dà una spiegazione dettagliata sulle porte di bronzo scolpite da __5__, che si chiamano le __6__. La veduta si trasferisce a Piazza della __7__ per farci vedere la Loggia dei __8__ e il Palazzo __9__. Il film ci ha fatto vedere anche alcuni famosi musei d'arte come: la Galleria degli __10__ e __11__, dove è esposto l'originale __12__ di Michelangelo. Abbiamo ammirato la chiesa di __13__, chiamata la "Westminster Abbey" dell'Italia, e la chiesa di __14__, dove si trovano le __15__ con le *Tombe di Giuliano e Cosimo dei Medici*. Infine, abbiamo visto centinaia di turisti che visitavano le botteghe di orefici situate sul __16__. "Firenze è veramente una cittadina incantevole senza paragoni," ha detto il nostro professore d'italiano.

E. Identify each item with a short sentence in Italian:

1. la "Superba"
2. la "Regina dell'Adriatico"
3. il Teatro Massimo
4. Piazza San Marco
5. il Bargello
6. Piazza dei Miracoli
7. la Garisenda
8. San Remo
9. Bolzano
10. il Castello Sforzesco
11. la Pinacoteca di Brera
12. il Canal Grande
13. Palazzo Pitti
14. il "Palio"
15. Carrara

6. L'Economia Italiana

L'Italia è ancora considerata un paese agricolo. Due terzi (2/3) della nazione è coltivabile, però solo una piccola percentuale della popolazione deriva il suo lavoro dalla terra.

1. La zona più fertile dell'Italia è **la Valle Padana**, lungo il fiume Po. Qui si trovano le fattorie (*farms*) più produttive del paese. Due altre zone produttive sono: **il Gran Tavoliere** (*Great Plain*) nella Puglia, noto per il grano, e **la Conca d'Oro** (*Golden Basin*) in Sicilia, nota per gli **agrumi** (*citrus fruits*).

2. Il **grano** è ancora uno dei principali prodotti agricoli. Con il grano si fa il pane, che gli Italiani mangiano in abbondanza. Legumi di tutti i tipi vengono coltivati anche in grande quantità.

3. L'Italia è la prima nazione nel mondo per la produzione del **vino.** Tra i vini più comuni: lo **Spumante**, il **Chianti**, il **Barolo**, il **Valpolicella**, il **Verdicchio**, il **Bardolino**, il **Soave**. Una zona di colline, chiamata I Castelli, vicino alla Città Eterna, produce anche il "vino dei Castelli."

4. L'Italia è in secondo posto mondiale nella coltivazione di olive e nella produzione dell'olio. La regione più produttiva per l'olio è la Puglia, seguita dalla Calabria, la Sicilia, e la Toscana.

5. La Campania produce la più grande quantità di **ortaggi** (*vegetables*) e offre una grande varietà di pomodori, patate, fagioli, cavoli, e cavolfiori. L'Emilia produce la migliore **frutta.** Ottime sono: le pesche, le ciliege, e le pere.

6. La coltivazione del **riso** è concentrata nel Piemonte e nella Lombardia, lungo il fiume Po. Il riso italiano è noto in tutto il mondo ed è anche coltivato negli Stati Uniti, con precisione nello stato della Virginia, ma in poca quantità.

7. La Sicilia è la maggiore produttrice di **agrumi**: arance, mandarini, limoni, pompelmi, ecc.

8. Altri prodotti d'importanza per l'Italia sono le **barbabietole da zucchero** (*sugar beets*), coltivate in abbondanza nel Veneto e nell'Emilia-Romagna; il **tabacco**, coltivato nel Veneto, nella Puglia, nell'Abruzzo, nella Campania e nell'Umbria. L'Italia è anche la maggiore produttrice di canapa (*hemp*) di tutta l'Europa.

9. La **floricultura** (*horticulture*) si concentra in Liguria, specialmente lungo la Riviera, tra Ventimiglia e Albenga. Fra i fiori più comuni ci sono i garofani (*carnations*), le rose, le tuberose, i gladioli, e i crisantemi. I **profumi** italiani vengono prodotti in gran parte dai fiori coltivati in questa zona.

10. L'**allevamento del bestiame** (*livestock breeding*) sta aumentando in Italia, però manca ancora carne in abbondanza per tutti gli Italiani. L'Italia ha circa 10 milioni di bovini (*cattle*), 7 milioni di suini (*pigs*), 9 milioni di ovini (*sheep*), 1 milione di equini (*equines*).

    Il **latte** non è sufficiente per tutta la nazione, ma il **formaggio** e altri **latticini** (*dairy products*) sono fra i più famosi del mondo. I formaggi rinomati sono: il **provolone**, il **gorgonzola**, il **Bel Paese**, la **fontina**, il **parmigiano**, il **pecorino**, la **ricotta**, e la **mozzarella**.

11. Gli Italiani mangiano molti prodotti del mare. Le coste lunghissime della penisola e delle sue isole grandi rendono ottima la pesca (*fishing*) italiana.

12. L'industria italiana è oggi in grande aumento. Però l'artigianato rimane ancora l'aspetto più importante dell'industria italiana. La qualità dell'artigianato italiano è conosciuta dovunque.

13. Il **turismo** è l'industria principale dell'Italia. Milioni di stranieri da tutte le parti del mondo visitano l'Italia ogni anno. Senza il turismo l'economia soffrirebbe immensamente.

14. Le altre industrie importanti all'economia italiana sono le **industrie meccaniche** e quelle **tessili.** Queste sono concentrate nel "triangolo industriale del nord." Le industrie meccaniche includono la produzione di autoveicoli (*motor vehicles*), di elettrodomestici (*appliances*), di macchine da scrivere, di calcolatrici, di frigoriferi, e di micromotori. L'industria dei giocattoli è anche aumentata recentemente.

15. Torino è il centro delle macchine **FIAT.** Modena è il centro delle **Ferrari** e **Maserati**; e Milano, delle **Alfa Romeo.**

16. L'industria tessile produce **lana, seta,** e **cotone** di ottima qualità. Si producono anche molti tessuti sintetici. Como è il centro della **seta** italiana.

17. L'industria chimica prospera in Italia. Si esportano **zolfo** (*sulfur*) e **bauxite** (con il quale si fa l'alluminio). L'Italia è una delle prime nazioni nella produzione di prodotti di plastica.

18. L'Italia non è ricca di risorse minerarie. C'è molto zolfo in Sicilia, ma poco carbone (*coal*), poco ferro, dello zinco, del piombo, e del mercurio. L'Italia è ricca di marmo, che si trova in abbondanza a Massa Carrara in Toscana.

19. L'industria idroelettrica è importante per gli Italiani perchè manca il carbone. Questa energia viene prodotta specialmente nell'Italia settentrionale dove c'è molta acqua.

20. I centri della **moda italiana** sono Torino, Roma, e Firenze. Fra i nomi più noti sono: le Sorelle Fontana, Emilio Pucci, e Valentino.

21. Firenze è il centro dell'artigianato del **cuoio** (*leather*). Borse, guanti, portafogli sono fra le specialità di questa industria. Firenze è anche il centro dell'oro italiano. Il Ponte Vecchio è il punto centrale per i prodotti d'oro lavorati in anelli, braccialetti, collane, ecc.

EXERCISES

A. Match each item in column I with the corresponding item in column II:

Column I	*Column* II
1. gorgonzola	*a.* vino
2. Barolo	*b.* Firenze
3. automobili	*c.* la Sicilia
4. olio	*d.* la Puglia
5. pesche, ciliege	*e.* Ponte Vecchio
6. agrumi	*f.* formaggio
7. anelli, collane	*g.* Milano
8. seta	*h.* Torino
9. cuoio	*i.* l'Emilia
10. Alfa Romeo	*j.* Como

B. If the statement is true, write **vero.** If it is false, rewrite the statement to make it true:

1. Il parmigiano è un vino.
2. Il Valpolicella è un formaggio.
3. Agli Italiani piacciono i prodotti del mare.
4. L'Italia ha molte risorse minerarie.
5. La zona più fertile è quella lungo il Po.

6. L'Italia non è più un paese agricolo.
7. I mandarini sono agrumi.
8. Le pere sono legumi.
9. Il turismo è importante per gli Italiani.
10. L'Italia è prima nella produzione del vino.
11. Il bestiame in Italia è sufficiente per la popolazione.
12. Le città che formano il "triangolo industriale del nord" sono Milano, Roma, e Firenze.
13. Firenze è il centro dell'industria meccanica.
14. La produzione dei prodotti di plastica occupa un posto principale in Italia.
15. Il provolone è un formaggio.
16. La Ferrari è il nome di un vino.
17. Gli elettrodomestici non sono manifatturati in Italia.
18. Il marmo è abbondante.
19. Il Gran Tavoliere è in Sicilia.
20. L'Italia è prima nella produzione dell'olio.
21. La "Conca d'Oro" è in Sicilia.
22. Gli Italiani non producono tessuti sintetici.
23. La coltivazione del riso è concentrata nella Basilicata.
24. Il tabacco è un prodotto principale.
25. L'industria tessile produce molto vino.

C. Complete each sentence in Italian:

1. Il vino dei Castelli è prodotto nella zona dei _____.
2. La regione che produce più olio d'oliva è _____.
3. Fra gli agrumi ci sono _____, _____, _____, e _____.
4. Como, in Lombardia, è il centro della produzione della _____.
5. La _____ produce la più grande quantità di ortaggi.
6. Ottimi oggetti di cuoio vengono prodotti nella città di _____.
7. La FIAT e la Ferrari sono nomi di _____.
8. Lo zolfo italiano viene dalla _____.
9. Lo Spumante è un _____.
10. L'acqua è necessaria per la produzione dell'energia _____.
11. Il _____ si usa per fare il pane.
12. Le Sorelle Fontana ed Emilio Pucci sono nomi conosciuti nel mondo della _____.
13. Massa Carrara è celebre per le sue risorse di _____.
14. I turisti interessati in oggetti d'oro visitano il Ponte _____ a _____.

15. L'industria tessile italiana produce lana, _____, e _____ in grande quantità.
16. Il Barolo e il Verdicchio sono due _____ italiani.
17. La floricultura italiana è concentrata in _____.
18. Bel Paese e fontina sono _____ italiani.
19. Lo zucchero è prodotto da _____.
20. L'aspetto più importante dell'industria italiana è _____.

D. Complete the following paragraph in Italian:

L'economia italiana è basata principalmente sull'__1__. Le tre zone più fertili sono __2__, lungo il fiume Po; __3__, nella Puglia; e __4__, in Sicilia. L'Italia è la prima nazione nel mondo per la produzione __5__, come, per esempio, __6__ e __7__. Produce anche molto olio di oliva. La regione che produce più olio è __8__ seguita dalla __9__. La Campania, invece, produce una grande quantità di __10__, mentre l'Emilia produce la migliore __11__. L'Italia è anche rinomata per i suoi latticini. Due di questi formaggi ben conosciuti negli Stati Uniti sono __12__ e __13__. L'industria in Italia, invece, si concentra in due triangoli geografici, uno nel nord, l'altro nel sud. Le tre città che formano il "triangolo industriale del sud" sono __14__, __15__, e __16__; ma l'economia italiana dipende principalmente dal __17__, che attrae ogni anno sempre più gente per godere la bellezza della penisola.

E. Identify each item with a short sentence in Italian:

1. il pecorino
2. lo zolfo
3. la Ferrari
4. le Sorelle Fontana
5. la Maserati
6. Emilio Pucci
7. agrumi
8. il Bel Paese
9. il Verdicchio
10. il "vino dei Castelli"

7. La Repubblica Italiana

1. La Costituzione della Repubblica Italiana fu approvata nel dicembre del 1947 e andò in vigore (*into effect*) il 1.o (*first*) gennaio del 1948, quando iniziò l'attuale Repubblica.

2. L'organizzazione dello Stato Italiano si basa sulla Costituzione. Il primo articolo indica: "L'Italia è una Repubblica democratica fondata sul lavoro. La sovranità appartiene al popolo che la esercita (*exercises*) nelle forme e nei limiti della Costituzione."

3. La Costituzione garantisce l'uguaglianza (*equality*) di tutti i cittadini. Il voto è universale e segreto. Tutti gli Italiani, uomini e donne, di 18 anni, hanno diritto al voto.

4. Il ramo esecutivo è composto (*a*) del **Presidente** della Repubblica e (*b*) del **Primo Ministro**, che dirige il Governo.

5. Il **Presidente** della Repubblica ha la carica (*post*) più alta dello Stato. È eletto per sette anni dal Parlamento. È lui che assicura il funzionamento e la continuazione dello Stato. Egli nomina il Presidente del Consiglio (o Primo Ministro) e promulga (*decrees*) le leggi. Ha il comando supremo delle Forze Armate (*Armed Forces*) e presiede al Consiglio Supremo della Difesa. Può sciogliere (*dissolve*) sia l'una che l'altra Camera del Parlamento. La sua residenza ufficiale è nel **Palazzo del Quirinale** a Roma.

6. Il **Primo Ministro**, nominato dal Presidente, e il **Consiglio dei Ministri,** formano il Governo. Loro assicurano l'amministrazione delle leggi e dirigono la politica della nazione. Il Governo è responsabile al Parlamento (il Senato e la Camera dei Deputati). Il Governo può essere sciolto se il Parlamento vota la sfiducia (*vote of no confidence*).

7. Il **Parlamento,** che esercita il potere legislativo, comprende due assemblee: la **Camera dei Deputati** (*House of Representatives*) e **il Senato.** I Deputati sono eletti a suffragio (*vote*) universale, da persone oltre i 18 anni. I Senatori sono eletti a suffragio universale da persone oltre i 21 anni di età. La Camera è la più grande con 630 membri. Il Senato ha 315 membri.

8. Il Parlamento ha due funzioni essenziali: la formazione delle leggi e il controllo dell'operazione del Governo con il voto di fiducia o di sfiducia.

9. La Costituzione garantisce l'indipendenza dell'autorità giudiziaria (*judiciary*) che difende la libertà individuale.

10. Come si è detto prima, l'Italia è divisa in 20 regioni. Ogni regione è governata dal **Consiglio regionale,** formato dalla **Giunta** (*junta*), e dal **Presidente** della Giunta.

11. Le regioni sono divise in 93 **province,** e ogni provincia ha un **Prefetto,** nominato dal Governo. Le province sono amministrate da un **Consiglio provinciale,** formato dalla Giunta, e dal Presidente della Giunta.

12. Le province sono divise in **comuni** (circa 350) che hanno tre organi: il Sindaco, il Consiglio comunale, e la Giunta.

13. L'emblema nazionale italiano è la bandiera tricolore: *bianco*, *rosso*, e *verde*. L'inno nazionale è *L'Inno di Mameli*. La musica fu scritta da Michele Novaro nel 1847 basata sulle parole scritte dal giovane poeta, Goffredo Mameli.

14. Il 2 giugno è la data della **festa nazionale.** Il 2 giugno 1946 fu il giorno in cui ci fu il referendum generale e l'elezione dei Deputati all'Assemblea Costituzionale. Questa Assemblea poi scrisse la Costituzione attuale della Repubblica. Fu la prima volta che le donne in Italia votarono.

EXERCISES

A. If the statement is true, write **vero.** If the statement is false, rewrite it to make it true:

1. La Repubblica è basata su una costituzione.
2. Il Parlamento consiste di un'assemblea.
3. Il Senato è eletto a suffragio universale.
4. Chi ha 18 anni può votare per il Senato.
5. Il Presidente è eletto per sei anni.
6. Il Primo Ministro è il Presidente del Consiglio.
7. Il Primo Ministro è eletto dal popolo.
8. L'Italia è una repubblica monarchica.
9. L'Italia è divisa in 18 regioni.
10. Il Sindaco è l'ufficiale principale del comune.
11. La magistratura non garantisce la libertà individuale.
12. Il Senato è più grande della Camera dei Deputati.
13. Il Governo può essere sciolto dal Parlamento.
14. La nuova Costituzione andò in vigore nel 1946.
15. La Costituzione garantisce uguaglianza solo agli uomini.

B. Complete the following sentences in Italian:

1. Il Parlamento è composto della _____ e del _____ .
2. Il _____ è eletto per sette anni dal Parlamento.
3. Il 2 _____ è la data della festa nazionale.
4. Le regioni sono divise in _____.
5. Il _____ nomina il Presidente del Consiglio.
6. Il Primo Ministro e il _____ formano il Governo.
7. Il Senato è eletto a suffragio _____ da chi ha _____ anni di età.
8. Le province sono divise in _____ .
9. L'inno nazionale fu scritto nel _____ .
10. L'organizzazione dello Stato si basa sulla _____ .
11. La Costituzione fu approvata nel _____ .
12. Il Presidente viene eletto dal _____ .
13. Il Presidente può sciogliere il _____ .
14. Il referendum generale ebbe luogo il _____ .
15. La bandiera italiana ha tre colori: _____ , _____ , e _____ .
16. La Camera dei Deputati ha _____ membri.
17. Il voto dei cittadini è _____ e segreto.
18. Il Presidente abita nel _____ .
19. L'Italia è una repubblica _____ fondata sul lavoro.
20. Tutti gli Italiani, uomini e _____ , hanno diritto al voto.

C. Complete the following paragraph in Italian:

L'Italia è una __1__ costituzionale. Per formare il Governo, il __2__ nomina il __3__, o __4__. Il Presidente promulga le leggi approvate dalle due Camere del __5__. Il ramo esecutivo è responsabile a queste due assemblee: __6__ e __7__, le quali formano il ramo legislativo. Sia il ramo __8__ che il ramo __9__ possono essere sciolti usando le procedure stabilite dalla Costituzione. L'unico ramo del governo che è indipendente sotto la Costituzione italiana è __10__ perchè questo deve garantire la libertà individuale del popolo.

D. Identify each item with a short sentence in Italian:

1. il Quirinale
2. Goffredo Mameli
3. il Tricolore
4. la Giunta
5. il comune
6. il Consiglio provinciale
7. Michele Novaro
8. il voto di fiducia
9. il Deputato
10. il Presidente del Consiglio

8. La Lingua Italiana

L'INFLUSSO SULL'INGLESE

1. L'italiano è una lingua romanza (*Romance language*) derivata soprattutto dal latino, la lingua dei Romani. Le altre lingue romanze sono: il francese, il portoghese, il rumeno, e lo spagnolo.

2. L'italiano è la lingua ufficiale dell'Italia ed è anche una delle lingue ufficiali della Svizzera. L'italiano viene anche parlato in alcune parti della Francia e della Iugoslavia e da molti emigrati sparsi per tutto il mondo.

3. Quasi ogni regione italiana ha il suo dialetto, che significa che quasi tutti gli Italiani parlano due lingue. Per esempio, una persona della Lombardia parla l'italiano e il lombardo, un Siciliano parla l'italiano e il siciliano, ecc.

4. Durante i primi anni del Trecento (*14th century*), Dante Alighieri scrisse il suo famoso poema *La Divina Commedia* nel volgare (la lingua del popolo), basata in maggior parte sul dialetto toscano. Altri giganti letterari italiani come Petrarca e Boccaccio scrissero anche nello stesso volgare. Così, il dialetto toscano divenne la lingua comune e ufficiale dell'Italia intera.

5. Ci sono molte parole inglesi e italiane che sono simili. Di solito queste parole hanno la stessa origine, e per questa ragione sono chiamate parole consanguinee (*cognates*).

Italiano	Inglese	Italiano	Inglese
annuale	annual	**memoria**	memory
balcone	balcony	**ombrello**	umbrella
cane	canine	**piede**	pedestrian
carnevale	carnival	**pilota**	pilot
compagno	companion	**solo**	solitude
concerto	concert	**teatro**	theater
coro	chorus	**visione**	vision
gazzetta	gazette	**vulcano**	volcano
libro	library		
manipolare	manipulate		

6. Molte parole ed espressioni italiane fanno parte oggi della lingua inglese. Ecco alcuni esempi:

CIBI E BEVANDE

antipasto, an appetizer consisting of cheese, meats, fish, peppers, olives, etc.
caffè espresso, a very strong black coffee

chianti, a dry red wine
gnocchi, Italian dumplings
gorgonzola, Italian blue cheese
lasagne, wide flat noodles used in the dish of the same name.
marsala, a light wine from Sicily
minestrone, a thick vegetable soup
mozzarella, a soft cheese used on pizza and in other Italian dishes
pizza, a dish consisting of a baked flat cake of leavened dough, covered with cheese, tomato sauce, etc.
provolone, a sharp cheese
ravioli, small square pieces of dough, filled with cheese or meat, which are boiled and usually served with tomato sauce
ricotta, Italian cottage cheese
salame, a thick, hard sausage
scaloppine, thin slices of veal cooked in wine, with mushrooms, etc.
spaghetti, thin strings of dried dough cooked in boiling water and then served with tomato sauce or butter
spumante, Italian sparkling wine
spumone, a kind of Italian ice cream with a whipped cream center
tortoni, a kind of Italian ice cream covered with almond paste

ESPRESSIONI MUSICALI

a cappella, singing without musical accompaniment
adagio, slow
allegro, fast and lively
cantata, a brief work for one or more vocal soloists and orchestra
crescendo, growing louder
finale, the ending of an act or of a movement, a scene, etc.
forte, strong and loud
legato, graceful and smooth
piano, soft
scherzo, a light, whimsical movement

ESPRESSIONI TEATRALI

bravo, a cheer used for performers, meaning "well done" or "excellent"
concerto, a musical composition for one or more principal instruments and orchestra
impresario, the manager of an opera, ballet, or concert company
maestro, a composer or conductor of music

opera, a play that is sung with the accompaniment of music
pastorale, an opera or other musical work with a pastoral theme
primadonna, the principal woman singer in an opera
scenario, an outline of a play, an opera, etc.
soprano, the highest singing voice
virtuoso, a person highly skilled in playing a musical instrument

ALTRE ESPRESSIONI

casinò, a building for public shows, dancing, gambling, etc.
costume, a style of dress
fiasco, a complete failure
ghetto, a section of a city heavily inhabited by a single minority group, usually quite poor
gondola, the typical boat used in the canals of Venice. In the U.S., a kind of river boat or a freight car or a car that hangs underneath a dirigible.
malaria, a disease transmitted by the bite of an infected mosquito
portico, a roof supported by columns, forming a covered walk or porch
regata, a boat race
stanza, a group of lines of poetry
stucco, a type of plaster
studio, the workroom of a painter, sculptor, photographer, etc.
villa, a country house, a vacation house
viola, a musical instrument of the violin family

EXERCISES

A Match each item in column I with the corresponding item in column II:

Column I	*Column* II
1. dialetto	*a.* *La Divina Commedia*
2. Dante Alighieri	*b.* Venezia
3. chianti	*c.* dialetto usato da Dante
4. l'italiano	*d.* lingua usata dai Romani
5. gondola	*e.* uno strumento musicale
6. il toscano	*f.* un formaggio
7. il latino	*g.* la seconda lingua
8. ricotta	*h.* una forma di gelato
9. viola	*i.* lingua ufficiale dell'Italia
10. spumone	*j.* un vino

B. Write an English cognate for each Italian word:

1. piede	**6.** contare	**11.** compagno	**16.** bibbia
2. naso	**7.** sorella	**12.** teatro	**17.** corte
3. dormire	**8.** immigrato	**13.** parco	**18.** maschile
4. femminile	**9.** spinaci	**14.** muro	**19.** appello
5. mano	**10.** amico	**15.** carnevale	**20.** cucina

C. Complete the following sentences in Italian:

1. La lingua italiana è una lingua romanza perchè deriva dal _____ .
2. Le altre lingue romanze sono _____ , _____ , _____ , e _____ .
3. Oltre a Dante, _____ e _____ scrissero in volgare.
4. L'italiano si parla in alcune parti della Francia e della _____ .
5. L'italiano è una delle lingue ufficiali della _____ .
6. Il dialetto della _____ è diventata la lingua ufficiale dell'Italia.
7. *La Divina Commedia* fu scritta nel _____ .
8. Il _____ è un vino leggero siciliano.
9. La protagonista di un'opera è la _____ .
10. I Siciliani parlano anche il _____ oltre all'italiano.

D. From the list below, use each word once only in the following sentences:

fiasco	maestro	villa	mozzarella	a cappella
viola	gondola	opera	bravo	studio

1. Abbiamo fatto un giro in _____ per i canali di Venezia.
2. Carlo abita in una bella _____ in campagna.
3. Arturo Toscanini era un grande _____ di musica.
4. Il coro ha cantato _____ , cioè, senza musica.
5. Ho fatto brutta figura ieri sera; è stato un _____ .
6. Maria è andata allo _____ del fotografo.
7. Non so suonare la _____ perchè è troppo difficile.
8. Il soprano ha cantato una bellissima aria nell'_____ di Giuseppe Verdi.
9. Quando mia madre fa la pizza, ci mette molta _____ .
10. Dopo che il coro ha finito di cantare, il pubblico ha gridato _____ !

E. Identify each item with a short sentence in Italian:

1. lingua romanza	**5.** Petrarca	**9.** mozzarella
2. dialetto	**6.** *La Divina Commedia*	**10.** marsala
3. il toscano	**7.** Boccaccio	
4. il volgare	**8.** gnocchi	

9. La Vita Quotidiana

LA RELIGIONE

La maggior parte degli Italiani sono cattolici. Con il Patto Laterano (*Lateran Pact*) del 1929 fra il Governo Italiano e il Vaticano, la religione cattolica divenne la religione ufficiale del paese. Il Vaticano divenne uno stato indipendente. La Costituzione della Repubblica, però, rispetta tutte le religioni.

LA SCUOLA

L'istruzione (*education*) in Italia è gratuita ed è aperta a tutti. Tutte le scuole, pubbliche e private, sono controllate dal Ministero della Pubblica Istruzione. I ragazzi italiani devono frequentare la scuola fino all'età di quattordici anni. I bambini dall'età di tre anni fino all'età di sei anni possono frequentare la **scuola materna** (*nursery school*) e l'**asilo infantile** (*kindergarten*). All'età di sei anni, incominciano la **scuola elementare** dove restano per cinque anni.

Dopo la scuola elementare, si passa alla **scuola media unica** (*junior high school*) per un periodo di tre anni. All'età di 14 anni, finisce l'obbligo scolastico, e lo studente è libero di scegliere se iniziare a lavorare o continuare lo studio. Gli studenti che vogliono imparare un mestiere cominciano a lavorare come apprendisti. Quelli, però, che vogliono studiare la tecnologia frequentano l'**istituto tecnico**; e quelli che vogliono diventare maestri di scuola elementare frequentano la **scuola magistrale** (*school of education*) per quattro anni. Altri, invece, che vogliono continuare gli studi fino all'università, devono iscriversi (*enroll*) per primo in un **liceo**, che equivale alla scuola superiore (*high school*) e ai primi due anni del "college" in America. Il liceo dura cinque anni, e ci sono tre licei diversi: il **liceo classico** (*liberal arts*), il **liceo scientifico**, e il **liceo artistico.**

Le **università** italiane non sono numerose come quelle negli Stati Uniti e ognuna ha la sua principale specializzazione. I corsi variano dai quattro ai sei anni, secondo il campo (*field*) di specializzazione. Gli studenti che finiscono i loro corsi ricevono una **laurea** che equivale al nostro "Master's Degree."

I ragazzi in Italia frequentano le scuole sei giorni la settimana, da lunedì a sabato. L'anno scolastico incomincia il l.o ottobre e termina il 28 giugno.

GLI SPORT E LE RICREAZIONI

Gli sport:

Lo sport nazionale è il **calcio** (*soccer*), seguito dal ciclismo (*bicycling*), dal pallacanestro (*basketball*), dal pugilato (*boxing*), dalla caccia (*hunting*) e dalla pesca. Le corse automobilistiche, la corsa dei cavalli, e la scherma (*fencing*) sono anche molto popolari.

Il **Giro d'Italia,** la corsa annuale di biciclette, in cui partecipano ciclisti di tutta l'Europa, dura 20 giorni. La corsa, in realtà, fa il giro della penisola.

Per le corse automobilistiche, come, per esempio, la **Mille Miglia,** le macchine italiane sono famose, specialmente le **Ferrari,** le **Maserati,** e le **Alfa Romeo.** Uno sport italiano che si giuoca anche negli Stati Uniti è quello delle **bocce** (*type of lawn bowling*).

Le ricreazioni:

Gli Italiani sono appassionati delle **passeggiate**, specialmente di sera, prima o dopo cena. Queste si fanno lungo le piazze, le strade, o sui lungomari (*boardwalks*). La piazza è un luogo molto importante per gli Italiani. Qui si radunano per chiacchierare, per camminare, o per godere un aperitivo in un caffè all'aperto. Il **caffè all'aperto** è diventato una tradizione molto cara agli Italiani ed è il posto dove si incontrano amici. Qui è dove si può anche leggere il giornale o una rivista, o ci si può divertire a guardare la gente che passa.

Il **bar,** che non è come il bar americano, è forse il luogo più caro agli Italiani. Ci vanno parecchie volte al giorno per un **caffè espresso** o un **cappuccino.** Spesso bevono in piedi, al banco. Le bevande alcooliche si prendono raramente nei bar italiani.

Agli Italiani piace anche andare al cinema e naturalmente frequentare l'opera. La televisione è anche diventata un aspetto integrale della vita italiana. Adesso c'è anche la televisione a colori ma attualmente ci sono soltanto due canali televisivi.

Il fine settimana, o il "weekend" (come si chiama oggi), è sacro per molti Italiani, specialmente durante la primavera e l'estate. È allora che tutti si recano in montagna o alle spiagge sparse per tutta la penisola. Infatti, quasi tutti gli Italiani vanno in ferie (*on vacation*) durante le prime due o tre settimane di agosto. Le vacanze culminano con la festa del **Ferragosto,** che si celebra il 15 agosto. Durante questo periodo, tutta l'Italia si ferma (*stops*).

LA CUCINA ITALIANA

Uno dei cibi basilari (*basic*) italiani è la **pasta,** che include una grande varietà: spaghetti, vermicelli, lasagne, ravioli, cannelloni, ecc. Olio e pomodori sono fra gli ingredienti più comuni della cucina italiana. Ogni regione ha la sua specialità. Fra i piatti più noti, ci sono:

pizza, a flat cake of dough that is covered with tomato sauce, mozzarella cheese, oil, and oregano and then baked. (In Italian, the word *pizza* refers to any type of pie, for example, pizza al pomodoro or alla napoletana. Recently, though, the general term *pizza* is used the world over to mean exclusively pizza as defined here.)
polenta, a thick porridge made of corn meal and served in various ways
scaloppine al marsala, veal cutlet cooked in Marsala wine sauce
pollo alla cacciatora, chicken cooked in oil, tomatoes, and wine
risotto alla milanese, rice cooked in broth and served with beef
tortellini di Bologna, egg noodles that are filled with meat, prosciutto, and parmesan cheese served in broth, with sauce or with cream
fritto misto, a mixture of fried seafoods
linguine o spaghetti alle vongole, pasta served with a red or white clam sauce. Italian clams used for this dish are extremely small but delicious.
linguine al pesto, linguini served in a sauce made with basil leaves and oil, a specialty of Genoa
abbacchio alla romana, roast lamb, a specialty of Rome
pasta alle sarde, pasta served with a sauce made with sardines, a specialty of Sicily

FESTE E GIORNI FESTIVI

1. **L'Anniversario della Repubblica** è la festa nazionale che ha luogo il 2 giugno.

2. **La Festa del Redentore** a Venezia ha luogo in luglio. Durante la celebrazione, c'è la famosa regata di gondole, dipinte in colori vivaci, con la gente che canta e suona strumenti musicali mentre viaggia per i canali. La festa finisce con una grande manifestazione di fuochi artificiali (*fireworks*).

3. **Lo Scoppio del Carro** a Firenze. Questo evento ha luogo il Sabato Santo, davanti al Duomo. A mezzogiorno, fuochi artificiali che adornano un carro (*float*) vengono accesi tramite una colomba artificiale appesa ad un filo lanciata verso il carro. L'esplosione indica la fine della Quaresima (*Lent*).

4. **Il Palio di Siena** è una corsa di cavalli rappresentanti le contrade (*districts*)

di Siena. La corsa ha luogo il 2 luglio e il 16 agosto, ed è preceduta da una sfilata in costumi medioevali e rinascimentali.

5. **La Festa di San Gennaro,** a Napoli, in settembre. San Gennaro è il patrono della città; e durante la festa, la statua del santo è portata per le strade accompagnata da una boccetta (*small bottle*) col sangue raggrumato (*coagulated blood*) del Santo. Se il sangue si liquefa, secondo la leggenda, allora il Santo farà dei miracoli. Se, invece, il sangue rimane raggrumato, allora ci sarà un disastro.

6. **Il Màggio Musicale Fiorentino,** a Firenze. È un festival musicale che ha luogo a maggio e durante il quale vengono presentati concerti, opere, e balletti.

7. **Il Festival dei Due Mondi** ha luogo a Spoleto per due settimane durante ogni estate ed è caratterizzato (*features*) da concerti, danze, opere, e rappresentazioni teatrali. Il direttore è **Gian Carlo Menotti,** compositore di opere moderne.

8. **Il Film Festival di Venezia** ha luogo ogni anno verso la fine di agosto o il principio di settembre.

9. **Il Festival della Canzone** a San Remo, dove le canzoni più moderne vengono presentate per la prima volta, e dov'è scelta la canzone che manterrà il primo posto fino al prossimo Festival.

10. **La Festa di Piedigrotta,** a Napoli, ha luogo ogni settembre. L'evento principale è il Festival delle Canzoni Napoletane.

11. **La Festa di San Nicola di Bari** ha luogo a maggio. Durante la celebrazione, una statua del santo viene messa su una barca e portata in processione accompagnata da musica, canti, e fuochi artificiali.

12. **La Festa di Santa Rosa,** a Viterbo. Sessanta uomini portano un campanile alto 19 metri (60 piedi) durante una processione fiaccolata (*torchlight procession*).

13. **Il Carnevale** è il periodo che di solito precede la Quaresima. Viene celebrato in tutta l'Italia con sfilate, mascherate (*masquerades*), e allegria generale. Le più note celebrazioni hanno luogo a Viareggio in Toscana e a Venezia.

14. **L'Epifania,** il 6 gennaio, è una festa religiosa. Secondo la leggenda, la Befana, una strega (*witch*) benevola, porta dei regali ai bambini durante la notte dal 5 al 6 gennaio.

15. **Il Ferragosto** è il periodo che va dal 10 al 20 agosto, quando tutti gli Italiani vanno in ferie. Il giorno forse più importante durante questo periodo è il 15 agosto. In questo giorno, si celebra la festa dell'Assunzione (*Assumption*), una festa religiosa.

EXERCISES

A. Match each item in column I with the corresponding item in column II:

Column I	*Column* II
1. la Befana	*a.* Napoli
2. il Palio	*b.* un campanile
3. la Festa di Piedigrotta	*c.* Spoleto
4. l'Anniversario della Repubblica	*d.* il 2 luglio
5. lo Scoppio del Carro	*e.* Quaresima
6. il sangue raggrumato	*f.* il 6 gennaio
7. il Festival dei Due Mondi	*g.* la regata
8. la Festa di Santa Rosa	*h.* Sabato Santo
9. il Carnevale	*i.* la Festa di San Gennaro
10. la Festa del Redentore	*j.* il 2 giugno

B. If the statement is true, write **vero**. If the statement is false, rewrite it to make it true:

1. La religione principale in Italia è quella protestante.
2. In Italia l'istruzione è gratuita.
3. Dopo la scuola elementare i ragazzi vanno al liceo.
4. Il bar italiano è come quello americano.
5. Il piatto principale italiano è la pasta.
6. La Festa di Piedigrotta è celebrata a San Remo.
7. La Befana porta dei regali ai bambini.
8. Il Palio è un museo.
9. Lo sport nazionale italiano è il "baseball."
10. Il Giro d'Italia è una corsa ciclistica.
11. Il caffè è importante agli Italiani.
12. L'istruzione italiana è sotto la direzione del governo nazionale.
13. L'Alfa Romeo è una festa siciliana.
14. La Costituzione rispetta tutte le religioni.
15. I giovani che non vogliono imparare un mestiere possono frequentare il liceo.

16. Non è necessario frequentare l'università per diventare insegnante di scuola elementare.
17. L'olio è importante per la cucina italiana.
18. Lo Scoppio del Carro ha luogo a Palermo.
19. Il Festival dei Due Mondi è una celebrazione religiosa.
20. Agli Italiani non piace fare le passeggiate.

C. Complete each sentence in Italian:

1. Il pollo alla cacciatora è pollo cotto in olio, _____, e _____.
2. Durante la Festa di Santa Rosa, _____ uomini portano un _____ alto 60 piedi.
3. Il formaggio che si usa sulla pizza è la _____.
4. Il Palio ha luogo il _____ luglio e il _____ agosto.
5. Il Patto Laterano fu l'accordo tra il Governo e il _____.
6. I ragazzini italiani devono frequentare la scuola, fino ai _____ anni d'età.
7. Dopo la scuola elementare, tutti frequentano la _____.
8. Il Giro d'Italia dura _____ giorni.
9. Le macchine da corsa sono le _____, le _____, e le _____.
10. Alla televisione italiana, ci sono _____ canali.
11. L'abbacchio è un piatto tipico _____.
12. _____ della Repubblica è celebrato il 2 giugno.
13. La regata a Venezia ha luogo durante la Festa del _____.
14. Il basilico è l'ingrediente basico per le linguine al _____.
15. La Festa di San Gennaro ha luogo a _____ nel mese di _____.
16. Gli studenti che finiscono i corsi universitari ricevono la _____.
17. Di solito, gli Italiani bevono il caffè _____ al banco del bar.
18. I ragazzi delle scuole elementari sono liberi soltanto la _____.
19. Pasta alle _____ è una specialità siciliana.
20. La Befana arriva durante la notte dal _____ gennaio al _____ gennaio.

D. Complete the following paragraph in Italian:

Ogni volta che vedo delle cartoline illustrate con vedute italiane, mi viene la voglia di ritornare in Italia. Sogno di trovarmi in montagna o alla spiaggia durante il periodo del __1__ come fanno quasi tutti gli Italiani fino al quindici agosto. Come sarebbe bello fare una gita insieme ai miei amici, il giorno di Ferragosto, per godere un bel piatto di __2__ alle __3__ in un ristorante all'aperto, vicino al mare! Dopo questa spaghettata faremmo la solita __4__, sul lungomare, fino a un caffè all'aperto dove prenderemmo un __5__, seduti a un tavolino, mentre la gente passeggia su e giù. Seduti, potremmo ammirare la processione della Madonna __6__, che passa proprio davanti al caffè. Dopo la processione, rimarremmo seduti ancora ad ascoltare la musica e a godere i __7__ artificiali.

E. Identify each item with a short sentence in Italian:

1. il bar
2. il due giugno
3. lo Scoppio del Carro
4. il Palio
5. Piedigrotta
6. il Festival dei Due Mondi
7. il Festival della Canzone
8. il Carnevale
9. l'Epifania
10. la Festa di San Gennaro

Una macchina per il caffè espresso e il cappuccino. **Nel disegno si vede anche il barista [bartender], in tipica giacca bianca, nell'atto di preparare una tazza di caffè.**

10. La Letteratura Italiana

IL DUECENTO E IL TRECENTO

1. **San Francesco d'Assisi** (1182-1226). Scrisse *Il Cantico delle Creature*, la prima poesia in lingua italiana. Ai tempi del Santo di Assisi, le poesie venivano scritte in latino.

2. **Dante Alighieri** (1265-1321). È considerato il più grande poeta della letteratura italiana e uno dei più grandi della letteratura mondiale. Le sue opere maggiori in italiano sono *La Vita Nuova* e *La Divina Commedia*. Dante è considerato il "padre della lingua italiana" non solo perchè scrisse in italiano, ma perchè perfezionò il volgare usato dai suoi contemporanei e lo rese utile come lingua letteraria.

3. **Francesco Petrarca** (1304-1374). È il più grande poeta lirico italiano. Ebbe un grande influsso (*influence*) su molti scrittori europei, specialmente quelli inglesi. Il suo capolavoro è *Il Canzoniere*, una raccolta di poesie che tratta dell'amore del poeta per la sua amata, Laura.

4. **Giovanni Boccaccio** (1313-1375). Generalmente considerato il più grande novelliere (*short-story writer*) della letteratura italiana. Scrisse *Il Decamerone*, una raccolta di 100 novelle raccontate da 10 giovani entro dieci giorni.

IL QUATTROCENTO E IL CINQUECENTO

5. **Niccolò Machiavelli** (1469-1527). Con la sua opera maggiore, *Il Principe*, viene acclamato il fondatore (*founder*) delle scienze politiche (*political science*) moderne. *Il Principe* è uno dei primi libri che considera un'Italia unita sotto un solo principe. Machiavelli scrisse anche *La Mandragola*, una delle migliori commedie del Rinascimento.

6. **Ludovico Ariosto** (1474-1533). Scrisse *L'Orlando Furioso*, forse l'unica epica letteraria italiana. È considerata anche fra le migliori del mondo.

7. **Baldassare Castiglione** (1478-1529). È autore di *Il Cortegiano*, che descrive la vita di corte nel Rinascimento. L'autore elenca il comportamento (*behavior*) ideale dei nobili dei suoi tempi.

8. **Torquato Tasso** (1544-1595). Grande poeta che scrisse il poema cavalleresco (*chivalric*) *La Gerusalemme Liberata*, che tratta della liberazione di Gerusalemme durante la prima crociata (*First Crusade*).

IL SETTECENTO

9. **Pietro Metastasio** (1698-1782). Autore dei primi libretti per melodrammi come: *L'Attilio Regolo* e *Didone Abbandonata.*

10. **Carlo Goldoni** (1707-1793). È considerato uno dei più grandi commediografi (*comedy playwrights*) della letteratura italiana e straniera. Scrisse molte commedie, parecchie delle quali furono tradotte in varie lingue. Fra le più famose: *La Locandiera* e *Il Ventaglio*.

11. **Giuseppe Parini** (1729-1799). Grande poeta satirico che criticò la corruzione della nobiltà dei suoi tempi nell'opera che ha per titolo *Il Giorno*. Questa è una poesia lunghissima, divisa in quattro parti: *Il Mattino*, *Il Mezzogiorno*, *Il Vespro*, e *La Notte*.

12. **Vittorio Alfieri** (1749-1803). Drammaturgo (*playwright*) e poeta che secondo i critici ha scritto le migliori tragedie della letteratura italiana. Molte delle sue tragedie trattano le idee della libertà e dell'odio della tirannide (*tyranny*), concetti che eventualmente portarono all'unificazione dell'Italia.

13. **Ugo Foscolo** (1778-1827). Grande scrittore lirico, noto per *I Sepolcri* e per *Le Ultime Lettere di Jacopo Ortis*, quest'ultima è un'autobiografia.

L'OTTOCENTO

14. **Alessandro Manzoni** (1785-1873). Il primo e forse il più grande romanziere (*novelist*) italiano. Fu anche fra i primi scrittori romantici dell'Italia. Oltre a scrivere bellissime poesie e tragedie, il suo capolavoro è il romanzo storico *I Promessi Sposi* (*The Betrothed*).

15. **Giacomo Leopardi** (1798-1837). Un gigante fra i poeti italiani. I suoi migliori poemi sono inclusi nella raccolta *I Canti*.

16. **Giosuè Carducci** (1835-1907). Ottimo poeta che fu il primo scrittore italiano a vincere il Premio Nobel, nel 1906. Una delle sue migliori raccolte poetiche ha per titolo *Odi Barbare*.

17. **Giovanni Verga** (1840-1922). Uno dei principali romanzieri italiani, conosciuto per il suo "verismo" (*realism*). Scrisse molti capolavori, fra i quali: *I Malavoglia* e *Mastro Don Gesualdo*.

18. **Antonio Fogazzaro** (1842-1911). Altro noto romanziere dell'Ottocento, ricordato specialmente per *Piccolo Mondo Antico*.

19. **Giovanni Pascoli** (1855-1912). Poeta lirico di ispirazione raffinata che

ci dà la poesia pura e quasi musicale. Fra le sue raccolte più note vi sono: *Myricae*, *Canti di Castelvecchio*, *Primi Poemetti*, e *Nuovi Poemetti*.

AUTORI MODERNI E CONTEMPORANEI

20. **Gabriele d'Annunzio** (1863-1938). Noto peota, drammaturgo, e romanziere. Fra le sue opere migliori vi sono: una raccolta di poesie, *Le Laudi*; i drammi *La Figlia di Iorio* e *Le Novelle della Pescara*; e i romanzi *Il Piacere* e *L'Innocente*.

21. **Benedetto Croce** (1866-1952). Grande critico-filosofo che ebbe molto influsso sulla critica letteraria ed artistica. Contribuì molto alla comprensione della letteratura spagnuola da parte degli Italiani.

22. **Luigi Pirandello** (1867-1936). Senza dubbio, il più grande drammaturgo italiano, le cui opere sono state tradotte in quasi ogni lingua importante del mondo. Due dei suoi drammi più famosi sono: *Sei Personaggi in Cerca d'Autore* e *Enrico IV*. Vinse il Premio Nobel nel 1934. È celebre anche per aver scritto alcuni romanzi. Il più noto di questi è *Il Fu Mattia Pascal*.

23. **Grazia Deledda** (1875-1936). Importante scrittrice di romanzi con lo sfondo sardagnolo (*Sardinian*). Vinse il Premio Nobel per la letteratura nel 1926. Fra le sue opere più note vi sono: *Cenere*, *Colombi e Sparvieri*, *L'Edera*, e *La Madre*.

24. **Aldo Palazzeschi** (1885-1974). Scrittore interessato nell'analisi del comportamento umano. Il suo romanzo più noto è *Le Sorelle Materassi*.

25. **Giuseppe Ungaretti** (1888-1970). Poeta originalissimo che ci ha lasciato poesie di una o poche parole. Fra le sue raccolte più importanti vi sono: *Sentimento del Tempo* e *Il Dolore*.

26. **Riccardo Bacchelli** (1891-). Noto in particolar modo per il romanzo *Il Mulino del Po*, considerato uno dei migliori romanzi europei dell'epoca.

27. **Giuseppe Tomasi di Lampedusa** (1896-1957). Autore del romanzo *Il Gattopardo*.

28. **Eugenio Montale** (1896-). Poeta contemporaneo, celebre per la sua poesia pessimistica. *Ossi di Seppia* è il suo maggior contributo alla letteratura italiana. Noto anche per *Le Occasioni* e *La Bufera*. Ha ricevuto il Premio Nobel nel 1976.

29. **Ignazio Silone** (1900-). Scrittore anti-fascista, che scrisse *Vino e Pane* e *Fontamara*.

30. **Salvatore Quasimodo** (1901-1968). Poeta moderno che riflette il tema contemporaneo del pessimismo. Vinse il Premio Nobel nel 1959. Alcune delle sue poesie più note sono: *Ed è Subito Sera*, *Giorno Dopo Giorno*, *La Terra Impareggiabile*.

31. **Carlo Levi** (1902-1975). Romanziere d'importanza che scrisse *Cristo si è Fermato a Eboli*, un romanzo anti-fascista, e *L'Orologio*.

32. **Alberto Moravia** (1907-). Uno dei più noti scrittori contemporanei. Fra le sue opere importanti vi sono: *La Romana*, *La Ciociara*, *La Bella Vita*, e *Gli Indifferenti*.

33. **Cesare Pavese** (1908-1950). Scrisse *La Luna e i Falò*, un romanzo-composizione.

34. **Elio Vittorini** (1908-1966). Noto particolarmente per aver scritto *Conversazione in Sicilia*, una narrativa che ha avuto molta influenza sugli scrittori del dopoguerra (*after World War II*).

35. **Italo Calvino** (1923-). Il migliore scrittore italiano di fiabe (*fables*), è anche autore di tre romanzi importanti: *Il Barone Rampante*, *Il Visconte Dimezzato*, e *Il Cavaliere Inesistente*.

EXERCISES

A. Match each item in column I with the corresponding item in column II:

Column I	*Column* II
1. Francesco Petrarca	*a. Il Piacere*
2. Baldassare Castiglione	*b. La Divina Commedia*
3. Gabriele d'Annunzio	*c. Odi Barbare*
4. Luigi Pirandello	*d. Il Canzoniere*
5. Giovanni Verga	*e. I Promessi Sposi*
6. Dante Alighieri	*f. I Malavoglia*
7. Ludovico Ariosto	*g. Le Sorelle Materassi*
8. Alessandro Manzoni	*h. Il Cortegiano*
9. Giosuè Carducci	*i. Orlando Furioso*
10. Aldo Palazzeschi	*j. Enrico IV*

B. Identify the Italian writers:

1. romanziere celebre per il suo verismo
2. scrisse le migliori tragedie italiane
3. autore di *Il Giorno*
4. il fondatore delle scienze politiche
5. poeta che scrisse per la sua Laura
6. autore di *La Gerusalemme Liberata*
7. uno dei più grandi commediografi
8. considerato il più importante romanziere italiano
9. vinse il Premio Nobel nel 1906
10. il più grande drammaturgo italiano
11. scrisse romanzi della gente sarda
12. autore di *Cristo si è Fermato a Eboli*
13. vinse il Premio Nobel nel 1959
14. autore di fiabe
15. vinse il Premio Nobel nel 1934

C. Complete the following sentences in Italian:

1. Il "padre della lingua italiana" è _____.
2. Luigi _____ vinse il Premio Nobel.
3. _____ scrisse *Piccolo Mondo Antico*.
4. San Francesco scrisse *Il Cantico* _____.
5. *Il Decamerone* è una raccolta di _____ novelle.
6. *Il Principe* fu scritto da _____.
7. *Il Cortegiano* elenca il _____ ideale della nobiltà.
8. *La Locandiera* e *Il Ventaglio* sono due opere di _____.
9. Giuseppe Parini criticò la _____ della nobiltà.
10. _____ è l'autore di *Myricae*.
11. _____ è un critico-filosofo moderno.
12. Giuseppe Tomasi di Lampedusa è l'autore di _____.
13. *Le Ultime Lettere di Jacopo Ortis* è un'opera di Ugo _____.
14. Le tragedie di Alfieri trattano dell'odio della _____.
15. *La Mandragola* di Machiavelli è una delle migliori _____ del Rinascimento.

D. Complete the following paragraph in Italian:

La letteratura italiana è ricca di magnifiche opere che hanno contribuito fortemente allo sviluppo di molti capolavori internazionali. Durante il Duecento e il Trecento, per esempio, vi furono tre colossi letterari italiani che ebbero molto influsso sulla letteratura inglese. Il primo è __1__, autore della *Divina Commedia* e della __2__. Il secondo è __3__ che scrisse una raccolta di poesie dedicate a Laura intitolata __4__. L'ultimo colosso di questo periodo fu il grande novelliere, __5__, che scrisse una raccolta di cento novelle intitolata __6__. Nel Quattrocento e nel Cinquecento, scrissero altri astri della letteratura italiana. __7__ è acclamato come il fondatore della scienza politica con il suo capolavoro __8__. La vita alle corti rinascimentali fu descritta da __9__ nella sua opera __10__, mentre __11__ scriveva commedie che ebbero un grande influsso su altri commediografi italiani e stranieri.

E. Identify each item with a short sentence in Italian:

1. *La Gerusalemme Liberata*
2. Ludovico Ariosto
3. Ugo Foscolo
4. Giovanni Pascoli
5. *Odi Barbare*
6. Giacomo Leopardi
7. *I Promessi Sposi*
8. Benedetto Croce
9. *Sei Personaggi in Cerca d'Autore*
10. Giuseppe Tomasi di Lampedusa
11. Ignazio Silone
12. *Il Mulino del Po*
13. Giovanni Verga
14. *La Luna e i Falò*
15. Elio Vittorini

11. Pittori, Scultori, Architetti

PITTORI

1. **Giovanni Cimabue** (1240-1302). Fondatore della Scuola Fiorentina, iniziò lo stile di pittura pre-rinascimentale.

2. **Giotto di Bondone** (1267-1337). Alunno di Cimabue, Giotto divenne il più grande pittore del primo Rinascimento. I suoi affreschi (*frescoes*) si trovano nella Cappella degli Scrovegni a Padova, nella Chiesa di San Francesco ad Assisi, e nella Chiesa di Santa Croce a Firenze.

3. **Fra Angelico** (1387-1455). Un frate domenicano che sviluppò la tecnica rinascimentale a Firenze. *L'Annunciazione* che si trova nel convento di San Marco a Firenze è uno dei suoi capolavori.

4. **Masaccio (Tommaso Guidi)** (1401-1428). Il primo pittore ad introdurre la prospettiva nella pittura. Le sue figure furono le prime a mostrare un effetto della terza dimensione.

5. **Fra Filippo Lippi** (1406-1469). Fu influenzato moltissimo da Masaccio. Le madonne e gli altri dipinti religiosi di Fra Filippo mostrano una qualità dolce ed umana.

6. **Pier della Francesca** (1416-1492). Considerato da molti come il più grande pittore del Quattrocento dopo Masaccio, è noto a sua volta per la prospettiva.

7. **Giovanni Bellini** (1430-1516). Uno dei pittori principali della Scuola Veneta. Diede enfasi allo sfondo campestre (*rustic*) con colori ricchi ma delicati.

8. **Andrea Mantegna** (1431-1506). Considerato il padre dell'intaglio pittorico (*engraving technique in painting*). Uno dei suoi capolavori è il ritratto di *San Sebastiano.*

9. **Sandro Botticelli** (1444-1510). Primo pittore a dipingere donne seminude. I suoi migliori quadri sono *La Primavera*, *La Nascita di Venere,* e *L'Adorazione dei Re Magi.*

10. **Leonardo da Vinci** (1452-1519). Uno dei più grandi artisti del Rinascimento. Introdusse innovazioni nell'uso dei colori e della prospettiva. Fra i suoi dipinti più celebri vi sono: *Il Cenacolo* (*L'Ultima Cena*), *Mona Lisa* (*La Gioconda*), e *La Madonna delle Rocce.*

11. **Michelangelo Buonarroti** (1475-1564). Forse l'artista più famoso del Rinascimento. Applicò la sua tecnica di scultore anche ai suoi dipinti e affreschi. I suoi capolavori nel campo della pittura sono gli affreschi del soffitto e della parete (*Il Giudizio Universale*) della Cappella Sistina.

12. **Giorgione** (1478-1510). Pioniere della Scuola Veneta. Conosciuto soprattutto per *La Tempesta* e *L'Adorazione dei Pastori.*

13. **Raffaello Sanzio** (1483-1520). Altro gigante del Rinascimento, noto per le sue madonne tranquille e ideali e per i suoi ritratti. Le sue opere includono Le Stanze del Vaticano; *La Scuola d'Atene*, *La Trasfigurazione di Cristo*, e *La Madonna del Cardellino.*

14. **Tiziano Vecellio** (1490-1576). Pittore di grande produzione, in colori vivaci, specialmente di ritratti di personaggi famosi. Fra i suoi dipinti più noti vi sono: *L'Assunta*, *Amor Sacro e Profano*, *L'Uomo del Guanto*, *Carlo V.*

15. **Tintoretto (Jacopo Robusti)** (1518-1594). Uno degli ultimi grandi pittori veneti del Rinascimento. Introdusse il "manierismo" in cui collocò (*combined*) la luminosità dei colori di Tiziano con l'azione vigorosa di Michelangelo, in modo originale.

16. **Paolo Veronese (Caliari)** (1528-1588). Grande pittore veneto rinascimentale, noto per i suoi dipinti di soggetto storico e mitologico. Dipinse *La Cena in Casa del Fariseo* e *Marte e Venere.*

17. **Caravaggio (Michelangelo Merisi)** (1569-1610). Noto come grande naturalista del Seicento. I suoi dipinti sono riconoscibili dalla luce radiante (*radiant*) che illumina l'oggetto principale del quadro. Influì su alcuni pittori stranieri come Velàzquez e Rembrandt. Dipinse *La Caduta di S. Paolo* e *Il Martirio di S. Pietro.*

18. **Gian Battista Tiepolo** (1696-1770). Il pittore più importante della Scuola Veneta del secolo. Uno dei suoi capolavori è *L'Incontro di Antonio e Cleopatra.*

19. **Amedeo Modigliani** (1884-1920). Artista moderno a cui piaceva dipingere figure isolate con corpi lunghi e teste ovali.

20. **Giorgio de Chirico** (1888-). Pittore surrealista con senso di immobilità. Ha dipinto *Piazza d'Italia.*

SCULTORI

1. **Niccolò Pisano** (1220–1278?). Precursore (*forerunner*) del Rinascimento, noto per aver scolpito due pulpiti (*pulpits*): uno nel Battistero a Pisa, l'altro nella Cattedrale di Siena.
2. **Lorenzo Ghiberti** (1378–1455). Famosissimo per le sue porte di bronzo del Battistero di San Giovanni a Firenze, che furono chiamate da Michelangelo "le porte del Paradiso."
3. **Donatello** (1386–1466). Il più grande scultore del primo Rinascimento. Scolpì il *Davide*, la bellissima statua equestre del *Gattamelata*, e *S. Giorgio.*
4. **Luca della Robbia** (1400–1482). Scultore noto per le sue figure e scene in terracotta.
5. **Michelangelo Buonarroti** (1475–1564). Fra i suoi lavori giganteschi ci sono il *Mosè*, quattro *Pietà*, il *Davide*, e le *Tombe di Giuliano e Cosimo dei Medici.*
6. **Benvenuto Cellini** (1500–1571). Grande scultore e ottimo orefice (*goldsmith*). La sua statua, *Perseo*, in bronzo, è una delle migliori sculture dell'epoca.
7. **Giovanni Lorenzo Bernini** (1598–1680). Scultore principale del periodo barocco. Scolpì statue enormi come il *Davide*, *Apollo e Dafne*, *Il Ratto di Proserpina*, e *Santa Teresa in Estasi.*
8. **Antonio Canova** (1757–1822). Massimo esponente dell'età neoclassica. Conosciuto principalmente per aver scolpito *Amore e Psiche*, *Paolina Borghese come Venere*, e *Napoleone I.*
9. **Marino Marini** (1901–   ). Noto per le sue statue di cavalli e cavalieri.
10. **Giacomo Manzù** (1908–   ). Ha scolpito i pannelli di bronzo per la Basilica di S. Pietro a Roma.

ARCHITETTI

1. **Filippo Brunelleschi** (1377–1446). Iniziò lo stile della cupola per le chiese. Disegnò per primo la cupola della Cattedrale di Santa Maria del Fiore a Firenze (il Duomo). Disegnò inoltre il Palazzo Pitti di Firenze, che è oggi un museo.

2. **Leon Battista Alberti** (1404–1472). Fra le sue opere, si devono segnalare la Chiesa di S. Francesco a Rimini, il Tempio Malatestiano a Rimini, e la Fontana di Trevi a Roma.

3. **Donato Bramante** (1444-1514). Stabilì le vaste dimensioni della Basilica di S. Pietro. Disegnò la cupola della Chiesa di Santa Maria delle Grazie a Milano, il luogo dove è esposta *L'Ultima Cena* di Leonardo.

4. **Michelangelo Buonarroti** (1475–1564) disegnò la cupola della Basilica di San Pietro.

5. **Andrea Palladio** (1518-1580). Il suo stile influenzò l'architettura inglese e americana. La sua architettura è conosciuta col nome inglese di "Georgian architecture" sia negli Stati Uniti che in Inghilterra.

6. **Giovanni Lorenzo Bernini** (1598-1680). Disegnò il colonnato di Piazza S. Pietro e il baldacchino (*canopy*) per l'altare maggiore della stessa basilica.

7. **Francesco Borromini** (1599-1667). Grande architetto del periodo barocco, disegnò la Chiesa di Sant'Agnese, in Piazza Navona, a Roma.

8. **Pier Luigi Nervi** (1891-   ). Il più noto architetto contemporaneo. Ha disegnato il Palazzetto dello Sport a Roma e lo Stadio Comunale di Firenze.

EXERCISES

A. Identify each of the following by writing *pittore*, *scultore*, or *architetto:*

1. Giotto
2. Niccolò Pisano
3. Bramante
4. Palladio
5. Cimabue
6. Leonardo da Vinci
7. Bernini
8. Ghiberti
9. Brunelleschi
10. Botticelli
11. Raffaello
12. de Chirico
13. della Robbia
14. Nervi
15. Fra Angelico
16. Tiziano
17. Donatello
18. Borromini
19. Canova
20. Caravaggio

B. Match each item in column I with the corresponding item in column II:

Column I	*Column* II
1. la *Pietà*	*a.* Donatello
2. "le porte del Paradiso"	*b.* Botticelli
3. *S. Giorgio*	*c.* Tintoretto
4. *S. Sebastiano*	*d.* Michelangelo
5. *La Primavera*	*e.* Bernini
6. le Stanze del Vaticano	*f.* Bramante
7. il "manierismo"	*g.* Giorgione
8. *Perseo*	*h.* Ghiberti
9. la cupola di Santa Marià delle Grazie	*i.* Giotto
10. il colonnato di Piazza S. Pietro	*j.* Cellini
11. gli affreschi di San Francesco	*k.* Mantegna
12. *La Tempesta*	*l.* Raffaello

C. Complete each sentence in Italian:

1. Sandro _____ dipinse *La Primavera.*
2. Michelangelo disegnò la _____ della Chiesa di S. Pietro.
3. _____ dipinse molti ritratti di persone note.
4. Caravaggio influenzò pittori stranieri come Velàzquez e _____ .
5. Niccolò _____ scolpì dei pulpiti rinomati.
6. Marino _____ è noto per le sue statue di cavalli.
7. Luca _____ è conosciuto per le sue scene in terracotta.
8. Amedeo Modigliani dipingeva figure isolate con corpi _____ e teste _____ .
9. Le "porte del Paradiso" fanno parte del _____ a Firenze.
10. La Scuola Fiorentina fu fondata da _____ .
11. La prospettiva nella pittura fu introdotta da _____ .
12. *La Gioconda* è un altro nome per la _____ .
13. Gian Battista _____ è considerato il pittore più importante della Scuola _____ .
14. Leon _____ _____ disegnò il Tempio Malatestiano a _____ .
15. "Georgian architecture" è lo stile creato da _____ .

D. Complete the following paragraph in Italian:

Il disegno e la scultura, come la musica, sembrano essere doni (*gifts*) di nascita del popolo italiano. Attraverso i secoli, gli Italiani hanno sempre iniziato nuovi stili o sviluppato nuove tecniche che stabilirono la supremazia dell'Italia nel campo delle belle arti. La prima scuola di pittura pre-rinascimentale fu quella __1__, fondata da __2__. Il suo alunno __3__ divenne il più grande pittore del primo Rinascimento, mentre __4__ fu il frate domenicano che sviluppò la vera tecnica rinascimentale. __5__, invece, fu il primo a dipingere donne semi-nude. Fra i grandi artisti del Rinascimento, dobbiamo includere: __6__, che dipinse *Il Cenacolo;* __7__, che scolpì il *Davide;* e __8__, che dipinse *La Madonna del Cardellino.* Se, invece, passiamo all'epoca moderna, risalgono altri artisti di fama come: __9__, a cui piaceva dipingere corpi lunghi e ovali; __10__, pittore surrealista con senso di immobilità; __11__, noto per le sue statue di cavalli e cavalieri; e __12__, il più noto architetto contemporaneo, che ha disegnato il Palazzetto dello Sport di Roma.

E. Identify each item with a short sentence in Italian:

1. *La Gioconda*
2. *L'Uomo del Guanto*
3. *Il Giudizio Universale*
4. *Il Martirio di S. Pietro*
5. Lorenzo Ghiberti
6. *Pietà*
7. Giovanni Bernini
8. Antonio Canova
9. Filippo Brunelleschi
10. Benvenuto Cellini
11. Luca della Robbia
12. Michelangelo Merisi
13. Jacopo Robusti
14. Tommaso Guidi
15. Francesco Borromini

12. Scienziati e Musicisti

SCIENZIATI

1. **Leonardo da Vinci** (1452-1519). È considerato il più grande scienziato sperimentale della sua epoca. Fu inventore, ingegnere, botanista, astronomo, anatomista, e geologo. Ideò il concetto dell'elicottero (*helicopter*), dell'aeroplano, del paracadute (*parachute*), e del carro armato moderno (*tank*).

2. **Galileo Galilei** (1564-1642). Astronomo, fisico, matematico, è considerato il padre della scienza moderna sperimentale. Scoprì la "legge del pendolo" (*pendulum*) e la "teoria della caduta dei gravi" (*falling objects*). Perfezionò il cannocchiale (*telescope*) e il termometro; e studiò i satelliti di Giove (*Jupiter*), gli anelli di Saturno, e le macchie (*spots*) della luna.

3. **Evangelista Torricelli** (1608-1647). Inventò il barometro e sviluppò il microscopio e il cannocchiale.

4. **Marcello Malpighi** (1628-1694). Anatomista che è considerato come il primo istologo (*histologist*) che abbia fatto degli studi sul sangue. Fu il primo ad usare il microscopio nella ricerca scientifica.

5. **Lazzaro Spallanzani** (1729-1799). Biologo e naturalista che studiò la circolazione del sangue, la digestione, e la riproduzione degli animali microscopici.

6. **Luigi Galvani** (1737-1798). Anatomista che scoprì la relazione fra organismi viventi e l'elettricità. Espressioni scientifiche come *ferro galvanizzato*, *galvanizzare*, e *galvanometro* sono derivate dal suo nome.

7. **Alessandro Volta** (1745-1827). Fu inventore della pila elettrica (*battery*) e del condensatore elettrico. Le espressioni *volt*, *voltaggio*, e *voltometro* derivano dal suo nome.

8. **Giovanni Schiapparelli** (1835-1910). Astronomo che era convinto di aver scoperto i canali su Marte (*Mars*). Scoprì invece la vera rotazione di Mercurio e l'asteroide Esperia.

9. **Guglielmo Marconi** (1874-1937). Famoso inventore che sviluppò la radiotelegrafia (radio senza fili) che eventualmente portò alla radio e alla televisione di oggi. Marconi vinse il Premio Nobel nel 1909.

10. **Enrico Fermi** (1901-1954). Noto fisico che nel 1942 produsse la prima reazione nucleare a catena (*nuclear chain reaction*). Vinse il Premio Nobel nel 1938 per il suo lavoro nella ricerca atomica.

11. **Giulio Natta** (1903-). Vinse il Premio Nobel per la chimica nel 1963 per aver cambiato il semplice idrocarbone in sostanze complesse molecolari.

12. **Daniele Bovet** (1907-). Vinse il Premio Nobel nel 1957 per lo sviluppo di droghe usate per distendere (*relax*) i muscoli in preparazione per le operazioni chirurgiche. Vinse un altro Premio Nobel nel 1963 per la fisica.

MUSICISTI

1. **Guido d'Arezzo** (995?-1050?). Stabilì la grafia musicale con il rigo musicale (*lines and staff*) con quattro linee. Si attribuisce a lui anche l'invenzione delle note musicali.

2. **Giovanni Pierluigi da Palestrina** (1525-1594) sviluppò la tecnica sistematica alla musica polifonica prima di Bach. Scrisse anche 93 messe.

3. **Claudio Monteverdi** (1567-1643). Compose la prima opera importante, *L'Orfeo*, ed è considerato il creatore della musica moderna.

4. **Alessandro Scarlatti** (1659-1725). È un compositore importante delle prime opere italiane. Le "overtures" delle sue opere diedero inizio alla musica sinfonica. Scrisse più di 100 opere oltre a molti oratori e cantate.

5. **Antonio Vivaldi** (1675-1741). Violinista e compositore, noto per le sue composizioni strumentali che includono sonate per violino e concerti per strumenti vari.

6. **Domenico Scarlatti** (1685-1757). Figlio di Alessandro, scrisse più di 550 pezzi di musica.

7. **Niccolò Paganini** (1782-1840). È forse il più grande violinista che il mondo abbia mai avuto. Scrisse parecchie composizioni per violino, come per esempio, *Moto Perpetuo* (*Perpetual Motion*).

8. **Gioacchino Rossini** (1792-1868). Grande compositore d'opera, noto per *Il Barbiere di Siviglia* e *Guglielmo Tell.*

9. **Vincenzo Bellini** (1801-1835). Altro famoso compositore di opere. Le sue opere più popolari sono: *La Sonnambula*, *Norma*, e *I Puritani.*

10. **Giuseppe Verdi** (1813-1901). Un gigante della storia musicale, scrisse molte opere di grande fama, fra le quali risplendono: *Il Trovatore*, *Aida*, *Rigoletto*, *La Traviata*, *Otello*, *La Forza del Destino*, e *Falstaff.*

11. **Amilcare Ponchielli** (1834-1886). Compose *La Gioconda*, nota per l'aria "Cielo e mare" e per il brano (*piece*) musicale "Il ballo delle ore."

12. **Arrigo Boito** (1842-1918). Fu il più noto librettista d'opere, specialmente per quanto riguarda le opere di Verdi. Scrisse anche un'opera completa (parole e musica), *Mefistofele.*

13. **Ruggiero Leoncavallo** (1858-1919). Compositore di parecchie opere, la più celebre delle quali è *I Pagliacci.*

14. **Giacomo Puccini** (1858-1924). Insieme a Verdi, Puccini è considerato l'altro grande gigante delle opere. Fra le sue opere più conosciute vi sono: *La Bohème, Tosca, Madama Butterfly*, *La Fanciulla del West*, e *Turandot.*

15. **Pietro Mascagni** (1863-1948). La sua opera più famosa è la *Cavalleria Rusticana*, che viene quasi sempre rappresentata insieme a *I Pagliacci*.

16. **Ottorino Respighi** (1879-1936). Noto compositore moderno, importante per la musica sinfonica. Alcune sinfonie composte da lui sono: *Le Fontane di Roma*, *I Pini di Roma*, e *Feste romane*.

17. **Arturo Toscanini** (1867-1957). Considerato forse il più grande direttore d'orchestra del mondo. Dal 1937 al 1953, Toscanini fu il direttore dell'orchestra sinfonica della NBC, nella città di "New York."

18. **Gian Carlo Menotti** (1911-). Compositore italiano che ha ottenuto molta fama con le sue opere scritte in inglese. Fra le più conosciute sono: *The Saint of Bleecker Street*, *The Medium*, *The Telephone*, *The Consul*, *Amahl and the Night Visitors.*

EXERCISES

A. Name the person associated with each of the following:

1. inventò la pila elettrica
2. il carro armato moderno
3. compose *L'Orfeo*
4. il primo istologo; studiò il sangue
5. l'inventore della radio senza fili
6. il compositore di *Rigoletto*

7. *Il Barbiere di Siviglia*
8. "galvanizzare"
9. l'inventore del barometro
10. il vincitore del Premio Nobel per la chimica nel 1963
11. librettista, compositore di *Mefistofele*
12. il più grande direttore d'orchestra
13. *La Bohème*, *Tosca*
14. grande violinista dell'Ottocento
15. lo "scopritore" dei canali su Marte

B. Complete the following sentences in Italian:

1. Gli esperimenti di Marconi portarono alla radio e alla _____ di oggi.
2. _____ studiò la circolazione del sangue e la riproduzione degli _____ microscopici.
3. Claudio _____ è considerato il creatore della musica moderna.
4. Domenico _____ scrisse più di _____ pezzi di musica.
5. *La Gioconda* fu composta da Amilcare _____.
6. Ruggiero Leoncavallo è conosciuto principalmente per _____.
7. I più grandi compositori di opere, secondo molti critici, sono Giuseppe _____ e _____ Puccini.
8. *Le Fontane di Roma* e *I Pini di* _____ sono composizioni di _____.
9. Gian Carlo Menotti ha scritto molte opere in _____.
10. La musica polifonica fu sviluppata da Palestrina prima di _____.

C. Match each item in column I with the corresponding item in column II.

Column I	*Column* II
1. Bellini	*a*. *Cavalleria Rusticana*
2. Leonardo	*b*. le note musicali
3. Bovet	*c*. Premio Nobel nel 1957
4. Mascagni	*d*. il paracadute
5. Menotti	*e*. la reazione nucleare
6. Fermi	*f*. le "overtures"
7. Guido d'Arezzo	*g*. il barometro
8. Torricelli	*h*. *Norma*
9. Scarlatti	*i*. *Guglielmo Tell*
10. Rossini	*j*. *The Medium*

D. Complete the following paragraph:

Domenica scorsa, Carla mi invitò a casa sua per ascoltare della musica e per dare un'occhiata ad alcuni libri scientifici. Il primo disco che ascoltammo fu un'aria dal *Trovatore* di Giuseppe __1__. Finito questo, Carla mise il disco con "Il ballo delle __2__" dalla *Gioconda* di __3__ Ponchielli. Ma la mia musica preferita è quella di Puccini. Allora, Carla mi fece sentire *La* __4__ *del West* e poi *Madama* __5__. Mentre ascoltavo questa musica dolce, diedi uno sguardo ai suoi libri scientifici e imparai che Evangelista __6__ fu l'inventore del barometro, e che Luigi __7__ scoprì la relazione fra organismi viventi e __8__. Sono rimasto affascinato del fatto che Galileo __9__ perfezionò il __10__, che usò per osservare i __11__ di Giove e gli anelli di __12__, come anche le __13__ della luna. Mentre leggevo, Carla mise l'ultimo disco del *Barbiere di* __14__ di Gioacchino __15__. Fu veramente una giornata indimenticabile!

E. Identify each person with a short sentence in Italian:

1. Enrico Fermi
2. Arturo Toscanini
3. Guglielmo Marconi
4. Gian Carlo Menotti
5. Guido d'Arezzo
6. Giacomo Puccini
7. Lazzaro Spallanzani
8. Pietro Mascagni
9. Evangelista Torricelli
10. Vincenzo Bellini
11. Giulio Natta
12. Antonio Vivaldi
13. Daniele Bovet
14. Ruggiero Leoncavallo
15. Alessandro Volta

13. Esploratori, Contributori alla Storia degli Stati Uniti, e il Cinema Italiano

ESPLORATORI

1. **Marco Polo** (1254-1324). Esploratore veneto che visitò l'Asia, e in modo particolare la Cina e il Giappone. Rimase alla corte del Kublai Khan per parecchi anni con il padre e con lo zio.
2. **Cristoforo Colombo** (1451-1506). Esploratore genovese che navigò sotto la bandiera spagnola. Scoprì il Nuovo Mondo (il continente americano) nel 1492. Fece quattro viaggi alle West Indies e lungo la zona dell'America Centrale.
3. **Giovanni Caboto (John Cabot)** (1450-1498). Esploratore veneto che navigò sotto la bandiera dell'Inghilterra. Attraversò l'Oceano Atlantico e scoprì la costa orientale dell'America del Nord nel 1497.
4. **Sebastiano Caboto** (1476-1557). Figlio di Giovanni Caboto, navigò per l'Inghilterra e per la Spagna. Sotto la bandiera spagnola, Sebastiano esplorò il Rio de la Plata, che si trova in Argentina. Sotto la bandiera inglese, comandò invece una spedizione che esplorò un passaggio nord-orientale, attraverso la Russia. Questa spedizione giunse fino alla città di Mosca.
5. **Amerigo Vespucci** (1454-1512). Navigatore e cartografo (*map maker*) che fece diversi viaggi al Nuovo Mondo. A causa delle sue carte geografiche e dei suoi scritti sulla nuova terra, l'America fu chiamata così per onorare le sue contribuzioni.
6. **Antonio Pigafetta** (1491-1534). Completò il viaggio di Magellano intorno al mondo dopo la morte dell'esploratore portoghese.
7. **Giovanni da Verrazano** (o **Verrazzano**) (1485-1528). Esploratore fiorentino che navigò per la Francia. Fu il primo ad entrare nel porto di New York, e scoprì il fiume Hudson parecchi anni prima di Henry Hudson.
8. **Luigi Amedeo di Savoia** (1873-1933). Fu il primo a scalare (*climb*) il Monte Saint Elias in Alaska nel 1897.
9. **Umberto Nobile** (1885-   ). Fu un generale dell'aeronautica (*Naval Air Force*) italiana, che esplorò l'Artico (*the Arctic*). Volò al di sopra del Polo Nord in un dirigibile nel 1926.

CONTRIBUTORI ALLA STORIA DEGLI STATI UNITI

Oltre ad Arturo Toscanini, Gian Carlo Menotti, Enrico Fermi, Cristoforo Colombo, Amerigo Vespucci, e Giovanni da Verrazano, i seguenti hanno anche contribuito alla storia del nostro paese:

1. **Enrico Tonti** (1650-1704). Esplorò i Grandi Laghi (*Great Lakes*) e il fiume Mississippi insieme a Robert de La Salle. Tonti viene frequentemente chiamato il "padre dell'Arkansas."

2. **Filippo Mazzei** (1730-1816). Amico intimo di Thomas Jefferson e patriota americano che viaggiò per tutta l'Europa per raccogliere (*raise*) denaro per aiutare la Rivoluzione Americana. L'espressione "tutti gli uomini sono creati uguali" (*all men are created equal*) fu usata da Mazzei in un libro scritto da lui e poi incorporata nella Dichiarazione d'Indipendenza da Thomas Jefferson. Scrisse anche la prima storia degli Stati Uniti pubblicata in Italia.

3. **William Paca** (1740-1799). Firmò, insieme ad altri, la Dichiarazione d'Indipendenza e prese parte a molti movimenti politici americani dal 1771 fino alla sua morte. Fu Governatore del Maryland e fu anche nominato Giudice della Corte del Maryland dal Presidente Washington nel 1789.

4. **Francesco Vigo** (1747-1836). Fu un eroe della guerra rivoluzionaria americana. Era amico del Generale Clark e contribuì molto denaro alla spedizione Lewis e Clark (*Lewis and Clark Expedition*).

5. **Lorenzo da Ponte** (1749-1838). Fondò la New York Italian Opera House nel 1833. Questo teatro fu il precursore della Metropolitan Opera House.

6. **Constantino Brumidi** (1805-1880). Conosciuto come il "Michelangelo degli Stati Uniti." Passò la maggior parte della sua vita a decorare e dipingere l'interno del Capitol nella città di Washington.

7. **Antonio Meucci** (1808-1889). Fu realmente il primo ad inventare il telefono alcuni anni prima di Alexander Bell.

8. **Paolo Busti** (1749-1824). Disegnò i piani per la città di Buffalo.

9. **Luigi da Cesnola** (1832-1904). Generale nell'esercito dell'Unione (*Union Army*), fu onorato con la Medaglia d'Oro del Congresso (*Congressional Medal of Honor*). Fu direttore del Metropolitan Museum of Art dal 1879 al 1904.

10. **Santa Francesca Saveria Cabrini** (1850–1917). La prima cittadina americana ad essere dichiarata santa dalla Chiesa Cattolica. Fece molto per gli immigranti italiani.

11. **Amedeo P. Giannini** (1870–1949). Stabilì la Banca d'Italia in America che nel 1930 divenne la Banca d'America (*The Bank of America*). Questa è oggi la banca commerciale più grande del mondo.

12. **Enrico Caruso** (1873-1921). Tenore della Metropolitan Opera House, considerato il più grande tenore nella storia dell'opera.

13. **Fiorello La Guardia** (1882–1947). Fu sindaco (*mayor*) di New York dal 1934 al 1945. Fu anche ideatore di molti programmi stabiliti per aiutare la gente di questa città.

IL CINEMA ITALIANO

Attori e Attrici

1. **Rossano Brazzi** (1917-   ). Attore italiano che ha avuto molto successo a Hollywood. Ha girato molti film negli Stati Uniti tra i quali: *Little Women* e *South Pacific*.

2. **Silvana Mangano** (1930-   ). Attrice italiana che fu molto acclamata negli Stati Uniti per due dei suoi film: *Riso Amaro* (*Bitter Rice*) e *Anna*.

3. **Vittorio De Sica** (1901–1975). Famoso attore italiano di cinema e di varietà che venne conosciuto negli Stati Uniti, per primo, nei film *Pane, Amore, e Fantasia* (*Bread, Love, and Dreams*) e *Pane, Amore, e Gelosia* (*Bread, Love, and Jealousy*). Questi film furono girati insieme a Gina Lollobrigida altra attrice ben conosciuta.

4. **Virna Lisi** (1936-   ). Attrice italiana che ha girato molti film negli Stati Uniti. Due suoi film che hanno avuto molto successo sono: *Divorzio all'Americana* (*Divorce American Style*) e *Il Miracolo di Santa Vittoria* (*The Miracle of Santa Vittoria*).

5. **Vittorio Gassman** (1922-   ). Attore italiano di grande abilità comica e drammatica. È stato il protagonista di molti film visti negli Stati Uniti come, per esempio, *Big Deal on Madonna Street*. È molto acclamato e apprezzato in Italia anche come attore di recita (*legitimate stage*).

6. **Giancarlo Giannini** (1942-   ). Il più recente degli attori italiani ad avere successo negli Stati Uniti. È il protagonista principale dei film della regista (*director*) Lina Wertmüller. Questi sono: *La Seduzione di Mimì*

(*The Seduction of Mimi*), *Naufragio* (*Swept Away*), e *Pasqualino Sette Bellezze* (*Seven Beauties*).

7. **Anna Magnani** (1909-1971). Grande attrice italiana diventata famosa negli Stati Uniti per la sua rappresentazione nel film *Roma, Città Aperta* (*Open City*). Nel 1957, girò il film *The Rose Tattoo*, per il quale ricevette un Oscar.

8. **Marcello Mastroianni** (1924-). Probabilmente l'attore italiano più famoso del mondo, è conosciuto negli Stati Uniti principalmente per le sue rappresentazioni nei film: *La Dolce Vita* (*The Easy Life*), *Divorzio all'Italiana* (*Divorce Italian Style*), e *Matrimonio all'Italiana* (*Marriage Italian Style*).

9. **Giulietta Masina** (1926-). È un'altra attrice italiana ben conosciuta negli Stati Uniti. È stata la protagonista di alcuni film che hanno avuto molto successo in questo paese: *La Strada* (*The Street*), *Le Notti di Cabiria* (*Nights of Cabiria*), e *Giulietta degli Spiriti* (*Juliet of the Spirits*).

10. **Gina Lollobrigida** (1927-). Anche questa attrice del cinema italiano e americano è conosciutissima negli Stati Uniti. La prima volta che una sua rappresentazione fu vista negli Stati Uniti fu quella del film *Pane, Amore, e Fantasia*, che girò in Italia con Vittorio De Sica. Dopo il successo di questo film, girò molti altri film sia in Italia che a Hollywood.

11. **Sophia Loren** (1934-) è probabilmente l'attrice italiana più famosa negli Stati Uniti. Fra tutti i film che ha girato in Italia e a Hollywood, il migliore si può considerare *La Ciociara* (*Two Women*), per il quale ricevette un Oscar.

Registi

1. **Roberto Rossellini** (1906-1977). Il primo dei registi italiani ad avere successo negli Stati Uniti. I suoi film *Roma, Città Aperta, Paisà* (*Countryman*), *Stromboli*, e *Il Generale della Rovere* (*The General della Rovere*) hanno introdotto, negli Stati Uniti, il movimento neo-realistico del cinema italiano del dopoguerra. Alcuni attori usati da Rossellini nei suoi film (e.g., *Stromboli* e *Paisà*) non erano attori professionali, ma individui il cui personaggio rappresentava il carattere e l'attitudine di un popolo che aveva sofferto la catastrofe di una guerra disastrosa.

2. **Luchino Visconti** (1906-1976). Considerato come il padre del movimento neo-realistico del cinema italiano del dopoguerra, venne conosciuto negli Stati Uniti molto più tardi degli altri registi che lo imitarono. I due suoi

film che furono molto acclamati sono: *Rocco e i suoi Fratelli* (*Rocco and his Brothers*) e *Il Gattopardo* (*The Leopard*).

3. **Vittorio De Sica** (1901-1975). Altro regista molto popolare del dopoguerra che seguì il movimento realistico del cinema. Venne conosciuto negli Stati Uniti nel 1945, quando fu presentato il suo film *Sciuscià* (*Shoeshine*). Continuò ad avere successo come regista e come attore fino alla sua morte, nel 1975. Altri suoi film ben conosciuti sono: *Ladri di Biciclette* (*Bicycle Thief*), *Umberto D*, *L'Oro di Napoli* (*The Gold of Naples*), *La Ciociara*, *Il Giardino dei Finzi-Contini* (*The Garden of the Finzi-Continis*), e il suo ultimo film *La Vacanza* (*The Vacation*), completato qualche mese prima della sua morte.

4. **Michelangelo Antonioni** (1912-   ). È un'altro regista i cui film hanno avuto molto successo negli Stati Uniti. Alcuni dei suoi film sono stati premiati, come, per esempio, *L'Avventura* (*The Adventure*), *La Notte* (*The Night*), e *L'Eclisse* (*The Eclipse*). Altri due suoi film più recenti sono anche ben conosciuti. Questi sono: *Blow-up*, che si svolge (*takes place*) in l'Inghilterra, e *Zabriskie Point*, che si svolge negli Stati Uniti.

5. **Giuseppe De Santis** (1917-   ). Non è molto conosciuto negli Stati Uniti. Nel 1949, però, diresse il film *Riso Amaro*, che ha avuto grande successo in molte parti del mondo. Anche questo film fa parte del movimento neo-realistico del dopoguerra.

6. **Pietro Germi** (1914-   ). È conosciuto negli Stati Uniti come il regista del film *Divorzio all'Italiana.* Di tutti i film italiani che sono stati mostrati negli Stati Uniti, questo è stato il più popolare.

7. **Federico Fellini** (1920-   ). È molto conosciuto negli Stati Uniti come regista, perchè i suoi film riflettono il movimento più recente del cinema italiano. Questo è il movimento "psicologico-simbolico" che sta dominando il cinema internazionale dalla fine del 1950 fino ad oggi. I suoi film principali sono: *La Strada*, *La Dolce Vita*, *8½*, *Giulietta degli Spiriti*, e *Amarcord* (*Bitter Memories*).

8. **Lina Wertmüller** (1928-   ). È la più recente dei registi italiani ad essere acclamata negli Stati Uniti. Finora, tre dei suoi film hanno avuto molto successo: *La Seduzione di Mimì*, *Naufragio*, e *Pasqualino Sette Bellezze*.

Note

I film di altri tre bravi registi italiani arrivano, di tanto in tanto, negli Stati Uniti. Finora, però, questi registi non sono ben conosciuti dalla maggioranza della popolazione. Si parla di **Mario Soldati** (1906–), di **Pier Paolo Pasolini** (1922–1975), e di **Bernardo Bertolucci** (1940–).

Produttori

1. **Dino De Laurentiis** (1919–). È uno dei produttori del cinema italiano più conosciuto negli Stati Uniti. Tra il 1950 e il 1957, De Laurentiis ha prodotto molti dei film già indicati come: *Riso Amaro*, *La Strada*, ecc. Ha prodotto e continua a produrre tuttora anche film e programmi per la televisione americana.

2. **Carlo Ponti** (1913–). È anche molto conosciuto negli Stati Uniti come produttore. Ha prodotto quasi tutti i film di sua moglie, Sophia Loren, e del comico italiano Totò.

Festival

Il Festival del Cinema di Venezia fu fondato nel 1932 dal Conte Volpi, un veneziano. Questo festival è rinomato in tutto il mondo per la mostra annuale dei migliori film internazionali.

EXERCISES

A. Identify each of the persons described:

1. il cartografo che diede il suo nome all'America
2. completò il viaggio di Magellano
3. esplorò i Grandi Laghi
4. un generale nell'esercito dell'Unione
5. il vero inventore del telefono
6. scoprì la costa orientale dell'America del Nord
7. il primo ad entrare nel porto di New York
8. volò al di sopra del Polo Nord
9. il fondatore della Banca d'America
10. il sindaco di New York
11. il migliore cantante del mondo
12. uno dei firmatari della Dichiarazione d'Indipendenza
13. il "Michelangelo degli Stati Uniti"
14. la prima santa americana
15. un amico del Generale Clark

B. Complete each sentence in Italian:

1. Luigi _____ fu il primo a scalare il Monte Saint Elias.
2. Marco _____ era amico del Kublai _____ .
3. _____ Caboto esplorò il Rio de la Plata.
4. Giovanni da _____ scoprì il fiume Hudson prima di _____ Hudson.
5. Filippo _____ era amico di Thomas Jefferson.
6. _____ fu direttore del Metropolitan Museum of Art.
7. Amedeo _____ fondò la _____ d'Italia.
8. _____ fece i piani per la città di Buffalo.
9. Umberto Nobile fu esploratore dell' _____ e sorvolò il Polo _____ .
10. Lorenzo _____ stabilì la New York Italian _____ House.
11. _____ è la protagonista del film *Riso Amaro*.
12. Anna Magnani è la protagonista del film _____ , diretto da Roberto Rossellini.
13. Il film *Pane, Amore, e Fantasia* ha per protagonista l'attrice _____ .
14. _____ è l'attrice italiana che si puo vedere nel film *La Strada*.
15. Il film per il quale Sophia Loren ha ricevuto l'Oscar ha per titolo _____ .

C. Complete the following sentences by choosing the correct word or expression in parentheses:

1. Filippo Mazzei scrisse la prima storia (dell'Italia, degli Stati Uniti) in italiano.
2. (Lorenzo da Ponte, Enrico Tonti) esplorò il Mississippi con Robert de La Salle.
3. Brumidi fu pittore a (Roma, Washington).
4. La prima santa americana è (Santa Margherita, Santa Francesca Cabrini).
5. (Cristoforo Colombo, Amerigo Vespucci) scoprì il Nuovo Mondo nel 1492.
6. William Paca firmò la (Dichiarazione d'Indipendenza, la Costituzione) americana.
7. Antonio Meucci fu il primo ad inventare (la radio, il telefono).
8. Enrico Caruso era (cantante, esploratore).
9. L'esploratore che visitò la Cina fu (Cristoforo Colombo, Marco Polo).
10. Giovanni Caboto viaggiò per la bandiera (inglese, italiana).
11. (*Ladri di Biciclette*, *Paisà*) è un film diretto da Roberto Rossellini.
12. Uno dei film diretti da Vittoria De Sica è (*Il Gattopardo*, *Sciuscià*).
13. Il produttore del film (*Riso Amaro*, *La Ciociara*) è stato Dino De Laurentiis.

14. Luchino Visconti ha diretto il film (*Rocco e i suoi Fratelli, Il Giardino dei Finzi-Contini*).
15. (*L'Avventura, Amarcord*) è un film diretto da Michelangelo Antonioni.

D. Complete the following paragraph in Italian:

Dal viaggio di __1__ in Cina al contributo di __2__ all'opera del Metropolitan di New York, possiamo elencare (*to list*) una schiera di personaggi italiani che diedero al mondo il loro ingegno. Molti di questi ebbero un influsso significativo sugli Stati Uniti. Dopo la scoperta dell'America per opera di __3__ nel __4__, altri Italiani lo seguirono per esplorare varie zone del nuovo continente. __5__, per esempio, disegnò le prime carte geografiche della nuova terra in base ai propri viaggi. __6__ scoprì la costa orientale dell'America, mentre, __7__ fu il primo a scoprire il fiume Hudson.

E. Identify each person with a short sentence in Italian:

1. Federico Fellini
2. Sebastiano Caboto
3. Antonio Pigafetta
4. Vittorio Gassman
5. Carlo Ponti
6. Filippo Mazzei
7. Francesco Vigo
8. Enrico Caruso
9. Amedeo P. Giannini
10. Constantino Brumidi
11. Marcello Mastroianni
12. William Paca
13. Luigi da Cesnola
14. Vittorio De Sica
15. Lorenzo da Ponte

14. Mastery Exercises

A. Choose the word or expression that does *not* belong with the others:

1. regioni: Basilicata, Lazio, Alpi, Puglia
2. monti: Bianco, Rosa, Cervino, Cimabue
3. scultori: Palestrina, Bernini, Canova, Michelangelo
4. compositori: Rossini, Verdi, Puccini, da Cesnola
5. pittori: Caravaggio, Stromboli, Tintoretto, Tiepolo
6. città: Napoli, Capri, Firenze, Pisa
7. scienziati: D'Annunzio, Fermi, Bovet, Spallanzani
8. esploratori: Verrazano, Polo, da Vinci, Caboto
9. architetti: Nervi, Brunelleschi, Bramante, Puccini
10. vini: mozzarella, Barolo, spumante, chianti
11. chiese: Santa Maria del Fiore, San Pietro, Colosseo, Santa Croce
12. porti: Spoleto, Palermo, Trieste, Venezia
13. laghi: Garda, Adige, Como, Maggiore
14. fiumi: Arno, Tevere, Po, Etna
15. automobili: Ferrari, Soave, Alfa Romeo, FIAT
16. piazze: di Spagna, Navona, Venezia, Sistina
17. contributori alla storia americana: Cabrini, da Ponte, Polo, Caruso
18. piatti: linguine al pesto, ravioli, marsala, cannelloni
19. vulcani: Como, Stromboli, Etna, Vesuvio
20. musei: Uffizi, Pitti, Bargello, Colosseo
21. strade famose: Veneto, Appia, Condotti, Parma
22. scrittori: Boccaccio, Petrarca, Borromini, Moravia
23. scienziati: Malpighi, Volta, Galvani, Michelangelo
24. musicisti: Leopardi, Respighi, da Palestrina, Leoncavallo
25. artisti: Tiziano, Barolo, Raffaello, Modigliani

B. Choose the correct response in parentheses:

1. L'Italia ha (20, 18, 15) regioni.
2. La Festa del Redentore si celebra a (Palermo, Venezia, Napoli).
3. Andrea Mantegna era noto come (architetto, pittore, scultore).
4. La *Cavalleria Rusticana* fu composta da (Leoncavallo, Mascagni, Verdi).
5. Il Quirinale è (un museo, la residenza del Presidente, una chiesa).
6. La mozzarella è (un formaggio, un vino, una canzone).
7. L'Italia ha la forma di (un'isola, uno stivale, un cerchio).
8. Il più grande poeta d'Italia è (Respighi, Dante, D'Annunzio).

9. L'istruzione in Italia è obbligatoria fino all'età di (16, 12, 14) anni.
10. L'anniversario della Repubblica Italiana è festeggiato il (1.o maggio, 2 giugno, 16 aprile).
11. Il Colosseo è un monumento nella città di (Roma, Venezia, Firenze).
12. Gli Appennini sono (fiumi, montagne, laghi).
13. *Il Principe* è il capolavoro di (Machiavelli, Michelangelo, Modigliani).
14. Il Giro d'Italia è (un'opera, una corsa di biciclette, un dipinto).
15. La sede della FIAT è a (Milano, Torino, Pisa).
16. La Sardegna è (un'isola, un fiume, una catena di montagne).
17. Una delle nazioni che confina con l'Italia è (la Germania, la Spagna, l'Austria).
18. Alessandro Manzoni era noto come (musicista, romanziere, scienziato).
19. Un compositore italiano che ha scritto molte opere in inglese è (Leoncavallo, Menotti, Puccini).
20. La Festa di Piedigrotta viene celebrata a (Pisa, Napoli, San Remo).
21. L'Arno è un (monte, lago, fiume).
22. La prima santa americana è (Maria Goretti, Grazia Deledda, Francesca Cabrini).
23. Il calcio è (un piatto, un formaggio, uno sport) italiano.
24. La scuola magistrale è per gli studenti che vogliono diventare (architetti, insegnanti, dottori).
25. Uno scienziato che vinse il Premio Nobel nel 1938 è (Fermi, Natta, Bovet).
26. Capri è (un'isola, una città, una regione).
27. Una delle città del "triangolo industriale del nord" è (Bari, Milano, Firenze).
28. Fra gli scrittori moderni c'è (Moravia, Tasso, Ariosto).
29. Il Palio di Siena ha luogo il (30 ottobre, 2 luglio, 2 giugno).
30. La "Serenissima" è il nome dato a (Pisa, Genova, Venezia).
31. Oltre all'italiano, in tutte le regioni si parla anche (un dialetto, il francese, il tedesco).
32. L'Umbria è nell'Italia (centrale, settentrionale, meridionale).
33. Enrico Fermi era una grande (astronomo, fisico, pittore).
34. La Torre Pendente è a (Bologna, Torino, Pisa).
35. La "Città Eterna" e (Siena, Roma, Firenze).
36. Pierluigi da Palestrina era un celebre (scrittore, architetto, musicista).
37. Il Piemonte è (una penisola, una regione, un monte).
38. Guglielmo Marconi è l'inventore (della televisione, della radio, del cannocchiale).
39. Il capoluogo della Sardegna è (Sassari, Cagliari, Nuoro).

40. La *Mona Lisa* è opera di (Michelangelo, Leonardo da Vinci, Raffaello).
41. Il fiume più lungo d'Italia è (l'Arno, il Tevere, il Po).
42. *Il Cenacolo* è un dipinto di (Botticelli, Leopardi, Leonardo da Vinci).
43. Il Vesuvio è (un vulcano, uno stretto, un lago).
44. Fra i vini italiani c'è (il Barolo, lo Stromboli, la Ferrari).
45. Le Catacombe venivano usate dai primi (scrittori, cristiani, imperatori) romani.
46. Pirandello è l'autore del romanzo (*Il Gattopardo*, *I Malavoglia*, *Il Fu Mattia Pascal*).
47. *La Nascita di Venere* fu dipinto da (Modigliani, Botticelli, Raffaello).
48. Trinacria era il nome antico (della Toscana, dell'Umbria, della Sicilia).
49. *Il Decamerone* è una raccolta di (poesie, novelle, romanzi).
50. La *pasta alle sarde* è un piatto tipico (della Puglia, della Sicilia, della Lombardia).
51. Carlo Ponti è il produttore dei film principali di (Virna Lisi, Giulietta Masina, Sophia Loren).
52. Il Festival del Cinema ha luogo a (Trieste, Venezia, Roma).
53. Giancarlo Giannini è il protagonista del film (*l'Avventura*, *Divorzio all'Italiana*, *Naufragio*).
54. Il regista Giuseppe De Santis è conosciuto negli Stati Uniti per il film (*Roma, Città Aperta*; *Riso Amaro*; *Amarcord*).
55. Un protagonista nel film *La Dolce Vita* è (Vittorio Gassman, Rossano Brazzi, Marcello Mastroianni).

C. Write **vero** if the statement is true. If the statement is false, rewrite it to make it true:

1. Bologna ha l'università più antica del mondo.
2. Tutti gli studenti italiani devono frequentare il liceo.
3. Giuseppe Verdi era un celebre scrittore.
4. Il Presidente della Repubblica viene eletto dal popolo.
5. Tra le città industriali italiane ci sono Milano, Genova, e Torino.
6. Le Alpi separano l'Italia dalla Francia e dalla Svizzera.
7. Salvatore Quasimodo era musicista.
8. Enrico Caruso era un grande tenore.
9. Piazza di Spagna è a Firenze.
10. Paganini era un noto violinista.
11. "Le porte del Paradiso" furono scolpite da Michelangelo.
12. Torino è un centro della moda italiana.
13. La Costituzione italiana fu approvata nel 1956.
14. Pier Luigi Nervi è un noto architetto.

15. Il provolone è un vino squisito.
16. Firenze è il capoluogo della Toscana.
17. L'Arno attraversa Roma.
18. Guido d'Arezzo inventò le noti musicali.
19. Il Ferragosto si celebra in aprile.
20. La lingua italiana deriva dal latino.
21. Filippo Mazzei era amico di Thomas Jefferson.
22. Il bar non è importante per gli Italiani.
23. L'abbacchio è una specialità toscana.
24. William Paca firmò la Dichiarazione d'Indipendenza.
25. Cortina d'Ampezzo è nota per gli sport estivi.
26. La Befana è una festa religiosa.
27. Lo spagnolo è una lingua romanza.
28. Brumidi era "il Michelangelo dell'Italia."
29. Antonio Fogazzaro era drammaturgo.
30. Marco Polo viaggiò in Francia e in Inghilterra.

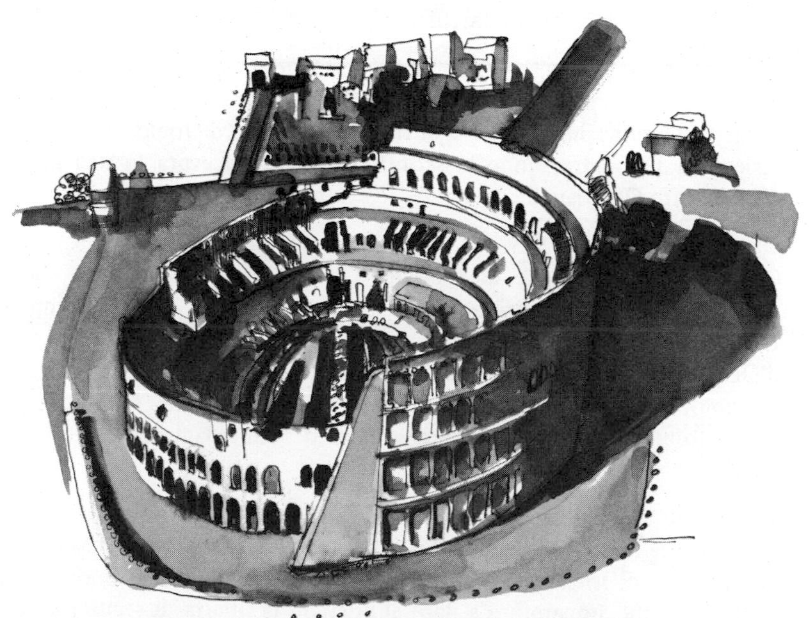

L'interno del *Colosseo*, famoso anfiteatro dell'antica Roma, visto dall'alto. Milioni di turisti lo visitano ogni anno.

15. Personaggi Importanti della Storia d'Italia (Optional)

Note

In Lessons 15 and 16, both the historical present and the past absolute are used to make students aware of the possibility of using either tense to describe distant historical events.

IL PERIODO ROMANO

1. **Giulio Cesare** (c. 102 a.C.–44 a.C.) (a.C. = avanti Cristo). Generale romano che conquistò molti popoli. Sotto il suo comando, Roma divenne la più grande potenza del mondo occidentale. Fu ucciso il 15 marzo, 44 a.C. da un gruppo di repubblicani, fra i quali c'era il suo figlio adottivo, Bruto. Cesare fu ucciso perchè stava per (*was about to*) convertire la Repubblica in monarchia.

2. **Marco Antonio** (83 a.C.–30 a.C.). Console romano e parente di Giulio Cesare, fu il primo a dichiarare (*declare*) guerra contro gli assassini di Cesare. Divenne imperatore dell'Impero Romano d'Oriente e si uccise, insieme a **Cleopatra**, dopo la sconfitta (*defeat*) ricevuta in una guerra civile contro Ottaviano.

3. **Ottaviano (Augusto)** (63 a.C.–14 d.C.) (d.C. = dopo Cristo). Pronipote (*great-grandson*) e figlio adottivo di Giulio Cesare, si unisce a Marco Antonio per vendicare (*revenge*) la morte del nonno. Forma l'Impero Romano insieme a Marco Antonio e diventa imperatore dell'Impero d'Occidente. In seguito a una guerra civile nella quale sconfigge Marco Antonio, Ottaviano unisce i due imperi in un solo regno. Diventa così imperatore di tutto l'Impero, e il Senato romano gli dà il nome di **Augusto.**

4. **Costantino** (c. 288–337). Ultimo grande imperatore romano. Divise nuovamente l'Impero in quello d'occidente e quello d'oriente. La capitale dell'Impero d'Oriente fu chiamata Costantinopoli in suo onore. Fu anche il primo imperatore a dare ai cristiani la libertà di seguire la loro religione apertamente (Editto di Milano, 313).

5. **Giustiniano** (483-565). Imperatore dell'Impero d'Oriente che fece salvare e regolare le leggi romane. Questo sistema di leggi fu usato come base per la formazione dei codici delle leggi moderne di tutto il mondo occidentale.

LA DOMINAZIONE STRANIERA

6. **Odoacre** (434-493). Primo imperatore "barbarico" di Roma. Con la sua conquista dell'Impero d'Occidente, cominciano le dominazioni "barbariche" della penisola. L'Impero d'Oriente, invece, continua sotto il dominio degli eredi (*heirs*) di Costantino.
7. **Teodorico** (c. 454-526). Generale degli Ostrogoti, altro popolo barbarico. In accordo con l'Imperatore d'Oriente, invade Roma e si stabilisce (*establishes himself*) come imperatore romano. I suoi eredi, però, non furono capaci di mantenere la pace. Con questa scusa, l'imperatore bizantino invade l'Italia e la pone sotto il dominio dell'Impero d'Oriente (chiamato già Impero Bizantino).
8. **Liutprando** (re dal 712 al 744). Generale dei Longobardi, altro popolo "barbarico," che scaccia (*drives out*) i Bizantini dal centro e dal nord della penisola. Per conseguenza, l'Italia viene divisa in due domini (*kingdoms*): il dominio longobardo (centro e nord) e il dominio bizantino (Meridione e Sicilia). Alla fine di questa guerra, il Papa ottiene Sustri, e si sviluppa così il potere "temporale" della Chiesa.
9. **Pipino** (?-768). Re dei Franchi, altro popolo "barbarico," che sconfigge i Longobardi. Come risultato di questa sconfitta, la Romagna e il Lazio passano alla Chiesa e si forma così lo Stato Pontificio. (Il Papa Stefano II aveva chiesto l'aiuto di Pipino contro i Longobardi.) L'Italia si divide così in tre parti: L'Impero dei Franchi (centro e nord), lo Stato Pontificio (Romagna e Lazio), e l'Impero Bizantino (Meridione e Sicilia).
10. **Carlo Magno** (742-814). Figlio di Pipino ed erede dell'Impero dei Franchi, conquista i Sassoni (Germania), gli Arabi (Spagna), e stabilisce il primo Regno d'Italia. Viene incoronato (*crowned*) dal Papa come imperatore del Sacro Romano Impero, e con questa incoronazione si crea nuovamente l'Impero d'Occidente sotto il dominio "spirituale" della Chiesa.
11. **Federico I** (c. 1123-1190) (detto **il Barbarossa**). Re di Germania che, dopo una serie di guerre fra gli eredi di Carlo Magno, scende in Italia per stabilire l'ordine. Rimane in Italia e riceve anche lui la corona del Sacro Romano Impero. L'imperatore attaccò i Comuni italiani, formati da

recente, ma non gli fu possibile conquistarli. Si formò contro di lui la prima Lega Lombarda, alla quale presero parte (*took part*) i Comuni e lo Stato Pontificio. Questa lega ottenne la sconfitta dell'imperatore alla famosa battaglia di Legnano (1176).

12. **Innocenzo III** (1160-1216). Papa severo e autoritario che proclamò l'autorità della Chiesa su tutti i regnanti della terra con il famoso decreto: "Ogni autorità viene da Dio." Divenne padrino (*godfather*) e tutore di Federico II di Svevia alla morte dei genitori di questo quando Federico era ancora bambino.

13. **Federico II** (1194-1250). Nipote di Federico I (Barbarossa) fu posto sul trono di Germania dal Papa Innocenzo III a condizione che affidasse (*entrust*) il Regnò di Sicilia ad altri. Federico II non mantenne la parola data al Papa e si trasferì (*moved*) invece in Sicilia, dove fondò la corte più famosa del Medioevo. In questa corte, situata a Palermo, si sviluppò la base della letteratura e della lingua italiana. Inoltre (*In addition*), Federico II fondò l'Università di Napoli e la Scuola Medica di Salerno.

    L'odio di Federico II verso il Papa causò nuove lotte con i Comuni e con lo Stato Pontificio. Si formò così la seconda Lega Lombarda per la difesa dei Comuni e della Chiesa. Durante queste lotte, si formarono in Italia due fazioni politiche: i Guelfi, a favore della Chiesa, e i Ghibellini, a favore dell'imperatore.

14. **Manfredi** (c. 1232-1266). Figlio di Federico II, continua la lotta, iniziata dal padre, contro i Comuni e contro lo Stato Pontificio. Il Papa chiede l'aiuto della Francia, e così scende in Italia Carlo d'Angiò. Manfredi viene ucciso nella battaglia di Benevento (1266), e il Regno di Sicilia passa agli Angioini.

15. **Carlo d'Angiò** (1226-1288). Fratello del re di Francia, stabilisce la dinastia angioina nell'Italia meridionale e in Sicilia. Durante il suo regno, scoppia (*breaks out*) una rivoluzione sull'Isola che si conosce con il nome di Vespri Siciliani (1282). Questa rivoluzione si conclude con una guerra nella quale i Siciliani, con l'aiuto della Spagna, cacciano (*chase away*) i Francesi (Angioini) dalla Sicilia.

16. **Bonifazio VIII** (Papa dal 1294 al 1303). Ultimo Papa teocratico il quale voleva portare il potere della Chiesa nuovamente al livello dell'autorità di Innocenzo III. Questo suo tentativo non ebbe successo perchè il re di Francia (Filippo IX) si rifiutò di accettare l'autorità assoluta del Papa. Inoltre, Bonifazio VIII è anche noto per aver mandato in esilio (*exile*) Dante Alighieri.

17. **Clemente V** (Papa dal 1305 al 1314). Vescovo (*Bishop*) francese che divenne Papa alla morte di Bonifazio VIII. Fu autore dello spostamento (*movement*) della sede papale in Francia, perchè si rifiutò di trasferirsi a Roma. Dopo la sua morte, questo rifiuto causò il famoso scisma della Chiesa perchè furono eletti (*elected*) due papi nello stesso periodo: **Urbano VI** a Roma e **Clemente VII** in Francia.

18. **Lorenzo dei Medici** (1449-1492) (detto **il Magnifico**). Grande uomo di stato che governò Firenze nel periodo in cui la città diventò "la culla dell'arte." Fu capace di ottenere un lungo periodo di pace in tutta l'Italia usando la diplomazia e mantenendo così il bilancio (*balance of power*) fra le varie potenze. È conosciuto anche come grande appassionato delle belle arti.

19. **Girolamo Savonarola** (1452-1498). Frate domenicano fiorentino che predicava (*preached*) sempre contro il governo dei Medici. Dopo la caduta di questi, i Fiorentini formarono una repubblica ed elessero Savonarola come capo del governo. Questa repubblica, però, non durò a lungo. I Medici presero un'altra volta il potere, e il Papa proibì a Savonarola di predicare contro di loro. Savonarola si rifiutò e fu, per primo, scomunicato (*excommunicated*) e poi impiccato (*hanged*) e bruciato (*burned*) in Piazza della Signoria a Firenze.

20. **Alessandro VI** (1431-1503). Papa della famiglia spagnuola dei Borgia che passò alla storia come il Papa più nepotista di tutti. Lo conosciamo anche come il padre di Cesare Borgia e per avere scomunicato Girolamo Savonarola.

21. **Cesare Borgia** (1476-1507). Capitano generale (Gonfaloniere) della Chiesa, titolo datogli da suo padre Alessandro VI. Conquistò la Romagna e le Marche, uccidendo i "Signori" che le governavano, e formò, di questi, uno stato unico. Cesare Borgia fu usato da Machiavelli come modello per il suo *Principe*, un trattato politico che espone la dottrina dell'uso di qualsiasi mezzo, anche l'uccisione degli avversari, per arrivare ad un obiettivo considerato giusto.

22. **Giulio II** (Papa dal 1503 al 1513). Papa che si dedicò più ad essere principe che pontefice (*pontiff*). Fu tenace nemico dei Borgia e per questo causò la caduta di Cesare Borgia dal potere dello stato che aveva formato (Romagna-Marche).

23. **Carlo V** (1500-1558). Re asburgo (*Austrian*) che diventa anche re di Spagna. Carlo V impone al Papa Clemente VII (Sacco di Roma, 1527) di dargli la corona del Sacro Romano Impero come erede di Carlo Magno.

Durante la prima metà del secolo XVI, diventa il più forte uomo di stato dell'Europa. Questo porta alle guerre di supremazia che si combattono, principalmente in Italia, tra la Francia e la Spagna.

24. **Napoleone Bonaparte** (1769-1821). Nato in Corsica, da genitori italiani, diventò per primo generale e poi imperatore di Francia. Napoleone invase l'Italia dando alla penisola una certa libertà. Scacciò gli Austriaci dalla Lombardia e formò il Regno Italico sotto il "codice napoleonico."

IL RISORGIMENTO

25. **Giuseppe Mazzini** (1805-1872). Nato a Genova, Mazzini tentò molte volte di unificare l'Italia. I suoi scritti dettero l'impeto agli altri patriotti del Risorgimento di scacciare lo straniero dall'Italia a tutti i costi. Per questa ragione, Mazzini, venne chiamato "la penna del Risorgimento." Dobbiamo anche segnalare che oltre ai suo scritti, Mazzini tentò più volte di unificare il paese con la forza. Abbiamo come esempio, la fondazione della Repubblica romana (1849) che, però, non durò a lungo.

26. **Giuseppe Garibaldi** (1807-1882). Chiamato "l'eroe dei due mondi," fu un altro patriotta del Risorgimento. Garibaldi prese il comando di parecchi tentativi per unificare la penisola. Lo vediamo per primo nella rivoluzione contro Roma, poi al comando delle truppe piemontesi in una spedizione (*expedition*) contro l'Austria. La sua impresa più grande però fu la Spedizione dei Mille con la quale conquistò la Sicilia e il Meridione. In ultimo, riapparve nello scontro (*battle*) di Aspromonte, dove le truppe del Regno d'Italia sconfissero i Garibaldini e presero Garibaldi prigioniero (*prisoner*). Quest'ultimo avvenimento fu causato dal fatto che Garibaldi riteneva che Vittorio Emanuele II agisse troppo lentamente nel risolvere la "questione romana." Garibaldi morì in ritiro, a Caprera, nel 1882, passando alla storia come "la spada del Risorgimento."

27. **Camillo Benso di Cavour** (1810-1861). Primo Ministro del Re Vittorio Emanuele II, fu capace di usare l'arte della diplomazia per ottenere l'unificazione dell'Italia. Usò l'amicizia con Napoleone III di Francia per scacciare l'Austria e per stabilire definitivamente il Regno d'Italia. Cavour passò alla storia come "il pensiero del Risorgimento."

28. **Silvio Pellico** (1788-1854). Scrittore e patriotta del Risorgimento, scrisse un famoso libro intitolato (*entitled*) *Le mie Prigioni*, nel quale descrive le sofferenze passate nel carcere austriaco di Spielberg, sia da lui che da

altri patriotti italiani del Risorgimento come **Pietro Maroncelli e Federico Confalonieri.**

29. **Carlo Alberto di Savoia** (re dal 1831 al 1849). Re di Piemonte e di Sardegna, fu il primo sovrano italiano a dedicare la sua vita alla liberazione dell'Italia dal dominio straniero.

    L'indipendenza e l'unificazione del paese si ottenne finalmente, durante il regno di suo figlio, Vittorio Emanuele II.

30. **Vittorio Emanuele II** (re dal 1849 al 1878). Figlio di Carlo Alberto, Re di Piemonte e di Sardegna, Vittorio Emanuele II fu il re che salì sul primo trono del Regno d'Italia dopo l'unificazione. Insieme al suo Primo Ministro Camillo Benso di Cavour, ottenne l'unificazione del nord e del centro della penisola.

L'ITALIA MODERNA

31. **Vittorio Emanuele III** (1869-1947). Erede del primo Re d'Italia, salì al trono nel 1900. Questo re ebbe la sfortuna di trovarsi al potere durante il periodo del regime fascista e dunque durante il disastro della seconda guerra mondiale.

32. **Giovanni Giolitti** (1842-1928). Primo Ministro italiano durante il periodo della prima guerra mondiale, fu capace di stabilire il bilancio economico della penisola e di portare l'Italia ad un certo livello di prosperità.

33. **Benito Mussolini** (1883-1945). Dittatore che governò l'Italia dal 1922 al 1943. Fu fondatore del Partito Fascista. Dai disordini che seguivano la prima guerra mondiale, portò l'ordine al paese con la forza.

    Usò il nazionalismo e il desiderio degli Italiani di ritornare alla "gloria di Roma" per fare accettare al popolo la politica fascista. Questa politica di espansione risultò in un'alleanza (*alliance*) con la Germania conosciuta con il nome di "patto d'acciaio" (1939). Tramite questa alleanza, l'Italia entrò nella seconda guerra mondiale al lato della Germania (Tedeschi). Perduta la guerra, Mussolini fu ucciso (1945) dagli Italiani stessi.

34. **Pietro Badoglio** (1871-1956). Maresciallo (*Field Marshal*) delle forze armate italiane durante la seconda guerra mondiale, toccò a lui di firmare l'armistizio con gli alleati (*allies*) e di governare l'Italia dal 1943 al 1945.

35. **Alcide De Gasperi** (1881-1954). Primo Ministro d'Italia subito dopo la seconda guerra mondiale, fu capace di stabilire un governo che diede inizio alla ripresa economica nazionale del dopoguerra.

EXERCISES

A. Match each item in column I with the corresponding item in column II. There will be one item left over.

Column I	*Column* II
1. Carlo Magno	*a.* "patto d'acciaio"
2. Augusto	*b.* *Le mie Prigioni*
3. Federico II	*c.* Impero Romano
4. Bonifazio VIII	*d.* prima Lega Lombarda
5. Alcide De Gasperi	*e.* re longobardo
6. Benito Mussolini	*f.* l'Università di Napoli
7. Girolamo Savonarola	*g.* Sacro Romano Impero
8. Manfredi	*h.* esilio di Dante
9. Silvio Pellico	*i.* battaglia di Benevento
10. Liutprando	*j.* primo ministro italiano
	k. Repubblica fiorentina

B. Complete the following sentences by choosing the correct item in parentheses:

1. Giuseppe Garibaldi fu chiamato ("la penna del Risorgimento," "la spada del Risorgimento," "il pensiero del Risorgimento").
2. Clemente V fu responsabile per (l'Editto di Milano, i Vespri Siciliani, lo scisma della Chiesa).
3. Federico Barbarossa apparteneva alla Casa (Sveva, Angioina, Normanna).
4. Lorenzo dei Medici era "Signore" di (Ravenna, Firenze, Mantova).
5. Costantino fu incoronato imperatore (del Sacro Romano Impero, della Chiesa, dell'Impero Romano).
6. Cesare Borgia fu figlio di (Giulio II, Alessandro VI, Innocenzo III).
7. Camillo Benso di Cavour fu primo ministro di (Carlo Alberto, Vittorio Emanuele III, Vittorio Emanuele II).
8. Giuseppe Mazzini fu un grande scrittore del periodo (del Risorgimento, del Rinascimento, del Fascismo).
9. Carlo Alberto apparteneva alla Casa (Savoia, Asburga, Borbonica).
10. Carlo d'Angiò occupò (la Sardegna, la Sicilia, la Lombardia).

C. If the statement is true, write **vero.** If the statement is false, write the word or expression that will make it true:

1. Marco Antonio uccise Giulio Cesare.
2. Giustiniano fondò la città di Costantinopoli.
3. Carlo Magno era anche conosciuto come il Barbarossa.

4. Federico I prese parte alla battaglia di Legnano.
5. I Comuni si formarono durante il Risorgimento.
6. I Guelfi erano a favore della Chiesa.
7. La seconda Lega Lombarda si formò per difendere i Comuni da Federico II.
8. Carlo d'Angiò era il fratello del re di Francia.
9. Bonifazio VIII proclamò, "Ogni autorità viene da Dio."
10. Teodorico fu ucciso alla battaglia di Benevento.
11. Innocenzo III portò la sede dello Stato Pontificio in Francia.
12. Alessandro VI fu il padre di Cesare Borgia.
13. Giuseppe Mazzini è chiamato "la spada del Risorgimento."
14. Carlo Alberto di Savoia dedicò la sua vita all'indipendenza dell'Italia.
15. Pietro Badoglio governò l'Italia dal 1943 al 1945.

D. Complete the following sentences in Italian:

1. Benito Mussolini fondò il _____.
2. _____ fu il primo ministro che stabilì il bilancio economico prima della prima guerra mondiale.
3. Il primo re d'Italia dopo l'unificazione fu _____.
4. Il re che fece salire al potere Mussolini fu _____.
5. Il primo ministro italiano subito dopo la fine della seconda guerra mondiale fu _____.
6. Nella prima guerra mondiale, l'Italia combattè contro la _____ e l'_____.
7. Giuseppe Mazzini prese parte alla fondazione della _____.
8. Nella seconda guerra mondiale, l'Italia combattè al lato dei _____.
9. Giuseppe Garibaldi è anche popolarmente chiamato _____.
10. _____ fu primo ministro di Vittorio Emanuele II.
11. Due patriotti del Risorgimento messi in prigione insieme a Silvio Pellico furono _____ e _____.
12. _____ fu usato come modello del *Principe*, scritto da Machiavelli.
13. _____ formò il Regno Italico al principio del Risorgimento.
14. Il "patto d'acciaio" fu firmato dall' _____ e dalla _____.
15. Il Papa _____ era grande nemico di Cesare Borgia.

E. Use a short Italian sentence to identify each of the following names:

1. Giulio Cesare
2. Pipino
3. Teodorico
4. Odoacre
5. Giustiniano
6. Marco Antonio
7. Carlo V
8. Girolamo Savonarola
9. Carlo Alberto
10. Vittorio Emanuele III

16. Brevi Avvenimenti della Storia d'Italia (Optional)

IL PERIODO PRE-ROMANO

La storia italiana è molto complicata perchè, fin dall'inizio, l'Italia fu occupata da diversi popoli primitivi, detti **popoli italici.** Questi popoli si stabilirono nelle zone della penisola che, più o meno, rappresentano le regioni di oggi. Infatti, i nomi di queste regioni corrispondono, in largo modo, ai nomi dei popoli primitivi che le occuparono originalmente.

I Veneti, per esempio, occuparono la zona che oggi si chiama il Veneto; i Liguri, la Liguria; gli Etruschi, la Toscana (dalla pronuncia romana "Tusci" per "Etruschi"); i Latini, il Lazio (dalla parola latina "Latium"); gli Umbri, l'Umbria; i Siculi, la Sicilia; ecc.

Fra questi popoli, quelli che contribuirono di più allo sviluppo del paese furono i **Latini.** Anzitutto (*above all*), i Latini furono responsabili per la fondazione della città di **Roma.** (Secondo la leggenda, la città fu fondata da due fratelli, Romolo e Remo, e fu chiamata inizialmente **Città Quadrata**). Dopo la fondazione di Roma, questo popolo aggressivo si dedicò alla conquista di tutti gli altri popoli primitivi che abitavano la penisola come pure (*as well as*) all'espulsione della Grecia, che da secoli, dominava l'Italia meridionale e la Sicilia. Tutta questa zona meridionale si chiamava, in quei tempi, **Magna Grecia.**

I Latini, inoltre, insieme agli altri popoli già conquistati, si chiamarono **Romani.** I Romani furono capaci di unificare la penisola da Rimini fino allo Stretto di Messina. La Grecia fu costretta (*forced*) così a ritirarsi in Sicilia, dove continuò a dominare l'isola fino alle invasioni arabe (Saraceni).

Due città siciliane, Siracusa e Agrigento, sono tuttora (*still*) modelli della cultura avanzata e del progresso politico-sociale che i Greci stabilirono in tutta l'Italia meridionale e in Sicilia.

Note

1. **Gli Etruschi,** altro popolo primitivo, contribuirono molto nel campo dell'agricoltura e dell'architettura. Questi loro sistemi furono usati con grande successo dai Romani. Di questo popolo, però, non conosciamo nè le origini nè la lingua.

2. Il nome **Italia** non è stato applicato a tutta la penisola fino al principio dell'Impero Romano (c. 27 a.C.). Prima, si chiamava Italia soltanto la regione che oggi conosciamo con il nome di Calabria.

IL PERIODO ROMANO (753 a.C.–476 d.C.)

Dalla fondazione di Roma (753 a.C.) alla caduta dell'Impero (476 d.C.), la storia d'Italia è essenzialmente la storia di Roma.

Durante il suo predominio, Roma passò da **monarchia** (i sette re) a **repubblica** (fino alla morte di Giulio Cesare) e, per ultimo, ad **impero**. Dopo le grandi conquiste di Giulio Cesare, il dominio di Roma si estese (*extended*) dall'Inghilterra all'Egitto (*Egypt*). Questo periodo di dominazione fu chiamato il periodo dell'Impero Romano.

L'Impero fu creato da Ottaviano, figlio adottivo di Giulio Cesare, con l'aiuto di Marco Antonio, parente di Giulio Cesare e Console romano. Ottaviano si prese la corona d'occidente, mentre quella d'oriente passò a Marco Antonio. Questa divisione, però, non durò a lungo. Scoppiò una guerra civile tra Ottaviano e Marco Antonio alla fine della quale Marco Antonio si uccise insieme a Cleopatra, regina d'Egitto, sua amante. Ottaviano divenne così imperatore dell'Impero Romano (oriente e occidente). Ottaviano è anche conosciuto nella storia con il nome di *Augusto*, titolo dato a lui dal Senato romano.

Una schiera (*group*) di imperatori seguirono il regno di Ottaviano (Augusto). Alcuni sono ricordati per le loro atrocità contro i Romani e contro i cristiani. Fra questi si possono segnalare (*mention*) Nerone e Caligola. Altri, invece, hanno contribuito molto allo sviluppo della civiltà europea. Costantino e Giustiniano sono esempi di quest'ultima categoria.

L'Impero Romano d'Occidente cadde (476 d.C.) con la sconfitta dell'imperatore Romolo Augustolo. (Costantino aveva di nuovo diviso l'Impero in due parti: occidente e oriente.) Questa sconfitta fu imposta dal generale "barbarico" Odoacre.

Termina così la gloria di Roma come "padrona del mondo." Non si elimina, però, tutto l'Impero perchè quello di oriente continua il suo dominio fino al medioevo con il nome di **Impero Bizantino**.

IL MEDIOEVO (SECOLI V-XIII)

Il principio del medioevo trova l'Italia tutta frazionata: il centro e il nord sotto il dominio di diversi popoli **barbarici**, e il Meridione e la Sicilia sotto il dominio **bizantino**. Allo stesso tempo, in altri luoghi dell'Europa si cominciavano a formare alcune potenze (Francia, Spagna, ecc.) che dovevano influire molto sulla storia d'Italia.

Con le invasioni "barbariche," già indicate, cominciò una serie di dominazioni straniere che durò per tredici secoli. A queste dominazioni dobbiamo aggiungere anche quella dello **Stato Pontificio**, che, durante il dominio "barbarico," cominciò a svilupparsi come potenza "temporale."

Fra gli invasori "barbarici" ci furono i **Longobardi**, considerati i più barbari dei "barbari." Dobbiamo segnalare che questo popolo tentò di unificare la penisola. Questo tentativo, però, non ebbe successo perchè il Papa, per paura di doversi sottomettere (*placed under*) al dominio longobardo, impedì la loro espansione. A questo scopo (*purpose*), il Papa ebbe l'aiuto di Carlo Magno, re di un altro popolo "barbaro," i **Franchi**, che già aveva conquistato la **Gallia.** I Longobardi furono sconfitti, e Papa Leone III dette la corona del **Sacro Romano Impero** a Carlo Magno. Quest'ultimo avvenimento stabilì definitivamente il potere "temporale" dello Stato Pontificio.

Note

Si può dire che con l'incoronazione di Carlo Magno, si pone il Papa simbolicamente al di sopra (*above*) di ogni principe, re, o imperatore. Il concetto simbolico stabilito in questa occasione si convertirà, più tardi, in una proclamazione ufficiale della Chiesa quando il Papa Innocenzio III dichiara che: "Ogni autorità viene da Dio." Questa proclamazione stabilisce il potere assoluto della Chiesa su di ogni sovrano d'Europa.

La discesa (*descent*) di Carlo Magno in Italia poteva anche avere dei risultati benefici rispetto all'unificazione della penisola. L'Imperatore aveva già ottenuto l'unificazione del centro e del nord, che si chiamò **Regno d'Italia.** Sfortunatamente, però, Carlo Magno morì prima di conquistare il Meridione e la Sicilia, e così non si ottenne l'unificazione completa. La morte dell'Imperatore causò la divisione del nuovo regno, e si formarono così dei piccoli poteri governati da sovrani indipendenti.

Approfittando (*Taking advantage*) delle lotte che si svilupparono fra questi nuovi sovrani, alcune città dichiararono la loro autonomia. Queste città cominciarono a combattere fra di loro per ottenere più territorio e in questo modo si crearono i **Comuni.** I Comuni si convertirono, poi, in forti stati che diventarono ancora più potenti tramite (*through*) lo sviluppo del commercio. Si passò così al governo delle **Signorie**, famiglie ricche che prendevano in mano il governo dei Comuni e formavono vere e proprie dinastie. I Signori che governarono gli stati principali del centro e del nord furono i seguenti:

Signori	*Stati*
i Visconti gli Sforza	Milano
i Da Polenta	Ravenna
i Malatesta	Rimini
i Medici	Firenze
i Montefeltro	Urbino
i Gonzaga	Mantova
gli Este	Ferrara

A questi dobbiamo aggiungere la città di **Venezia**, che rimase una repubblica indipendente sotto il governo dei **Dogi**; lo **Stato Pontificio**, governato dal Papa; e i conti e principi di **Savoia (Sabaudi)**, che in questo periodo cominciarono a prendere piede in Italia.

Dal Medioevo alla fine del **Risorgimento** (*Unification*), il Meridione e la Sicilia passarono da una dinastia (*dynasty*) straniera all'altra.

Durante il dominio bizantino, la Sicilia venne conquistata dagli **Arabi (Saraceni)**. In seguito, i **Normanni** conquistarono l'Italia meridionale dai Bizantini e la Sicilia dagli Arabi. Si formò così il **Regno di Sicilia**, governato dalla dinastia normanna. Questo regno passò poi alla dinastia tedesca (**Casa Sveva**) con la sconfitta dei Normanni. Di tutti gl'imperatori della Casa Sveva, il più famoso fu Federico II, il quale stabilì, alla sua corte di **Palermo**, il centro principale per la diffusione della cultura italiana. Creò, inoltre, l'Università di Napoli e la Scuola Medica di Salerno.

Dopo la dinastia sveva, vennero al trono del Regno di Sicilia gli **Angioini** di Francia (Carlo d'Angiò). Durante il regno di Carlo d'Angiò, scoppiò (in Sicilia) una rivoluzione contro i Francesi che si conosce tuttora con il nome di **Vespri Siciliani** (1282).

Questa rivoluzione si convertì in una lunga guerra durante la quale i Siciliani chiesero l'aiuto di Pietro III di Aragona (Spagna). Alla fine di questa guerra, gli Angioini lasciarono l'isola e formarono il **Regno di Napoli** (Italia meridionale), mentre la Spagna prese possesso della Sicilia.

IL RINASCIMENTO (SECOLI XIV E XV)

Se il Rinascimento ha dato all'Italia una incomparabile grandezza materiale e intellettuale, le gelosie interne impedirono parecchi tentativi, da parte di uomini illustri, di unificare la penisola come, per esempio: Lorenzo dei Medici, Machiavelli, Giulio II, ecc. La scoperta del Nuovo Mondo (1492) e la nuove vie di commercio che si aprirono come risultato di questa scoperta fecero diminuire l'importanza di tutte le città marinare italiane. Il controllo del commercio passò così ad alcune potenze straniere (Spagna, Inghilterra, ecc.).

La Spagna, che in questo periodo era la più forte delle potenze europee, si trovò coinvolta (*mixed up*) in una serie di guerre contro le altre potenze. Molte di queste guerre furono combattute in Italia e durarono fino alla metà del secolo XVIII (guerre di successione). Con la caduta della potenza spagnuola, l'Italia si trovò divisa sotto quattro domini diversi:

1. I **Savoia** in Sardegna
2. Gli **Asburgo Lorena** (Austria) in Toscana
3. I **Borboni** (Francia) nel Regno di Napoli e in Sicilia (chiamato **Regno delle Due Sicilie** dopo la caduta di Napoleone)
4. Lo **Stato Pontificio**, che aggiungeva al suo territorio anche le città di Ferrara e di Bologna

IL RISORGIMENTO (1820–1871)

La rivoluzione francese aveva talmente (*so*) esposto (*exposed*) gl'Italiani ai nuovi ideali di libertà e di uguaglianza che anche il dominio tirannico imposto nuovamente in Italia dopo la caduta di Napoleone Bonaparte non ebbe la forza di sopprimere il movimento d'indipendenza. A scopo di questa indipendenza, si crearono delle "società segrete": La **Massoneria**, la **Carboneria**, e, in ultimo, la **Giovane Italia** creata da Giuseppe Mazzini.

Il movimento principale dell'unificazione ebbe, però, inizio a Milano ("cinque giornate"), dove scoppiò una rivoluzione contro l'Austria che andò a finire in una guerra–**prima guerra d'indipendenza, 1848–49**. In questa guerra, prese anche parte Carlo Alberto di Savoia, Re di Piemonte e di Sardegna. I Savoia si stabilirono così come i difensori dell'ideale italiano d'indipendenza e di unificazione. Alla fine di questa guerra, il Regno di Savoia passò a Vittorio Emanuele II (figlio di Carlo Alberto), il quale nominò, come suo Primo Ministro, il Conte Camillo Benso di Cavour.

Cavour, tramite la sua astuta tattica politica, riesce ad avere l'aiuto della Francia per cacciare l'Austria dalla Lombardia e dal Veneto–**seconda guerra d'indipendenza, 1859**. Poco dopo l'inizio di questa guerra, la Francia e l'Austria giungono ad un accordo di pace nel quale la Lombardia passa ai Savoia e il Veneto resta all'Austria.

Nel 1860 ha inizio la **spedizione dei mille** (corpo di volontari in camicie rosse), che, sotto il comando di Giuseppe Garibaldi, invadono la Sicilia e cacciano i Borboni sia dall'isola che dall'Italia meridionale. Le truppe di Vittorio Emanuele II, per tanto, scendono dal Piemonte per venire incontro ai Garibaldini. Si ottiene così l'unificazione della penisola (1861) e si forma il **Regno d'Italia** sotto il governo di Vittorio Emanuele II.

Restano ancora fuori del regno due regioni: il **Veneto**, che rimane sotto l'Austria, e il **Lazio**, che rimane al Papa ("questione romana").

Il Veneto viene dato all'Italia come risultato di una guerra in cui l'Italia combatte al lato della Prussia e contro l'Austria–**terza guerra d'indipendenza, 1866**. Il Lazio, invece, protetto dalle truppe francesi, resta sotto il dominio del Papa fino al 1870. In questo stesso anno, però, le truppe italiane occupano Roma (breccia di Porta Pia) e anche il Lazio entra nel Regno d'Italia. Occupata Roma, la sede del regno passa a questa città, che diventa allo stesso tempo capitale d'Italia. (Altre capitali furono Torino e Firenze.)

Restava ancora da risolvere la questione del Papa. Questa questione viene risolta con il decreto del primo parlamento italiano (1871) che proclama: "Libera Chiesa in libero Stato." Il Papa si chiude così in **Vaticano**, e si rifiuta di uscire fino al 1929–il **Patto Laterano.**

L'ITALIA MODERNA

Dopo l'unificazione, la monarchia intraprende (*undertakes*) una serie di riforme: si sviluppano le industrie, si ottengono delle riforme agricole, la scuola diventa obbligatoria, ecc. L'Italia comincia così ad aggiornarsi (*to modernize itself*) e, per altro, a mettersi alle pari con gli altri paesi europei. Arriviamo di questo modo alla vigilia della **prima guerra mondiale** (1914-1918).

L'Italia prende parte in questa guerra al lato della Francia, dell'Inghilterra, e degli Stati Uniti. La guerra si conclude con la vittoria di questi sull'Austria e sulla Germania.

L'Italia, come risultato del trattato di pace (1919), ottiene il Trentino con l'Alto Adige, Trieste con l'Istria, e Zara. Anche la città di Fiume viene annessa (*annexed*) all'Italia nel 1924, dopo che Gabriele d'Annunzio la occupa con una spedizione di soldati italiani.

Dopo la fine della prima guerra mondiale, i problemi interni dell'Italia diventano sempre più intensi. Mancanza (*lack*) di lavoro, scioperi (*strikes*), conflitti tra partiti politici, ecc. portano il paese all'orlo (*edge*) di un disastro economico. Questi furono eventi che portarono alla "rivoluzione fascista" (i "fasci di combattimento," fondati da Benito Mussolini, esistevano già dal 1919).

Le "squadre di azione" (dette anche "squadrismo") usarono il senso del nazionalismo e la mancanza di rispetto verso la legge per riorganizzare il paese e per mantenere l'ordine con la violenza. Questa dottrina dittatoriale fu accettata sia dal re che dalla maggior parte del popolo italiano.

Il 28 ottobre del 1922, Benito Mussolini marcia su Roma con un gruppo di squadristi, e in quello stesso giorno Mussolini assume la **dittatura**.

Una volta al potere, Mussolini abolisce la libertà di stampa, la Costituzione, il Parlamento, e i partiti politici. Sotto il Fascismo, l'Italia comincia a ristabilire l'economia e l'ordine nazionale. Mussolini intraprende, però, una politica di espansione territoriale in Africa che si conclude, per l'Italia, con i disastrosi risultati della **seconda guerra mondiale** (1939-1945). Inoltre, le idee del Fascismo di riportare l'Italia alla grandezza dell'Impero Romano formano la base di un trattato con la Germania, chiamato il **patto d'acciaio**. Non appena la Germania comincia le invasioni di certe nazioni europee (1939), la Francia e l'Inghilterra le dichiarano guerra. L'Italia scende in guerra al lato della Germania, ed inizia così la seconda guerra mondiale. Durante questa guerra, l'Italia diventò di nuovo campo di battaglia e dovette sopportare tutti i disastri della guerra: bombardamenti, invasioni, fame, disordine, ecc. Nel 1943 gli alleati (Inghilterra, Stati Uniti, Francia, Russia) forzarono l'Italia a firmare un armistizio e cadde così il regime fascista. Dopo l'armistizio, il Re Vittorio Emanuele III mise il governo nelle mani del Maresciallo Pietro Badoglio, il quale governò l'Italia dal 1943 al 1945.

Durante questi ultimi due anni della seconda guerra mondiale, l'Italia doveva soffrire grandissime pene alle mani della Germania, che considerava gl'Italiani come traditori. In questo periodo, la penisola fu quasi totalmente distrutta da bombardamenti e da battaglie.

L'episodio del Fascismo si conclude con la rovina (*ruin*) nazionale e con l'uccisione di Benito Mussolini (1945).

Dal 1945 in poi, si stabilisce in Italia una forma di governo democratico (*see page 317*) che la porta verso la riabilitazione. Questo succede principalmente sotto la guida del Primo Ministro Alcide De Gasperi e con l'aiuto finanziario degli Stati Uniti.

Dal 1960 ad oggi, l'Italia ha raggiunto uno sviluppo industriale e commerciale che la pone fra i paesi più progrediti (*advanced*) del mondo. Con questo sviluppo, però, sono giunti anche i problemi economici e sociali che confrontano tutti i paesi dell'occidente. Soltanto facendo parte di questa comunità internazionale, l'Italia potrà risolvere i problemi che tuttora l'affliggono (*afflict*). Perciò, le famose parole di Benito Mussolini—"l'Italia può fare da sè"—non hanno oggi alcun significato perchè il modo di vivere italiano è legato alle sorti (*fates*) di tutti gli altri paesi del mondo.

EXERCISES

A. Match each item in column I with the corresponding item in column II. There will be one item left over.

Column I	*Column* II
1. Magna Grecia	*a*. Milano
2. Etruschi	*b*. Mazzini
3. Da Polenta	*c*. Venezia
4. Malatesta	*d*. Roma
5. Dogi	*e*. Ravenna
6. Giovane Italia	*f*. Sicilia
7. Città Quadrata	*g*. Carlo Magno
8. Leone III	*h*. Rimini
9. Sforza	*i*. Toscana
10. Savoia	*j*. Augusto
	k. Sabaudi

B. Complete the following sentences by choosing the correct item in parentheses:

1. Durante il periodo della monarchia, Roma fu governata (dai sette re, della Grecia, dai Bizantini).
2. Cleopatra era l'amante di (Marco Antonio, Cesare Augusto, Romolo Augustolo).
3. I Latini si stabilirono (nel Lazio, in Toscana, in Liguria).
4. I Saraceni occuparono (il Veneto, la Sicilia, la Lombardia).
5. I Gonzaga erano "Signori" di (Ferrara, Urbino, Mantova).
6. I Borboni erano (austriaci, francesi, spagnuoli).
7. Pietro III era (spagnuolo, arabo, normanno).

8. Una città siciliana che dimostra ancora la cultura greca è (Palermo, Siracusa, Messina).
9. Lo Stato Pontificio fu governato dai (papi, re, imperatori).
10. Il Regno di Napoli fu creato (dai Francesi, dagli Spagnuoli, dagli Arabi).

C. Write **vero** if the statement is true. If the statement is false, write the word or expression that will make it true:

1. La città di Venezia era independente tra il Medioevo e il Rinascimento.
2. Gli Angioini formarono il primo Regno di Napoli.
3. Carlo Alberto apparteneva alla Casa Sveva.
4. I Saraceni invasero la Sicilia.
5. I Comuni si convertirono in Signorie.
6. Gli Etruschi unirono l'Italia.
7. I Medici governarono Firenze.
8. La Calabria si chiamava anticamente Italia.
9. I Longobardi furono più barbari dei barbari.
10. Napoleone Bonaparte unificò la penisola.
11. I "Garibaldini" erano soldati di Vittorio Emanuele II.
12. L'Italia fu unita nel 1849.
13. La seconda guerra d'indipendenza fu combattuta tra la Francia e l'Austria.
14. Il primo parlamento italiano si creò nel 1871.
15. La monarchia dell'Italia unita fu quella dei Savoia.

D. Complete the following sentences in Italian:

1. La rivoluzione siciliana del 1282 si chiama _____.
2. Al periodo della caduta di Roma, l'Italia meridionale e la Sicilia erano dominate dai _____.
3. I _____ fu il popolo primitivo che si stabilì in Sicilia.
4. Il primo imperatore romano d'Oriente fu _____.
5. Il secondo imperatore del Sacro Romano Impero fu _____.
6. Il primo Regno d'Italia fu fondato da _____.
7. Nerone e Caligola sono famosi per aver commesso atrocità contro i _____ e i _____.
8. _____ fu il Papa che stabilì la supremazia della Chiesa su tutti i regnanti d'Europa.
9. I _____ furono una delle famiglie che governò lo Stato di Milano.

10. Come risultato della terza guerra d'indipendenza, l'Italia ottenne la regione del _____.
11. La "breccia di Porta Pia" si riferisce all'occupazione della città di _____.
12. Dopo la prima guerra mondiale, l'Italia ottenne _____, _____, e _____.
13. I "fasci di combattimento" furono fondati da _____.
14. La città di Fiume fu occupata dalle truppe di _____.
15. La seconda guerra mondiale si concluse con la sconfitta dell'_____ e della _____.

E. Use a short Italian sentence to identify each of the following items:

1. Medioevo
2. Rinascimento
3. Risorgimento
4. invasioni "barbariche"
5. Carboneria
6. "cinque giornate"
7. "questione romana"
8. "squadre di azione"
9. armistizio del 1943
10. "patto d'acciaio"

Monumento con statua equestre (a cavallo) di *Giuseppe Garibaldi* situato sul colle Gianicolo a Roma. Questo monumento commemora anche il periodo del Risorgimento.

Part VI—Auditory Comprehension

A. COMPLETION OF ORAL SENTENCES

Directions to the Pupil: The teacher will read aloud a sentence, in Italian, and will repeat it. After the *second* reading of the sentence, write the letter of the answer that best completes the sentence.

B. SUITABLE RESPONSES TO QUESTIONS OR STATEMENTS

Directions to the Pupil: The teacher will read aloud a question or statement, in Italian, and will repeat it. After the *second* reading of the question or statement, write the letter of the alternative that is the most suitable response to the oral question or statement.

1. *a*. Piove.
   b. È mezzogiorno.
   c. È primavera.
   d. È notte.

2. *a*. C'è del tè.
   b. C'è della neve.
   c. C'è del pane.
   d. C'è della musica.

3. *a*. A piedi.
   b. Un po' meglio.
   c. A buon mercato.
   d. In biblioteca.

4. *a*. Non fa niente.
   b. Parlo con tutti.
   c. Ecco Mario.
   d. È un giovane alto.

5. *a*. Piove tanto.
   b. Che bel regalo.
   c. Siamo in estate.
   d. Mangiamo molto.

6. *a*. La macelleria è chiusa.
   b. Hai scritto una lettera?
   c. Ho un bel posto qui.
   d. Abbiamo ricevuto una cartolina.

7. *a*. È mezzogiorno.
   b. È giovedì.
   c. C'è un bel sole.
   d. Non metterci del sale.

8. *a*. Non parla mai con nessuno.
   b. È caduto sul ghiaccio.
   c. Non fa bel tempo.
   d. Facciamo una passeggiata.

9. *a.* Che bel colore!
b. A che ora parte?
c. Le strade sono strette.
d. Dove hai messo le calze?

10. *a.* Non mi piacciono le riviste.
b. D'accordo. Ho una fame tremenda.
c. Quel cavallo è grande.
d. Hai pagato troppo.

11. *a.* È una bella sorpresa.
b. Questi stivali sono stretti.
c. Qualcuno mi aspetta.
d. Ho sempre torto.

12. *a.* La messa è bella.
b. Chi è l'artista?
c. Di chi è questa penna?
d. È tardi.

13. *a.* Peccato.
b. Non mi sento bene.
c. Ho molta sete.
d. Non c'è niente da bere.

14. *a.* Costano troppo.
b. Mi piace il colore.
c. È presto.
d. I pantaloni sono lunghi.

15. *a.* Un romanzo antico.
b. Una sedia nuova.
c. Una Coca-Cola.
d. Pasta asciutta.

16. *a.* Vanno spesso alla spiaggia.
b. Sono sempre al cinema.
c. Cantano in coro.
d. Ci vanno in macchina.

17. *a.* In aula.
b. In treno.
c. In biblioteca.
d. In autunno.

18. *a.* Parli troppo.
b. Sei andato a letto troppo tardi.
c. È a buon mercato.
d. Il treno è in ritardo.

19. *a.* La musica era bellissima.
b. L'artista non dipinge bene.
c. Il televisore non funziona.
d. Ho comprato una radio.

20. *a.* Andare in campagna.
b. Il calcio.
c. Viaggiare in aereo.
d. Fare delle spese.

21. *a.* Ce ne sono dieci.
b. È molto piccola.
c. Sediamoci qui.
d. La frutta è matura.

22. *a.* È un bel quadro.
b. È caduto per la strada.
c. Preferiamo le banane.
d. Mangio alle sette ogni sera.

23. *a.* Andiamo su per le scale.
b. Siamo andati alla Scala di Milano.
c. Prendiamo l'aereo.
d. Facciamo colazione.

24. *a.* Ne siamo orgogliosi.
b. Ci siamo lavati sabato scorso.
c. I nostri amici arriveranno oggi.
d. Il televisore è nuovo.

25. *a.* È così allegra.
b. Poverina, è così triste.
c. Ha una bella voce.
d. È andata a fare la spesa.

26. *a.* Ha un appartamento.
b. Non aveva niente da fare.
c. La carne era buona.
d. Sono le quattro.

27. *a.* Dell'insalata.
b. Un tappeto.
c. Una vacca.
d. Un gatto.

28. *a.* Le piacciono queste?
b. A che ora parte?
c. L'uscita è a sinistra.
d. Non ho l'orologio.

29. *a.* Hai comprato molto?
b. Non ti senti bene?
c. Era bello il film?
d. Ti ha tirato un dente?

30. *a.* Che tempesta!
b. Andiamo a nuotare allora.
c. I fiori sono belli.
d. La neve non mi piace.

31. *a.* Facciamo un viaggio.
b. La Germania è lontana.
c. Il treno ci passa.
d. Non mi piace studiare le lingue.

32. *a.* Ti porto il giornale.
b. Guarda il programma.
c. Mangia attentamente.
d. Non scrivere così rapidamente.

33. *a.* Perchè, hai sete?
b. Perchè, piove?
c. Perchè, hai torto?
d. Perchè, hai fame?

34. *a.* È greco.
b. È ingegnere.
c. È simpatico.
d. È giovane.

35. *a.* Ecco una nazione grande.
b. C'è molto da vedere.
c. Ecco un bel braccialetto.
d. Il lago è magnifico.

36. *a.* È andato al negozio.
b. È tornato dalla luna.
c. Il sole è troppo lontano.
d. Le stelle brillano stasera.

37. *a.* Fa novanta.
b. Fa diciannove.
c. Fa uno.
d. Fa diciassette.

38. *a.* È in viaggio?
b. Il telegiornale è interessante.
c. Il pesce è un cibo nutriente.
d. Il treno non è comodo.

39. *a.* Non mangia troppo.
b. Lava i panni ogni sabato.
c. Mi fa piacere.
d. Non sono ancora le quattro.

40. *a.* Che tempo fa?
b. Chi ha vinto?
c. Non mangiarne troppi.
d. Cantate insieme.

41. *a.* Di chi è questa macchina?
b. Questo programma è interessante.
c. Non mi piace sciare.
d. Ha preso la medicina?

42. *a.* Perchè non comprate questa gonna?
b. Ma Gianni non sente bene.
c. È un amico di mia zia.
d. La medicina è amara.

43. *a.* Ha sentito un rumore.
b. Susanna ha preparato la cena.
c. Le cotolette sono squisiste.
d. Studiate troppo.

44. *a.* È un giovane intelligente.
b. Non ho il pettine.
c. La radio non funziona.
d. Le banane sono troppo mature.

45. *a.* C'è molta neve per terra?
b. C'è dell'insalata verde.
c. C'è una lettera per me?
d. C'è un posto al centro.

46. *a.* È una festa nazionale.
b. Il sole è brillante.
c. La cabina è qui vicino.
d. Venezia è una città incantevole.

47. *a.* Sì, eccone due fogli.
b. Le foglie sono già cadute.
c. Sì, c'è un buon film stasera.
d. La geografia è molto interessante.

48. *a.* Ma non ci voglio andare.
b. Non sente tanto bene.
c. L'ho comprato a buon mercato.
d. Ho perso il pettine.

49. *a.* Pasqua.
b. Natale.
c. Capodanno.
d. Primavera.

50. *a.* Lo zio è arrivato ieri.
b. L'aereo va a Roma.
c. Andranno in Francia.
d. Il tedesco è difficile.

C. AUDITORY COMPREHENSION PASSAGES

Directions to the Pupil: The teacher will read aloud, in Italian, a question followed by a paragraph, and will repeat the reading of both the question and the paragraph. After the second reading, write the letter of the alternative that best answers the question. Base your answers only on the content of the paragraph.

1. Dove sono andate queste ragazze?
a. a fare spese
b. al museo
c. al mercato
d. a casa

2. In quale negozio siamo?
   a. dal panettiere
   b. dal fruttivendolo
   c. dal barbiere
   d. dal macellaio

3. Perchè questo giovane è andato in Francia?
   a. per studiare
   b. per visitare i genitori
   c. per visitare i nonni
   d. per prendere aria

4. Quante cose beve Alberto durante la colazione?
   a. una
   b. due
   c. tre
   d. quattro

5. Cosa non piace a Maria?
   a. la musica popolare
   b. i dischi
   c. l'opera
   d. suonare

6. Di quale stagione si parla?
   a. dell'estate
   b. dell'inverno
   c. dell'autunno
   d. della primavera

7. Come sta la zia?
   a. Benissimo.
   b. Male.
   c. Triste.
   d. Allegra.

8. Dov'è Firenze?
   a. lontano da Pisa
   b. in una università
   c. a poca distanza da Pisa
   d. accanto ad una torre pendente

9. Dove siamo?
   a. in una libreria
   b. dal barbiere
   c. in chiesa
   d. dalla modista

10. Perchè è famosa Bologna?
   a. Ha molte antichità.
   b. È nell'Emilia-Romagna.
   c. È una città del Medio Evo.
   d. È nota per la sua università antica.

11. Come viaggiano questi giovani?
   a. A piedi.
   b. In aereo.
   c. In macchina.
   d. A cavallo.

12. Di che cosa si parla?
   a. di una statua
   b. di un'opera musicale
   c. di una chiesa
   d. di un quadro

13. Perchè non possono andare in mare i bambini?
   a. La madre è malata.
   b. Fa cattivo tempo.
   c. Ci sono delle lampade.
   d. Il pianoforte suona.

14. Perchè Dante Alighieri è importante per l'Italia?
- *a*. Scrisse molte poesie in latino.
- *b*. Era padre dell'Italia.
- *c*. Iniziò l'uso dell'italiano nella letteratura.
- *d*. Nacque a Firenze.

15. Che tipo di giovane è Roberto?
- *a*. È disonesto.
- *b*. Non è diplomatico.
- *c*. È triste.
- *d*. È uno studente intelligente.

16. Quando si celebra questa festa?
- *a*. d'inverno
- *b*. d'estate
- *c*. d'autunno
- *d*. in primavera

17. Perchè Giacomo vuole dare del denaro al vecchio?
- *a*. È malato.
- *b*. Vuole comprare un giornale.
- *c*. Vuole comprare qualcosa da mangiare.
- *d*. Deve viaggiare.

18. Cosa si impara da questo paragrafo?
- *a*. Gli Italiani sono studiosi.
- *b*. Gli Italiani si riposano dopo mezzogiorno.
- *c*. I negozi si aprono presto la mattina.
- *d*. Le tradizioni non piacciono agli Italiani.

19. Dove sono i giovani?
- *a*. in biblioteca
- *b*. ad una partita di calcio
- *c*. al museo
- *d*. ad una corsa automobilistica

20. Dov'è questa signorina?
- *a*. in chiesa
- *b*. in città
- *c*. in campagna
- *d*. al mare

21. Qual è la professione del signore che parla?
- *a*. È professore.
- *b*. È medico.
- *c*. È ingegnere.
- *d*. È avvocato.

22. Perchè ha telefonato il ragazzo?
- *a*. Desidera invitare l'amica al cinema.
- *b*. Vuol fare i compiti.
- *c*. Preferisce parlare con Rossellini.
- *d*. Gli piace parlare al telefono.

23. Cosa cerca la signora?
- *a*. un commesso
- *b*. un giocattolo per il marito e per il figlio
- *c*. una bambola per sua figlia
- *d*. un ragazzino

24. Di che si parla?
a. di un film nuovo
b. di una scena d'inverno
c. di un programma televisivo
d. di un quadro

25. Quando cominciò a dipingere quest'artista?
a. quando era uomo
b. quando dipinse la Cappella Sistina
c. dopo che visitò Roma
d. quando era ragazzo

26. Qual è il risultato di questa visita?
a. L'impiegato è malato.
b. L'impiegato ha trovato quello che ha perso.
c. Il medico è stanco.
d. La posta non è arrivata.

27. Perchè il commesso è irritato?
a. La signora non compra niente.
b. La signora compra tutto.
c. La signora parla troppo.
d. La signora ha i piedi grandi.

28. Dove siamo?
a. in un ristorante
b. a scuola
c. dal macellaio
d. dal dottore

29. Perchè sono chiusi tutti i negozi?
a. È l'anniversario del re.
b. La regina celebra il compleanno.
c. È domenica.
d. Non ci sono lezioni.

30. Perchè è solo il signore?
a. Voleva andare a lavorare.
b. L'amico non è venuto.
c. Voleva mangiare bene.
d. Non aveva fame.

31. Cosa fa questa studentessa?
a. Sta studiando.
b. Apre una finestra.
c. Non studia affatto.
d. Giuoca con i compagni.

32. Perchè è così popolare questo soggetto?
a. Perchè è così drammatico.
b. Perchè piove sempre.
c. Perchè è facile parlarne.
d. Perchè è presto.

33. A cosa serve quest'oggetto?
a. a leggere bene
b. a comunicare
c. a mangiare rapidamente
d. a telefonare ad un amico

34. Cosa è successo dopo una settimana?
a. Marco non sente più dolore.
b. Il medico ha un dolore al piede.
c. Marco non è più tornato.
d. Il dolore c'è ancora.

35. Cosa pensa l'uomo del film?
a. Crede che non sia tanto buono.
b. Gli piace molto.
c. Gli piace guardare le signorine.
d. I film musicali sono interessanti.

36. Cosa c'era da mangiare?
a. dei panini imbottiti
b. un'insalata verde
c. quasi niente
d. un frigorifero

37. Cosa vuol fare la bambina?
a. Le piacerebbe sporcarsi.
b. Vorrebbe giuocare con l'amica.
c. Vuol uscire con la mamma.
d. Vuole andare a comprare una bambola.

38. Dove vanno questi uomini?
a. Vanno a visitare un'amica.
b. Partono per le vacanze.
c. Visitano Cape Canaveral.
d. Partono per lo spazio.

39. Dove si trovano questi amici?
a. in un parco
b. in classe
c. al cinema
d. al mercato

40. Perchè questo signore è entrato nel negozio?
a. Vuole comprare un abito.
b. Ha visto una sedia antica.
c. Vuole evitare il caldo.
d. Ha visto un letto grande.

41. Dove s'incontrano questi giovani?
a. davanti al parco
b. vicino al ponte
c. nell'Arno
d. in biblioteca

42. Cosa fecero i fratelli?
a. Si alzarono.
b. Rimasero a letto.
c. Guardarono un programma.
d. Comprarono una sveglia.

43. Di cosa si parla?
a. di una chiesa famosa
b. di una pietra preziosa
c. di una luce grande
d. del pubblico veneziano

44. Cosa si celebra a Napoli?
a. una festa di canzoni
b. il compleanno di qualcuno
c. il santo patrono di Napoli
d. la veduta del Vesuvio

45. Dove ci troviamo?
a. a scuola
b. in macchina
c. al giardino botanico
d. al giardino zoologico

46. Cosa desiderava il signore?
a. Voleva denaro dalla signora.
b. Voleva sapere l'ora.
c. Stava cercando un poliziotto.
d. Cercava un suo compagno.

47. Cosa ha capito la mamma?
a. che la signorina ama la musica
b. che è tardi per mangiare
c. che la figlia ama un giovane
d. che domani sera danno un concerto

48. Perchè si sposa il giovane?
a. Ha paura degli amici.
b. La futura moglie ha molto denaro.
c. Non gli piace stare solo.
d. Si sente poco bene.

49. Cosa s'impara da questo paragrafo?
a. Il cane è amico della signora.
b. Il cane è molto timido.
c. È un cane coraggioso.
d. Il cane abbaia molto.

50. Che cosa era quasi successo a Colombo?
a. I marinai volevano fargli del male.
b. Aveva perso speranza di vedere la terra.
c. I marinai volevano fare una festa.
d. Stava per diventare superstizioso.

Part VII—Passages for Reading Comprehension

A. BRIEF PASSAGES FOR COMPREHENSION

Read the following passages. Then write the letter of the alternative that is the most suitable response to the question or statement.

1. Oggi è stata una giornata orribile per Marisa. Ha piovuto continuamente. Non c'era nessun programma interessante alla televisione e i suoi amici non potevano venire perchè avevano molto da fare. Peggio ancora, neanche il giradischi funzionava e naturalmente non ha potuto sentire i suoi dischi preferiti.

   Come ha passato la giornata questa ragazza?

   a. Ha studiato tutto il giorno.
   b. Non ha fatto niente.
   c. È andata a trovare degli amici.
   d. Ha guardato dei programmi interessanti.

2. Tonino e i suoi genitori hanno fatto una scampagnata vicino al lago. Il ragazzo ha mangiato troppo perchè il pesce che ha preparato la mamma era magnifico. Dopo un'ora però, Tonino non si sente bene e sente dei rumori strani allo stomaco.

   –Mamma–dice Tonino, –ho paura che il pesce che abbiamo mangiato non sia morto ancora.

   Perchè non sta bene Tonino?

   a. È andato a pescare.
   b. È con i suoi genitori.
   c. Ha mangiato troppo.
   d. Il padre gli ha fatto male.

3. Giovanni Boccaccio, figlio di un mercante italiano, nacque probabilmente a Parigi e morì nella città di Certaldo vicino a Firenze l'anno dopo la morte di Francesco Petrarca. Quand'era ancora giovane, il padre lo portò a Firenze e più tardi a Napoli dove studiò e dove incontrò studiosi illustri alla corte del re.

Secondo questo racconto, Boccaccio

a. viaggiò alcune volte col padre.
b. rimase in Francia.
c. diventò re di Napoli.
d. visitò la nonna.

4. Un giorno vorrei avere la casa ideale che sarà vicina a un lago. Nella casa ideale ci dovranno essere delle stanze grandi con le finestre che danno sul lago. Davanti ci sarà un giardino e dietro una piccola spiaggia con della sabbia pulita e bianca. Sarà un luogo incantevole.

L'autore parla

a. di un giorno ideale.
b. delle finestre grandi.
c. di un luogo ideale dove abitare.
d. del mare.

5. Le Alpi, quelle montagne gigantesche al nord dell'Italia, separano la penisola dalla Francia, dalla Svizzera, dall'Austria, e dalla Iugoslavia. Formano una barriera naturale tra l'Italia e le altre nazioni e ciò aiuta anche d'inverno quando i venti freddissimi sono bloccati e non portano nè troppo freddo nè troppa neve agli Italiani.

A cosa servono le Alpi?

a. Proteggono gli Italiani.
b. Separano l'Italia dalla Russia.
c. Non servono a niente.
d. Rendono lo studio facile.

6. La prima colazione in Italia è molto diversa da quella americana. La prima colazione italiana è molto semplice e consiste di una tazza di caffè, dei panini, con burro o marmellata. Gli Italiani non sono abituati a mangiare molto la mattina, mentre invece il pasto principale per loro è il pranzo.

Com'è la prima colazione italiana?

a. C'è troppo da mangiare.
b. È semplice ma abbondante.
c. È come la colazione americana.
d. Non c'è niente da bere.

7. Una sera Pietro aiuta la mamma ad asciugare i piatti ma non lo fa volentieri. Allora la mamma, per farlo sentire meglio, gli dice:

–Devi lavorare con più velocità. Sai che non bisogna mai lasciare fino a domani ciò che si può fare oggi.

–Allora–risponde Pietro–finiamo tutta la torta stasera invece di lasciarla fino a domani.

Cosa vuole fare il ragazzo?

a. Vuole asciugare i piatti.
b. Vuole mangiare tutto in un giorno.
c. Deve andare dall'amico.
d. Preferisce guardare la televisione.

8. Nicola prende il treno delle otto ogni mattina e di solito legge il giornale fino alla sua stazione. Stamattina, però, non ha il giornale e può guardare in giro. Ed ecco che vede una signorina molto bella, con i capelli lunghi e neri e con gli occhi azzurri. Poverino, rimane incantato e non nota che la sua stazione è passata dieci minuti fa.

Il giovane non è sceso alla sua stazione perchè

a. ha perso il giornale.
b. gli hanno tagliato i capelli.
c. c'è troppa gente.
d. ha visto una ragazza bella.

9. Susanna e la madre camminano per i viali di un parco vicino a casa loro. È domenica mattina e c'è molta gente nel parco. Ad un tratto la bambina vede un cane e gli va vicino. L'uomo che è col cane dice:

–Sta' attenta, non ti avvicinare troppo. Non lo toccare. Ti può fare male perchè non ti conosce.

–Ebbene, ditegli che mi chiamo Susanna!

Perchè la bambina non dovrebbe andare vicino al cane?

a. Non lo conosce.
b. È domenica mattina.
c. Perchè si chiama Susanna.
d. La mamma ha paura.

10. Dopo che Colombo scoprì l'America, fece altri tre viaggi, ritornando in Spagna ogni volta con molto oro e con alcuni Indiani. Però, poco dopo l'ultimo viaggio nel 1506, Colombo fu messo in prigione dove passò lunghi mesi di miseria. Morì povero e abbandonato da tutti. Nessuno aveva apprezzato la sua grande scoperta.

Come morì Colombo?

a. in compagnia di amici
b. solo e abbandonato
c. come uomo famoso
d. mentre viaggiava

11. Il grande pittore italiano Raffaello aveva soltanto venticinque anni quando dipinse le Stanze del Vaticano. Oltre a quelle dipinse circa trenta madonne e in tutte le madonne di Raffaello c'è pura bellezza e un profondo affetto materno. Secondo alcuni critici la Madonna della Cappella Sistina è la più bella del mondo.

Questo artista è noto perchè

a. visitò la Cappella Sistina.
b. morì a venticinque anni.
c. le sue madonne sono bellissime.
d. la madre gli regalò un quadro.

12. Renzo è venuto a Milano da Roma per vedere il famoso dipinto di Leonardo da Vinci, *L'Ultima Cena*. Prende un tassì e va direttamente alla Chiesa di Santa Maria delle Grazie. Entra e chiede ad una guardia dove si trova il famoso dipinto. Ma la guardia gli dice:

–Mi dispiace, ma oggi è lunedì e quella parte della chiesa è chiusa.

Perchè Renzo non ha visto il dipinto?

a. Non c'erano tassì a Milano.
b. Faceva troppo caldo.
c. Leonardo non era in chiesa.
d. Quel giorno non si poteva vedere.

13. È da un anno che Lucia aspetta questo momento. Fra un'ora sposerà Roberto, e naturalmente è nervosa. Arriva in chiesa col padre, e insieme aspettano che incominci la musica per iniziare la cerimonia. Aspettano venti minuti, quaranta minuti, un'ora. Ma la musica non incomincia mai. Roberto non c'è. Ha cambiato idea.

Lucia non si è sposata perchè

a. lo sposo non è arrivato.
b. il padre non voleva.
c. l'orologio non funzionava.
d. la chiesa era piena di gente.

14. Il francobollo in Italia ha le stesse caratteristiche che hanno i francobolli in tutto il mondo, con la sola differenza che in Italia il francobollo acquista anche valore di moneta corrente (*cash*); cioè, che per piccoli pagamenti fatti per posta si possono inviare francobolli invece di contanti (*cash*) o assegni bancari (*checks*).

I francobolli italiani si usano anche

a. per spedire lettere.
b. come denaro.
c. per spedire cartoline.
d. per entrare in un ristorante.

15. Come in tutti gli altri paesi latini, anche in Italia la religione cattolica ha

un posto importante nella vita pubblica del cittadino. Esistono altre religioni, ma queste sono in minoranza e non hanno molto influsso sulla vita del pubblico in generale.

Di che cosa si parla?

a. del pubblico italiano
b. della religione
c. della lingua latina
d. dell'arte italiana

16. Un cane e un leone entrano in un ristorante. Il cameriere dà loro il menù e il cane ordina un osso enorme e delle polpette. Il leone non dice niente e il cameriere gli suggerisce una bistecca.

–Il leone non prende niente–dice il cane.
–Perchè? Non ha fame?
–Se avesse fame, io non sarei qui ad ordinare!

È evidente che

a. il leone ha molta fame.
b. il cane non ordina niente.
c. il leone non ha fame.
d. il cameriere non sente bene.

17. Sandra vuole andare alla spiaggia con le amiche ma non sa come chiedere permesso ai genitori. Ha paura che le diranno di no. Allora domanda al fratello, Mario, di chiedere permesso per lei. Mario risponde di "sì" ma si fa promettere un dollaro come regalo.

Mario ha deciso di aiutare la sorella perchè

a. le vuole bene.
b. vuole del denaro.
c. la mamma non c'è.
d. i genitori sono a casa.

18. Laura, Giovanni, e Paolo sono fra i cento passeggeri che volano da Roma a Madrid. Hanno avuto permesso dai loro genitori di andare a visitare la capitale spagnuola durante la settimana di Pasqua. Dal finestrino vedono montagne altissime e dei mari azzurri e verdi. È un viaggio meraviglioso che dura troppo poco per i tre amici.

Dove sono gli amici?

a. in aereo
b. in montagna
c. in mare
d. a Madrid

19. Uno scienziato sta per ricevere un premio per una sua scoperta. Prima, però, un giornalista chiede allo scienziato:

–Scusi, professore, ma Lei quando trova il tempo migliore per pensare?

–Di solito quando mi faccio la barba perchè è più facile a quell'ora pensare a cose scientifiche.

–Allora–risponde il giornalista–le persone che hanno la barba non avranno mai l'opportunità di pensare.

Chi non avrà mai l'opportunità di pensare?

a. gli scienziati
b. le persone che non si fanno la barba
c. quelli che si fanno la barba
d. i giornalisti

20. Una bambina nella prima classe della scuola elementare torna a casa, e la mamma le chiede immediatamente:

–Cosa hai imparato a scuola oggi?

–Ho imparato che quattro più quattro fa nove.

–Ma ciò non è corretto!

–Allora–risponde la bambina–in quel caso non ho imparato niente affatto oggi.

La bambina parla

a. di matematica.
b. della mamma.
c. del maestro.
d. della scienza.

21. Gino ha invitato Anita al cinema ma prima di andarci Anita ha voluto preparare un bel pranzo. Mentre Gino aspetta gioca col cane di Anita. Butta un giornale da una parte del salone all'altra, e il cane corre a prenderlo e lo riporta a Gino. Mentre Gino lancia il giornale per la quarta volta, Anita entra col piatto di pasta asciutta e il giornale cade proprio nel piatto. Che disastro!

Come è finita questa storia?

a. Il cane non ha potuto leggere.
b. Il pranzo è stato rovinato.
c. Anita ha comprato un giornale.
d. Gino ha preparato la pasta asciutta.

22. Il signor Bello ha accompagnato la moglie a fare delle spese. Vanno da un negozio all'altro, e il povero signor Bello ha le braccia piene di scatole e di pacchi di ogni genere. Ci sono abiti, scarpe, guanti, eccetera che la signora ha comprato. Il signor Bello è stanco.

–Ma non possiamo prendere un tassì e andare a casa? –chiede il signor Bello.

–Impossibile–risponde la signora–non vedi che abbiamo speso già troppo denaro? Possiamo camminare.

Come hanno passato la giornata?

a. Hanno viaggiato in un tassì.
b. Hanno comprato parecchie cose.
c. Hanno spedito delle scatole.
d. Si sono sposati.

23. Giuseppe ha avuto una nuova chitarra per Natale, e vuole imparare a suonarla al più presto possibile. Va dall'amico Vincenzo, il quale sa suonare molto bene.

–Mi puoi dare qualche lezione? –domanda Giuseppe.

–Certo. Ma soltanto se tu prometti di aiutarmi con la biologia.

–D'accordo.

Giuseppe è andato dall'amico per

a. imparare a suonare.
b. studiare biologia.
c. vendergli la chitarra.
d. celebrare il Natale.

24. Giosuè Carducci è considerato uno dei più grandi poeti d'Italia. Nacque in Toscana e per molti anni fu professore di letteratura italiana all'Università di Bologna. La sua poesia, che tratta dei tempi gloriosi di Roma, descrive gli eventi principali della storia italiana ed esprime il suo immenso amore per la giustizia, la libertà, e l'umanità.

Oltre ad essere professore, quest'uomo era

a. scrittore.
b. romano.
c. avvocato.
d. architetto.

25. La settimana prossima vi sarà un banchetto enorme a cui prenderanno parte duecento persone. Le tavole saranno apparecchiate e siccome il banchetto avrà luogo all'aperto le tavole saranno illuminate da migliaia di lampadine. Il banchetto durerà fino a mezzanotte e gli invitati si divertiranno a cantare, a ballare, a mangiare, e a bere.

Cosa succederà fra una settimana?

a. Avrà luogo una partita.
b. Ci sarà una festa.
c. Si costruiranno delle tavole.
d. Due giovani si sposeranno.

B. LONGER PASSAGES FOR COMPREHENSION

1. Read the following passage. Then write **vero** or **falso** for each sentence that follows the paragraph.

L'ora di cui si servivano i Romani non era l'ora come la conosciamo oggi, cioè l'ora di 60 minuti che divide il giorno in ventiquattro parti uguali. Il giorno di luce, il tempo cioè in cui il sole rimaneva all'orizzonte, era diviso in dodici ore uguali, e d'estate quindi le ore erano più lunghe che d'inverno. L'ora sesta era il mezzogiorno. Ai tempi romani esistevano due tipi di orologi: quello a sole e quello ad acqua. L'orologio come lo sappiamo oggi fu inventato soltanto alla fine del Medio Evo.

a. L'ora di oggi è come quella dei Romani.
b. L'ora romana era divisa in 60 minuti.
c. La giornata del sole dei Romani era divisa in 24 ore.
d. Il mezzogiorno nostro è come l'ora sesta romana.
e. Le ore d'inverno erano più lunghe di quelle d'estate.
f. Ai tempi dei Romani l'ora si misurava usando il sole.
g. Gli orologi moderni furono inventati dopo il Rinascimento.

2. Read the following passage. Then answer the questions in complete English sentences.

Il re di Spagna voleva invitare Cristoforo Colombo a pranzo. L'invito fu mandato al navigatore tramite un capitano del re. Colombo ascoltò il capitano e poi rispose:

–Mi dispiace ma non posso accettare l'invito del re.

–Ma perchè? –chiese il capitano. È impossibile che rifiutate.

–E perchè? –domandò Colombo. –Ho detto di no al principe Giovanni quando mi invitò ad accompagnarlo ai laghi in montagna. Avrebbe potuto mettermi in prigione, ma non lo fece. Perchè non dovrei rifiutare l'invito del re?

–Sta bene–disse il capitano–ma mi dia almeno una buona scusa qualsiasi che io possa dire al re.

–Ditegli che vado a letto tutte le sere alle nove e mezza.

Il re non si offese, e l'invito a pranzo fu cambiato in un invito a colazione che Colombo non rifiutò.

a. Chi aveva invitato Colombo a pranzo?
b. Come fu invitato Colombo?

c. Quale fu la risposta di Colombo?
d. Dove voleva andare il principe Giovanni?
e. Quale fu la scusa di Colombo?
f. Cosa fece il re alla fine?

3. Read the following passage. Then answer the questions in complete English sentences.

Una vecchia aveva gli occhi malati e subito chiamò il medico. Il dottore venne subito e mise della medicina negli occhi della donna. Mentre la vecchia aveva gli occhi chiusi, il dottore prese un orologio e se lo mise in tasca. Venne a mettere la medicina negli occhi della donna ogni giorno per una settimana. Ed ogni volta prendeva qualche oggetto prezioso. Alla fine della settimana la vecchia si rifiutò di pagare il medico. Naturalmente fu portata in corte e andò davanti al giudice.

—Sì—disse la donna al giudice. —È vero; io gli avevo promesso il denaro quando avrei veduto meglio. Ma ora dopo tanta medicina io sto peggio di prima. Prima vedevo tutti gli oggetti della mia casa, e adesso non li vedo più!

a. Perchè la vecchia chiamò il medico?
b. Cosa mise negli occhi della donna il medico?
c. Cosa prendeva il medico ogni volta?
d. Per quanto tempo andò il medico a casa della vecchia?
e. Cosa rifiutò di fare la vecchia?
f. Perchè sta peggio la donna?

4. Read the following passage. Then answer the questions in complete English sentences.

Un uomo aveva due figlie, una sposata a un contadino (*farmer*), l'altra a un costruttore di case. Un giorno il padre va a visitare la figlia, moglie del contadino, e le domanda come sta, come vanno le cose per lei e per suo marito.

—Tutto andrebbe bene—risponde la figlia—se Dio mandasse la pioggia a questa frutta e verdura.

Pochi giorni dopo il padre va a trovare l'altra figlia, la moglie del costruttore di case. E le fa la stessa domanda.

—Ho tutto. Tutto va bene. Non ho nulla da chiedere. Basta che il tempo rimanga bello così e che il sole continui a brillare così mio marito può continuare a costruire molte case.

—Ma se tu vuoi il sole e tua sorella la pioggia, per chi dovrò pregare a Dio?

a. A chi è sposata la prima figlia?
b. A chi è sposata la seconda figlia?
c. Cosa voleva la prima figlia?
d. Cosa voleva la seconda figlia?
e. Cosa dice il padre alla fine?

5. Read the following passage. Then answer the questions in complete English sentences.

Era il primo giorno che Gianni si metteva gli occhiali. Fino a quel giorno non aveva potuto vedere le cose da lontano. Ignorava i colori magnifici delle cose che lo circondavano. Allora la madre lo portò dal dottore, prima per la visita generale, e pochi giorni dopo per gli occhiali. Ed oggi gli occhiali erano pronti. Il medico gli mise gli occhiali e Gianni per la prima volta vide bene la faccia bellissima della madre. Poi andò alla finestra e guardò giù nella strada. Vide bambini che giocavano, macchine di ogni colore che passavano, uomini e donne che camminavano insieme. E soprattutto vide i fiori bellissimi nei giardini e gli alberi grandi, verdi e giganteschi. Era un miracolo!

a. Cosa stava per succedere a Gianni per la prima volta?
b. Cosa aveva ignorato fino a quel momento?
c. Dove lo aveva portato la madre? Perchè?
d. Cosa vide bene per la prima volta?
e. Cosa vide dalla finestra?
f. Cosa facevano i bambini?
g. Com'erano i fiori e gli alberi?

6. Read the following passage. Then answer the questions in complete English sentences.

Pinocchio, il famoso libro di Carlo Lorenzini, ha avuto un'origine curiosa. Lorenzini era uno scrittore fiorentino che non pensava affatto di dedicarsi alla letteratura per ragazzi. Una sera giocava a carte, ma invece di vincere perdette un migliaio di lire e non le poteva pagare. Naturalmente non era molto felice. Mentre pensava come fare per pagare il denaro perso, l'editore (*publisher*) Felice Paggi gli domandò a cosa pensava.

—Ho perso—Lorenzini rispose—e non so come pagare.

—Quanto hai perso?

–Mille lire e non le ho.

–Le vuoi?

Lorenzini credeva che l'editore non dicesse la verità. Ma Paggi gli dette le mille lire e gli fece firmare un contratto che lo obbligò a scrivere un libro per fanciulli entro un anno. Quel libro fu *Pinocchio.*

a. Qual era la professione di Lorenzini?
b. Come perse il denaro?
c. Come si sentiva dopo aver perso il denaro?
d. Chi offrì di aiutarlo?
e. Quali erano le condizioni del contratto?

7. Read the following passage. Then select the alternative that best answers each question.

Nel 1903 lo scienziato Guglielmo Marconi fu invitato da Edison a colazione ad Orange, New Jersey. Era domenica. Marconi arrivò ad Orange verso l'una. Edison gli fece visitare il laboratorio dove lavorava sulle sue invenzioni. Poi iniziò una conversazione assai interessante con Marconi sulle loro esperienze. La conversazione continuò per circa un'ora. Finalmente Marconi disse:

–Caro Edison, sono quasi le due. A che ora si fa colazione?

–Colazione? Ma io ho già mangiato–disse Edison.

–Ma Lei mi ha invitato a colazione.

–Ha ragione–disse Edison. –Me ne ero dimenticato.

(1) Perchè Marconi era andato a trovare Edison?

a. Fu invitato a fare una conferenza.
b. Voleva vedere il laboratorio.
c. Fu invitato a mangiare.
d. Pensava di vedere Orange.

(2) Dove abitava Edison?

a. in Italia
b. negli Stati Uniti
c. nel Sud America
d. nel Canadà

(3) Cosa fecero dopo che visitarono il laboratorio?

a. Si misero a parlare.
b. Iniziarono a mangiare.
c. Fecero una conferenza.
d. Visitarono Orange.

(4) Cosa voleva fare Marconi?

a. inventare qualcosa
b. fare un viaggio
c. mangiare
d. scrivere una lettera

(5) Perchè non avevano fatto colazione?

a. Edison non c'era.
b. Marconi aveva mangiato.
c. Edison si era dimenticato.
d. Marconi se n'era andato.

8. Read the following passage. Then choose the appropriate answer in parentheses that completes each sentence.

Una bella signorina va da un famoso medico al quale non piace parlare troppo. Senza parlare gli mostra la mano che era stata morsa (*bitten*) da un gatto. Il dottore domanda:

–Caduta?
–Morsa.
–Cane?
–Gatto.
–Ieri?
–Oggi.
–Soffre?
–No.

Il medico mette della medicina sulla mano e chiede:

–Signora?
–Signorina.
–Sola?
–Sì.
–Libera?
–Sì.
–Sposiamoci?
–Sì.

Ed il giorno dopo sono marito e moglie.

a. Una signorina va da un medico (che parla troppo, che dice poco, che fa pagare molto).
b. È andata perchè le fa male (il dottore, il braccio, la mano).
c. La signorina si è fatta male (ieri, oggi, due giorni fa).
d. La signorina abita (con i genitori, da sola, con una compagna).
e. Il medico la vuole (sposare, aiutare, accompagnare).

9. Read the following passage, which has been adapted from *I Promessi Sposi* by Alessandro Manzoni. Then select the phrase or sentence that correctly answers each question.

Renzo andò verso la casa di Lucia, che era un po' fuori dal villaggio.

Davanti a quella casetta, c'era un piccolo cortile (*courtyard*) circondato da un muretto. Il giovane entrò nel cortile e sentì delle voci che venivano da una stanza di sopra. S'immaginò che erano le amiche, venute ad accompagnare Lucia, e non volle farsi vedere. Una ragazzina che si trovava nel cortile gli andò incontro e gridò:

–Lo sposo! Lo sposo!

–Zitta Bettina, zitta–disse Renzo. –Vieni qui; va' su da Lucia e dille all'orecchio . . . ma di maniera che nessuno senta . . . che devo parlarle, che aspetto nella stanza al pianterreno, e che venga subito.

(1) Dove abitava Lucia?

a. in una casa grande
b. nel centro del villaggio
c. a poca distanza dal villaggio
d. in un cortile

(2) Cosa circondava il cortile?

a. molte case grandi
b. un giardino meraviglioso
c. un muro basso
d. dei bambini che giocavano

(3) Secondo Renzo chi parlava?

a. delle donne
b. una bambina
c. un uomo
d. lo sposo

(4) Cosa fece la bambina che vide Renzo?

a. Incominciò a cantare.
b. Si mise a parlare con le amiche.
c. Incominciò a giocare nel cortile.
d. Annunciò che era arrivato lo sposo.

(5) Perchè Renzo era venuto da Lucia?

a. per sposarla
b. per parlare con lei
c. per accompagnarla
d. per darle un regalo

10. Read the following passage. Then select the phrase or sentence that best answers each question or completes each statement.

Al caffè c'erano il professor Giulio Buono, il signor Carlo Siano, ingegnere, e il dentista Mario Esposito. Erano seduti ad un tavolo e chiacchieravano. Era la vigilia di Natale.

Il professor Buono disse:

–Sapete che cosa ho scoperto? A Babbo Natale (*Santa Claus*) i ragazzi non ci credono più. Quando arrivano all'età di sei o sette anni d'un tratto diventano tanto intelligenti, secondo loro. Ieri ho sentito mia figlia che parlava con un'amica. L'amica le ha chiesto: "Ma tu hai scritto ancora a Babbo Natale?" Mia figlia ha risposto: "Certo. Cosa vuoi, devo far contenti i miei genitori, perchè sono sicuri che io ci credo ancora. Meglio così, altrimenti non riceverei nessun regalo affatto!"

(1) Cosa facevano questi uomini?

a. Giocavano a carte.
b. Parlavano in un caffè.
c. Facevano del caffè.
d. Leggevano il giornale.

(2) Che giorno era?

a. il giorno prima di Natale
b. il compleanno di uno degli amici
c. il giorno dopo Natale
d. il giorno di Natale

(3) Cosa aveva scoperto il professor Buono?

a. I ragazzi hanno sei anni.
b. I ragazzi non credono più a Natale.
c. Doveva pagare per il caffè.
d. I ragazzi non credono più a Babbo Natale.

(4) La figlia del professore ha scritto

a. all'amica.
b. a Babbo Natale.
c. al padre.
d. alla nonna.

(5) Se non scrive la lettera

a. non potrà andare a scuola.
b. non avrà regali.
c. riceverà molti regali.
d. potrà fare un viaggio.

11. Read the following passage. Then select the answer that best completes each statement.

Mio padre, uomo di poche parole ma molto intelligente, mi portava ogni domenica, da quando ero bambino, per una passeggiata. Andavamo da soli, dopo mangiato, senza parlare. Mio padre sapeva delle strade solitarie, deserte, dove si camminava piano piano per ore intere e senza incontrare quasi mai nessuno. Quasi mai perchè ogni tanto s'incontrava un contadino, una vecchia, una donna con una bambina. Mio padre pensava continuamente mentre io cercavo qualcosa con cui giocare.

(1) Il padre del ragazzo

a. parlava molto.
b. diceva poco.
c. partiva ogni domenica.
d. mangiava da solo.

(2) Uscivano insieme

a. ogni settimana.
b. prima di mangiare.
c. raramente.
d. con la mamma.

(3) Camminavano sempre

a. per le strade affollate.
b. dove non c'era quasi nessuno.
c. in un deserto.
d. con una bambina.

(4) Mentre camminavano il padre

a. parlava al figlio.
b. non diceva niente.
c. cantava da solo.
d. leggeva il giornale.

(5) Il figlio, invece,

a. parlava ad alta voce.
b. si divertiva cercando qualcosa.
c. chiacchierava da solo.
d. preparava da mangiare.

12. Read the following passage. Then select the alternative that best answers the question or completes each statement.

Quando Carla andava in montagna, le sembrava di nascere un'altra volta. Sentiva il vento sulla faccia e senza nessun pensiero sentiva di vivere come avrebbe voluto vivere sempre. Quando invece scendeva da lassù si sentiva sempre triste e tornava in città malinconica. Ciò che la aiutava a sentirsi un po' allegra era quel che portava con sè da lassù: un fiore, un ramo, una foglia. Allora soltanto si sentiva ancora legata a quella montagna distante da casa sua. Era con quella foglia o ramo che andava a scuola; ma invece di studiare pensava alla campagna montagnosa lontana, bella, e verde.

(1) Cosa succedeva a questa ragazza in montagna?

a. Si sentiva di avere una vita nuova.
b. Si faceva male spesso.
c. Doveva studiare molto.
d. Mangiava troppo.

(2) Come si sentiva lontana dalla montagna?

a. allegra
b. infelice
c. studiosa
d. bene

(3) Quando scendeva in città portava

a. un panino.
b. dei libri.
c. qualcosa dalla montagna.
d. un abito nuovo.

(4) La montagna era

a. lontana da casa sua.
b. vicino a casa sua.
c. in città.
d. malinconica.

(5) Cosa faceva a scuola Carla?

a. Studiava molto.
b. Scriveva delle lettere.
c. Non pensava agli studi.
d. Leggeva dei romanzi.

13. Read the following passage. Then select the answer that best completes each statement.

Giuseppe Marotta, uno dei più importanti scrittori umoristici italiani, nacque a Napoli nel 1902. Suo padre, che era avvocato, morì quando Marotta aveva nove anni. Dopo alcuni anni, siccome non c'era nessuno che potesse lavorare per la famiglia, il giovane fu costretto a lasciare gli studi all'età di quindici anni per cercare lavoro. Tentò molti lavori diversi mentre studiava di sera da solo. Incominciò a scrivere poesie e novelle che vennero pubblicate nei giornali locali. A ventitrè anni andò a Milano per trovare lavoro da scrittore. Infatti, due mesi più tardi fu assunto (*hired*) dalla casa editrice Mondadori e così iniziò la sua carriera letteraria.

(1) Marotta è conosciuto per le sue storie

a. tristi.
b. allegre.
c. vecchie.
d. nuove.

(2) Il padre morì quando Giuseppe Marotta

a. era vecchio.
b. era ragazzo.
c. era appena nato.
d. si era sposato.

(3) All'età di quindici anni dovette

a. rimanere a scuola.
b. cercare del lavoro.
c. scrivere delle poesie.
d. pubblicare dei giornali.

(4) Alcuni dei suoi lavori letterari furono

a. pubblicati.
b. persi.
c. abbandonati.
d. mangiati.

(5) A Milano trovò

a. molta gente.
b. la carriera che cercava.
c. un giornale.
d. la madre.

14. Read the following passage. Then select the alternative that best answers each question or completes each statement.

Mio fratello ed io siamo due persone completamente diverse. A lui piace studiare tutto il giorno, mentre a me non piace studiare affatto. Lui ha sempre freddo ed io sempre caldo. La notte d'inverno, quando dormiamo insieme nel nostro letto, io rimango solo col lenzuolo, mentre lui invece si copre totalmente con la coperta (*blanket*). Lui non mangia carne affatto, soltanto verdura e insalata. A me invece piace carne di ogni tipo e odio verdura e insalata. A lui non piacciono i dolci. Io invece mangio tutto—torte, gelati, caramelle. Purtroppo, lui è così snello e io sono così grasso!

(1) Come sono questi fratelli?

a. uguali
b. differenti
c. simili
d. alti

(2) A chi piace studiare sempre?

a. a tutti e due
b. a nessuno
c. a uno solo
d. ai genitori

(3) Di notte, uno si copre tutto, ma l'altro che fa?

a. Non dorme affatto.
b. Si copre soltanto col lenzuolo.
c. Legge i libri.
d. Mangia tutto.

(4) Un fratello mangia quasi tutto; l'altro invece

a. preferisce carne.
b. mangia solo verdura.
c. mangia dolci.
d. dorme da solo.

(5) Il fratello che mangia quasi tutto

a. pesa più del fratello.
b. è snello.
c. è alto.
d. pesa meno del fratello.

15. Read the following passage. Then select the answer that best completes each question.

Ieri mi trovavo sul treno che va da Firenze a Pisa. Il vagone era pieno ma quasi nessuno parlava con la persona seduta accanto. Faceva bel tempo, e mi divertivo a guardare dal finestrino, godendo così il bel panorama lungo la strada. Ad una stazione fuori Firenze, salì una vecchia signora. Il treno continuò per Pisa. Il conduttore chiese alla signora il biglietto o le ottocento lire per il viaggio. La donna cercò dappertutto ma non trovò niente. Guardò in giro, ma nessuno faceva attenzione. Tutti guardavano fuori dal finestrino. Capii che qualcuno doveva aiutarla. E così facendo, mi ricordai che avevo ottocento lire in tasca. Le offrii alla signora. Lei le accettò e mi ringraziò continuamente fino a Pisa!

(1) Chi c'era nel treno?

a. C'erano poche persone.
b. Non c'era quasi nessuno.
c. C'era molta gente.
d. C'era soltanto il fattorino.

(2) Cosa si godeva dal finestrino?

a. la veduta
b. la gente
c. un film
d. il treno

(3) Chi era salito sul treno?

a. una ragazza
b. il padre
c. il fattorino
d. una donna anziana

(4) Cosa cercava la vecchia signora?

a. il panorama
b. il denaro per il biglietto
c. il treno
d. il finestrino

(5) Chi aiutò la signora?

a. il fattorino
b. il figlio
c. la figlia
d. l'autore

Part VIII—Practice in Directed Composition

Write a composition of five or more Italian sentences for each of the following topics. Each sentence or group of sentences should contain the information called for in the suggested guides for each topic.

1. You are asked to tell about your birthday. In your answer tell:
   a. the date of your birthday.
   b. how old you were on your last birthday.
   c. how you celebrated your last birthday.
   d. what gifts you received.
   e. what gifts you hope to receive for your next birthday.

2. You are asked to discuss the past school year. Talk about:
   a. the first day of school.
   b. the friends you met.
   c. the length of the school day.
   d. the subjects you studied.
   e. your impressions of the school.

3. You are walking along with a friend. Tell him:
   a. You will go to the country next summer.
   b. Your cousins go there, too.
   c. You always have a good time with them.
   d. When the weather is good, you go swimming.
   e. In the evening, you often go to the movies.

4. You are in a plane traveling to Italy. You speak to the passenger next to you.
   a. Introduce yourself.
   b. Ask him (her) if he (she) likes to travel by plane.
   c. Ask him (her) if he (she) knows when the plane will arrive in Rome.
   d. Tell him (her) the film you saw on the plane was good.
   e. Tell him (her) that you will be eating supper soon.

5. You are writing a composition for the Italian class. Tell your teacher that:
   a. You woke up at seven o'clock.
   b. After you washed, you had breakfast.

c. On the way to school, you met a friend.
d. Instead of going to school, you went to the movies.
e. You and your friend had a great time.

6. You were at a party. Tell:
a. that the party took place last Saturday.
b. who the party was for.
c. with whom you went.
d. what you did at the party.
e. what was served.

7. You are shopping in a large department store. You are speaking to a clerk.
a. Ask him to show you some ties.
b. Tell him you like red and blue ties only.
c. Ask him to show you some gloves, too.
d. Tell him the gloves are for your father.
e. Thank him and bid him good-bye.

8. It is a beautiful day in June. You are walking along a street.
a. Tell where you are.
b. Tell where you are coming from.
c. Tell where you are going.
d. Mention two articles of clothing you are wearing.
e. Tell about some other people you noticed.

9. You are asked to write a composition on your family. Tell:
a. who the members of the family are.
b. if you have brothers or sisters and who the oldest one is.
c. how old your parents are.
d. what your father or mother does.
e. something that you all do together.

10. Last night your mother prepared an excellent dinner. Tell that:
a. You ate at six o'clock.
b. It was your sister's 18th birthday.
c. You ate macaroni, chicken, salad, and cake.
d. For the first time, you had some wine.
e. You all had a great time.

11. Write a composition about your friend Mario.
a. He lives in Chicago with his parents.
b. You have invited him to come and spend a week with you.
c. He will arrive at 11 A.M. on Monday.
d. You and your sister will meet him at the station.
e. Mention two things you will be doing during the week.

12. You are writing a letter to your cousin.
a. You went to see a soccer game.
b. It was your first game.
c. You didn't understand all the rules (*regole*).
d. There were five thousand people in the stadium.
e. The Blue team won the game 2-0.

13. You are at the railroad station waiting for a train. Tell:
a. where you are.
b. where you are going.
c. that the train will arrive on time.
d. how long the ride will last.
e. when you expect to return.

14. You are in the library to study. Tell that:
a. You meet a friend there.
b. Instead of studying, you begin to talk.
c. You talked about the movie you both saw.
d. You both spoke too loudly.
e. You both decided to go outside and talk there, instead.

15. You and your friends have made plans for an outing. Say that:
a. You and your friends are going on a picnic.
b. It will take place on Saturday morning.
c. The girls will bring the food.
d. The boys will bring something to drink.
e. You will return at 7 P.M.

16. Imagine that you are in Rome. You approach a policeman.
a. Tell him that you have just arrived from the U.S.
b. Tell him how long you have studied Italian.
c. Ask him where St. Peter's Basilica is located.

d. Ask him if there is a good restaurant near the Basilica.
e. Thank him and tell him he has been very kind.

17. Write the following story.
a. Your uncle has just arrived from Naples.
b. Tell what he brought you as a gift.
c. Tell what he said about his trip.
d. Tell where he will go from here.
e. Tell when he will return to Italy.

18. A new boy has come into your class. Tell him:
a. how glad you are to meet him.
b. one fact about the school.
c. one fact about the teacher.
d. about the students in the class.
e. you would like to have lunch with him.

19. In a letter written to a friend, tell him:
a. where you are at present.
b. how you came to the place.
c. what the weather is like.
d. some things you have been doing.
e. that you will write again next week.

20. Write about looking for a friend's apartment. Say that:
a. You knocked on the door of an apartment.
b. A man asked you what you wanted.
c. You told him that you were looking for Giovanni Ranieri.
d. He told you that Mr. Ranieri lived on the next floor.
e. You thanked him and took the elevator.

21. You go to the doctor's office. As he examines you, you explain that:
a. Your left leg hurts.
b. You fell while coming down the stairs.
c. There was no one to help you.
d. You couldn't go to school for two days.
e. You would like to stay home three more days.

22. Write about your typical Sunday. Tell:
a. at what time you get up.
b. what you usually eat for breakfast.

c. what you do after breakfast (go to church, read the papers, etc.).
d. where you go after dinner.
e. how you spend the evening (watching television, going to the movies, etc.).

23. Write about your activities at home. Give the following information:
a. You help your mother (father) when possible.
b. the reason that you help.
c. the one thing you do to help.
d. what you are told when you help.
e. how you feel after you have helped.

24. You have had to visit a sick friend.
a. Ask him how he is feeling today.
b. Ask him when he became ill.
c. Ask him if the doctor came to visit him.
d. Tell him you had not been feeling too well either.
e. Tell him that you must go, and say good-bye.

25. A neighbor knocked on your door last night. Tell how:
a. You greeted her and asked how you could help her.
b. She wanted to borrow some milk.
c. You told her your mother wasn't home.
d. You looked in the refrigerator and found a bottle of milk to give her.
e. She thanked you, said good-bye, and left.

Part IX—Verb Summary Chart

Note

In Italian words of two or more syllables, the stress usually falls on the next-to-the-last syllable. Exceptions to this rule are indicated in Parts IX, X, and XI of this book by a dot below the vowel of the syllable to be stressed. In the following chart, verbs with one asterisk are conjugated with **ẹssere**; verbs with two asterisks are conjugated with **avere** or **ẹssere**. All other verbs in this chart are conjugated with **avere**.

Infinitive	Gerund; Past Participle	Present Indicative	Imperfect Indicative	Past Absolute
andare* *to go*	andando andato	vado vai va andiamo andate vanno	andavo andavi andava andavamo andavate andạvano	andai andasti andò andammo andaste andạrono
bere *to drink*	bevendo bevuto	bevo bevi beve beviamo bevete bẹvono	bevevo bevevi beveva bevevamo bevevate bevẹvano	bevvi bevesti bevve bevemmo beveste bẹvvero
chiẹdere *to ask*	chiedendo chiesto	chiedo chiedi chiede chiediamo chiedete chiẹdono	chiedevo chiedevi chiedeva chiedevamo chiedevate chiedẹvano	chiesi chiedesti chiese chiedemmo chiedeste chiẹsero
chiụdere *to close*	chiudendo chiuso	chiudo chiudi chiude chiudiamo chiudete chiụdono	chiudevo chiudevi chiudeva chiudevamo chiudevate chiudẹvano	chiusi chiudesti chiuse chiudemmo chiudeste chiụsero

Future	Conditional	Imperative	Present Subjunctive	Imperfect Subjunctive
andrò	andrei	. . . . . .	vada	andassi
andrai	andresti	va'	vada	andassi
andrà	andrebbe	vada	vada	andasse
andremo	andremmo	andiamo	andiamo	andassimo
andrete	andreste	andate	andiate	andaste
andranno	andrebbero	vadano	vadano	andassero
berrò	berrei	. . . . . .	beva	bevessi
berrai	berresti	bevi	beva	bevessi
berrà	berrebbe	beva	beva	bevesse
berremo	berremmo	beviamo	beviamo	bevessimo
berrete	berreste	bevete	beviate	beveste
berranno	berrebbero	bevano	bevano	bevessero
chiederò	chiederei	. . . . . .	chieda	chiedessi
chiederai	chiederesti	chiedi	chieda	chiedessi
chiederà	chiederebbe	chieda	chieda	chiedesse
chiederemo	chiederemmo	chiediamo	chiediamo	chiedessimo
chiederete	chiedereste	chiedete	chiediate	chiedeste
chiederanno	chiederebbero	chiedano	chiedano	chiedessero
chiuderò	chiuderei	. . . . . .	chiuda	chiudessi
chiuderai	chiuderesti	chiudi	chiuda	chiudessi
chiuderà	chiuderebbe	chiuda	chiuda	chiudesse
chiuderemo	chiuderemmo	chiudiamo	chiudiamo	chiudessimo
chiuderete	chiudereste	chiudete	chiudiate	chiudeste
chiuderanno	chiuderebbero	chiudano	chiudano	chiudessero

Infinitive	Gerund; Past Participle	Present Indicative	Imperfect Indicative	Past Absolute
conoscere *to know*	conoscendo conosciuto	conosco conosci conosce conosciamo conoscete conoscono	conoscevo conoscevi conosceva conoscevamo conoscevate conoscevano	conobbi conoscesti conobbe conoscemmo conosceste conobbero
dare *to give*	dando dato	do dai dà diamo date danno	davo davi dava davamo davate davano	diedi desti diede demmo deste diedero
dire *to say*	dicendo detto	dico dici dice diciamo dite dicono	dicevo dicevi diceva dicevamo dicevate dicevano	dissi dicesti disse dicemmo diceste dissero
dovere** *to have to,* *must*	dovendo dovuto	devo (debbo) devi deve dobbiamo dovete devano (debbono)	dovevo dovevi doveva dovevamo dovevate dovevano	dovetti (dovei) dovesti dovette (dovè) dovemmo doveste dovettero (doverono)
fare *to do,* *to make*	facendo fatto	faccio fai fa facciamo fate fanno	facevo facevi faceva facevamo facevate facevano	feci facesti fece facemmo faceste fecero

Future	Conditional	Imperative	Present Subjunctive	Imperfect Subjunctive
conoscerò	conoscerei	......	conosca	conoscessi
conoscerai	conosceresti	conosci	conosca	conoscessi
conoscerà	conoscerebbe	conosca	conosca	conoscesse
conosceremo	conosceremmo	conosciamo	conosciamo	conoscessimo
conoscerete	conoscereste	conoscete	conosciate	conosceste
conosceranno	conoscerebbero	conoscano	conoscano	conoscessero
darò	darei	......	dia	dessi
darai	daresti	da'	dia	dessi
darà	darebbe	dia	dia	desse
daremo	daremmo	diamo	diamo	dessimo
darete	dareste	date	diate	deste
daranno	darebbero	diano	diano	dessero
dirò	direi	......	dica	dicessi
dirai	diresti	di'	dica	dicessi
dirà	direbbe	dica	dica	dicesse
diremo	diremmo	diciamo	diciamo	dicessimo
direte	direste	dite	diciate	diceste
diranno	direbbero	dicano	dicano	dicessero
dovrò	dovrei	......	debba	dovessi
dovrai	dovresti	......	debba	dovessi
dovrà	dovrebbe	......	debba	dovesse
dovremo	dovremmo	......	dobbiamo	dovessimo
dovrete	dovreste	......	dobbiate	doveste
dovranno	dovrebbero	......	debbano	dovessero
farò	farei	......	faccia	facessi
farai	faresti	fa'	faccia	facessi
farà	farebbe	faccia	faccia	facesse
faremo	faremmo	facciamo	facciamo	facessimo
farete	fareste	fate	facciate	faceste
faranno	farebbero	facciano	facciano	facessero

Infinitive	Gerund; Past Participle	Present Indicative	Imperfect Indicative	Past Absolute
leggere *to read*	leggendo letto	leggo leggi legge leggiamo leggete leggono	leggevo leggevi leggeva leggevamo leggevate leggevano	lessi leggesti lesse leggemmo leggeste lessero
mettere *to put,* *to place*	mettendo messo	metto metti mette mettiamo mettete mettono	mettevo mettevi metteva mettevamo mettevate mettevano	misi mettesti mise mettemmo metteste misero
morire* *to die*	morendo morto	muoio muori muore moriamo morite muoiono	morivo morivi moriva morivamo morivate morivano	morii moristi morì morimmo moriste morirono
potere** *to be able,* *can*	potendo potuto	posso puoi può possiamo potete possono	potevo potevi poteva potevamo potevate potevano	potei potesti potè potemmo poteste poterono
prendere *to take*	prendendo preso	prendo prendi prende prendiamo prendete prendono	prendevo prendevi prendeva prendevamo prendevate prendevano	presi prendesti prese prendemmo prendeste presero
rimanere* *to remain*	rimanendo rimasto	rimango rimani rimane rimaniamo rimanete rimangono	rimanevo rimanevi rimaneva rimanevamo rimanevate rimanevano	rimasi rimanesti rimase rimanemmo rimaneste rimasero

Future	Conditional	Imperative	Present Subjunctive	Imperfect Subjunctive
leggerò	leggerei	......	legga	leggessi
leggerai	leggeresti	leggi	legga	leggessi
leggerà	leggerebbe	legga	legga	leggesse
leggeremo	leggeremmo	leggiamo	leggiamo	leggessimo
leggerete	leggereste	leggete	leggiate	leggeste
leggeranno	leggerebbero	leggano	leggano	leggessero
metterò	metterei	......	metta	mettessi
metterai	metteresti	metti	metta	mettessi
metterà	metterebbe	metta	metta	mettesse
metteremo	metteremmo	mettiamo	mettiamo	mettessimo
metterete	mettereste	mettete	mettiate	metteste
metteranno	metterebbero	mettano	mettano	mettessero
morrò	morrei	......	muoia	morissi
morrai	morresti	muori	muoia	morissi
morrà	morrebbe	muoia	muoia	morisse
morremo	morremmo	moriamo	moriamo	morissimo
morrete	morreste	morite	moriate	moriste
morranno	morrebbero	muoiano	muoiano	morissero
potrò	potrei	......	possa	potessi
potrai	potresti	......	possa	potessi
potrà	potrebbe	......	possa	potesse
potremo	potremmo	......	possiamo	potessimo
potrete	potreste	......	possiate	poteste
potranno	potrebbero	......	possano	potessero
prenderò	prenderei	......	prenda	prendessi
prenderai	prenderesti	prendi	prenda	prendessi
prenderà	prenderebbe	prenda	prenda	prendesse
prenderemo	prenderemmo	prendiamo	prendiamo	prendessimo
prenderete	prendereste	prendete	prendiate	prendeste
prenderanno	prenderebbero	prendano	prendano	prendessero
rimarrò	rimarrei	......	rimanga	rimanessi
rimarrai	rimarresti	rimani	rimanga	rimanessi
rimarrà	rimarrebbe	rimanga	rimanga	rimanesse
rimarremo	rimarremmo	rimaniamo	rimaniamo	rimanessimo
rimarrete	rimarreste	rimanete	rimaniate	rimaneste
rimarranno	rimarrebbero	rimangano	rimangano	rimanessero

Infinitive	Gerund; Past Participle	Present Indicative	Imperfect Indicative	Past Absolute
rispondere *to answer*	rispondendo risposto	rispondo rispondi risponde rispondiamo rispondete rispondono	rispondevo rispondevi rispondeva rispondevamo rispondevate rispondevano	risposi rispondesti rispose rispondemmo rispondeste risposero
salire** *to go up*	salendo salito	salgo sali sale saliamo salite salgono	salivo salivi saliva salivamo salivate salivano	salii salisti salì salimmo saliste salirono
sapere *to know*	sapendo saputo	so sai sa sappiamo sapete sanno	sapevo sapevi sapeva sapevamo sapevate sapevano	seppi sapesti seppe sapemmo sapeste seppero
scegliere *to choose*	scegliendo scelto	scelgo scegli sceglie scegliamo scegliete scelgono	sceglievo sceglievi sceglieva sceglievamo sceglievate sceglievano	scelsi scegliesti scelse scegliemmo sceglieste scelsero
scendere** *to go down*	scendendo sceso	scendo scendi scende scendiamo scendete scendono	scendevo scendevi scendeva scendevamo scendevate scendevano	scesi scendesti scese scendemmo scendeste scesero

Future	Conditional	Imperative	Present Subjunctive	Imperfect Subjunctive
risponderò	risponderei	· · · · · ·	risponda	rispondessi
risponderai	risponderesti	rispondi	risponda	rispondessi
risponderà	risponderebbe	risponda	risponda	rispondesse
risponderemo	risponderemmo	rispondiamo	rispondiamo	rispondessimo
risponderete	rispondereste	rispondete	rispondiate	rispondeste
risponderanno	risponderebbero	rispondano	rispondano	rispondessero
salirò	salirei	· · · · · ·	salga	salissi
salirai	saliresti	sali	salga	salissi
salirà	salirebbe	salga	salga	salisse
saliremo	saliremmo	saliamo	saliamo	salissimo
salirete	salireste	salite	saliate	saliste
saliranno	salirebbero	salgano	salgano	salissero
saprò	saprei	· · · · · ·	sappia	sapessi
saprai	sapresti	sappi	sappia	sapessi
saprà	saprebbe	sappia	sappia	sapesse
sapremo	sapremmo	sappiamo	sappiamo	sapessimo
saprete	sapreste	sappiate	sappiate	sapeste
sapranno	saprebbero	sappiano	sappiano	sapessero
sceglierò	sceglierei	· · · · · ·	scelga	scegliessi
sceglierai	sceglieresti	scegli	scelga	scegliessi
sceglierà	sceglierebbe	scelga	scelga	scegliesse
sceglieremo	sceglieremmo	scegliamo	scegliamo	scegliessimo
sceglierete	scegliereste	scegliete	scegliate	sceglieste
sceglieranno	sceglierebbero	scelgano	scelgano	scegliessero
scenderò	scenderei	· · · · · ·	scenda	scendessi
scenderai	scenderesti	scendi	scenda	scendessi
scenderà	scenderebbe	scenda	scenda	scendesse
scenderemo	scenderemmo	scendiamo	scendiamo	scendessimo
scenderete	scendereste	scendete	scendiate	scendeste
scenderanno	scenderebbero	scendano	scendano	scendessero

Infinitive	Gerund; Past Participle	Present Indicative	Imperfect Indicative	Past Absolute
scrivere *to write*	scrivendo scritto	scrivo scrivi scrive scriviamo scrivete scrivono	scrivevo scrivevi scriveva scrivevamo scrivevate scrivevano	scrissi scrivesti scrisse scrivemmo scriveste scrissero
sedere *to sit down*	sedendo seduto	siedo siedi siede sediamo sedete siedono	sedevo sedevi sedeva sedevamo sedevate sedevano	sedetti (sedei) sedesti sedette (sedè) sedemmo sedeste sedettero (sederono)
spendere *to spend*	spendendo speso	spendo spendi spende spendiamo spendete spendono	spendevo spendevi spendeva spendevamo spendevate spendevano	spesi spendesti spese spendemmo spendeste spesero
stare* *to stay,* *to be*	stando stato	sto stai sta stiamo state stanno	stavo stavi stava stavamo stavate stavano	stetti stesti stette stemmo steste stettero
tenere *to keep,* *to hold*	tenendo tenuto	tengo tieni tiene teniamo tenete tengono	tenevo tenevi teneva tenevamo tenevate tenevano	tenni tenesti tenne tenemmo teneste tennero

Future	Conditional	Imperative	Present Subjunctive	Imperfect Subjunctive
scriverò	scriverei	......	scriva	scrivessi
scriverai	scriveresti	scrivi	scriva	scrivessi
scriverà	scriverebbe	scriva	scriva	scrivesse
scriveremo	scriveremmo	scriviamo	scriviamo	scrivessimo
scriverete	scrivereste	scrivete	scriviate	scriveste
scriveranno	scriverebbero	scrivano	scrivano	scrivessero
sederò	sederei	......	sieda	sedessi
sederai	sederesti	siedi	sieda	sedessi
sederà	sederebbe	sieda	sieda	sedesse
sederemo	sederemmo	sediamo	sediamo	sedessimo
sederete	sedereste	sedete	sediate	sedeste
sederanno	sederebbero	siedano	siedano	sedessero
spenderò	spenderei	......	spenda	spendessi
spenderai	spenderesti	spendi	spenda	spendessi
spenderà	spenderebbe	spenda	spenda	spendesse
spenderemo	spenderemmo	spendiamo	spendiamo	spendessimo
spenderete	spendereste	spendete	spendiate	spendeste
spenderanno	spenderebbero	spendano	spendano	spendessero
starò	starei	......	stia	stessi
starai	staresti	sta'	stia	stessi
starà	starebbe	stia	stia	stesse
staremo	staremmo	stiamo	stiamo	stessimo
starete	stareste	state	stiate	steste
staranno	starebbero	stiano	stiano	stessero
terrò	terrei	......	tenga	tenessi
terrai	terresti	tieni	tenga	tenessi
terrà	terrebbe	tenga	tenga	tenesse
terremo	terremmo	teniamo	teniamo	tenessimo
terrete	terreste	tenete	teniate	teneste
terranno	terrebbero	tengano	tengano	tenessero

Infinitive	Gerund; Past Participle	Present Indicative	Imperfect Indicative	Past Absolute
uscire*	uscendo	esco	uscivo	uscii
to go out	uscito	esci	uscivi	uscisti
		esce	usciva	uscì
		usciamo	uscivamo	uscimmo
		uscite	uscivate	usciste
		escono	uscivano	uscirono
vedere	vedendo	vedo	vedevo	vidi
to see	veduto	vedi	vedevi	vedesti
	(visto)	vede	vedeva	vide
		vediamo	vedevamo	vedemmo
		vedete	vedevate	vedeste
		vedono	vedevano	videro
venire*	venendo	vengo	venivo	venni
to come	venuto	vieni	venivi	venisti
		viene	veniva	venne
		veniamo	venivamo	venimmo
		venite	venivate	veniste
		vengono	venivano	vennero
vivere**	vivendo	vivo	vivevo	vissi
to live	vissuto	vivi	vivevi	vivesti
		vive	viveva	visse
		viviamo	vivevamo	vivemmo
		vivete	vivevate	viveste
		vivono	vivevano	vissero
volere**	volendo	voglio	volevo	volli
to want, to wish	voluto	vuoi	volevi	volesti
		vuole	voleva	volle
		vogliamo	volevamo	volemmo
		volete	volevate	voleste
		vogliono	volevano	vollero

Future	Conditional	Imperative	Present Subjunctive	Imperfect Subjunctive
uscirò	uscirei	. . . . . .	esca	uscissi
uscirai	usciresti	esci	esca	uscissi
uscirà	uscirebbe	esca	esca	uscisse
usciremo	usciremmo	usciamo	usciamo	uscissimo
uscirete	uscireste	uscite	usciate	usciste
usciranno	uscirebbero	escano	escano	uscissero
vedrò	vedrei	. . . . . .	veda	vedessi
vedrai	vedresti	vedi	veda	vedessi
vedrà	vedrebbe	veda	veda	vedesse
vedremo	vedremmo	vediamo	vediamo	vedessimo
vedrete	vedreste	vedete	vediate	vedeste
vedranno	vedrebbero	vedano	vedano	vedessero
verrò	verrei	. . . . . .	venga	venissi
verrai	verresti	vieni	venga	venissi
verrà	verrebbe	venga	venga	venisse
verremo	verremmo	veniamo	veniamo	venissimo
verrete	verreste	venite	veniate	veniste
verranno	verrebbero	vengano	vengano	venissero
vivrò	vivrei	. . . . . .	viva	vivessi
vivrai	vivresti	vivi	viva	vivessi
vivrà	vivrebbe	viva	viva	vivesse
vivremo	vivremmo	viviamo	viviamo	vivessimo
vivrete	vivreste	vivete	viviate	viveste
vivranno	vivrebbero	vivano	vivano	vivessero
vorrò	vorrei	. . . . . .	voglia	volessi
vorrai	vorresti	vogli	voglia	volessi
vorrà	vorrebbe	voglia	voglia	volesse
vorremo	vorremmo	vogliamo	vogliamo	volessimo
vorrete	vorreste	vogliate	vogliate	voleste
vorranno	vorrebbero	vogliano	vogliano	volessero

Part X—Italian-English Vocabulary

a, ad, to, at, in
a bordo, on board
a causa di, because, owing to
a meno che. . .non, unless
abbaiare, to bark
abbandonato, abandoned
abbastanza, enough, very
abbigliamento, clothing; **negozio di abbigliamento,** clothing store
abbondante, abundant
abbracciare, to embrace, to hug
abbraccio, hug
abitante (*m., f.*), inhabitant
abitare, to live, to reside
ạbito, suit, dress
abituare, to accustom
abituarsi, to accustom oneself
abitụdine (*f.*), habit
accadere, to happen
accanto, next to
accendere, to ignite, to light, to turn on
accettare, to accept
acciạio, steel
acciuga, anchovy
accọgliere, to receive, to welcome
accomodarsi, to make oneself comfortable; to sit down
accompagnare, to accompany
accordarsi, to come to an agreement
accọrgersi, to notice
accostarsi, to approach someone
acqua, water; **acqua minerale,** mineral water
acquistare, to acquire, to buy
acre, acrid
acremente, acridly
adatto, suitable
addormentarsi, to fall asleep
adornare, to adorn, to decorate
adottivo, adoptive, foster; **figlio adottivo,** adopted son
aẹreo, airplane
aeronạutica, aeronautical, air force
affamato, hungry
affatto, at all
affetto, affection, love
affezionatamente, affectionately
affidare, to entrust
affinchè, so that, in order that
afflịggere, to afflict
affollato, crowded
affresco, fresco
affrettarsi, to hurry up
aggiornare, to bring up to date, to modernize
aggiụngere, to add
agire, to act
agnello, lamb
agosto, August
agrịcolo, agricultural
agricoltura, agriculture
agrumi (*m. pl.*), citrus fruits
aiutare, to assist, to help
ala, wing
albergo, hotel
albero, tree
Alberto, Albert
album (*m.*), album
alcuno, some, any
al di sopra, above
al lato, next to, at the side of
alleanza, alliance
alleato, ally
allegramente, happily
allegrịa, happiness
allegro, happy
allievo, pupil
allontanarsi, to go away from, to move away from
alluminio, aluminum
almeno, at least
Alpi (*f. pl.*), Alps

altamente, high, very high
alto, tall, high; loud; **alta voce**, aloud
altoparlante (*m.*), loudspeaker
altrimenti, otherwise
altro, other
altrui, of others
alunno, pupil, student
alzare, to raise
alzarsi, to get up
amạbile, amiable, lovable
amante (*m., f.*), lover
amare, to love
amaro, bitter
ambasciatore (*m.*), ambassador
ambasciatrice (*f.*), ambassadress
Ambrogio, Ambrose
americano, American
amicizia, friendship
amico, friend
ammazzare, to kill
amministrare, to administer
ammirare, to admire
amore (*m.*), love
analisi (*f. sing., pl.*) analysis
ancora, still, yet
ancora una volta, again, once more
andare, to go; **andare fuori**, to go out; **andare in effetto**, to go into effect
andạrsene, to go away (from)
andata, going, gone
Andrẹa (*m.*), Andrew
anello, ring (metal circle)
angoscia (*also* **angustia**), anguish
animale (*m.*), animal
annesso, annexed, attached
anniversario, anniversary
anno, year
annoiarsi, to get bored
annunziatore (*m.*), announcer
ansia, anxiety
antichità (*f. sing., pl.*), antiquity
anticamente, anciently
antico, old, ancient
antipasto, appetizer
antipạtico, disagreeable, unpleasant
Antonio, Anthony
anzitutto, above all
aperto, open; **all'aperto**, in the open air, outdoors
apparecchiare, to set (a table)
apparire, to appear
appartamento, apartment
appartenere, to belong to
appassionato, fond of; crazy about
appena, as soon as, just, hardly; **non appena**, no sooner
appẹndere, to hang
appetito, appetite
applicare, to apply
appoggiarsi, to lean on
apprezzare, to appreciate
approfittare, to take advantage of
appuntamento, appointment, date
appunto, exactly
aprile (*m.*), April
aprire, to open
Ạrabi (*m. pl.*), Arabs, Moors
ạrabo, Arab
arancia, orange
aranciata, orangeade
arancione, orange (color)
architetto, architect
architettọnico, architectural
architettura, architecture
ardire, to dare
arena, arena; drive-in movie
argento, silver
aria, air; song
aria condizionata, air conditioning
armadio, closet
arrivare, to arrive
arrivederci, so long, see you soon
arrivo, arrival
arrosto, roast
arte (*f.*), art
artịcolo, article
artigianato, craftsmanship

artista (*m.*, *f.*), artist
artịstico, artistic
Arturo, Arthur
ascensore (*m.*), elevator
asciugamano, hand towel
asciugare, to dry
asciutto, dry
ascoltare, to listen to
asfalto, asphalt
asilo infantile, kindergarten
ạsino, donkey
aspettare, to wait
aspro, harsh, bitter
assại, much
assassino, murderer, killer
assegno, check; **assegno bancạrio**, bank check
assente, absent
assicurare, to assure
assịstere, to assist
assụmere, to hire
astro, star
astrọlogo, astrologist
astronauta (*m.*, *f.*) astronaut
astronave (*f.*), spaceship
atleta (*m.*, *f.*), athlete
attaccare, to lash, to tie, to attack; **attaccato**, lashed, tied, attacked
attẹndere, to wait
attentamente, attentively
attento, attentive
attenzione (*f.*), attention; **fare attenzione**, to pay attention
ạttimo, moment
attirare, to attract
attivo, active
attore (*m.*), actor
attrice (*f.*), actress
attraversare, to cross
attuale, actual, presently
aula, classroom
australiano, Australian
autista (*m.*, *f.*), driver
ạutobus (*m.*), bus
automọbile (*f.*), automobile, car
automobilịstico, pertaining to a car
autore (*m.*), author
autrice (*f.*), author
autostrada, highway
autoveịcolo, motor vehicle
autunno, autumn
avanti Cristo (a.C.), Before Christ
avere, to have
aviogetto, jet plane
avvenimento, event, happening
avvenire (*m.*), future
avverso, adverse, against
avviarsi, to set out
avvicinarsi, to come near
avvocato, lawyer
azione (*f.*), action
azzurro, blue

babbo, dad; **Babbo Natale**, Santa Claus
baciare, to kiss
bacio, kiss
badare, to pay attention
bagaglio, baggage
bagnare, to wet; **bagnato**, wet
bagno, bath, bathroom
baldacchino, canopy
ballare, to dance
balletto, ballet
ballo, dance
bambino, child
bạmbola, doll
banana, banana
banca, bank
banchetto, banquet
banco, desk
bandiera, flag
bar (*m.*), bar (saloon)
barba, beard, whiskers
barbabiẹtola da zụcchero, sugar beet
bạrbaro, barbarian; **invasioni barbariche**, barbarian invasions
barbiere (*m.*), barber
barca, boat
barriera, barrier
basarsi, to be based on
basicamente, basically
basilare, basic
basịlica, basilica (church)
basso, low; **a bassa voce**, in a low voice
bastare, to suffice
battaglia, battle
battezzare, to baptize
battistero, baptistry
baule (*m.*), trunk (to pack things)
beato, lucky, blessed

Belgio, Belgium
bellezza, beauty
bellissimo, very beautiful, very handsome
bello, fine, beautiful, handsome
benchè, although, even though
bene, fine, well; **sta bene**, O.K., fine
benevolo, kind
benvenuto, welcome
bere, to drink
bevanda (*also* **bibita**), drink
bianco, white
biblioteca, library
bicchiere (*m.*), drinking glass
bicicletta, bicycle
bidello, custodian
biglietto, ticket
bilancio, balance, balance of power
biologia, biology
biondo, blond
birra, beer
biscotto, biscuit
bisognare, to need
bisogno, need
bistecca, steak
bizantino, Byzantine
bloccare, to block; **bloccato**, blocked
blu, blue
blusa, blouse
bocca, mouth
bocce (*f. pl.*), lawn bowling
boccetta, vial, small bottle
bocciare, to fail (someone)
bombardamento, bombardment, air raid
bontà (*f. sing., pl.*), goodness
borgo, village, suburb
borsa, bag, purse
bosco, woods
bottega, boutique, shop, store
bottiglia, bottle
bottone (*m.*), button
braccialetto, bracelet
braccio, arm
bravo, good, able
breve, brief, short
brillare, to shine
brocca, pitcher (for liquids)
broccoli (*m. pl.*), broccoli
brodo, broth
bruciare, to burn
bruciarsi, to burn oneself
brutto, ugly
bugia, lie
bruno, brunette
bue (*m.*), ox; **buoi** (*pl.*), oxen
buono, good
burro, butter
bussare, to knock
buttare, to cast, to throw

cabina, cabin
caccia, hunt; **a caccia**, hunting
cacciare, to expel, to chase away
cadere, to fall
caduta (*f.*), fall
calcio, soccer
calcolatrice (*f.*), calculator
caldo, hot, warm
calmo, calm
calza, stocking
calzino, sock
calzolaio, shoemaker
cambiare, to change
camera, bedroom
cameriera, waitress
cameriere (*m.*), waiter
camicetta, blouse
camicia, shirt
camino, chimney
camminare, to walk
campagna, field; country
campana, bell
campanello, doorbell
campanile (*m.*), bell tower
campestre, rustic
campo, field
Canadà (*m.*), Canada
canapa, hemp
candela, candle
cane (*m.*), dog
Canio, Kenneth
cannellone (*m.*), large macaroni most often filled with cheese
cannocchiale (*m.*), telescope
cantante (*m., f.*), singer
cantare, to sing
cantico, canticle, song
cantiere (*m.*), shipyard
canzone (*f.*), song

capace, able
capelli (*m. pl.*), hair
capire, to understand
capitale (*f.*), capital (of a country)
capitano, captain
capịtolo, chapter
capo, leader
Capodanno, New Year's
capolavoro, masterpiece
capoluogo, chief city, capital
cappello, hat
cappotto, overcoat
capra, goat
carabiniere (*m.*), Italian policeman belonging to the Army
caramella, candy, sweet
carạttere (*m.*), disposition
caratterịstica, characteristic
caratterizzato, featuring, distinguished by
carbone (*m.*), coal
cạrcere (*m.*), jail
cạrica, work, job
Carla, Carla
Carlo, Charles
Carlotta, Charlotte
carne (*f.*), meat
caro, dear, expensive
carota, carrot
carriera, career
carro armato, armored tank
carta, paper; **carta da scrivere**, writing paper; **carta geogrạfica**, map
carte (*f. pl.*), playing cards, official papers
cartọgrafo, map maker
cartoleria, stationery
cartolina, postcard
casa, house, home; **casa editrice**, publishing house
casetta, small house
caso, case, instance
castello, castle
catacombe (*f. pl.*), catacombs
catena, chain
Caterina, Catherine
cattedrale (*f.*), cathedral
cattivo, bad, wicked
cattolicẹsimo, Catholicism
cattọlico, Catholic
cavalleresco, chivalric
cavallo, horse
celebrare, to celebrate
cẹlebre, famous
cena, supper
cenare, to sup, to have supper
cẹnere (*f.*), ash (from a fire)
centinaio, about one hundred; **le centinaia** (*f. pl.*), several hundred
cento, one hundred
centrale, central
centro, center
cercare, to seek, to look for
cerimonia, ceremony
cerino, match (to make fire)
certamente, certainly
certo, certain
cessare, to stop
cestino, wastepaper basket
che, what; **che cosa?**, what?
che (*rel. pron.*), who, whom, that, which
chi, who, whom, which, whose; he who, him whom, the one who, whom, someone
chi . . . chi, some . . . others
chiacchierare, to chat
chiamare, to call
chiamarsi, to be called
chiaro, light, clear
chiave (*f.*), key
chiẹdere, to ask
chiesa, church
chilọmetro, kilometer
chịmica, chemistry; chemical
chinotto, bittersweet soft drink
chitarra, guitar
chiụdere, to close; **chiụdere a chiave**, to lock by key; **chiuso**, closed
chiụnque, anyone, whoever
ci, here, there, there is; us, to us, ourselves
cibo, food
cielo, sky, heaven
ciliẹgia, cherry

cima, peak
cimosa, chalkboard eraser
cinema, movies
cinese (*m., f.*), Chinese
cinquanta (*m.*), fifty
cinque (*m.*), five
cinquecento, five hundred; **il Cinquecento**, the 16th century
cintura, belt
ciò, that, that which; **ciò che**, what, that which
cioccolata, chocolate milk
cioccolato, solid chocolate
circa, about
circolazione (*f.*), traffic
circondare, to encircle, to surround
città (*f.*), city
Città Eterna, Eternal City (Rome)
cittadina, small town
cittadino, citizen
Clara, Claire
clarinetto, clarinet
classe (*f.*), class (school)
cliente (*m., f.*), client, customer
clinica, clinic, hospital
coda, tail
codice (*m.*), code, book of laws
cogliere, to gather, to pick
cognata, sister-in-law
cognato, brother-in-law
coinvolgere, to involve, to be mixed up in
colazione (*f.*), lunch; **prima colazione**, breakfast
collana, necklace
colle (*m.*) (*also* **collina**), hill
collega (*m., f.*) colleague
collo, neck
collocare, to place; to employ; to combine
colmo, full
colomba, dove
Colombo, Cristoforo, Christopher Columbus
colonnato, colonnade
colonnello, colonel
colore (*m.*), color
colossale, colossal
Colosseo, Coliseum
coltelleria, cutlery
coltello, knife
coltivabile, cultivable, farmable
comandare, to command, to lead
comando, command, leadership
combattere, to fight (battles)
come, how, as, like
come pure, as well as
cominciare, to begin, to start
commedia, comedy, play
commediografo, comedy playwright
commerciante (*m.*), businessman
commesso, salesman
commettere, to commit
comodino, night table
comodo, comfortable
compagnia, company
compagno, friend, companion
compera, purchase
compito, work, duty, task; **compito a casa**, homework
compleanno, birthday
complesso, complex, group
completamente, completely
comportamento, behavior
comprare, to buy
comprendere, to understand
compreso, including
con, with
concerto, concert
conchiudere, to conclude, to end, to finish
concludere, to conclude
condurre, to lead, to drive
conferenza, lecture
confessare, to confess
confine (*m.*), boundary, border
coniglio, rabbit
conoscenza, acquaintance
conoscere, to know; **conosciuto**, known, met
conquistare, to conquer

consacrato, consecrated
conseguenza, consequence
consentire, to consent
considerare, to consider
consigliare, to advise, to counsel
consịstere, to consist
cọnsole (*m.*), consul, general
contadino, farmer
contanti (*m. pl.*), cash
contemporạneo, contemporary
contentezza, happiness
contento, content, happy
continente (*m.*), continent
continuamente, continually, continuously
continuare, to continue
conto, bill (for money)
contrada, district
contrario, contrary
contratto, contract
contro, against
convegno, convention (meeting)
conversazione (*f.*), conversation
convịncere, to convince
coperta, blanket
coprire, to cover, to close
coraggio, courage
coraggioso, courageous
cordiale, cordial
coro, chorus
corrẹggere, to correct
correntemente, fluently
cọrrere, to run
correttamente, correctly
corruzione (*f.*), corruption
corsa, race (horse race)
corte (*f.*), court
cortese, courteous
cortesemente, courteously
cortesịa, courtesy
cortile (*m.*), courtyard
corto, short, brief
cosa, thing; **Cosa?**, What?
così, thus, so, like this, like that
così . . . come, as . . . as
costa, coast
costituzione (*f.*), constitution
costosissimo, very costly
costoso, costly, expensive
costrịngere, to force
costruire, to build, to construct
costruttore (*m.*), builder, constructor
cotoletta, cutlet
cotone (*m.*), cotton
cotto, cooked
cravatta, necktie
creare, to create
creatura, child, creature
crẹdere, to believe
crema, cream
crisantemo, chrysanthemum
crisi (*f. sing., pl.*), crisis
cristiano, Christian
crịtico, critic
crudele, cruel
cucchiaino, teaspoon
cucchiaio, spoon
cucinare (*also* **cuọcere**), to cook
cucire, to sew
cugina, cousin
cugino, cousin
cui (*rel. pron.*), who, which; **a cui**, to whom; **il cui, la cui, i cui, le cui**, whose, of which
culla, cradle
cuoco, cook
cuọio, leather
cuore (*m.*), heart
cụpola, dome, cupola
cura, cure
curioso, curious, strange
custodire, to keep, to house

da, from, at; **da chi?**, from whom?
d'accordo, O.K., agreed, all right
Daniela, Danielle
Daniele (*m.*), Daniel
dappertutto, everywhere
dapprima, at first
dare, to give; **dare il benvenuto**, to welcome
data, date (calendar)
dato che, since, because
dattilọgrafa, typist
davanti, in front of, before

davvero, really
dẹbole, weak
decịdere, to decide
dẹcimo, tenth
decreto, decree
dedicarsi, to dedicate oneself
degno di, worthy of
dei (*m. pl.*), gods
democrazịa, democracy
demọnio, demon, devil
denaro, money
dente (*m.*), tooth; **mal di dente**, toothache
dentista (*m., f.*), dentist
dentro, in, within, inside
depositare, to deposit
deputato, representative (of the Italian Assembly)
derivare, to derive
descrịvere, to describe
deserto, deserted; desert
desiderare, to desire
di, of, from, than; **di chi?**, whose?
di sọlito, usually; **sọlito**, usual
dialetto, dialect
diạlogo, dialogue
diạvolo, devil
dicembre (*m.*), December
dichiarare, to declare
dichiarazione (*f.*), declaration
diciannove, nineteen
diciassette, seventeen
diciotto, eighteen
dieci, ten
diecina, about ten
dietro, behind, in back of
difẹndere, to defend
difesa (*f.*), defense
differente, different
diffịcile, difficult
dignitoso, dignified
dimensione (*f.*), dimension
dimenticare, forget
dimora, home
dịnamo (*f.*) dynamo
dinastịa (*f.*), dynasty
dintorni (*m. pl.*), vicinity, neighborhood
dipịngere, to paint
diplomạtico, diplomatic
dire, to say, to tell
direttamente, directly
diretto, directed
direttore (*m.*), director, conductor of music; principal
dirigịbile (*m.*), dirigible
dirimpetto, opposite, across the way
diritto, right, privilege
disạstro, disaster
discẹndere, to descend, to come down
disco, record (music)
discorso, discourse, speech
discussione (*f.*), discussion
discụtere, to discuss
disegnare, to draw, to design
disobbedire, to disobey
disonesto, dishonest
dispiacere, to feel sorry for
disposto, disposed, ready
distante, distant, far
distinto, different, distinct
distrụggere, to destroy
disturbare, to disturb
dito, finger; **le dita** (*f. pl.*), fingers
ditta, company (business)
divano, sofa, divan
divenire (*also* **diventare**), to become
diverso, different
divertire, to enjoy
divertirsi, to enjoy oneself
divịdere, to divide
dizionario, dictionary
doccia, shower
documento, document
dọdici, twelve
dogana, customs
dolce (*m.*), dessert; sweet
dolersi, to be sorry
dọllaro, dollar
dolore (*m.*), pain, sorrow
doloroso, painful
domandare, to ask (for information)
domani, tomorrow
domattina, tomorrow morning
domẹnica (*f.*), Sunday

domẹstico, butler, valet, servant
dominio, rule, dominion, kingdom
dopo, after, afterward
dopo Cristo (d.C.), After Christ
dopodomani, day after tomorrow
dopoguerra (*m.*), after the war (used here with reference to World War II)
dormire, to sleep
dorso, back
dotto, learned
dottore (*m.*), doctor
dottoressa (*f.*), doctor
dottrina, doctrine
dove, where
dovere, to have to, must
dozzina, dozen
dramma (*m.*), drama, play
drammạtico, dramatic
drammaturgo, playwright
droga, drug
drogherịa, grocery store
dubbio, doubt
dubitare, to doubt
duca (*m.*), duke
duchessa, duchess
due, two
duecento, two hundred; **il Duecento**, the 13th century
durante, during
durare, to last
e, ed, and
ecc. (eccẹtera), etc. (and so on)
eco (*f.*), echo; **gli echi** (*m. pl.*), echoes
econọmico, economical, cheap
edificio, building, edifice
editore (*m.*), publisher
editto, edict, proclamation
effetto, effect
Egitto, Egypt
egiziano, Egyptian
elefante (*m.*), elephant
elegantemente, elegantly
elẹggere, to elect
elementare, elementary
elemento, element
elencare, to enumerate, to list
elettricista (*m., f.*), electrician
elettrodomẹstici (*m. pl.*), electrical appliances
elevare, to elevate, to raise
elicọttero, helicopter
emblema (*m.*), emblem
emigrante (*m., f.*), emigrant
energịa, energy
enfasi (*m.*), emphasis
enorme, enormous
Enrico, Henry
entrare, to enter
entrata, entrance
entusiasmo, enthusiasm
ẹpica, epic
Epifanịa, Epiphany
ẹpoca, epoch, era
equestre, equestrian
equivalere, to equal
erba, grass
erede, heir
erẹggere, to erect; **eretto**, erected
eroe (*m.*), hero
eroina, heroine
errore (*m.*), error, mistake
esame (*m.*), examination
esaminare, to examine
esatto, exact
esecutivo, executive
esempio, example
esercitare, to exercise
esercizio, exercise
esilio, exile
esịstere, to exist
esitare, to hesitate
esperienza, experience
esperto, expert
esplorare, to explore
esploratore (*m.*), explorer
esponente (*m., f.*), exponent
esporre, to expose, to show
esprịmere, to express
essenziale, essential
ẹssere, to be
est (*m.*), east
estate (*f.*), summer
estendersi, to extend itself

ẹstero, abroad
estremamente, extremely
età, age
Europa, Europe
evento, event, happening
evidente, evident
evitare, to avoid, to evade

fa, ago; **poco fa**, a short time ago
fạbbrica, factory
fabbricare, to build, to make, to construct
faccia, face
fạcile, easy
fagiolini (*m. pl.*), string beans
fagiolo, bean
falegname (*m.*), carpenter
fame (*f.*), hunger; **aver fame**, to be hungry
famiglia, family
famoso, famous
fanciullo, child
fango, mud
fare, to do, to make
farina, flour
farmacịa, pharmacy, drugstore
farmacista (*m.*, *f.*), pharmacist
fattorịa, farm
fattorino, ticket checker; errand boy
farsi, to do to oneself; **farsi male**, to hurt oneself
favorito, favorite
fazione (*f.*), faction
fazzoletto, handkerchief
febbraio (*m.*), February
febbre (*f.*), fever
felicità (*f.*), happiness
fermarsi, to stop
fermata, stop
feroce, ferocious
Ferragosto, mid-August (Feast of the Assumption)
ferro, iron
ferrovịa, railroad
fẹrtile, fertile
festa, holiday, feast, party
festeggiare, to celebrate
fiaba, fable
fiaccolata, torchlight procession
fiammịfero, match (to make fire)
fico, fig
fiducia, faith
fiera, fair, exhibit
figlio, son; **figli** (*m. pl.*) children
figura, figure; showing
fila, row, file, line
film (*m.*), film
fịlobus (*m.*), trolley bus
filọlogo, philologist
finalmente, finally
finchè, until
fine (*f.*), end
finestra, window
finestrino, window (of a car, train, bus, etc.)
finire, to end, to finish
finto, false, mock
fiore (*m.*), flower
fiorentino, Florentine
fiorire, to bloom
Firenze (*f.*), Florence
firmare, to sign
fịsica, physics
fịsico, physicist
fiume (*m.*), river
floricoltura, horticulture
foglia, leaf
foglio, sheet (of paper)
folla, crowd
folle, foolish, insane
follemente, foolishly, madly
follịa, madness
fondare, to found, to establish
fontana, fountain
forchetta, fork
foresta, forest
forma, form
formaggio, cheese
formare, to form
fornire, to furnish
forte, strong
fortezza, fort
fortuna, luck, fortune
forza, strength
foto (*f.*) (*also* **fotografịa**), photograph
fra, between, among; **fra poco**, in a little while

frạgola, strawberry
francamente, frankly
francese (*m.*, *f.*), French
Francia, France
franco, frank
Franco, Frank
francobollo, stamp
frase (*f.*), sentence
fratellino, little brother
fratello, brother
frazionare, to fraction, to divide
frazionata, fractioned, divided
frazione (*f.*), fraction
frequentare, to attend, to frequent
frequente, frequent, often
frequenza, frequency
fresco, fresh; cool
fretta, hurry; **avere fretta**, to be in a hurry
frịggere, to fry
frigorịfero, refrigerator
fronte (*f.*), forehead; front
frontiera, frontier, border
frutta, fruit
fruttivẹndolo, fruit vendor
frutto, the fruits (of one's labor)
fumare, to smoke
funzionamento, function
funzionare, to function, to work
fuochi artificiali (*m. pl.*), fireworks
fuoco, fire
fuori, out, outside

gallerịa d'arte, art gallery
gallina, hen
gallo, rooster
galvanizzare, to galvanize
gamba, leg
garage (*m.*), garage
garantire, to guarantee
garọfano, carnation
gassosa, soft drink
gastronomịa, gastronomy
gelato, ice cream
geloso, jealous
generale (*m.*), general
generalmente, generally
gẹnere (*m.*), type
genitore (*m.*), father; **genitori** (*pl.*), parents
gennaio, January
Gẹnova, Genoa
gente (*f.*), people
gentile, gentle
gentilezza, gentleness, kindness
geografịa, geography
Germania, Germany
gesso, chalk
Gesù (*m.*), Jesus
gettone (*m.*), token
ghiaccio, ice
già, already
giacca, jacket
Giacomo, James
giallo, yellow
Gianni (*m.*), John
Giappone (*m.*), Japan
giapponese (*m.*, *f.*), Japanese
giardino, garden; **giardino botanico**, botanical gardens; **giardino zoologico**, zoo
gigante (*m.*, *f.*), giant
gigantesco, gigantic
ginocchio, knee; **le ginocchia** (*f. pl.*), knees
giocare (*also* **giuocare**), to play
giocạttolo, toy
giọia, joy
gioiello, jewel
Giorgio, George
giornale (*m.*), newspaper
giornalista (*m.*, *f.*), news reporter
giornata (*also* **giorno**), day; **giorno libero**, day off
giọvane (*m.*, *f.*), young man, young woman
Giovanni (*m.*), John
giovanotto, young man; lad
giovedì (*m.*), Thursday
gioventù (*f.*), youth
giradischi (*m. sing.*, *pl.*), record player
giraffa, giraffe
girare, to turn, to wander about

gita, ride
giụdice (*m.*), judge
giudiziaria, judiciary
giugno (*m.*), June
Giulietta, Juliet
giụngere, to arrive
giuoco, game
giustizia, justice
giusto, just, right
gladiatore (*m.*), gladiator
gladiolo, gladiola
gli, to him
glorioso, glorious
gnocco, potato-filled macaroni (dumpling)
godere, to enjoy
gola, throat
golf (*m.*), golf; sweater
golfo, gulf
gomma, rubber, pencil eraser
gonna, skirt
gọtico, gothic
governo, government
grado, degree
grammatica, grammar
grano, grain, wheat
grasso, fat
grattacielo, skyscraper
gratụito, free, gratis
grave, serious
grazioso, graceful, pretty
Grecia, Greece
Gregorio, Gregory
grigio, gray
gruppo, group
guadagnare, to earn
guancia, cheek
guanto, glove
guardare, to look at, to watch
guardia (*m., f.*), guard
guardiano, guardian
guarire, to heal
guerra, war
guida (*m., f.*), guide
guidare, to drive, to guide
Guido, Guy
gusto, taste

idea, idea, thought
ideale (*m., f.*), ideal
ideatore (*m.*), inventor, creator
idroelẹttrica, hydroelectric
ieri, yesterday
ignorare, to ignore
il, the
illuminare, to illuminate, to light
illustre, famous, illustrious
immaginarsi, to imagine
immediatamente, immediately
immenso, immense
immigrante (*m., f.*), immigrant
immobilità (*f.*) immobility
imparare, to learn
impaziente, impatient
impedire, to prevent
impermeạbile (*m.*), raincoat
ịmpeto, impetus
impiccare, to hang (someone)
impiegato, employee; office worker
imporre, to impose, to compel
importante, important
impossịbile, impossible
improbạbile, improbable
improvviso, sudden; suddenly
in, in; **in caso che**, in the event that; **in modo che**, so that
incamminarsi, to set out
incantato, enchanted, spellbound
incantẹvole, enchanting
inchiostro, ink
incominciare, to begin, to commence
incontrare, to meet
incontrarsi, to meet (each other), to meet themselves
incoronare, to crown
incorporare, to incorporate
Indiano, Indian
indipendenza, independence
indirizzo, address
indossare, to wear
indụstria, industry
industriale (*m.*), industrial businessman
infatti, in fact
infelice, unhappy, sad
inferiore, inferior

infermiera (*f.*), nurse
infermiere (*m.*), male nurse
ịnfimo, inferior, very small
influsso, influence
ingegnere (*m.*), engineer
Inghilterra, England
ingiallire, to yellow
inglese, English
iniziare, to begin
inizio, beginning
innamorarsi, to fall in love
innovazione (*f.*), innovation
inoltre, furthermore
insalata, salad
insegnare, to teach
in sẹguito, later on
insieme, together
insịstere, to insist
intaglio, carving
integrale, integral
intelligenza, intelligence
intelligentemente, intelligently
interessante, interesting
interesse (*m.*), interest
intero, whole, entire
intitolato, entitled
intraprẹndere, to undertake
inụtile, useless
invạdere, to invade
invasione (*f.*), invasion
invece, instead
inverno, winter
inviare, to send
invitare, to invite
invitato, invited (guest)
io, I
ira, ire, anger, rage
irritato, irritated, nervous
ịsola, island
istọlogo, histologist (blood specialist)
istruzione (*f.*), education, instruction
Italia, Italy
italiano, Italian
Iugoslavia, Yugoslavia

là, there
labbro, lip; **le labbra** (*f. pl.*), lips
laboratorio, laboratory
laggiù, over there, down there
lago, lake
lạmpada, lamp
lampadina, light bulb
lampo, lightning
lana, wool
lanciare, to cast, to throw
larghezza, width
largo, wide
lasciare, to leave (something); **lasciar fare**, to allow, to permit
lassù, up there
latino, Latin
lato, side
latte (*m.*), milk
lattuga, lettuce
laurea, university degree
lavagna, chalkboard
lavare, to wash
lavarsi, to wash oneself
lavatrice (*f.*), washing machine
lavorante (*m., f.*) (*also* **lavoratore**, *m.*), worker
lavorare, to work
lavoro, work
lega, league
legare, to tie
legge (*f.*), law
leggenda, legend
lẹggere, to read
leggero, light (in weight)
legno, wood
legumi (*m. pl.*), vegetables (not leafy—peas, beans, etc.)
lentamente, slowly
lento, slow
lenzuolo, sheet (for bed); **le lenzuola**, (*f. pl.*), sheets
leone (*m.*), lion
letịzia, gladness
lẹttera, letter
letterario, literary
letteratura, literature
letto, bed
lettura, reading
levante (*m.*), east
levare, to raise
lezione (*f.*), lesson
lì, there
libbra, pound
libertà (*f. sing., pl.*), liberty
librerịa, bookstore
libro, book

liceo, state secondary school
lieto, happy
Liliana, Lillian
limonata, lemonade
limone (*m.*), lemon
linea, line
lingua, tongue; language
lino, linen
lista, list; **lista delle vivande**, menu
livello, level
lo, him, it
locale, local
Lombardia, Lombardy
Londra, London
lontano, far
loro, them, to them, theirs
Loro, to you, yours, your
lotta, struggle
lottare, to struggle
luce (*f.*), light
Lucia, Lucy
Lucio, Luke, Lucius
luglio, July
lui, him, to him
Luigi (*m.*), Louis
Luisa, Louise
luminosità (*f.*), brilliance
luna, moon
lunedì (*m.*), Monday
lunghezza, length
lungo, long
luogo, place; **aver luogo**, to take place
lupo, wolf
lussuoso, luxurious
ma, but
macchè, Are you kidding? Go on!
maccheroni (*m. pl.*), macaroni
macchia, spot
macchina, car; machine; **macchina da scrivere**, typewriter
macellaio, butcher; **dal macellaio**, at the butcher's (shop)
Maddalena, Madeline
madonna, Madonna
madre (*f.*), mother
maestoso, majestic
maestro, teacher
maggio, May
maggiore, older, major
magia, magic
magnetofono, tape recorder
magro, thin, slender
mai, never
maiale (*m.*), pork
malato, sick; sick person
malattia, illness
male, ache; **mal di testa**, headache; **mal di stomaco**, stomachache
malinconico, melancholy
mamma, mom, mother
mancanza, lack
mancare, to fail
mancia, tip
mandare, to send
mandarino, tangerine
mangiare, to eat
manicotti (*m. pl.*), a kind of macaroni filled with cheese
maniera, manner
manierismo, mannerism
mano (*f.*), hand; **le mani** (*f. pl.*), hands
mantello, cape
manzo, beef
marciapiede (*m.*), sidewalk
marciare, to march
Marco, Mark
mare (*m.*), sea
maresciallo, field marshall
Maria, Mary
marinaio, sailor
marinara (*f. sing.*), maritime; **repubbliche marinare**, maritime republics
marito, husband
marittimo, maritime
marmellata, jelly, marmalade
marmo, marble
marrone, brown
Marta, Martha
martedì (*m.*), Tuesday
marzo, March
maschera, mask; **ballo in maschera**, masquerade ball
mascherata, masquerade
massimo, very big, maximum
matematica, mathematics
materia, subject, course

materno, maternal
matita, pencil
matrimọnio, wedding, matrimony
mattina (*also* **mattino**), morning
mattone (*m.*), brick
mạturo, ripe
me, me, to me
meccạnico, mechanic; mechanical
medicina, medicine
mẹdico, doctor
medioevale, medieval
Medio Evo (*also* **Medioevo**), Middle Ages
Mediterrạneo, Mediterranean
meglio, better
mela, apple
menare, to lead
meno, less
mento, chin
mentre, while
menzogna, lie
meraviglia, marvel
meravigliarsi, to be amazed
meraviglioso, marvelous
mercante (*m.*), merchant
mercato, market
mercoledì (*m.*), Wednesday
meridionale, southern
meridione (*m.*), south
meritarsi, to deserve
merletto, lace
merluzzo, whiting (fish)
mese (*m.*), month
messa, Mass
messicano, Mexican
Mẹssico, Mexico
mestiere (*m.*), trade
metà (*f.*), half
metallo, metal
metro, meter
metropolitana, subway
mẹttere, to place, to put; **mẹttere piede**, to set foot
mẹttersi, to place oneself; to wear; **mẹttersi d'accordo**, to come to an agreement
mezzanotte (*f.*), midnight
mezzo, half
mezzogiorno, noon
Mezzogiorno, South of Italy
mi, me, to me, myself
Michele (*m.*), Michael
micromotore (*m.*), micromotor
migliaio, about one thousand; **le migliaia** (*f. pl.*), several thousands
miglio, mile; **le miglia** (*f. pl.*), miles
migliore, better, best
Milano, Milan
miliardo, billion
milione (*m.*), million
mille, one thousand
minaccia, threat
minacciare, to threaten
minestra, soup (vegetable)
minestrone (*m.*), thick vegetable soup
mịnimo, minimum, very small
ministro, minister
minoranza, minority
minore, minor, younger
minuto, minute
mirạcolo, miracle
miseria, misery
misto, mixed
misurare, to measure
mite, mild
mitolọgico, mythological
mobilia, furniture
mọbile (*m.*), piece of furniture
moda, fashion
modista, milliner
moglie (*f.*), wife
molecolare, molecular
molo, pier
molto, much
molti, many
momento, moment
mọnaca, nun
mọnaco, monk
mondo, world
moneta, moneta corrente (*also* **contanti**), money, cash
montagna (*also* **monte**, *m.*), mountain
montagnoso (*also* **montuoso**), mountainous
mọrbido, soft
mọrdere, to bite; **morso**, bitten; bite

morire, to die; **morto**, dead
morte (*f.*), death
mostra, exhibit
motocicletta, motorcycle (popularly referred to as **la moto**)
mucca, cow
muro, wall (exterior)
museo, museum
musica, music
musicale, musical

nailon (*m.*), nylon
Napoli (*f.*), Naples
narrare, to narrate
nascere, to be born
nascondere, to hide
nascondersi, to hide oneself
naso, nose
nastro, tape, ribbon
Natale (*m.*), Christmas
natio, native
naturale, natural
naturalmente, naturally
nave (*f.*), boat, ship
navigare, to navigate, to sail
navigatore (*m.*), navigator
nazione (*f.*), nation
neanche, not even
ne, of it, of him, of her, of them; from there
nè . . . nè, neither . . . nor
necessario, necessary
negare, to deny
negozio, store
nemico, enemy
nemmeno, not even
neonato, newborn
nepotista (*m.*, *f.*), nepotist (known for hiring relatives)
nero, black
nervoso, nervous
nessuno, no one
neve (*f.*), snow
Nicola (*m.*), Nicholas
nido, nest
nient'altro, nothing else
niente, nothing
nipote (*m.*, *f.*), nephew, niece; grandson, granddaughter
no, no
nobile (*m.*, *f.*), noble; nobleman, noblewoman
nobiltà (*f.*), nobility
noi, we, us
noioso, tiresome, boring
nome (*m.*), name
nominare, to nominate, to appoint
non, not
nonna, grandmother
nonno, grandfather
nono, ninth
nonostante, although, despite
nord (*m.*), north
notare, to note, to notice
notizia, news
notte (*f.*), night
novanta, ninety
nove, nine
novecento, nine hundred; **il Novecento**, the 20th century
novella, short story
novelliere (*m.*, *f.*), short-story writer
novembre (*m.*), November
numero, number
nuotare, to swim

o, or
obbedire, to obey
obbligare, to oblige
obbligo, obligation
occasione (*f.*), occasion, opportunity
occhiali (*m. pl.*), eyeglasses
occhio, eye
occidente (*m.*), west, occident
occidentale, western
occorrere, to be in need of
occupare, to occupy, to invade
oceano, ocean
odiare, to hate
odio, hate
offendersi, to be offended
offrire, to offer
oggetto, object
oggi, today
oggigiorno, nowadays
ogni, each, every, all, any

Olimpiade (*f.*), Olympics
ombra, shadow
ombrello, umbrella
ombrellone (*m.*), beach umbrella
ọpera, work, task; opera
operạio, worker
operịstico, operatic
opporre, to oppose
opportunità (*f.*), opportunity
ora, hour
ora (*adv.*), now
orario, schedule, timetable
orchestra, orchestra
ordinare, to order
ọrdine (*m.*), order, stability
orecchio, ear
orẹfice (*m.*), goldsmith
orientale, oriental, eastern
oriente (*m.*), east, orient
orịgine (*f.*), origin
orizzonte (*m.*), horizon
orlo, brink, edge
ornamentare, to decorate, to ornament
oro, gold
orologio, watch, clock
orrịbile, horrible
orso, bear
ortaggi (*m. pl.*), vegetables
ospedale (*m.*), hospital
ospitare, to give hospitality to, to house
osso, bone; **le ossa** (*f. pl.*), bones of the body
ottanta, eighty
ottavo, eighth
ọttimo, very good, the best
otto, eight
ottobre (*m.*), October
ottocento, eight hundred; **l'Ottocento**, the 19th century
ovale, oval
ọvest (*m.*), west
ovunque, everywhere

pacco, package
pace (*f.*), peace
padella, frying pan
padre (*m.*), father
padrino, godfather
paesaggio, countryside
paese (*m.*), town; country, nation
pagamento, payment
pagano, pagan
pagare, to pay
pagella, report card
pạgina, page
pạio, pair; **le pạia** (*f. pl.*), pairs
palazzo, palace, building
palla, ball
pallacanestro (*f.*), basketball
panchina, bench
panetterịa, bakeshop
panettiere (*m.*), baker
panettone (*m.*), typical Milanese sweet bread
panino, roll (bread); **panino imbottito**, sandwich
panorama (*m.*), panorama
pantaloni (*m. pl.*), pants
pantọfola, slipper
Pạolo, Paul
papa (*m.*), pope
papà (*m.*), father
paracadute (*m.*), parachute
paragonare, to compare
parco, park
parecchio, some, considerable; **parecchi**, several
parente (*m., f.*), relative
parere, to seem
parete (*f.*), wall (interior wall)
parlare, to speak, to to talk
parola, word; **parola consanguinea**, cognate word
parrucchiere (*m.*), hairdresser
parte (*f.*), part
partenza, departure
partire, to depart (town)
partita, game, match
partito, political party
Pasqua, Easter
passaporto, passport
passare, to pass; to spend time
passato, past

passeggero, passenger
passeggiata (*also* **passeggio**), walk
pasta (*also* **pasta asciutta**), macaroni
pasticciere (*m.*), confectioner, baker
pasto, meal
patata, potato
pạtria, country, fatherland
patriota (*also* **patriotta**) (*m.*, *f.*), patriot
patriọttico, patriotic
Patrizia, Patricia
patrono, patron
patto, pact, treaty
paura, fear; **aver paura**, to be afraid
pavimento, pavement, floor
pazientemente, patiently
pazienza, patience; **aver pazienza**, to be patient
pazzịa, madness
peccato, sin; it's a pity; too bad
pẹcora (*f. sing.*), sheep
peggio (*adv.*), worse
peggiore (*adj.*), worse; **il peggiore**, worst
pelle (*f.*), skin
pelliccia, fur
pena, pain; sentence
pendente, leaning
pẹndolo, pendulum
penịsola, peninsula
pensare, to think
pensiero, thought
pensione (*f.*), boarding-house
pẹntola, pot
pepe (*m.*), pepper (spice)
Peppe (*m.*), Joe
per, for, via, through, in order to
pera, pear
percentuale (*m.*), percentage
perchè, why, because
perciò, therefore
pẹrdere, to lose
perfetto, perfect
perfezionare, to perfect
pericoloso, dangerous
perịodo, period (of time)
permẹttere, to permit, to allow
però, but, however
persona, person
persuadere, to persuade
pesante, heavy
pesarsi, to weigh oneself
pesca, peach; fishing
pescare, to fish
pescatore (*m.*), fisherman
pesce (*m.*), fish
peschereccio, fishing
pescherịa, fish market
pescivẹndolo, fishmonger
peso, weight
pẹssimo (*adj.*), very bad
pettinarsi, to comb oneself
pẹttine (*m.*), comb
petto, chest
pezzettino, small piece
pezzo, piece
piacere, to like
piacẹvole, pleasing, pleasant
piạngere, to cry
pianista (*m.*, *f.*), pianist
piano, floor (1st, 2nd, etc.)
pianoforte (*m.*), piano
pian piano, slowly
pianta, plant
pianterreno, ground floor
piattino, saucer; small dish
piatto, plate, dish
piazza, square, plaza
pịccolo, small; **da pịccolo**, as a small child
piede (*m.*), foot
Piero, Pietro, Peter
pietra, rock, stone
pigro, lazy
pila elẹttrica, battery
pilota (*m.*, *f.*), pilot
pioggia, rain
piombo, lead
pioniero, pioneer
piscina, swimming pool
piselli (*m. pl.*), peas
pistola, pistol
pittọrico, pictorial
pittura, painting
più, more
più tardi, later
pochissimo, very little; very few (*pl.*)

pochi, some, few
poco, little
poesịa, poem, poetry
poeta (*m.*), poet
poetessa (*f.*), poet
poi, then, afterward
politicamente, politically
polịtico, political
polizịa, police
poliziotto, policeman
pollerịa, chicken market
pollo, chicken
polpetta, meatball
poltrona, armchair
pomeriggio, afternoon
pomodoro, tomato
ponente (*m.*), west
ponte (*m.*), bridge
pontẹfice (*m.*), pope, pontiff
popolare, popular
popolarmente, popularly
popolato, populated
popolazione (*f.*), population
porco, pig
porre, to place, to put
porta, door
portabagagli (*m. sing., pl.*), porter
portacẹnere (*m.*), ashtray
portafoglio, wallet
portare, to bring; to wear; to carry
portiere (*m.*) (*also* **portinaio**), doorman
porto, port
portone (*m.*), front door, main door
possedere, to possess, to own
possịbile, possible
possibilità (*f.*), possibility
posta, mail; post office
postino, mailman
posto, seat, place, spot
potenza, power, powerful nation
potere (*m.*), throne, seat of government
potere, to be able, can, may
poverino, poor man
pọvero, poor
povertà (*f.*), poverty
pranzare, to dine
pranzo, dinner
prato, meadow
precise (*f. pl.*), precise, sharp, exactly
precisione (*f.*), precision
precursore (*m.*), forerunner
predicare, to preach
preferire, to prefer
preferito, preferred
pregare, to pray
pregiatịssimo, highly regarded, highly desirable
premiato, rewarded
premio, award, prize
prẹndere, to take; **prẹndere (parte)**, to take (part)
prenotare, to reserve
preoccuparsi, to worry about
preparare, to prepare
prepararsi, to prepare oneself
presente (*m.*), present
presidente (*m.*), president
presiedere, to preside
presso, near
prestare, to lend
presto, quickly, quick
prete (*m.*), priest
prezioso, precious
prezzo, price
prigione (*f.*), prison
prigioniero, prisoner
prima, first; before
primavera, spring
primo ministro, prime minister
principale, principal, leading
prịncipe (*m.*), prince
principessa, princess
probạbile, probable
probabilmente, probably
problema (*m.*), problem
proclamare, to proclaim
produrre, to produce
produttivo, productive
profumo, perfume
professione (*f.*), profession
professore (*m.*), professor, teacher
professoressa, professor, teacher

profondo, profound, deep
programma (*m.*), program
progredito, advanced
progresso, progress
proibire, to forbid, to prohibit
promẹttere, to promise
promulgare, to decree
promulgazione (*f.*), decree
pronipote (*m., f.*), great grandchild
pronto, ready; hello; hurry
proporre, to propose
prospettiva, perspective
prọssimo, next
protẹggere, to protect
protestante (*m., f.*), Protestant
provare, to try; to prove
proverbio, proverb
provincia, province
prugna, plum
pubblicare, to publish
pụbblico, public
pugilato, boxing
pugno, fist
pulire, to clean
pulito, clean
pụlpito, pulpit
punire, to punish
punta, point
punto, period
può darsi, it is possible
purchè, provided that
puro, pure

qua, qui, here
quaderno, notebook
quadrato, square
quadro, picture, painting
qualche, some, any
qualche cosa (*also* **qualcosa**), something
qualcuno, someone
quale, which
qualità (*f.*), quality
qualsiasi, any, any other
quantità (*f.*), quantity
quanti, how many
quanto, how much
quantunque, although
quaranta, forty
quartiere (*m.*), section, district
quarto, quarter; fourth
quasi, almost
quattọrdici, fourteen
quattro, four
quattrocento, four hundred; **il Quattrocento**, the 15th century
quel che, what, that which
quelli, those
quello, that
quello che, what, that which
questo, this
questi, these
quịndici, fifteen
quinto, fifth

rabbia, anger, rage
raccolta, collection
raccontare, to narrate
radente, grazing, skimming over
rạdersi, to shave
radio (*f.*), radio
radunarsi, to gather together, to meet
raffinato, refined
raffreddarsi, to catch cold
raffreddore (*m.*), cold
ragazza, girl
ragazzino, small boy
ragazzo, boy
raggiụngere, to arrive, to reach
raggrumato, coagulated
ragione (*f.*), reason, right; **avere ragione**, to be right
ragioniere (*m.*), accountant
rame (*m.*), copper
rammentarsi, to remember
ramo, branch
rapidamente, rapidly, quickly
rapidità (*f.*), rapidity
raramente, rarely
raro, rare
ravioli (*m. pl.*), cheese- or meat-filled macaroni
re (*m.*), king
reale, real; royal
realtà (*f.*), reality
reazione nucleare (*f.*), nuclear reaction

regalo, gift
regata, boat race
regime (*m.*), regime
regina, queen
regione (*f.*), region
regnante (*m.*, *f.*), ruler
regno, reign, kindgom
regolare, regular
regolarmente, regularly
relativamente, relatively
religione (*f.*), religion
religioso, religious
reliquia, relic
remare, to row
rẹndere, to render, to give; **rẹndere ụtile**, to render useful
repụbblica, republic
repubblicano, republican
restare, to remain, to stay
resti (*m. pl.*), remains
rete (*f.*), net, network
ribassare, to lower
ricco, rich
ricerca, research
ricẹvere, to receive
riconoscịbile, recognizable
ricordare (*also* **ricordarsi**), to remember
rịdere, to laugh
rientrare, to reenter; to go back home
rifiutare, to refuse
riflẹttere, to reflect
riforma, reform
rifornire, to provide, to supply
riga, ruler (straightedge)
rilasciare, relax; release
rimanere, to remain, to stay
Rinascimento, Renaissance
rinascimentale, of the Renaissance
rincasare, to go back home
rinfrescante, refreshing
rinfrescarsi, to refresh oneself
ringraziare, to thank
rinomato, well-known
rinunciare, to renounce, to give up
riportare, to bring back
riposarsi, to rest
riposo, rest
riproduzione (*f.*), reproduction
risalire, to date back to; to climb up again
riso, rice; laughter
Risorgimento, revival, awakening (Italy's unification)
risorsa, resource
rispettare, to respect
rispọndere, to answer, to respond
risposta, answer
ristorante (*m.*), restaurant
risultato, result
ritardo, late, delay; **in ritardo**, late
ritirarsi, to withdraw
rito, rite
ritornare, to return, to come back
ritorno, return
ritratto, picture, drawing
ritrovo, resort
riuscire, to succeed; to go out again
riva, shore, bank
rivista, magazine
rivoluzione (*f.*), revolution
Roma, Rome
Romani (*m. pl.*), Romans
romanza, Romance (language)
romanziere (*m.*), novelist
romanzo, novel
rọmpere, to break
rosa, rose; pink
rosso, red
rotazione (*f.*), rotation
rovinare, to ruin
rubare, to rob
rumeno, Romanian
rumore (*m.*), noise, sound
ruscello, brook
russo, Russian

sabato (*m.*), Saturday
sabbia, sand
sacro, sacred
sala, room; **sala da bagno**, bathroom; **sala da pranzo**, dining room

salame (*m.*), salami
salario, salary
sale (*m.*), salt
salire, to go up, to climb, to ascend
salone (*m.*), living room, salon
salotto, living room
salsa, sauce, gravy
salsiccia, sausage
salumeria, delicatessen
salutare, to greet
salute (*f.*), health
saluti (*m. pl.*), greetings, regards
sangue (*m.*), blood
sano, whole, safe
santo, saint
sapere, to know
sapone (*m.*), soap
saporosịssimo, very tasty
Saràceni (*m. pl.*), Saracens
sarcọfago, sarcophagus
sardagnolo (*also* **sardo**), Sardinian
Sardegna, Sardinia
sardina, sardine
sarta, dressmaker
sarto, tailor
satịrico, satirist; satirical
sbagliarsi, to be mistaken
sbaglio, mistake
sboccare, to flow (into)
scacchi (*m. pl.*), chess
scacciare, to expel
scaffale (*m.*), shelf
scala, staircase, stairs
scalare, to ascend, to climb, to scale
scalinata, stairway
scampagnata, picnic, outing
scantinato, cellar
scarpa, shoe
scạtola, box
scẹgliere, to choose, to pick, to select
scelta, choice
scena, scene
scẹndere, to descend, to go down
scherma, fencing
scherzare, to joke, to jest
scherzo, joke, trick
schịera, flock, herd; **una schiera di imperatori**, a long line of emperors
sciare, to ski
sciatore (*m.*), skier
scienze politiche (*f. pl.*), political science
scienziato, scientist
scimmia, monkey
sciọpero, strike
scisma (*m.*), schism
scoiạttolo, squirrel
scolaro, scholar
scolạstico, scholastic
scolpire, to carve, to chisel
scommẹttere, to bet
scomunicare, to excommunicate
sconfiggere, to defeat
scontento, unhappy
scontro, battle
scoperta, discovery
scopo, purpose
scoppiare, to explode
scoppio, explosion
scoprire, to discover
scordare, to forget
scorso, last, preceding
scortese, discourteous
scrittore (*m.*), writer
scrivanịa, desk
scrịvere, to write
scultore (*m.*), sculptor
scuola, school; **scuola magistrale**, school of education; **scuola materna**, nursery school; **scuola media**, junior high school
scuro, dark
scusa, excuse
scusare, to excuse
sdraiarsi, to stretch out
sebbene, although
sẹcolo, century
secondo, second; according to
sede (*f.*), seat
sedersi, to sit down
sedia, chair
sẹdici, sixteen
segnalare, to point out
segretaria, secretary
segreto, secret
seguire, to follow
sẹguito, following
sei, six
seicento, six hundred; **il Seicento**, the 17th century
selvạtico, savage, wild
sembrare, to seem

sẹmplice, easy, simple
sempre, always
senato, senate
senatore (*m.*), senator
sentire, to hear; to feel
sentirsi, to feel
senza, without
separare, to separate
sera (*also* **serata**), evening
sereno, serene; clear
serio, serious
servire, to serve
servirsi di, to use, to make use of
sessanta, sixty
se stesso, himself
sesto, sixth
seta, silk
sete (*f.*), thirst; **avere sete**, to be thirsty
settanta, seventy
sette, seven
settecento, seven hundred; **il Settecento**, the 18th century
settembre (*m.*), September
settimana, week
sẹttimo, seventh
settentrione (*m.*), north
severo, severe
sfiducia, lack of confidence
sfilata, parade, procession
sì, yes
siccome, since
Sicilia, Sicily
Siciliani (*m. pl.*), Sicilians
sicuro, sure, certain
sicuramente, surely
sigaretta, cigarette
sịgaro, cigar
significare, to mean
signora, lady, madam, Mrs.
signore, sir, gentleman, Mr.
signorina, Miss, young lady
sịmile, similar, equal
simpạtico, nice, pleasant
sinceramente, sincerely
sincerità (*f.*), sincerity
sinfonịa, symphony
sinistra, left
sintẹtico, synthetic
sito, site, place
situato, situated
slitta, sled
smẹttere, to stop
smoking (*m.*), tuxedo
snello, thin, slender
società (*f.*), society
sọffice, soft
soffitto, ceiling
soffrire, to suffer
soggetto, subject, topic
soggiorno, stay; den
sogno, dream
solamente, only
soldato, soldier
soldi (*m.*), money
soldino, penny
sole (*m.*), sun
solitario, solitary, lonely
solo, alone, only
soltanto, only
sonno, dream
sopra, on, above
soprạbito, topcoat
soprannominato, nicknamed
soprano (*m.*), soprano
sorella, sister
sorellina, little sister
sorprẹndere, to surprise
sorpresa, surprise
sorriso, smile
sorte (*f.*), fate
sotterraneo, underground
sotto, under
sottomettersi, to place oneself under
sovranità (*f.*), sovereignty
sovrano, king, ruler
spaghetti (*m. pl.*), spaghetti
spagnolo (*also* **spagnuolo**), Spanish
spalla, shoulder
spạrgere, to disperse, to spread
spazio, space
specchio, mirror
speciale, special
specializzazione (*f.*), specialty
specialmente, especially
spedire, to send, to remit
spedizione (*f.*), expedition
spẹgnere, to put out, to extinguish
spẹndere, to spend
speranza, hope
sperare, to hope

sperimentale, experimental
spesa, food shopping
spese (*f. pl.*), shopping (in general)
spesso, often
spettạcolo, show
spezzare, to break
spiaggia, beach
spiccare, to stand out
spịccioli (*m. pl.*), small change (money)
spiegare, to explain; to unfold
spiegazione (*f.*), explanation
spinaci (*m. pl.*), spinach
spina dorsale, spinal column
spirituale, spiritual
splẹndido, splendid, wonderful
spolverare, to dust
sporcarsi, to dirty oneself
sporco, dirty
sport (*m.*), sport
sportello, ticket window
sportivo, sportsman, athlete
sposare, to marry
sposarsi, to get married
sposa, bride
sposo, bridegroom
spostamento, shift, movement
squadra, team, squad
squisito, exquisite, delicious
sta bene, all right
stabilirsi, to establish oneself, to settle
stadio, stadium
stagione (*f.*), season
stamattina, this morning
stanchẹvole, tiring
stanco, tired
stanotte, tonight
stanza, room
stare, to be
stasera, this evening
Stati Uniti (*m. pl.*), United States
stato, state
statua, statue
stazione (*f.*), station; **stazione ferroviaria**, railroad station
Stẹfano, Stephen
stella, star
stesso, same
stile (*m.*), style
stivale (*m.*), boot
stọmaco, stomach
storia, story; history
strada, street
straniero, stranger; foreigner
strano, strange
stretto, narrow, tight
strịngere, to tighten, to press, to bind, to clasp
studente (*m.*), student
studiare, to study
studio, study, office
studioso, studious
su, on, upon, over, above, about, toward
sụbito, quickly
succẹdere, to happen
successione (*f.*), succession
successo, success
succo, juice
sud (*m.*), south
suddiviso, subdivided
sufficiente, sufficient, enough
suffragio, suffrage, vote
suggerire, to suggest
suicida (*m., f.*), suicide
suo, his, its
suonare, to play (an instrument); to sound; to ring
superfịcie (*f.*), area, surface
superiore, better; higher
supermercato, supermarket
superstizioso, superstitious
supplicare, to beg, to implore
supremazịa, supremacy
supremo, best; highest
Susanna, Susan
susina, plum
sussidio, assistance
svedese, Swedish
sveglia, alarm clock
svegliare, to awaken
svegliarsi, to wake up
sviluppare, to develop
Svịzzera, Switzerland

tabaccaio, tobacconist

tabacco, tobacco
tacchino, turkey
tacco, heel
tacere, to be silent
tagliare, to cut
tagliarsi, to cut oneself
tanti, so many
tanto, so much
tanto . . . quanto, as . . . as; as much . . . as; as many . . . as
tappeto, rug
tardi, late
tasca, pocket
tassa, tax
tassì (*m.*), taxi
tavola, table (on which to eat)
tavolo, table (on which to work)
tazza, cup
tè (*m.*), tea
te, you, to you
teatro, theater
tẹcnica, technique
tedesco, German
telefonare, to telephone
telẹfono, telephone
telegramma (*m.*), telegram
televisione (*f.*), television
televisivo (*adj.*), television
televisore (*m.*), television set
temere, to fear
temperato, temperate
temperino, pocket-knife, penknife
tempesta, storm
tempo, time; weather; tense
temporale, temporal, earthly
tenace, tough
tenere, to have, to hold
tẹnero, tender
tenore (*m.*), tenor
tentare, to tempt; to attempt, to try
teocrạtico, theocratic, absolute
Teodoro, Theodore
teọlogo, theologian
Teresa, Theresa
terminare, to end, to terminate
terra, land, earth, ground; floor
territorio, territory
terzo, third
tesoro, treasure
tẹssile (*m.*), textile
testa, head
tetto, roof
ti, to you; yourself
tigre (*m.*), tiger
tịmido, timid
timore (*m.*), fear
tịpico, typical
tipo, type
tirare, to pull; to throw
tiretto, drawer
toccare, to touch
tọgliere, to take from, to remove
tọgliersi, to take off (clothes)
tomba, tomb
Tommaso, Thomas
tonno, tuna
topo, mouse
torcia, torch; torchlight
tornare, to turn; to return
torre (*f.*), tower
torta, cake, pie
torto, wrong; **avere torto**, to be wrong
Toscana, Tuscany
totalmente, totally
tovaglia, tablecloth
tovagliolo, napkin
tra, between, among
traditore (*m.*), traitor
tradizione (*f.*), tradition
tradurre, to translate
trạffico, traffic
tram (*m.*), trolley
trạmite, by means of, through the process of
tranquillo, tranquil, peaceful
tranquillamente, tranquilly
trarre, to pull, to extract
trasferirsi, to move, to transfer oneself
trasportare, to transport
trattare, to treat, to deal with
trattato, treaty
trattorịa, family-style restaurant
traversare, to cross
tre, three

trecento, three hundred; **il Trecento**, the 14th century
trẹdici, thirteen
tremendo, tremendous
treno, train
trenta, thirty
triạngolo, triangle
trionfare, to triumph
triste, sad
tristemente, sadly
tristezza, sadness
trono, throne
troppi, too many
troppo, too much
trovare, to find
trovarsi, to be situated; to find oneself
truppe (*f. pl.*), troops
tu, you
tuberosa, tuberose (flower)
tuffarsi, to dive
tuo, your; yours
tuono, lightning
turco, Turkish
Turchịa, Turkey
turista (*m., f.*), tourist
tutore (*m., f.*), tutor
tutti, everyone; **tutti e due**, both, the two of them
tutto, all, everything; **tutto il giorno**, all day long
tuttora, still

uccello, bird
uccịdere, to kill
udire, to hear
ufficiale, official
ufficio, office; **ufficio postale**, post office
uguaglianza, equality
uguale, equal
ụltimo, last
umanità (*f.*), humanity
umidità (*f.*), humidity
umorịstico, humorous
un, uno, one
ụndici, eleven
ụnico, only, alone, unique; **senso ụnico**, one way
unificare, to unify
unificazione (*f.*), unification
un po' di, a little (of), some
universale, universal
università (*f.*), university
uomo, man
uovo, egg; **le uova** (*f. pl.*), eggs
usare, to use
uscire, to go out (of the house)
uscita, exit
ụtile, useful
uva, grape

vacanza, vacation
vacca, cow
vagone (*m.*), car (of a train)
valere, to be worth
valigia, suitcase
valore (*m.*), worth
vano, vain
variạbile, variable
varietà (*f.*), variety
variò, various
vaso, vase
Vaticano, Vatican
vecchiạia, old age
vecchio, old; old man; **vecchissimo**, very old
vedere, to see
veduta, view
veli (*m. pl.*), curtains
veloce, fast, speedy
velocemente, fast, speedily
velocità (*f.*), velocity, speed
vẹndere, to sell
vendicare, to avenge
venditore (*m.*), vendor, seller
venerdì (*m.*), Friday
Venezia, Venice
venire, to come
venti, twenty
ventina, about twenty
vento, wind
veramente, really
verde, green
verdura, leafy vegetables
Vẹrgine (*f.*), Virgin
vergogna, shame
verità (*f.*), truth
vero, true
verso, toward
vẹscovo, bishop
Vespa, motorscooter
veste (*f.*), dress

vestirsi, to dress oneself
vestiti (*m. pl.*), clothes
vetrina, store window
vetro, glass
vettura, coach (of a train)
vi, here; there; you; to you; yourself
via, street
viaggiante (*m., f.*) (*also* **viaggiatore**, *m.*), traveler
viaggiare, to travel
viaggio, trip, voyage
viale (*m.*), avenue
vicino, near; neighbor
vigilia, eve
villa, villa
villaggio, village
vịncere, to win
vino, wine
viola, violet
Violetta, Violet
violino, violin
vịsita, visit
visitare, to visit
viso, face
vita, life
vite (*f.*), vine
vitello, veal; calf
vịvere, to live, to reside
Viviana, Vivian
vivo, alive
vocabolario, vocabulary; dictionary
voce (*f.*), voice
voglia, desire
voi, you
volare, to fly
volentieri, gladly, willingly
volere, to want, to wish
volgare, vulgar; vulgate (language of the masses of people)
volo, flight
volpe (*f.*), fox
volta, time; **una volta**, one time, once
voltare, to turn
volto, face
vostro, your; yours
voto, vote; grade, mark
vulcano, volcano
vuoto, empty

zaino, knapsack
zia, aunt
zio, uncle
zịngaro, gypsy
zitto, quiet
zolfo, sulfur
zona, zone
zụcchero, sugar

Part XI—English–Italian Vocabulary

able: **to be able**, potere
about, di, circa, verso
accompany, accompagnare
actor, attore (*m.*)
actress, attrice (*f.*)
add, aggiụngere
admire, ammirare
affectionately, affezionatamente
afraid: **to be afraid**, avere paura
airport, aeroporto
almost, quasi
alone, solo
although, sebbene, nonostante, quantunque, benchè
always, sempre
American, americano
anchovy, acciuga
answer: **to answer**, rispọndere
appear, apparire, sembrare
appetizer, antipasto
apple, mela
architect, architetto
arm, braccio
arrive, arrivare
ascend, salire
ask, domandare, chiẹdere
astrologist, astrọlogo
at, to, a
aunt, zia
author, autore (*m.*), autrice (*f.*)
automobile, automọbile, mạcchina

bank, banca
be, ẹssere, stare
bean, fagiolo
before, prima (*adv.*), davanti (*prep.*)
begin, cominciare, incominciare
believe, crẹdere
best, mẹglio (*adv.*), il migliore (*adj.*)
bet: **to bet**, scommẹttere
bicycle, bicicletta
bill, conto
bind: **to bind**, strịngere, legare
birthday, compleanno
book, libro
bored: **to become bored**, annoiarsi
born: **to be born**, nạscere
boy, ragazzo
bread, pane (*m.*)
break: **to break**, rọmpere, spezzare
brother, fratello
burn: **to burn oneself**, bruciarsi
bus, ạutobus
butcher, macellạio
butter, burro
buy, comprare
by, at, da

cake, torta
call: **to call**, chiamare
can (to be able), potere
capital, capitale (*f.*)
car, mạcchina, automọbile (*f.*)
careful: **to be careful**, stare attento
carry, portare
cathedral, cattedrale (*f.*)
Catholic, cattọlico
celebrate, celebrare, festeggiare
central, centrale
century, sẹcolo
certain, certo, sicuro
chair, sẹdia
change: **to change**, cambiare
Charles, Carlo
chemistry, chịmica
children, figli (*m. pl.*), bambini, ragazzini
choose, scẹgliere
church, chiesa
city, città (*f.*)
clasp: **to clasp**, strịngere, abbracciare

class, classe (*f.*)
clean: **to clean**, pulire
climb: **to climb**, salire
close: **to close**, chiụdere
coat, cappotto
coffee, caffè (*m.*)
cold: **to catch cold**, raffreddarsi
comb oneself, pettinarsi
come, venire; **come near**, avvicinarsi
commit, commẹttere
conclude, conclụdere, conchiụdere
convince, convịncere
cook, cuoco, cuoca; **to cook**, cuọcere, cucinare
correct: **to correct**, corrẹggere
cost: **to cost**, costare
country, campagna, paese, nazione
cousin, cugino (*m.*), cugina (*f.*)
cover: **to cover**, coprire
cross: **to cross**, attraversare, traversare
cut: **to cut oneself**, tagliarsi

dance: **to dance**, ballare
dare: **to dare**, ardire
dear, caro
decide, decịdere
defend, difẹndere
deny, negare
depart, partire
descend, scẹndere
desk, banco (student's), scrivanịa
die, morire
difficult, diffịcile
dine, pranzare
discover, scoprire
dish, piatto
disobey, disobbedire
divide, divịdere
do, fare
doctor, dottore (*m.*), dottoressa (*f.*), mẹdico
dog, cane (*m.*)
door, porta
doubt: **to doubt**, dubitare
down, giù
drama, dramma (*m.*)
dress, ạbito, vestito; **to dress oneself**, vestirsi
drink: **to drink**, bere
drive: **to drive**, guidare
driver, autista (*m.*, *f.*)
dry, asciutto
during, durante
dynamo, dịnamo (*f.*)

early, presto, di buon'ora
earn, guadagnare
eat, mangiare
echo, eco (*f.*)
elephant, elefante (*m.*)
enemy, nemico
English, inglese
enjoy, divertire; **to enjoy oneself**, divertirsi
enter, entrare
evening, sera, serata
every, ogni
everywhere, dappertutto
evident, evidente
explain, spiegare
eyeglasses, occhiali (*m. pl.*)

face, fạccia, volto, viso
fall, autunno
fall: **to fall**, cadere; **to fall asleep**, addormentarsi
family, famịglia
famous, famoso
far, lontano
fear: **to fear**, temere
feel, sentire; **to feel sorry**, dispiacere
few, pochi
find, trovare
fine, bene (*adv.*), buono (*adj.*)
finish: **to finish**, finire
first, primo
floor, piano, pavimento
flower, fiore
fly: **to fly**, volare
follow, seguire
foot, piede (*m.*)
forbid, proibire
forget, dimenticare, scordare
France, Frạncia
Friday, venerdì (*m.*)
friend, amico (*m.*), amica (*f.*)
from, da

fruit, frutta
furnish, fornire
furniture, mobilia

gather, cogliere, raccogliere
generally, generalmente
gentle, gentile
gently, gentilmente
German, tedesco
girl, ragazza
give, dare, rendere
go, andare; **to go down**, scendere; **to go out**, uscire; **to go out again**, riuscire; **to go up**, salire
gold, oro
grandparents, nonni (*m. pl.*)
green, verde
greet, salutare

happen, succedere
happy, contento, felice; **to be happy**, essere allegro
hat, cappello
have, avere; **to have to, must**, dovere
he, egli, lui
heal, guarire
hear, sentire, udire
help: **to help**, aiutare
hide: **to hide**, nascondere
his, suo, sua, suoi, sue
hold: **to hold**, tenere
home, casa
hope: **to hope**, sperare
horse, cavallo
hour, ora
hunting, caccia

I, io
ice cream, gelato
idea, idea
ill, malato
important, importante
impossible, impossibile
improbable, improbabile
in, in
in order that, affinchè, per
in order to, per
in the event that, in caso che
inhabitant, abitante (*m.*,*f.*)
inside, dentro
insist, insistere
intelligent, intelligente
invite, invitare
island, isola
Italian, italiano

Japanese, giapponese
Joe, Peppe

kill, uccidere
king, re (*m.*)
kiss: **to kiss**, baciare
kitchen, cucina
knife, coltello
knock: **to knock**, bussare
know, conoscere, sapere
lady, signora
lake, lago
lamp, lampada
language, lingua
large, grande
last, ultimo, scorso; **to last**, durare
late, tardi
laugh, riso; **to laugh**, ridere
lawyer, avvocato
lead: **to lead**, condurre
lean: **to lean**, appoggiarsi
learn, apprendere, imparare
leave (something), lasciare
lesson, lezione (*f.*)
letter, lettera
lettuce, lattuga
library, biblioteca
lie, bugia
lip, labbro; **lips**, le labbra (*f. irreg.*)
listen (to), ascoltare
little, poco, un po'
live: **to live**, abitare, vivere
living room, salotto
look at, guardare
look for, cercare
lose, perdere
loudly, ad alta voce

magazine, rivista
maid, cameriera, domestica
mail: **to mail**, inviare, spedire, mandare

make, fare
make oneself comfortable (to sit down), accomodarsi
man, uomo
many, molti
marry, sposare
Mary, Maria
mathematics, matematica
may, potere
meat, carne (*f.*)
meatball, polpetta
meet, incontrare
memory, memoria
milk, latte (*m.*)
minister, ministro
Miss, young lady, signorina
mistaken: **to be mistaken**, sbagliarsi
Monday, lunedì (*m.*)
money, denaro, moneta, soldi
monk, monaco
month, mese (*m.*)
morning, mattina, mattino
mother, madre, mamma
mountain, montagna, monte (*m.*)
movies, cinema (*m.*)
Mr. and Mrs., coniugi (*m. pl.*)
museum, museo
my, mio, mia, miei, mie

narrate, raccontare, narrare
necessary: **to be necessary**, essere necessario, occorrere, bisognare
newspaper, giornale (*m.*)
noted, noto
novel, romanzo

obey, obbedire, ubbidire
offer: **to offer**, offrire
often, spesso
old, vecchio, antico; **old man**, vecchio
only, solo; **only one**, unico
open (*adj.*), aperto; **to open**, aprire
opera, opera
order: **to order**, ordinare
outside, fuori

package, pacco, pacchetto
paper, carta
patience, pazienza
Paul, Paolo
pay: **to pay**, pagare
pen, penna
pencil, matita
photograph, fotografia, foto (*f.*)
piano, pianoforte (*m.*)
pick: **to pick**, cogliere, scegliere
picture, ritratto, fotografia, quadro
pig, porco, maiale (*m.*)
pity, peccato
place: **to place**, mettere, porre; **to place oneself**, mettersi
play: **to play (a game),** giuocare, giocare; **to play (an instrument),** suonare
please: **to please,** piacere
port, porto
possess, possedere
postcard, cartolina
precious, prezioso
prefer, preferire
prepare, preparare
president, presidente (*m.*)
press: **to press**, stringere
prince, principe (*m.*)
probably, probabilmente
professor, professore (*m.*), professoressa (*f.*)
program, programma (*m.*)
prohibit, proibire
promise: **to promise**, promettere
propose, proporre
protect, proteggere
provided that, purchè
punish, punire
put, mettere, porre; **put on**, mettersi

quickly, presto, subito

raise: **to raise**, alzare
rapidly, rapidamente
reach: **to reach**, raggiungere

read, lẹggere
receive, ricẹvere
red, rosso
reflect, riflẹttere
remain, restare, rimanere
remember, ricordarsi, ricordare
render, rẹndere
reside, abitare, vịvere
respond, rispọndere
rest: **to rest**, riposarsi
restaurant, ristorante (*m.*)
return: **to return**, tornare, ritornare
rich, ricco
right, giusto, destra; **right away**, presto
road, strada
run: **to run**, cọrrere
Russian, russo

sad, triste
Saturday, sạbato (*m.*)
say, dire
school, scuola
season, stagione (*f.*)
see, vedere
seek, cercare
seem, parere, sembrare
select, scẹgliere
sell, vẹndere
send, inviare, mandare, spedire
serve, servire
set: **to set (a table)**, apparecchiare
several, parecchi
shave: **to shave**, rạdersi, farsi la barba
she, lei, essa
shelf, scaffale (*m.*)
shirt, camịcia
short, corto
shout: **to shout**, gridare
silent: **to be silent**, tacere
silver, argento
since, dato che, siccome
sing, cantare
sir, signore
sister, sorella
sit down, sedersi, accomodarsi
situated: **to be situated**, trovarsi
sleep: **to sleep**, dormire
slow, lento
slowly, lentamente
small, pịccolo
snow, neve (*f.*); **to snow**, nevicare
sofa, divano, sofà
softly, leggermente
soldier, soldato
some, alcuno, qualche, di (+ *def. art.*)
song, canzone (*f.*)
sorry: **to be sorry**, dolersi
so that, affinchè, di modo che
sound: **to sound**, suonare
Spanish, spagnolo, spagnuolo
speak, parlare
spend, spẹndere, passare
spinach, spinaci (*m. pl.*)
spring, primavera
square, piazza
stamp, francobollo
stay, rimanere
stocking, calza
stomach, stọmaco
stop, fermata
store, negọzio
storm, tempesta
story, stọria, racconto
student, studente (*m.*), studentessa (*f.*)
study: **to study**, studiare
succeed, riuscire
suffer, soffrire
suggest, suggerire
summer, estate (*f.*)
Sunday, domẹnica (*f.*)
supper, cena
surprise, sorpresa
Susan, Susanna
sweet, dolce
sweetbread, panettone (*m.*)
swim: **to swim**, nuotare

table, tạvola, tạvolo
tailor, sarto
take, prẹndere; **to take from, to remove**, tọgliere
talk: **to talk**, parlare
tall, alto
tea, tè (*m.*)
teach, insegnare
teacher, insegnante (*m., f.*), professore, maestro

telephone, telẹfono; **to telephone**, telefonare
television, televisione (*f.*); **television set**, televisore (*m.*)
tell, dire
terrible, terrịbile
that, quello
theater, teatro
their, il loro, i loro, la loro, le loro
these, questi, queste
they, essi, esse, loro
think, pensare
this, questo, questa
Thursday, giovedì (*m.*)
ticket, biglietto
tie, cravatta
tighten, strịngere
time, hour, tempo, ora
today, oggi
together, insieme
tomato, pomodoro
tomorrow, domani
too much, troppo
town, paese (*m.*)
train, treno
translate, tradurre
travel, viaggiare
tree, ạlbero
true, vero
truth, verità (*f.*)
Tuesday, martedì (*m.*)
turn, return, tornare, ritornare

uncle, zio
understand, capire, comprẹndere
unfold, spiegare
unless, a meno che . . . non
until, fino a, finchè
up, su
up: **to get up, to arise**, alzarsi

variety, varietà (*f.*)
vase, vaso
very, troppo, molto
virtue, virtù (*f.*)
visit: **to visit**, visitare

wait: **to wait**, aspettare
wake up, svegliarsi
walk: **to walk**, camminare
want, wish: **to want, to wish**, volere
wash: **to wash**, lavare; **to wash oneself**, lavarsi
water, ạcqua
we, noi
wear, portare, indossare
Wednesday, mercoledì (*m.*)
week, settimana
weigh: **to weigh oneself**, pesarsi
well, bene (*adv.*)
what, cosa, che cosa, che
when, quando
where, dove
while, mentre
who, chi
wife, mọglie (*f.*)
win, vịncere
window, finestra
wine, vino
winter, inverno
withdraw, ritirarsi
without, senza
work: **to work**, lavorare
worry: **to worry about**, preoccuparsi
worth: **to be worth**, valere
write, scrịvere

year, anno
yesterday, ieri
you, tu, voi, Lei, Loro
young, giọvane; **young lady**, giọvane (*f.*), signorina; **young man**, giọvane (*m.*)